07
09

CITY OF BURBANK
Public Library

JUN 1 3 2001

NOTE DATE DUE

EACH BORROWER is required to sign an application and is responsible for books drawn in his name.

FINES are charged for each book kept overtime (including Sundays and Holidays.)

THE BROKEN TOWER

ALSO BY PAUL MARIANI

POETRY
Timing Devices (1979)
Crossing Cocytus (1982)
Prime Mover (1985)
Salvage Operations: New & Selected Poems (1990)
The Great Wheel (1996)

BIOGRAPHY
William Carlos Williams: A New World Naked (1981)
Dream Song: The Life of John Berryman (1990)
Lost Puritan: A Life of Robert Lowell (1994)

CRITICISM
A Commentary on the Complete Poems of Gerard Manley Hopkins (1970)
William Carlos Williams: The Poet and His Critics (1975)
A Usable Past: Essays on Modern and Contemporary Poetry (1984)

PAUL MARIANI

W. W. NORTON & COMPANY

New York / London

THE
BROKEN
TOWER

A LIFE *of* HART CRANE

The Hart Crane poetry is from *Complete Poems of Hart Crane*, edited by Marc
Simon. Copyright 1933, © 1958, 1966 by Liveright Publishing Corpora-
tion. Copyright © 1986 by Marc Simon. Reprinted with the permission of
the publishers. "Oda a Walt Whitman" by Frederico García Lorca from
Obras Completas (Galaxia Gutenberg, 1996 edition) © Heredos de Frederico
García Lorca. Translation by Paul Mariani © Heredos de Frederico García
Lorca. All rights reserved. For information regarding rights and permis-
sions for works by Frederico García Lorca, please contact William Peter
Kosmas, Esq., 8 Franklin Square, London W14 9UU, England.

For information about permission to reproduce selections from this book,
write to Permissions, W. W. Norton & Company, Inc.,
500 Fifth Avenue, New York, NY 10110.

The text of this book is composed in Bembo, with the display set in Centaur.
Composition by Chelsea Dippel
Manufacturing by Maple-Vail Book Manufacturing Group
Book design by Judith Stagnitto Abbate/Abbate Design

Library of Congress Cataloging-in-Publication Data
Mariani, Paul L.
The broken tower : a life of Hart Crane / Paul Mariani.
p.   cm.
Includes bibliographical references and index.
ISBN 0-393-04726-1
1. Crane, Hart, 1899–1932.   2. Poets, American—20th century—
Biography.   3. New York (N.Y.)—In literature.   4. New York (N.Y.)—
Biography.   I. Title.
PS3505.R272Z753 1999
811'.52—dc21
[B]   98-37726
CIP

W. W. Norton & Company, Inc., 500 Fifth Avenue,
New York, NY 10110
http://www.wwnorton.com

W. W. Norton & Company Ltd., 10 Coptic Street, London WC1A 1PU

1 2 3 4 5 6 7 8 9 0

CONTENTS

PART IV

The slant light of late afternoons across the backs
Of silent Adirondack chairs. The lovely ghosts
Of those men & women I loved so much, strolling
Across the gold green lawn of Bread Loaf,
Laughing, discoursing lightly as we did
When all the world was young & we were young.

PROLEGOMENON

THERE WAS ONLY ONE CITY for Hart Crane, and that was New York. At seventeen, already on his own with the breakup of his parents' marriage, he left Cleveland to make a go of it in New York. Without a job, he could not hold on for very long, and soon he was back in Ohio, working for his father. Still, New York's rivers and bridges, its towers and brownstones and canyoned white buildings, had already claimed him for their own. Even away from the city, New York was always on his mind: not only when he was in Akron, Cleveland, and Washington, but in the hills seventy miles north of New York, or on the Isle of Pines, or in Hollywood, London, or Paris, Ermononville or Marseilles, or even during his last year in Mexico. Had he lived, it is possible he might have made the old city of Mexico over into his image as well, but hardly without the language, any more than Lorca could finally make New York his own. The fact is that when Crane died, it was to a truculent, depression-ravaged, yet still vital New York that he was returning.

But since the city has ten thousand faces, one particular New York: Manhattan seen from the window of an apartment on Columbia Heights, overlooking the twentieth century's towering skyscrapers as Georgia O'Keeffe and Walker Evans saw them: white buildings rising above the East River, with Liberty off to the left, and his beloved Gothic bridge spanning the river off to the right. When the great love of his life, Emil Opffer, brought him to this place in the spring of 1924, it was, Crane said, to discover a scene already in his mind's eye "more familiar than a hundred factual previsions could have rendered it." At the window of Number 110, in a building that has long since disappeared, Crane looked out over New York—his New Atlantis—as it rose majestically before him. *That*, he said, was where he wanted to be remembered most of all, along with "the ships, the harbor, and the skyline of Manhattan, midnight, morning or evening—rain, snow or sun."[1]

It was his city, rising from the confluence of the Atlantic with the Hudson and the East Rivers. Here, he said, the sea that would one day claim him for her own had thrown herself upon him, kissing his eyes with "speech . . . beyond words entirely." And the still majestic, besotted "River that is East," with its ships and tugs plying the river at all hours and seasons, moaning buoys out in the fogged-in harbor, traffic riding "the unfractioned idiom" of the bridge's surface on clear winter nights like the man-made zodiac it is. Or those cyclopean giants standing guard across the way, winking back the light of the rising sun. New York, with its erotic charge and tantalean promise, friends and lovers waiting, the energy of writers and artists, the bon mot, the electric glance, the ecstasy, the sharp dismissal, the great publishing houses that would disseminate the ineffable Word and make him famous.

Crane made New York, made it in his own inimitable image, the majesty and awe of it, breathing its white buildings into white rings of tumult and freedom and ecstasy:

> How many dawns, chill from his rippling rest
> The seagull's wings shall dip and pivot him,
> Shedding white rings of tumult, building high
> Over the chained bay waters Liberty . . .[2]

And of course he made New York in the other way as well, all of his lovers and one-night stands emblems of his insatiable drives and desires, as he made one man after another. He made the city, at the height of his powers, before life broke him, made it over into his own image, as every New York artist—driven by eros and invention—must make it over.

Yet, although Poe and Melville both walked its cobbled streets, Walt Whitman turns out to have been New York's first great poet:

The blab of the pave, tires of carts, sluff of bootsoles,
    talk of the promenaders,
The heavy omnibus, the driver with the interrogating thumb,
    the clank of the shod horses on the granite floor . . .
The excited crowd, the policeman with his star quickly
    working his passage to the centre of the crowd,
The impassive stones that receive and return so many echoes . . .[3]

"Song of Myself," 1855, Whitman rendering a New York still familiar to Crane seventy years after, and to us seventy years after that. And other poets too, taking their cue from Whitman. William Carlos Williams, of Rutherford, New Jersey, New York's first suburban town, a busy doctor on his appointed round of house calls, for a moment pulling his flivver over to the side of the bend at the crest above Ridge Road, there by the cemetery, gazing with love at the city with its lights winking back at him. Love and fame and time and money. "In the distance/over/the meadows," he would write, "A dream/a little false/toward which/now/we stand/and stare/transfixed. . . ."[4] Women, smart women, with the arched grace of a beauty driving a man to despair. He too ached to steal—if necessary—his own piece of the city, even as he understood all too well that city's undersides, its defeats, its tabloids speaking cynically of the latest bank hoist, this one pulled off by the guards themselves. Thinking too of the whole root system of that impossible white flower: the rivers, beautiful as they were in the late afternoon sun, become "the foulest/sink in the world," off which Crane's seagulls fed.

New York holds its poets fast. They stare into the vortex and the vortex stares unblinking back. Langston Hughes's jazz-saturated Harlem, Frank O'Hara's brash, fay, midtown Manhattan with its art galleries and pop-art glitz and melancholy, John Ashbery's Manhattan as an experiment in abstract expressionism, white noise and elegy beating against the void, Robert Lowell's Central Park, the expensive apartments with their bad plumbing, the hustlers rubbing up against this improper Bostonian, the *clip-clop* of mounted police in forsythia yellow raincoats writing out tickets on the Upper West Side. Or—a thousand miles away across town—Allen Ginsberg's Lower East Side Manhattan with its bums and angry hipsters, Galway Kinnell's Avenue A. Or, on the Upper West End, Sharon Olds's old men and streetwise kids, Philip Levine's meditations from an apartment overlooking the

Hudson, Bill Matthews's Horatian meditations on a New York super-imposed on the in-your-face imperial city of Rome, its twins suckling the dugs of a steel-eyed wolf. Or Donald Justice's haunting image of an umbrella blown down some street, "Whose very cobbles once the young Hart Crane/Had washed with a golden urine mixed with rain."[5]

It has been sixty years since Philip Horton's spirited biography of Crane, fifty since Brom Weber's critical study, thirty since John Unterecker gave us his immensely researched 800-page life. In that last thirty years, new readings and new information have both become available, giving us further access to Crane's brilliant, multifoliate world. The century that ushered Crane in is itself about to be ushered out. And those odd, little culture wars which involved Crane's contemporaries—Munson and Tate and Winters—and their skewed assessments of this magnificent poet have long been fought, to be succeeded by new culture wars.

Finally, as the third millennium approaches, we can begin to take stock of what this phenomenon called modern American poetry was. However we sum up the age, however we read Williams and Stevens, Pound and Eliot, however we read Frost, or Moore, Plath or Bishop, Berryman or Lowell, Hughes or Wilbur, Merrill or Ashbery, Levine or Justice, or so many other extraordinary voices, Crane seems destined to have a central place in any serious assessment of the age. In fact, the hard gemlike flame that burns about his name seems to brighten rather than to dim, as Catullus' does, as Villon's or Baudelaire's or Hopkins's. In short, something in the man continues to draw us irresistibly, and to survive his own self-willed oblivion.

It would be difficult to find a serious poet or reader of poetry in this country today who has not been touched by something in Hart Crane's music. Ask any one of them, and they will tell you that they read Crane—usually when young—and that Crane resonated for them in unexpected ways. When I was Crane's age, I thought about writing his life, only to realize I was not ready to undertake that task. The hand of fire he extended toward me then felt in truth rather like the rapidly vanishing one Keats extended toward his readers in the months before his death. And so I flinched, pulled back, went on to other things. Teaching—thirty years and more of it—and poems, and the lives of poets, other poets: Hopkins, Williams, Berryman, Lowell. Yet, through it all, Crane winked. Sitting now at his ease on the other side of the great divide, he was no longer in any hurry for this book or, for that matter, any other.

As a New Yorker, raised in the shadow of the Third Avenue El, I think I feel something of what Crane felt about New York. My heart still lifts when I come in view of the Brooklyn Bridge, whether from the Brooklyn side or driving south on the FDR. When I look upon the gray patina of the rotting piers, the tugs wheezing upriver with their garbage scows, the dank, urine-scented subways, the yellow cabs, the long avenues undulating uptown, the incessant traffic, the neon lights, "the nightly sessions,/Refractions of the thousand theatres" along Times Square, Hell's Kitchen, "the glass doors gyring at your right": all of these remind me of the young Crane who sang this maddening, heartbreaking, voluptuous city, and loved it bitterly, ecstatically, until he died.

Once, standing in the middle of Brooklyn Bridge, he watched the U.S. Fleet sail up the East River as if it were streaming between his legs. Such was his fantasy. Love and poetry being part of the same creative drive, it is no wonder he strove heroically, sadly, to make New York. Alcohol and excess exacted its toll on him, and took him much too early. But for a splendid moment we had a poet in the right time and in the right place to grace us with a vision of what God might look like if God should ever visit us as a city, as I must believe he came and came again to Crane.

PAUL MARIANI
Montague, Massachusetts
6 June 1998

PART I

1 / STARTING OUT

CLEVELAND *and* NEW YORK
1899–1918

WHEN HAROLD HART CRANE walked out of the canyoned sunlight of Grand Central into the cold air of Manhattan four days after Christmas, 1916, he was—at seventeen—already a poet, with two published poems to his credit. Now, he was sure, he was ready to begin the life he'd dreamed of for the past six years. Back in Cleveland, in the room which had served as his ivory tower for those six years, he'd abandoned a sheaf of unpublishable poems—false, necessary starts—along with the fragments of a family torpedoed by recriminations and counterrecriminations, with only flotsam and jetsam left bobbing in the aftermath. Somehow, amid the detritus, he too had managed to surface and to find his way to New York City, where he was determined, the Muse willing, to undergo the necessary sea change that would make of him a poet. First, he knew, New York would work its transformations on him, after which he would proceed to make New York over in his own image.

The genesis of Hart Crane's particular odyssey begins in the spring of 1898, when a twenty-year-old debutante from Chicago, one Grace Edna Hart, traveled by rail to Garrettsville, Ohio, for an extended visit with her aunt and cousin. Among the first families of that provincial center, and already known to the Harts, were the Cranes. A successful middle-class entrepreneur, Arthur Crane ran both a maple

syrup business and the town's general store, as well as serving as direc-
tor of the town's First National Bank. Arthur had one son, Clarence
Arthur (C.A.), who had turned twenty-three that spring. C.A. had
already put in two years at Allegheny College in western Pennsylvania.
That was before he'd decided to strike out on his own and make his
fortune. At twenty, he'd taken to the open road, selling cookies for
the National Biscuit Company of Akron. But soon he was back in
Garrettsville, working for his father's maple syrup business. C.A. was
built like a bull and had the drives of one. Passionate, headstrong,
good-natured, innocent in the murderous way of many young "red-
blooded" Americans, he had an eye for women as well as for money,
both of which he regarded—until he learned better—as commodities.
Like other young American men of his generation, what he set his
mind to having for himself he pursued relentlessly, until he had made
it his own. Only afterwards, when it was too late, did he come to tally
up the real costs.

Introduced to Grace, he decided at once that he had to have her.
So insistent was he that by the time she was ready to return home to
Chicago, C.A. had already proposed. Rebuffed (mildly), he showered
her with gifts and flowers, made trips (frequent) to Chicago, met
Grace's parents, acted the beau, fantasized, waited, plotted, waited, took
no refusal as final. And so, just two months after meeting, the couple
were married in Chicago. The wedding—a big, noisy affair—took place
on June 1, 1898, after which C.A. and Grace returned to Garrettsville,
where C.A.'s father had built for them a substantial clapboard house
with wraparound porch and vine trellis. Up until this point C.A. had
followed the standard rules of courtship. But now it was back to business. He had a wife to support and an important job in his father's
maple syrup cannery. Grace was his wife, and he would expect her to
act like one. What he could not understand was why she seemed to
deflect his amorous advances. He had his duties, he reasoned, and she
had hers.

Initially, Grace complied, for thirteen months after the wedding,
on 21 July 1899, she gave birth to their only child, a son, whom they
named Harold Hart Crane. A good baby, not given to severe childhood illnesses, though asthma would develop as tensions between the
couple increased. Harold spent his first two years—the crucial, forma-
tive ones, for which there is so little information—in Garrettsville,
before C.A. moved his family in 1901 to nearby Warren to begin what

would become, within half a dozen years, the largest maple syrup business of its kind in the world. This C.A. managed with the help of a substantial loan from Grace's father, Clinton Hart.

Cane sugar was the wave of the future, C.A. could see. Cane with a bit of maple sugar to give the whole the taste of maple syrup, but at a cost far less than the real thing. One of the pure products of America. C.A.'s father had not been keen on such adulteration, but C.A., shrewd businessman that he was, knew most Americans were not so much interested in quality as in finding a bargain. He was right, of course, in assessing the American temper, and the maple/cane sugar business grew. Knowing a good thing when he saw it, Clinton, who'd made his own money in steel, helped finance a sugar cannery for his prospering son-in-law: a brown-tiled building at Franklin and South Pine there in Warren, complete with its own rail siding to get his products to market.

"Behind/My father's cannery works I used to see/Rail-squatters ranged in nomad raillery," Crane would write twenty years later on an island off the southern coast of Cuba. The bums, the hoboes, the outsiders, the runaways, the homeless, the ragged remnant of the old pioneers, so different from his industrious father:

> . . . ancient men—wifeless or runaway
> Hobo-trekkers that forever search
> An empire wilderness of freight and rails.
> Each seemed a child, like me, on a loose perch,
> Holding to childhood like some termless play.[1]

Little of the Garrettsville years ever found their way into Crane's poetry, at least in any recognizable sense, but there is one passage, an image of his mother sitting at the piano and singing. She sings a song with a French tag, "Do you know the place?" But there is a sense of claustrophobia about the memory, a need on the speaker's part to break free and walk among the roses, the mystical roses that would later populate his long poem, *The Bridge*.

> "Connais tu le pays . . . ?"
> Your mother sang that in a stuffy parlor
> One summer day in a little town
> Where you had started to grow.
> And you were outside as soon as you

Could get away from the company
To find the only rose on the bush
In the front yard . . .[2]

And other boyhood images, remembered or reconfigured. The poet strolling along New York's Avenue A, recalling his boyhood years in Warren as he walked to the old Central Grammar School on Harmon Street ("It is the same hour though a later day"), recalling Pizarro and Cortés and the New England pilgrims, Priscilla and Captain Smith, and Rip Van Winkle, all names embedded in his history primer. A house at 249 High Street, followed by a bigger one on North Park Avenue, with its "cinder pile at the end of the backyard," where he had once "stoned the family of young/Garter snakes under." The heady years following the Wright brothers' flight, a space age in the offing: "the monoplanes/We launched—with paper wings and twisted/Rubber bands."[3] The serpent and the eagle: a sense of conquest even here in these boyish images of Einsteinian time and space, signaling the twentieth century's grasping after its own pragmatic, palpable definition of transcendence.

In 1908, C.A. sold his maple business to the Corn Products Refining Company and began working for the new owners as manager of the packaging plant they'd just completed. Still, he kept coming up with other bright ideas. Cellophane, he told them, cellophane from France rather than paper bags—that was the wave of the future. The idea caught on. With his new wealth, C.A. bought Grace a horse-drawn carriage and for his father one of those new-fangled motorcars beginning to put-put along the main streets of America. And now long business trips away, periods when Grace too was away on trips to Chicago. During these absences, Harold was left behind to stay with aunts. Symptomatically, his asthmatic attacks became more and more frequent and intense. He plunked away at his Aunt Bess's piano, eking out a sweet, haunting tune. What was it called? she asked him. "The Lamb's First Morning," he told her.

Once, he got dressed up to deliver a birthday card to a Miss Hall and wound up giving it to the wrong woman. Still, the wrong Miss Hall invited him in, sat him down, and served him tea and cookies. When he returned home and explained where he had been, Grace began tweaking him about his error, then tweaked him again and again, until finally, understanding that he was just a little fool, he fled the room in tears. And once, on Mackinac Island, breakfasting with his parents in the big sunny hotel dining room, he failed to rise at the approach of a lady friend of his mother's. Afterwards, Grace roundly upbraided the boy for his boorishness. Humiliated, he began running a fever until he was forced to take to his bed. Afterwards his mother came to him, bending over him to chafe his wrists and place cool compresses on his brow. It delighted him to see her worried like this. Driven to it, he learned early on how to make illness serve his own ends.

In the late summer of 1908, after ten years of blistering marriage, C.A. and Grace agreed to a trial separation. While Grace had herself admitted to a sanitarium for a regimen of complete rest, C.A. moved into a rooming house in Chicago, near the main offices of his employer. For his part, the nine-year-old Harold was shipped off to live with Grace's parents in Cleveland. The Hart home—at 1709 East 115th Street—was a three-storied, twin-towered late Victorian structure, the massive wooden towers as if inspired by the medieval city walls of Carcassonne. Seeing the strategic advantage of those twin towers looming over the surrounding houses, Harold moved into the north one, the view from his window looking out over the surrounding trees and—in the evenings—catching the light from the setting sun. It was a room of his own, which he was free to decorate and arrange as he pleased. There were other advantages as well: servants, a cook, a grandmother who adored him.

Shortly, Grace rejoined Harold in Cleveland, and by winter—after he had profusely and abjectly apologized and courted his wife all over again—C.A. was also allowed to move back. The house in Warren was sold and the Cranes became Clevelanders. Having her daughter back under her roof, Grace's mother, Elizabeth, a fervent Christian Scientist, could work on her until she too was ready to become a believer. Even C.A., sometime Methodist, followed suit, becoming a lukewarm follower of Mary Baker Eddy. In time too young Harold became outwardly a Scientist, though later he would confess to friends that he'd done so to appease his mother. Sundays, he attended the Christian Scientist Sunday School; weekdays, it was the Fairmount Elementary School, where he proved to be a lackluster student.

On a trip to Victoria, British Columbia, C.A. made the discovery of a chocolate so wonderfully good he was convinced it would make him rich. He tried to get a franchise for it for the Cleveland area, but when the Canadian company balked, he had the chocolate chemically analyzed and then began producing and selling a clone of it locally. Once again, his father and father-in-law bankrolled him, and by 1911, the thirty-five-year-old entrepreneur was making and selling his own "Queen Victoria Chocolates" in stores all over Cleveland. It was this same C.A., in fact, who invented the original Life Savers, "the candy with a hole in the middle." Always the ideas man, he found a way to use a pharmaceutical punch (for making pills) that could punch holes in hard candy without shattering it. "Crane's Peppermint Life Savers," the wrapper read. "For That Stormy Breath." He packaged them to sell for a nickel a roll, a picture of an old sailor tossing a lifesaver to a young girl adorning the wrapper. Packaging indeed was the thing in America, and C.A. became a genius at it. Later still he would employ a well-known artist, Maxfield Parrish, to design his line of Mary Garden Chocolates. Then, in 1913, C.A. sold the trademark and formula for what would become a multi-million-dollar industry to one Edward Noble for the modest sum of $2,900. C.A.'s business instincts were good, but they were not unerring.

He had high hopes of passing his candy empire on to his boy; but his boy, even early on, seemed to have other ideas about the direction of his life. For one thing, Harold seemed more interested in dressing up in his mother's clothes. At the age of eleven, he typed a letter to his mother noting that the actress, Eva Tanguay, whom he'd seen at a performance at the Hippodrome in Warren, had worn *seven* different gowns during her performance. This sort of behavior C.A. found difficult to understand. In fact, Harold, C.A. was discovering, was becoming one strange boy: introverted, uninterested in sports, preferring reading (Musset's *Mr. Wind* and *Madame Rain*, in translation), dancing, piano (which he played poorly), vaudeville shows, musicals, and even art lectures over football and baseball.

By the time he was sixteen, Harold also had a collection of mild pornography and had become an inveterate smoker of big cigars. Intense, nervous, and shy—a loner, in fact—he came to believe in friendship and loyalty with a passion hard for many to fathom, and when that friendship was not returned, he could feel utterly betrayed. Given the instability of his family life, it is no wonder he craved friendships that would survive the corrosions all friendships, alas, are subject to.

In January 1913, Clinton Hart died, leaving Harold a bequest of $5,000, to be held in trust until after the death of his wife, Elizabeth. In his mind, Harold would spend that $5,000 hundreds of times over before it came—briefly—into his possession following the eventual death of his grandmother. More immediately, because the death of Clinton left a large house to a widow now in her seventies, C.A. and Grace took over the management of things, leaving Elizabeth, like Harold, with a single room of her own. Three months later, C.A.'s parents bought the house directly across the street from them, a move that caused more friction than anything else between the Harts and the Cranes as the marriage of C.A. and Grace continued once again to disintegrate. In early 1914, Harold—at fourteen—at last enrolled in Cleveland's East High School, where he would attend classes irregularly for the next three years.

Irregularly, for Grace had no problem in withdrawing Harold from school for long periods so that he could accompany her and see something of America's vast spaces, or winter with her on her mother's decaying plantation on the Isle of Pines. When the island, located fifty miles off the southern coast of Cuba, became a U.S. protectorate after the Spanish-American War, a number of enterprising Americans saw their chance to scoop up cheap land on which to grow fruit for American consumption. Clinton had been one of these entrepreneurs, and now that he was dead and the estate in shaggy disrepair, his wife and daughter came to spend their winters there. The plantation had long since ceased producing anything and had been left to decay genteelly in the hands of various caretakers.

In high school Harold continued his career as an indifferent student, except in English, the one subject he excelled in because he liked it. Enrolled in the "Classical" program, geared to the college-bound student, he took three years of Latin, three of a modern language (German), English, math (algebra and geometry), physics. In most courses he received a simple Pass, a grade designed for bright students with a history of sporadic attendance or other problems. In class he said as little as possible, preferring to blend in with the other students. He played tennis passionately, badly. He had few school friends, but the three he did have, he kept. Kenneth Hurd, with whom he would lose contact after he left high school, was one; George Bryan, with whom he would keep in touch for years, the second; and Bill Wright, who would remain his friend for life, the third.

He also began dating, in particular, a frail girl named Vivian Brown, to whom on special occasions he presented boxes of his father's chocolates. Somewhere in junior high or high school he had his first homosexual encounter, which may have been a case of sexual abuse by an older man. Only years later did he come to brag about the incident, and by then it had been transformed into a comic myth, with Crane seducing the man rather than his having been coerced. Was it one of his tutors? a handyman? Or simply an experiment, no different from what so many other boys, exploring their own pubescent sexuality, have encountered?

In the summer of 1914, a writer and self-promoter from East Aurora, New York, one Elbert Hubbard, a man who'd modeled himself after William Morris by dabbling in everything from bookbinding to textiles and design, visited the Cranes in Cleveland. Because Hubbard was a self-styled entrepreneur as well as an artist, C.A. hailed him as someone after whom Harold might model himself. If one had to dabble in writing, C.A. reasoned, Hubbard's was the way to go. For years after, in fact, C.A. would quote Hubbard's Yankee self-start maxims in letters to his son. As for Harold, it did not take him long to realize how little substance there was to Hubbard. Whatever an artist was, he understood, Hubbard was not it.

In January 1915, Harold joined his parents for his first trip south to the Isle of Pines for a ten-week vacation in the sun. Within days of his arrival, however, C.A., restless with so much enforced leisure and champing to get back to his desk, insisted on the family's returning to Cleveland. When Grace refused, a ferocious argument ensued, after which C.A. packed his bags and left. "We may never talk again," Grace warned him as he walked out the door.

That was fine by C.A. They'd been this route before. But by the time he reached Florida, he was bombarding his wife and son with telegrams and letters, begging for forgiveness and understanding. He tried enlisting Harold on his side. "I guess you must have thot [sic] that dad behaved badly," he wrote from the Hotel Seminole in Jacksonville on the 24th. He hoped Harold and his mother would see that he was still "worth saving" and come back home real soon.[4] Perhaps a new Cadillac 8 might entice Grace back? But Grace steadfastly refused, knowing she could have the car *and* the vacation. Magnanimous but

undeterred, she allowed C.A. to send her daily assurances of his undy-
ing devotion while she stayed on at the plantation with her devoted
Harold.

Meanwhile, unnoticed, Harold himself sank deeper and deeper
into a depression. Twice that February he tried to kill himself. The first
time, he slashed his wrists. The second time, he stole all his mother's
packets of Veronal sleeping powders (eighteen, she discovered) and
swallowed the contents. Though the family never discussed the incident, Harold seems to have taken the drugs one night after being awakened by his mother, told there were cows roaming about the
plantation—and ordered to shush them away. What should have taken a
few minutes became an hour, and when he returned out of the darkness, his eyes were dilated and he was lapsing into semiconsciousness.
He was taken to a local Spanish-speaking doctor and, after explaining
the situation, given an injection to counteract the effects of the powders. C.A. was summoned and returned at once to the Isle of Pines to
see that his family made it safely back to the States.

Years later Crane would tell Bill Wright what had happened on
the island that winter of 1915. And once—in Paris in 1929, when he
was visibly going to pieces—he confided to Allen Tate that his parents'
incessant quarreling and making up afterwards, replete with its attendant cooing and heavy lovemaking (short, nasty, violent), had sworn
him forever off all heterosexual lovemaking.

In April 1915 Harold spent several weeks as an apprentice at Roy-
croft, Hubbard's art colony in western New York. Three months later,
the boy escorted his mother on a tour of the eastern United States,
staying at posh hotels in Rye Beach and Boston. Already an accomplished ballroom dancer, the sixteen-year-old Harold—in the absence
of his father—led his mother about the dance floor at various socials
and dinner dances. The following winter, C.A. and Grace tried the
Isle of Pines adventure a second time. C.A. would combine business
with pleasure, seeking new outlets for his chocolates as he and Grace
made their way by train down the coast to Florida. This time, Harold
was left behind to catch up on his studies. Mostly he spent his days
alone, seeing no one besides the maid, Aunt Zell Deming (his mother's
sister-in-law), and a few friends. Each day he wrote poems, hating the

fact that school was taking up time he might better have spent in writing. Somehow he survived.

That summer, he traveled with his high school friend, George Bryan, to Chautauqua, New York, to mingle with the local artists, afterwards stopping at Jamestown on the western New York/Pennsylvania border to visit with his sometime "girlfriend," Vivian Brown, her sister, and her parents, who were summering there. But if Harold was on his best behavior in the presence of the Brown sisters, especially under the ever vigilant eye of their mother, he was still the same Harold who, with the help of Bryan, had once spent an afternoon crushing the ceramic heads of Bryan's sister's dolls under the tread of a rockinghorse, laughing wildly as he did so.

He was back home in Cleveland only a short while before he was on the road once more, escorting his mother on yet another trip, this one through the western states by Pullman and back via the Canadian Rockies. He was now old enough to be particularly irked by his mother's insistence that they share the same compartment. Still, there were extraordinary vistas to be seen from the observation car, and he could not help but feel a sense of awe as the New World offered itself to him: the barely tamed Yellowstone National Park, the great Canadian Rockies, Lake Louise, the international resort at Banff.

When they returned home at the end of August, rumors had begun circulating—thanks to Grace's friends—that C.A. had been seen about town in the company of other women. What followed were accusations and denials, many of which Harold could not help overhearing, until he was choking with asthmatic fits and his body had erupted into a mass of angry welts. Finally, in early November, C.A. moved out of the house and took a room at the Athletic Club. For Grace, it was the last straw. This time she contacted the family lawyer and immediately filed for divorce on the grounds of extreme cruelty and gross neglect. Within days, a contrite C.A. was sending her roses and violets, even a bad poem. Then he was on the phone, begging her to let him at least talk to her. But Grace was adamant, especially since she could count on having Harold on her side.

As divorce proceedings went forward, Harold at last saw his chance. He could see that the family was coming unraveled and that there would be no one left now with the strength to get in his way. Time then to strike out on his own and become what he already knew he was destined to become. Not in Cleveland, God forbid, but where the real action was, in New York. His plan was simple. He would drop out of boring school, get a job in a local picture shop—Korner & Woods—to help support himself, and then go to New York as soon as he had enough money saved up. Once there, he would find a job, hire tutors in math and French to prepare him for the entrance exams to Columbia University, get his degree, and find a full-time job. At least that was the scenario he laid out for his mother. Sensing how romantic it would be to have a son in New York whom she could eventually join—parties, socials, dances—Grace agreed to the plan. As for C.A., that adulterous pariah, he could do little more than scratch his head and pay his son's expenses. The one thing Harold had not yet told either of them was that he was going to New York for one purpose only: to become a poet.

Once, when he was ten, awed by the sight of wall-to-wall books in his mother's sister's home, Harold had announced that he meant someday to become a poet. Already he had his ivory tower to which he could escape, the place he called—not without some irony and linguistic fumbling—his "*sanctum de la tour.*" This was his real, his palpable world, with the afternoon light and evening shadows playing across the off-gray walls lined with his favorite prints and paintings. By sixteen, he was listening to his collection of classical and pop records on his windup Victrola every chance he got. Here, too, he kept the latest literary magazines, purchased from Laukhuff's Bookstore, and hid his cache of forbidden books, among them Boccaccio's *Decameron*, Oscar Wilde, and Aubrey Beardsley's decadent, woman-mocking prints. He stole perfume from his mother's desk to sprinkle in his room. His senses stimulated by the pricky stings and perfumed scents of his surroundings, he pecked away at his Corona typewriter, composing long, sensuous poems in the style of the yellow nineties, stealing his drugged rhythms from Swinburne, Lionel Johnson, and Wilde. Here, too, he read Coleridge, Shelley, and Poe, chewed endlessly on cigars, or sank his nose into an old pair of the maid's leather shoes for the exquisite scents to be found there.

By Christmas 1915, he was already deep into a long, confused poem about the quest of the visionary poet, written in rhymed quatrains that evoked Swinburne's mesmeric, galloping anapests. In the poem—one he had the good sense finally to abandon—he pictured himself as a blind moth raised among butterflies, which for a brief moment had found itself rising upward into the empyrean to behold "Great horizons and systems and shores all along,"[5] only to find its wings crumpling and itself falling—like Icarus—back to earth. He was that moth, blessed too with an intense, too-brief glimpse of beauty, though unable to convey what he'd seen before he found himself falling from a great height.

Did he put on the poem's knowledge with its power? For, clotted as the poem was, it seemed uncannily to foreshadow his own visionary flight and fall. Years later he would evoke the Icarian airman reaching into the dizzying empyrean before spinning back to earth to die. A leap followed by a fall. It was an image deep-wired into Crane's psyche from an early age.

In the spring of 1916, he read a series of essays on Oscar Wilde's wretched life in Reading Gaol following his trial for homosexuality. These he'd found in a small Greenwich Village magazine called *Bruno's Weekly*, which he'd picked up at Laukhuff's. The fruit of Crane's meditation on the incarceration of this disgraced poet was a thirteen-line lyric that he finally sent off to *Bruno's* in the late summer of 1916, along with a letter praising the magazine's editor for daring to champion the work of the modern imagination.

The poem itself was in the late Romantic mode found in *Palgrave's Treasury*, not unlike the sort of thing the young William Carlos Williams and Ezra Pound had committed to paper a few years earlier. It was titled "C 33" (Wilde's cell number), and in it Crane praised the poet for wringing beauty out of the pain of his humiliation and incarceration. The poem also began that punning on Harold Hart ("Heart") Crane's own name that would become a signature of his poetry, as here he wove rose-vines "About the empty heart of night." The lyric also suggested that Grace, his beloved mother, hurt by life's betrayals, was to be his first, last Muse. And though his was as yet but "song of minor, broken strain," in time he hoped his words might come to enrich the "gold head/And wavering shoulders" of his "Materna."[6]

"C 33" appeared in the September issue of *Bruno's*. After that, Crane's name was elevated to grace the masthead as contributing editor. It was his first publication and he was ecstatic with his good fortune. Additional attempts he sent to William Carlos Williams at *Others*, one of the most avant garde of the new little magazines in the New York area. "Damn good stuff," Williams wrote back in mid-November. "*Others* is in a state of transition—to say the least, so—We'll keep your things in the hope that someday—someday—when we get some money—we may print them."[7] Promises there, but no cigar. Crane had better luck with another Greenwich Village magazine, *The Pagan*, which used Beardsley prints to decorate its covers. "Dear Sir," Harold wrote the editor, Joe Kling, in a butter-up letter that appeared in the October number, "I am interested in your magazine as a new and distinctive chord in the present American Renaissance of literature and art. Let me praise your September cover: it has some suggestion of the exoticism and richness of Wilde's poems." To the letter he appended an exotic and rich exercise of his own: a ten-line imagist description of sunlight and moonlight alternately transforming a rural scene, perhaps seen from his own backyard. It was called "October–November," and Kling ran that in his November issue. Crane now had a second poem to his credits.

There was one friend of the family, ten years Harold's senior, a painter who hailed from Warren, and who'd been helped substantially by Harold's aunt Zell and whom Harold had met earlier in the year in Cleveland. This was Carl Schmitt, and he had recently rented a studio apartment in New York on the Lower East Side. "With pipe, solitude and puppy for company, I am feeling resplendent," Crane wrote him at Thanksgiving. "After a day's work in a picture store selling mezzotints and prints, you may not think it, yet there comes a great peaceful exaltation in merely reading, thinking, and writing." He needed such quiet moments, he confided, because his family was coming apart under the strain of the imminent divorce. True, there'd been "tremendous struggles" in his life, but he had to believe there was also light at the end of it all.[8]

Working evenings at the bookstore gave him time during the days to write. After all, he was still only seventeen and sure he had the wherewithal to shape his destiny. Some day, he hoped, he would join Schmitt in New York and talk all this over with him man to man. Crane spoke about it as if it might happen in some distant future. But, as the fates would have it, with his father rooming at the Athletic Club and his mother off visiting friends in Chicago, he would find himself pounding the streets of New York within a month, ready to begin a life that was already half over. Two months earlier, returning with his friend Bill Wright from their Saturday afternoon dancing class, he'd told Wright of his plans to be a poet. So far he'd written only a few pale, imitative verses in an exhausted idiom. But seven years later, once more walking with Wright, this time down Fifth Avenue, Crane said he now believed he had it in him not only to become a poet—he'd long since passed that hurtle—but the greatest singer of their generation. He was twenty-three when he made that pronouncement, and already well on his way to fulfilling it.

But now, four days after Christmas, as 1916 ran out, Crane stood poised at the beginning of his odyssey. Out on the streets of New York, he headed for Carl Schmitt's studio over on East 15th Street, and within hours he and Schmitt were searching for a place for Harold to live. What they found was a dirty cold-water flat two blocks west of Schmitt's studio, at 139 East 15th. The apartment crawled with roaches and bedbugs and Harold was dismayed to learn he would have to share a filthy toilet out on the gaslit landing; but the place, he consoled himself, was merely a stopgap measure. In a few days he would look for something better. In the meantime, he began exploring the city he meant to make his own. On New Year's Eve, he boarded a doubledecker for the long ride up Fifth Avenue, marveling at the marble facades gleaming like crystal in the benzine-rinsed winter sunshine.

It was like finding oneself in the midst of some vast ocean, this being here in New York, he wrote his father breathlessly, a place that—for a boy from Ohio—had already turned out to be both "a great shock" and "a good tonic." Somewhere out there among those "countless multitudes," that "sea of humanity," he hoped—if only his father would help him—to find his own "lost identity."[9] He waded awed through the city's Egyptian splendor, although, like Walt Whitman before him, it was among the city's vibrant teeming masses that he felt most at home. Within days he discovered Little Italy, with its freshly baked bread, garlic, and translucent yellow-green olive oils. He visited Carnegie Hall, Madison Square Garden, and—more practically—his father's office on East 33rd Street, managed by Hazel Hasham, a friend of C.A. and Grace's. A good place to visit, Harold knew, especially if he needed cash.

Still, a stranger amid the chambered vastnesses of New York, he clung desperately to Schmitt, hanging about his studio, unwilling to leave, and talking far into the night about aesthetics, as Schmitt carried on with his pet thesis: that all things—artistic and spiritual—had to be kept in balance. That was it. If he could only keep mind and heart balanced, Harold was beginning to understand, he too might some day "mount to extraordinary latitudes." He would study Latin, German, and philosophy, and these, he told his father, would balance his emotions and lead him to a "more exact expression" in his poetry.[10]

He even began meeting some of the Big Ones, like Conrad Aiken and Alfred Kreymborg, co-editor with Williams of *Others*. And then there was Schmitt's fellow Ohioan, Earl Biggers, author of the "Charlie Chan" detective mysteries, whom Harold took to at once for his "quietness and un-worldliness."[11] Day after day Harold returned to Schmitt's studio for talk and more talk, until finally, if only to get some work done, Schmitt began locking his door. Once, after Harold had knocked and waited, knocked and left, Schmitt opened the door to find a forlorn plant sitting there, a gift from his young friend. As if that weren't enough to make him feel guilty, he had to listen while Harold later told him he'd heard Schmitt walking around inside. Schmitt tried to explain, but things were never the same between the two after that.

To prepare for the French exams that, once passed, he hoped would allow him entrance to Columbia, Harold hired first one tutor, then another. He attended concerts. He wrote poems. He visited his editor friends, Guido Bruno at *Bruno's Weekly* and Joseph Kling at *The Pagan*. And through the widow of a Chicago poet, William Vaughn Moody, he came to meet several New York writers. Mrs. Moody herself he'd met in Cleveland the year before, and had followed up the meeting with a spirited correspondence. She was a golden contact, Harold realized, and he was not about to let her slip away. In her time Mrs. Moody had hosted both Rabindranath Tagore and W. B. Yeats when they'd lectured in Chicago. She knew Vachel Lindsay, knew Sandburg, knew the writer and poet Padraic Colum. When Harold sent her some poems, she was kind enough to encourage him.

Five days into 1917, thanks to Mrs. Moody, he finally met Colum and his wife, Mary. Mary Colum's impressions, recalled thirty years later, would be of a raw western boy, gangling, semiliterate, who for a while had visited her and her husband twice a week to discuss the French Symbolists, the new crop of Irish writers, and the New York scene. Harold was duly impressed: by them, and by all they seemed to know, delighted that a poet of Colum's stature had actually taken the time to learn a few lines of his poetry by heart, which Colum quoted as Crane walked through the door into the Colums' apartment. It was a smart touch on Colum's part, and it worked, for Crane began turning all his attention to them, discussing poetry, and dining with them—their treat—at a local Italian restaurant called Gonfarones. He expected Harold to have a book in two years' time, Colum was soon telling Crane, and he would write the preface. "O this is the place to live," a delirious Crane wrote his mother.[12]

It was several weeks before Crane heard from his father, annoyed that he'd not been informed earlier of Harold's flight to New York, and professing still to be in the dark about what his son was up to. It would be better, C.A. wrote now, if Harold returned home at once and got himself ready to enroll in some military academy like Culver, where he could get "a liberal amount of outdoor exercise," as well as crack a book from time to time.[13] *That* was how one prepared for life. When Harold wrote back that Culver was the last place in the world he wanted to be, C.A. in turn retorted that it was too bad that Harold was such "a victim of moods."[14]

In those first weeks Harold passed his time walking, talking, or reading in the halls of the New York Public Library. He listened to chamber music in Mrs. Moody's Washington Square salon, viewed William Merritt Chase's paintings at the Metropolitan Museum, and attended a reading by Vachel Lindsay of his poems. In March, the third of Harold's poems appeared, this one in *The Pagan*. It was called "The Hive," and it spoke of the inestimable cost to the psyche of living alone in a city where "Humanity pecks, claws, sobs, and climbs" up the "chasm-walls" of the poet's "bleeding heart."[15] But the pain was well worth it, the poet insisted, for he could feel the bitter loneliness of the exile transforming itself into the honey of art. He was still composing in a diction three decades old.

Then, suddenly, Grace was in New York after a winter at the luxurious Hotel Royal in Palm Beach, where she'd watched several beauty pageants, as well as "real 'coons'" performing the annual hotel cakewalk.[16] For three weeks that March she stayed at the Waldorf-Astoria, doing eurhythmics—dance exercises—and visiting with Harold and his friends, especially Carl Schmitt, and the Yale-educated, mildly successful writer of light dramas, Charles Brooks, whom the Cranes had known back in Cleveland. Wherever she went, Grace insisted on being treated like royalty, and it was Harold—strapped for funds himself—who had to borrow $160 from his father's office to pay her expenses. It was of course only a matter of time before C.A. learned what his estranged wife and son were doing. Once he did, however, he sent a telegram off, ordering his son to return home at once. That was on March 21st, by which time Grace decided she should return to Cleveland, since the divorce would become final on April 1st. It was left to Harold to write his father, explaining that, much as he wanted to comply with C.A.'s wishes, he was too busy studying for his entrance exams. The truth was he was not leaving New York if *he* had any say in the matter.

In April, two more poems appeared in *The Pagan*: a nine-line cryptic piece entitled "Annunciations," and an eight-line lyric that was, by contrast, a model of clarity. "Fear," it was called, and it lifted the image of night licking at the poet's window from another young poet named T. S. Eliot. Then came a letter from Grace. "Harold Crane, poet," indeed, she wrote mockingly. Did he intend to ignore completely the Hart side of the family? Why not split the glory and begin signing himself Harold *Hart* Crane? Or even better, Hart Crane? Dutifully, he published his next poem under the name Harold H. Crane, and from then on simply as Hart Crane. His father was not impressed.[17]

Hostilities on two fronts: On 6 April, 1917, the United States declared war on Germany, and America was at last drawn into the cataclysm that had gripped Europe for the past thirty months. Overnight, the docks of New York became a major port of embarkation for troops, medical supplies, munitions, trucks, horses. On the 7th, with the divorce now official, Harold was summoned back to Cleveland to help his mother pack for an extended stay in New York. Back home, he wrote his father to say he was thinking of joining the army and doing his part. Not eager to see his only child shot up, C.A. cautioned Harold not to let the war news disturb him too much. Better to wait and see how things turned out. If the time came when the country really needed them, they could both go. True, at forty-one he would "make a very poor marcher," but someone would need to drive cars and trucks and he could certainly do that.[18] In the meantime, by the stipulations of the divorce settlement, Harold received an allowance of $140 a month, and Grace a good deal more.

By the beginning of May, Harold was once more back in New York, this time with his mother and grandmother, looking for accommodations. Finally, after two weeks, they found a handsome brownstone apartment (two rooms, bath, and kitchenette) at 44 Gramercy Park off 21st Street, where Charles and Minerva Brooks were already living. Once settled, Grace's mother returned to Cleveland. Now, under the guidance of the Brookses, serious Christian Scientists like Grace's mother, Grace renewed her interest in its tenets and urged Harold to do likewise. For her sake he was willing to pretend an interest, though he would never be a disciple of anything but poetry. He was careful to write his father to say he was still preparing for his entrance exams to Columbia, though with a war going on he wasn't sure if it was the right time to be thinking about school. In fact, Dartmouth, Yale, and Harvard were virtually empty now, he reported, with so many young men enlisting. If C.A. suspected that Harold was simply waffling, he trod gently, for he had undertaken once again to try to woo Grace back. In mid-July, a week before Hart's eighteenth birthday, C.A. at last proposed and Grace accepted. With that, she and Hart returned to Cleveland to prepare for the wedding.

But nothing had really changed. All the old tensions were still there, lying dormant for the moment, crackling, waiting to explode, as they did finally on the eve of the reunion, when Grace and C.A. quarreled bitterly over whether or not their son was going to be allowed to return to New York to live alone. Finally, C.A. stormed out of the house and back to the club, and Grace tried to take her own life by overdosing on bichloride of mercury. She was discovered, rushed to the hospital, and treated. Afterwards, she lapsed into a severe depression and took to her bed for weeks, lying in a darkened room and seeing no one but her mother. Beside himself over this bizarre turn of events, Harold stormed out of the house and took the train back to New York. Still, if the marriage was definitely over, C.A. was not quite ready to give up his only child.

"My dear Boy," he wrote Harold once calm had returned, "You are the only treasure I have on God's green earth, and your father's love for you is equal to any emergency."[19] Whether Harold decided to stay on in New York or return home, it was important that he build up his mind and character. Harold let a week elapse before he felt strong enough to write back. Once Grace was up and about, she would join him in New York, he told his father. In fact, he himself had been "diabolically nervous" since the final breakup and he was still trying to regain some equilibrium by resting out on one of Long Island's beaches. He was there now, on a Sunday morning, with two friends, Carl Schmitt and Stanislaw Portapovich, listening to the breakers crash against the shore.[20]

Schmitt, his father already knew. Portapovich, whom Harold had met through Schmitt, was a ballet dancer who had performed with Diaghilev's *Ballets Russes* and was now doing several shows a night at a restaurant up on Broadway and 145th. It was this same Portapovich who would later teach Crane the "gotzotzsky," an impossible Russian peasant dance Crane performed many times over during the next dozen years, arms folded and legs kicking out from a half-sitting position. Fueled with alcohol, he would dance it wherever a crowd of partygoers could be assembled: in country living rooms in the dead of winter, outdoors on the Fourth, on the streets of New York, in Los Angeles, in ballrooms aboard a liner crossing the Atlantic.

But now, lying under a blazing sun, Harold was trying to understand that there was more to life than just talk. He had a body to care for, too, a body that had been badly shaken by the reality of his parents' divorce. He knew his father cared for him, and he was hoping, now that the family had been finally torn apart, that nothing would "ever again break the foundation of sincerity" that had been forged between C.A. and himself. For the first time in writing his father, Harold signed himself "Hart Crane."[21] It was a gesture of independence, meant kindly but firmly. Although his father would continue to address him as Harold for the rest of his life, Hart Crane was how he now saw himself. It was a name meant to bridge the abyss that from this point on would separate his parents.

In August, Grace made one more halfhearted attempt at reconciliation before even she realized that the marriage was finally over. Three weeks after the fight that had sent Hart packing, C.A. wrote Grace a short, sharp note: "Forget C.A. Crane does or ever did *live*."[22] Within a week of receiving that note, she was back in New York, her mother with her, ready at thirty-nine to try to begin life again. But not yet, for she spent her first few weeks in New York confined to her bed. When C.A. wrote his son in mid-September, he could not help taking a few shots at his hysterical ex-wife. Caught in the middle, Hart begged his father to desist. "If, when you write me," the son pleaded, "you are thinking of Mother in a distasteful way, please conceal it, remaining silent on the subject. And if, in thinking of her, one kind thought should occur (as I know it does) express it."

As for himself, if he'd told his father they were through that last night in Cleveland, his anger had long passed. He loved both his parents. How could he not? But he'd heard only words of "forgiveness, tenderness, mercy, and love" on his mother's part, and only hard words from his father. How long this "purgatory" he and his parents were going through was going to last, he had no way of knowing. But he did know that his own fate was linked irrevocably to theirs. If they fought, he bled too.[23]

C.A.'s response to his son's mild rebuke was short and murderous. If the father meant to hurt his son, he clearly succeeded. Hart's asthma returned and his face broke out in welts. Now it was Grace who wrote C.A. His latest missive, she raged, had struck Hart "the hardest blow" he'd ever dealt him, with the result that his feelings for his father had congealed to ice.[24] With that, she closed the lease on the Gramercy Street apartment and returned to Cleveland, leaving her son to settle into a dingy apartment on East 11th Street. "Forget him," Hart wrote his mother when she was back in Cleveland. His father was "too low" even to think about. Nothing for it now but to bleed the bastard for all he was worth. "Why be scrupulous in one's dealings with unscrupulous people, anyway?" he added, heartbroken. It was time to get on with his own life.[25]

Among those Crane met in New York that fall of 1917 was the irrepressible Maxwell Bodenheim, poet, at twenty-four already a Greenwich Village fixture. At the moment he was working with Williams and Kreymborg as a sometime editor for the on-again, off-again *Others*. In late September, Bodenheim called on Crane at his apartment on 11th Street to compliment him on some poems of his he'd recently come across in *The Pagan*. When he left, he took several of Crane's new poems to show to James Oppenheim, co-editor with Waldo Frank, Van Wyck Brooks, and Paul Rosenfeld of *The Seven Arts*, a magazine that had been in existence now for the past year. Its purpose had been to call America's attention to the fact that the country was undergoing a period of national self-consciousness. America was destined for greatness, the editors believed, and Walt Whitman was the movement's guiding spirit.

No matter that the magazine would fold in a matter of weeks. It

was important to Crane that a man of Bodenheim's stature and importance to the new national movement should have sought him out. He
could identify with Bodenheim, who had just wrestled his way out of
"four years of absolute obscurity," Crane told his mother afterwards, and
he'd done it by flattering and cajoling editors—most of them disappointed writers themselves—until they'd been ready to notice him.
Bodenheim had also told Crane that as soon as *Others* could get back
on its feet and begin publishing again, he would personally see to it that
Crane's poems got a hearing there. "Success," Crane smiled, seemed
more imminent now than ever.[26] Five months earlier, Williams himself
had written him that, although *Others* was at the moment "floating precariously somewhere under and somewhere over something" for lack
of money, he liked Crane's stuff and would publish him as soon as possible.[27] But in spite of these reassurances, nothing of Crane's ever
appeared in the magazine.

Instead, he turned to pastures new. By October, in fact, he was col-
laborating with his landlady, Frances Walton, on a novel set in Havana
and the Isle of Pines, based on the caretaker of the Hart estate—one
Walter Wilcox—whom he envisioned as falling in love with a New
York "society maiden . . . attending the races in Havana."[28] But when
Grace wrote back that a hurricane had just smashed into the island,
destroying much of the plantation, so that Wilcox had been forced to
abandon the place, Crane abandoned his project. Instead, again with
Mrs. Walton's help, he began dreaming up short story plots for the well-
paying monthly *Smart Set*, as well as movie scripts. He even tried to
convince Grace—the eurhythmics dancer—to come back to New York
and dance for the movies. He was sure his landlady, who frequented
movie houses, would be able to help her land suitable work.

The long and short of it was that, nine months after arriving in
New York, Crane had yet to find a paying job. What money he received
from his father went for rent, food, clothing, and entertainment, and it
hurt to be beholden to his father, whom—he confided to Schmitt,
since returned to Ohio—he'd heard through the rumor mill now
thought of him as a "weakling . . . totally incapable of anything at all."
Still, he'd be damned if he was "going to . . . drudge at completely foreign tasks" at the expense of his poetry. Certainly not if he had any say
in the matter.[29]

By October, there were signs everywhere in New York that America was on a war footing. Every few days Crane seemed to run into

yet another parade making its way down Fifth Avenue, in the process tying up traffic for hours. In fact, there were patriotic parades for everyone and everything: dog parades, cat parades, all marching, he complained, to "that eternally rapturous and boring melody, 'Over There.'"[30] At Thanksgiving, he became ill, and Grace returned to New York to be with him. Then she too became ill. She tried enlisting C.A.'s sympathy and support, and wrote begging him to come east and help take care of their boy. But C.A., sniffing a trap, refused. He'd be damned if he'd come, he told her, even if Harold was dying.

When Grace informed him of his father's rejection, Crane's illness became more pronounced. He was barely managing to hold "on to health and sanity with both hands," he confessed to Schmitt,[31] and was relieved when Aunt Zell decided to take matters into her own hands and arrived to help Grace and Harold out. A month later, with the approach of Christmas, mother and son returned to Cleveland, only to find themselves the guests of honor at a dinner party C.A. had arranged. But this gesture too, like all the others, went nowhere. In early January 1918, Grace and Hart returned once more to New York—Grace to hotel accommodations, Hart to his miserable flat on East 11th.

"I am really getting a reputation for poetry and can find space now in at least two magazines for most of my better work," he'd told his mother back in October.[32] He had continued to write his Yellow Decade poetry for both *Bruno's Weekly* and *The Pagan* during these months. Then, at Halloween, he'd been invited to the offices of *The Little Review* to meet with the editors, Margaret Anderson and Jane Heap, "and perhaps dispose of a poem."[33] The office—in a three-story building on West 16th Street that had once served as William Cullen Bryant's home—was located above a funeral parlor and embalming school. With its Chinese gold wallpaper, off-white woodwork, dark plum floors, old mahogany furniture, and divan suspended from the ceiling by black chains, the magazine's offices were meant to make a statement, and they did. Crane was duly impressed.

Months earlier, Pound had been named foreign editor of the magazine, and soon he was sending poems and essays by Eliot, Yeats, and Wyndham Lewis on to New York. Thanks in part to Pound, *The Little Review* also began running James Joyce's *Ulysses* in its pages, that is, until the U.S. government brought obscenity charges and the magazine would be forced to stop publication for a year. Here, then, was *the* place to be published.

In late September Crane received a letter from Margaret Anderson. "Dear *Hart* Crane, poet!!" she saluted him. "I'm using 'Shadow' in the December issue. . . . It's the best thing you've sent yet."[34] Crane had written the poem only weeks earlier, inspired by the lyrics of Wallace Stevens, a poet he'd been reading in the pages of *Poetry*. Composed of four interlocking rhymed quatrains, "In Shadow" is a subtle, understated seduction piece, in which the poet appears to be following someone, perhaps a prostitute. There was about the poem a quiet authority and a finer music than Crane had yet been able to manage, and he knew instinctively that he was onto something here:

> Out in the late amber afternoon,
> Confused among chrysanthemums,
> Her parasol, a pale balloon,
> Like a waiting moon, in shadow swims.[35]

When, the following spring, Pound wrote Crane an Easter sonnet as part of his foreign editor column, he wisecracked that, while beauty was "a good enough egg," as far as he could see, Crane didn't have "the ghost of a setting hen or an incubator" of hatching that beauty. The truth was that unless Pound himself discovered a writer, he had little use for him. Crane wrote back, tactfully measuring the older man. Really, he retorted, Pound's literary judgment was "too good a douche" to waste on a poor novice like himself. Then he turned the tables by praising Pound as "second only to Yeats of living poets writing in English." That must have soothed even Pound's enormous ego for the moment.[36]

Still, now that he had made it into the pages of *The Little Review*, Crane began reassessing his involvement with *Bruno's Weekly* and *The Pagan*. Joe Kling had been delighted to have Crane on his masthead, and had already called him the equal of any poet writing in America. This was certainly more generous than Pound's assessment, but Crane no longer trusted Kling's criticism or the general tone of Kling's magazine. He knew Kling was guilty of hyperbole in speaking of his own modest achievements, but that he could live with. Moreover, the magazine was still providing a ready outlet for his poems. In fact, he would publish six more in its pages between the fall of 1917 and the following summer—poems with titles like "Echoes," "The Bathers," "Modern Craft," "Carmen de Bohème," "Exile," "Postscript," "Forgetfulness." He even began publishing reviews there, the first of which, "The Case Against Nietzsche," appeared in the spring of 1918.

It was a spirited defense of Nietzsche against the strong anti–German feeling created by America's entry into the war, feeling that had already spilled over into violence against German Americans. Crane followed up the piece with a second, entitled "The Last Chord," which examined various concerts, exhibitions, and plays going on about New York that winter. He focused on several poetic dramas being performed in the Village: the Provincetown Players in Eugene O'Neill's *Ile;* the Other Players' rendering of Kreymborg's puppet play *Manikin and Miniken;* and Edna St. Vincent Millay's *Two Slatterns and a King.*

For a few weeks that March Crane found work in the basement of Brentano's Bookshop at 26th and Fifth, selling books, as he phrased it, on "wet nursing, care of mothers during pregnancy, the Montessori method, and how to know the wild flowers."[37] No one, he noticed with dismay, ever seemed to ask him where the poetry section was. When Grace at last returned to Cleveland in April, he moved into an apartment at 78 Washington Place, between Sixth and Washington Square. It was a larger apartment than he'd rented before and boasted all the twentieth-century luxuries: double bed, stove, closet, even running water. His old high school chum, George Bryan, who had enrolled in Carleton Academy just across the Hudson in New Jersey, spent a weekend with him in the new apartment soon after he moved in. "Write soon, George," Crane wrote afterwards, using green ink (for spring! spring!), because Bryan was the one person now who seemed to be able to bring him any "sense of restfulness and satisfaction."[38] He even began making plans to share rooms with Bryan somewhere in the country that summer. But those plans were shattered a few weeks later by a letter from his mother begging him to return home as soon as possible. Come August, she'd just learned, C.A. was planning to remarry.

2 / SHUTTLECOCK

CLEVELAND/NEW YORK
JUNE 1918–NOVEMBER 1919

C.A. HAD SET HIS HEART on a black-haired, docile Irish beauty named Frances Kelley. The marriage would turn out to be a good one for both of them. As for Grace, she went at once into denial, keeping up a feverish round of activities to try to forget C.A.'s perfidy. She took part in amateur plays, began riding and driving lessons, and tried to find comfort in a handsome Roadster. Then, as the wedding day drew nearer, she made plans to take a long trip east with Hart and her mother. Part of the plan was to have her son act as companion and chauffeur, but Crane artfully dodged those tortures by finding "essential" war-related work at Warners, a munitions plant on the Cleveland waterfront. There he worked grueling eight-hour shifts, tightening bolts on machine parts as they rolled past one after the other on the assembly line. When Grace at last left for her trip on the Fourth of July, 1918, she and her mother in the backseat, it was Charles, the hired hand up front, who was doing the driving. The three were New York–bound, and along the route Grace would stop to look over no less than twelve colleges to see if any of them might prove suitable for her son.

But after just two weeks at Warners, with Grace too far away to protest, Crane quit his job. His nineteenth birthday he celebrated with his old friend Bill Wright, working that summer as a counselor in a boys' camp outside Cleveland. With all the time in the world on his hands, Crane had his teeth fixed, looked around for work when the mood took him, scribbled a bit, and pored over Joyce's *Portrait of the Artist as a Young Man*. He even played with the idea of getting married, joking to Wright—perhaps to hide his real feelings about such matters—that if he could only dig up some "lonely young lady (or old) with a lot of money," he would tie the knot.[1]

When, that July, a Los Angeles critic attacked *Portrait of the Artist* as a study in decadence, Crane became infuriated enough to send a letter off to *The Little Review*. Decadent? The only decadent writing was *bad* writing. "A piece of work is art, or it isn't," he insisted; there was no middle ground. He'd already put Swinburne and Wilde behind him—Swinburne because he was a poet of "beautiful, though often meaningless mouthings," all sound and "irrelevant metaphors," and Wilde because, after one sorted out and analyzed his paradoxes, "very little evidence of intellect" remained.[2] By 1918, he had graduated to two new heroes—Baudelaire and Joyce—because these two had somehow managed to penetrate to the heart of life as only the greatest artists could. Decadent? Except for Dante, *Portrait of the Artist* had turned out to be the most spiritual book he'd ever read.

By early August, Grace and her mother were back in Cleveland. For a day or two things were fine, but Grace was edgy, and soon she was twitting Hart about all the fine, young red-blooded American boys she saw walking around now in uniform. And here was her son without so much as a job to help the country out in its time of need. Two days of this was as much as he could take before he went down to the local recruiting center to enlist. That very day—August 12th—Crane had heard from Wright, who had written to say that because he might soon be drafted, he'd been thinking of volunteering for the ambulance corps. As it turned out, the government, assessing the progress of the war, had decided that same day not to accept any more young recruits. "You will not be drafted," Crane told Wright that afternoon, at least not for the coming year. He himself had been stopped by a guard at the entrance to the recruiting station, and when he'd asked why, been told to read the papers.

If he were in fact drafted now, he would no doubt be assigned to a factory or a machine shop, work he'd already tried and found distasteful. In any event, by the time he was sent overseas, the war would probably be over. "Some would call me a demon of the Huns for whispering this in your ear," Crane added, but there it was. It had been

neither patriotism nor bravery but the August heat, as well as the heat
at home, that had prompted him to rush down to the draft board that
morning. He had certainly not tried to join up for the ladies. Still,
having made up his mind, and having "disposed of so many seductive
distractions, such as, (well—) love, poetry, career, etc.," he was sorry to
have been turned away. Now all those "damned things" were back
again, "sporting about me with all too much familiarity." He might go
to New York, he ended; he might stay put; he might just explode.[3]

He may also have decided to join up as a way of getting his father's
attention, for C.A. was due to marry his new bride out in Kansas City
in just two days' time. When that happened, the tension at home would
become unbearable. Anxious to get away, Crane went back to the
docks, finding new war-related work as a riveter. For three weeks he
crouched in the bellies of the huge tankers, crawling precariously from
girder to girder amid shouts, curses, and the incessant flare of acety-
lene sparks, as he hammered away in the debilitating heat. What put an
end to the job, finally, was a severe case of hay fever that nearly blinded
him, his doctor ordering him to quit before he really hurt himself. Then
he learned that, without war-essential work, and with the war dragging on, he was once again eligible for the draft. Within weeks, however, a deadly influenza epidemic began killing off civilians and soldiers
together, shutting down one boot camp after another as late summer
gave way to fall. And then—overnight—the war was over. He celebrated by writing an armistice sonnet and sending it to the *Cleveland
Plain Dealer*, which not only published it but also hired him on as a
cub reporter at a salary of twenty dollars a week.

Having landed a literary job of sorts, Crane lost no time in sending off six poems to the Reverend Charles Bubb of Cleveland, editor
of the modest Church Head Press. If he wasn't ready to publish a book,
then perhaps a pamphlet published locally. It would be a start. He was
offering this "meager sheaf," he wrote Bubb, as the best work he'd so
far done. Five of the poems had already been published in *The Pagan*, the
sixth in *The Little Review*. Perhaps they might be printed as a little pamphlet under the title "Six Lyrics." Because he knew the Reverend Bubb's
critical judgment was "of the highest standard," and because he knew
there might still be "flaws and aberrations" in his work, Crane asked
Bubb to be especially "alive to whatever beauty" the poems might contain. And since he was only nineteen, he added coyly, he knew there
might no doubt still be room for improvement. As he was now work-

ing full time as a newspaperman, he regretted he could not call on the Reverend in person. Instead, he would leave the poems with Mr. Laukhuff at his bookstore.[4] But there was no reply, no nibble, nothing.

Crane's initiation into the bleaker aspects of reporting came on the night of December 12th, when he was called to the scene of a "smash-up" on Cleveland's west side. Bodies everywhere. Six dead, four taken by ambulance to the city hospital. Crane followed the ambulances to the morgue, where for the next three hours five of the dead remained unidentified. Repulsed and fascinated, he watched as the mangled bodies were undressed, washed, and laid out on slabs. "I didn't puke nor anything else," he confessed to George Bryan afterwards, "but for a first experience it was a trial."[5] But only a first experience. In the weeks to follow he would spend more than his share of cold nights covering accidents or waiting around the morgue for something to happen. He was there Christmas Day and there again on "First Night," when he was sent to identify a woman "who had celebrated the holiday season" by drowning herself in Lake Erie.[6] Mercifully, he had Christmas night off, and spent it drinking and smoking Cincos cigars in his tower room with Bryan, unburdening himself of the rage he felt toward his parents for the goddamn mess they'd made of his life.

After seven weeks Crane was ready to call it quits. By New Year's, whatever glamour he thought there might have been in being a cub reporter had long ago worn off, and he was sure the routine was simply making him dull and stupid. On 8 January 1919, he finally resigned and began looking for another job. But this time he came up with nothing. He tried writing movie scripts, again without any luck. Hearing of his son's plight, C.A. offered to give him an allowance until he could once again get back on his feet. Then Grace sank into another of her depressions, taking to her bed and pulling the covers over her head. Crane did what he could to help her, but all he succeeded in accomplishing was to become more and more depressed himself. There was nothing for it but to get out of Cleveland and back to New York as soon as he could.

At last, on the evening of February 20th, he boarded a Pullman sleeper bound for Manhattan. The following morning, back in the city again, having arrived this time in freezing rain, he sent a postcard off to Bryan: "It sure seems good to be back in the old town."[7] The first thing he did was to return to his old apartment on East 11th Street to see his former landlady, Mrs. Walton, and spend the night there. The following day he found a dollar-a-night flat uptown at 119 West 76th Street. Then he began looking up his old friends: Alfred Kreymborg and his wife, Dorothy; his former tutor, Mme Lebegue; Joe Kling, editor of *The Pagan*; and his old friend Mrs. Spencer over by Gramercy Park, who provided him with a decent dinner.

Afterwards, he and Mrs. Spencer sat in front of a wood fire and talked about the efficacy of Christian Science. She spoke of friends of hers who had, she was convinced, been saved from certain death because of their faith. Crane listened politely and said little. Then, while she washed the dishes, he played the piano. Even in this wet weather, he wrote his mother, it was good to be back in New York, for the whole city was "ablaze with life." The avenues sparkled in the rain and there was so much wealth everywhere that money seemed to "roll in the gutters." It was like being in New York that first time, only better, for he saw things now "with different, keener, happier eyes than ever before."[8] To George Bryan, he was more matter-of-fact. "I find all my old friends either married or making loads of money," he wrote him, "seldom both."[9]

But he too was looking to make some much-needed money and movie scripts were still high on his list of ways of doing just that. Somebody he knew in New York had recently been offered $2,000 "for a scenario it won't take him a day to write,"[10] he wrote Bryan. But when the movie script idea fizzled, he turned his attention instead to ad writing. The trouble was that finding any kind of work in New York in the spring of 1919 was becoming impossible. "Every day a couple of troupe-ships [sic] dumps [sic] a few thousand more unemployed men in the town," he complained to his mother three weeks after arriving, so that there seemed a real danger of economic depression and even the possibility of "general panic" unless the government did something, and soon.[11]

"Don't give up your job until you have to, is my advice these days to almost everybody," he wrote Bryan on March 17th. It was impossible even to find work waiting on tables or pushing a street broom; not that he'd actually "applied for these elevated positions."[12] He tried finding work on several Sunday newspapers as a writer, but again without luck. Through the intervention of his old friend, Padraic

Colum, he was offered an interview with Colum's publishers, Boni & Liveright, for work as a proofreader, but nothing came of this either. He contacted his cousin, eighteen-year-old Alice Calhoun, an aspiring actress who'd found work with one of the New York–based movie companies, hoping to interest her in one of his movie scripts. Again nothing.

There were other troubles as well. After two weeks in his apartment, his landlady having by then "committed enough atrocities . . . to fill a book,"[13] he was ready to move on. The woman, it turned out, was actually crazy. A friend had called his hall telephone three times, only to be told by the landlady that there was no one named Hart Crane living there. Only after another tenant had overheard her and had taken down the caller's name and number did Crane learn what had happened. Several times she had come up to his room, pointing at something only she could see and asking if the thing was his. Once he'd been interrupted by a knock on the door to find her whispering that the thing was down there. It was time to move on.

What he found with the help of another tenant, Alex Baltzly, was a basement apartment at 307 West 70th Street, just off Riverside Drive. Baltzly was a Harvard grad and one more ex-army officer who had just found himself coming off a transport and being decommissioned right there in New York. Since he'd once roomed at the West End apartment, he promised Crane that the little Irish landlady who ran the place was not only sane but actually competent. By late March, the two men were sharing a room for $3.50 each a week. Spring, Crane sighed, and now he found himself doing what he'd long dreamed of doing: walking up along the Hudson River and watching the lights on the Jersey shore shining like millions of stars.

Adrift and without a job, he spent his days hanging around Joe Kling's bookstore, its walls hung with reproductions of the Ashcan School—George Bellows and John Sloan—as well as of more avant-garde artists like Stuart Davis, Gaudier-Brzeska, Paul Signac, William Gropper. It was here, in early March, that Kling introduced him to another young writer who was also writing for *The Pagan*, another new arrival to the city like himself: Gorham Munson. The discussion turned to the brilliance of Joyce's *Ulysses*, then appearing in installments in *The Little Review*. In Munson, Crane at once sensed a kindred spirit, and soon the two men were seeing a good deal of each other.

It was Art Crane was after now, not religion, and within weeks of returning to New York, he finally told his mother he was no longer interested in Christian Science. "The fact that I do not talk and write about it continually is no sort of testimony that I am not as much interested as ever in it," he wrote in early April, trying to appease her after she'd written to ask why he'd cooled toward it.[14] But he was constitutionally incapable of pursuing the Science wholeheartedly, he tried to explain. The truth was that the Scientists who did follow it zealously frankly bored him because they seemed afraid to accept life with all its uncertainties. With Bill Wright, he was even blunter. He no longer gave a damn about Christian Science, though he was anxious to have his mother think he did because she needed "to depend on that hypocrisy as an additional support for her own faith in it." It was only because her belief in the Science had done her some good that he'd lied to her about his own interest in it, though God knew "lying to both Lord and Devil" was no pleasure.[15] If the method worked—and he believed it often did—it was because an optimistic outlook on life really did seem to make a difference. As a way of dealing with stress, he had no problem with it, and in fact it had often acted as a balm on his own too-taut nerves. But when it came to denying the reality of the physical world, he drew the line. If God was to be found in experience, He had to be found in all experience, the bad along with the good, and not just in some sanitized version of life.

In early May, Alex Baltzly left New York for an insurance job in Boston, and Crane moved downtown to a room above the offices of *The Little Review* on West 16th Street. The rent there was just ten dollars a month for a large, unheated room on the third floor. He also found work as the magazine's unpaid advertising manager, and soon he was pounding the streets looking for prospective advertisers, though without much success. (But who besides a handful of intellectuals had ever heard of *The Little Review*?) He'd hoped to make $4,000 a year with the job, and instead he'd come up with nothing. How hard it was, he was learning, to get through the door of "some of these huge and ominous mechanisms, New York offices," especially if you were trying to sell them ad space for some literary magazine.[16]

In fact, the only takers he found were his father, who bought several full-page ads for his Mary Garden line of chocolates, and Stan Portapovich, who took out an ad as "Maître de Danse," figuring he owed Crane that much for the poem Crane had recently published praising Portapovich's dance skills. "To Portapovich" had just appeared in the pages of yet another New York–based little magazine, this one called *The Modern School*. On his return to New York, Crane had visited with Portapovich and his wife, Anna, but the magic he'd found in Portapovich the year before was gone. The man who could put on two shows a night at Healey's seven nights a week, the man who had vaulted "on the opal carpet of the sun," this "Barbaric Prince Igor," this Daphnis, this "blind Pierrot" whose gestures had seemed "More real than life,"[17] had now settled into a life of smug conventionality, offering dancing lessons to a few mediocre students as a way of getting by.

Thanks to the generosity of a new friend, Crane was paying very little for rent. The new friend was Harrison (Hal) Smith, young, affluent, an editor at Harcourt, who had recently married Claire Spencer, the girl Crane had lived next door to in Gramercy Park the year before. Crane and Spencer had taken a liking to each other then, going on long walks and talking about all sorts of things, so that Crane had gone back to Cleveland thinking he and Claire had come to some vague sort of understanding. But if they had, Claire herself knew nothing about it, believing—from the way he'd acted—that she and Crane were simply good friends. In any case, she was now married, and Crane would simply have to readjust his thinking. As it turned out, the young couple took a liking to Crane, amused by his high spirits and hearty laughter, his crazy antics, his intelligence. Besides, Hal Smith, who fancied himself a writer, was delighted to find himself in the presence of a rising young New York poet. He had money, and he knew how to be generous with it.

In effect, Crane had all but taken over Smith's study, which adjoined his own room, and was now using Smith's desk and typewriter. It was just as well, for Crane was down to his last fifteen cents. He'd already cashed his mother's emergency checks, but having learned that the money she'd given him was from her own allowance and not set aside for him by C.A., he could not bring himself to ask her for more. Luckily, when the Smiths discovered that he had no furniture and no money to buy any, Claire bought him a bed, then found him some sheets, pillows, and blankets, along with a few sticks of furniture. For the rest, Crane asked his mother to forward his rugs and some other things from his room back home. By that gesture he broke the news to her as gently as possible that, job or no job, at nineteen he was in New York to stay.

If he hated being at the mercy of his father, especially now that he'd severed all personal contact, he hated even more taking what his mother needed for herself. He could not resist writing her and asking why she didn't insist on the provisions of the divorce settlement being carried out. All he wanted was what was due him by the terms of that settlement, and he did not want to have to hear her tell him down the line that she'd been forced to curtail her own pleasures to take care of him. He had not forgotten her "twitting" him the summer before for not paying board when he was living at home, so that he no longer welcomed her "generosity quite so much," for fear she would some day throw it in his face.[18]

Here he was, the son of well-to-do parents who had managed not only to destroy their own marriage but were now destroying his future. For eight years, his youth had been a "bloody battleground" for his parents' "sex life and troubles."[19] Had he had a normal youth, he told her, he would now be in college on his way to a career, rather than looking at the prospect of sweeping streets or washing dishes for a living. He put the best spin he could on his so-called job at *The Little Review*. Yes, someday it just might pay a decent salary, but he could no longer fool himself. He had no real experience in copywriting, and each day now he trudged the city streets looking for a real job. If only he could find the money to take courses in business and advertising at Columbia, he had to believe he might still land on his feet.

After all, as he confessed to Bill Wright, America *was* big business, and sooner or later everyone bowed to that inevitability. That did not mean, of course, surrendering one's "nobler and better" aspirations.[20] He still had Plato for company each night, and Chaucer and Cervantes, and Twain and James and Lawrence. And he still managed to meet interesting people from time to time. One night, after a theater party, he'd walked Robert Frost's daughter, Lesley, back to her rooms at Barnard. She'd been "worth looking at," he told Wright, and he hoped "to see more of her."[21] But, like everything else, it was—as Carl Schmitt kept telling him the year before—all a matter of keeping things in balance. Work and relaxation, and money to do what he wanted. But as the weeks passed and he could still find nothing, he was reduced almost to begging. Whatever rose-colored visions he'd had of New York, the poverty of his situation made him see the city now as one vast wasteland. Perhaps there was wisdom in having one's illusions shattered, no matter how painful, he told Wright. Certainly there was a strange kind of freedom in that. Yes, New York really could be savage, much more savage than Cleveland had ever been. And yet, what vistas it offered: its rivers, its bridges, its skyscrapers, its multitudes. There was really no other city quite like it, either for sublimity or for slapstick comedy.

As with Crane and the Baroness. Only in New York was someone like this woman possible—a woman who had already struck fear not only in Wallace Stevens but in William Carlos Williams as well. The Baroness was Elsa von Freytag-Loringhoven, widow of the late Baron Loringhoven, who, summoned to serve in the German Army in 1914, had decided instead to put a bullet through his brain, leaving his wife stranded in New York. But the Baroness had proved herself infinitely resourceful, becoming in the process the very symbol of Dadaism. She acted and dressed the part, affecting the most outlandish and daring costumes: coal scuttle hats, and teaballs suspended from her nipples; a head with two different faces in profile, one yellow, one purple. She sported hats with feathers and ice cream spoons, wore black vests and kilts, tam o'shanters.

Once, when Stevens, seeing her on the streets of Greenwich Village, had applauded one of her costumes, she'd chased after him so that he'd refused to go below 14th Street for years after. Once, she hid in Williams's car outside his house and attacked him when he was called out to see a patient in the middle of the night. After that he practiced with a punching bag in his basement, in case she came too close again. She published long, rambling, sporadically brilliant missives in *The Little Review,* where she became something of a fixture. As for Crane, he was soon performing hilarious little parodies of her heavily accented speech and exaggerated gestures for friends. But when the Baroness decided she needed a typewriter, she simply walked into Crane's room and took his—the one belonging to Hal Smith—and lugged it back to her own apartment. After a week of waiting to get it back, Crane had to explain to Smith what had happened. Together, they decided to descend on the Baroness and demand the typewriter back. Once in her apartment, they could see it sitting there in plain view on a table, while they wracked their brains over how to get it back. Finally, they quit, leaving the typewriter behind. It was easier, Smith had decided, simply to buy another.

Summer swept down over the city like a succubus. For relief, the Smiths took a cottage across the Hudson River in West Englewood, New Jersey, inviting Crane to spend long weekends with them. The place was "perfection itself," Crane wrote Bill Wright on June 17th. Here was a retreat where one could escape the congestion of the city and actually "see the moon and stars and hear the frogs croak" and do nothing "but live in one's bathing suit and go canoeing and play tennis and eat amazingly."[22] He enjoyed himself outdoors immensely, until he came down with a terrible case of sunburn. In July, the Smiths found another place out in Brookhaven, Long Island, for the month, and again they invited Crane to spend as much time with them as he could.

But again Crane was penniless. On July 10th, just before leaving to join the Smiths, he wrote his mother begging for enough money to get a haircut and some razor blades. By then he'd been reduced to asking Smith for rent money and enough extra to buy some food. He was going without meals rather than ask for any more, though the Smiths had been unstintingly generous with him. True, he might find work in some machine shop or on the docks; but work like that barely kept body and soul together, and neither job was going to help him write poetry. He even wrote his father, asking if he would pay for his class in business and advertising at Columbia; but C.A., miffed at his son's rejection of his new marriage, did not write back. Worse, C.A. had yet to pay for the ads he'd taken out in *The Little Review.* Rage, impotent rage, was what Crane felt for his father now.

Then the Brookhaven interlude became strained. True, there were idyllic moments, with Crane joking, telling stories, dancing with Claire under a moonlit sky with the scratchy windup Victrola playing Wagner and *Valse Bleu* and *Valse Triste.* But by then Claire was expecting a child and becoming more and more withdrawn. Feeling himself somehow displaced and helpless, Crane became increasingly irritable, going so far as to leave his diary open for her to see just how upset he was with her. Then, late one night, after everyone had gone to bed, the Smiths heard Crane noisily packing his trunk. A scene of mutual recrimination and contrition followed, until the Smiths relented, and begged Crane to stay.

Finally, C.A. wrote his son, asking him to be in New York on July 29th for a job interview at the offices of Rheinthal & Newman, a firm that supplied C.A. with Maxfield Parrish reproductions for his Mary Garden line of chocolates. The meeting proved very satisfactory, Crane wrote his mother afterwards, and he was to begin work in the order department there on September 1st. Until then, he planned to stay on in Brookhaven. Instead, there was another blowup with the Smiths a week after the interview. This time Crane stormed out and returned to New York, where he began work at once. What had proved most important about the new job, from Crane's point of view, was his father's having gone out of his way to help him. His mother had blown hot, cold, and indifferent toward C.A., Hart told her bluntly now, largely because she'd been hurt by her husband's leaving her for another woman. But that was her problem. As far as he was concerned, he was ready to believe his father really was a decent man after all, someone who had cared enough to help him out when he most needed it.

Then, in September, Crane's hay fever returned. The condition became so bad that he had to stop working for a week. On top of which, there was the intense late summer heat in a stifling study to contend with. That, and bedbugs in his mattress, which kept him up half the night. As a gesture of reconciliation, Hal Smith turned his room completely over to Crane, though he continued to pay for it. He also gave him all the extra furniture he could find from his New Jersey bungalow. But the damage there had been done, and the Smiths began to recede into the background, as others had before them. With the coming of fall, new people took their places: Gorham Munson, and then Munson's literary friend, Matthew Josephson, the latter part of a new breed of New York writers—cool, cynical, worldly, urbane, detached.

There was also a young woman Crane had met through Alex Baltzly, one Charmion von Wiegand, an aspiring writer recently married to Hermann Habicht, an executive with the Habicht-Braun import-export firm in New York, which—as it turned out—did business with Crane's father. With the Habichts, and especially with Charmion, Crane could relax and enjoy intelligent conversation on almost any topic. More, Charmion looked to Crane as to a mentor and teacher. Bill Wright had also recently moved to New York, where he was about to begin classes at Columbia. On a Saturday in mid-September, Crane took Wright and another Cleveland friend for a tour of New York: Chu Chin Chow's in Chinatown for a show, followed by beer, sandwiches, and cabaret music at Churchill's.

Back in August, Crane had sent Munson a picture postcard of the Brooklyn Bridge with a note saying he meant to get over to the offices of *The Modernist* on East 14th to meet James Waldo Fawcett, the magazine's editor and a friend of Munson's. "Knowing your predilection for bridges," he'd written over the photo on the postcard, "I send you this!"[23] But it wasn't until early October that Crane finally got around to *The Modernist*'s offices to drop off some poems. Three of these—"Legende," "Interior," and "North Labrador" (all early works, all short)—were published in the November issue, the sole issue of the magazine to appear.

"Legende" spoke of the loss of an unnamed woman (Crane probably altering genders here), where only the memory remained, "Like a shell surrendered to evening sands," until the all-devouring sea would erase eventually even that.[24] "Interior" spoke of a stolen hour of love in some lamplit room, hidden from a jealous world. And "North Labrador," the most controlled of the three, described the poet in the face of an intractable Sublime, a land of eternal ice beyond hope of change, a place of "No birth, no death, no time nor sun."[25] The first two poems had returned to the theme of love won and lost, with all particulars erased except for the loneliness and *tristesse* inevitably following such assignations. "North Labrador" rounded out the triad by presenting the claustrophobic image of a self forever locked in ice.

Ice: with November and the onset of colder weather, Crane was at last forced to abandon his unheated apartment and find a furnished room at the Hotel Albert on University Place and 11th Street. By then he knew the job at Rheinthal & Newman's—stocking shelves and jumping at the bidding of secretaries—was going nowhere, and now he decided to abandon that as well. He'd taken it as a gesture of goodwill toward his father, and look where that had gotten him. A child could do what he did, and—as the weeks had passed—he'd felt more and more demeaned. Sensing that Harold had now played out his hand at independence and failed, C.A. wrote to say that, with business booming, there would always be a place for him if he ever came back to Cleveland. His options depleted, Crane realized he had no choice but to return home.

On November 5th, he wrote his friend Charmion Wiegand from his hotel room at the Albert, bitter and self-mocking about the way the New York experiment had turned out. He was leaving "the big city" the following evening and taking the train back to those "great expanses of cornfields so much talked about and sung." Eight months in New York had yielded almost nothing in the way of poetry. Ironically, on the very eve of his departure, he began a poem "in an entirely new vein with the luscious title: 'My Grandmother's Love Letters.'" He didn't want "to make the dear old lady too sweet or too naughty," he joked, "and balancing on the fine line between these two qualities" was going to be fun. He hoped being in the same house again with his grand-mother didn't kill the poem for him.[26] In fact, "My Grandmother's Love Letters" would turn out to be the best poem he'd written yet.

3 / ABOUT MY FATHER'S BUSINESS

FIVE DAYS AFTER RETURNING HOME, Harold went with his father to visit his father's new store in Akron, forty miles south of Cleveland. Harold would have to start from the bottom—it would be C.A.'s way of breaking in his son—and he would be expected to put in seventeen-hour days, from six in the morning until eleven at night, six days a week. In 1919, Akron was a bustling metropolis, home of the rubber tire; and with hundreds of thousands of new cars hitting the road each year, all needing tires, Akron was like one of those earlier frontier gold rush towns in California and Alaska. The same month that Crane arrived in Akron, the local papers saluted the news that the net worth of the city had just reached the half-billion-dollar mark.

C.A. was in there with the best of them. His new store had been outfitted with an enormous soda fountain on one side and counters of chocolates ranging alongside opposite. *CRANE'S: A store that would be distinguished on Fifth Avenue,* the ads ran. *CRANE'S WONDERFUL CANDIES.* But it was not this store that C.A. had chosen for Harold. Harold would work out of the Portage Drug Store, where a one-man counter had been installed, behind which Harold would sell Mary Garden Chocolates specially packaged for the Christmas season.

He was game enough, though it seemed a shame to waste a store as delicious-looking as his father's new one on a place like Akron. Still, Akron was bustling, no doubt about it, with new buildings going up everywhere. In fact, the main thoroughfares were littered with rubble from old buildings being torn down to make way for new factories. It was like something out of Bret Harte, Crane mused, with as many Slavs and Jews on the streets as he used to see along New York's Sixth Avenue, but without the El darkening overhead. Moreover, with his father's business "whizzing," he enjoyed dreaming of the millions C.A. would be worth before he was finished.[1] If only he could prove himself to his father, he stood to get a son's share of all that wealth.

In mid-November, he settled into the Hotel Akron, ready to go to work, knowing that his other work—writing—would have to be sandwiched in between midnight and dawn. But because C.A. had failed to advertise the Portage Drug Store location until just before Christmas, Crane found himself with all the time in the world on his hands. Much of it he spent at the nearby Temple Book Store, reading copies of *The Little Review*, as well as de Maupassant, Pound's *Pavannes & Divigations,* and T. S. Eliot. There were his New York friends to keep in touch with: Charmion, Munson, Josephson. And now a new correspondent: Sherwood Anderson. Back in September, Crane had praised Anderson's *Winesburg, Ohio* in *The Pagan,* comparing the book favorably to Edgar Lee Masters, de Maupassant, Balzac, even Lucretius. "America should read this book on her knees," his review closed. "It constitutes an important chapter in the Bible of her consciousness." Reading that, Anderson had written back to thank Crane.[2]

In the months to come, the correspondence would flourish. When Crane wrote Anderson about his job in Akron, Anderson wrote back telling him about his own early business experiences in Cleveland and Elyria. When Crane complained that his father did not understand his attraction to the arts, Anderson tried to explain C.A.'s side of the issue. "The arts [C.A.] ridicules have not been very sturdy and strong among us," he wrote in early December. "Our books are not much, our poetry not much yet. The battle has scarcely begun. These men are right too when they ridicule our pretensions."[3] Artists could do worse, Anderson added, than to model themselves on the rugged individualism of businessmen like Crane's father. Soon Crane was pitting Anderson against Josephson, Josephson representing the "classic, hard and glossy" aspects of modernism, Anderson the "crowd-bound, with a smell of the sod about him, uncouth." It was Eliot versus Whitman. And somewhere between them Hart Crane, "with a kind of wistful indetermination, still much puzzled."[4]

Within weeks of leaving New York, Crane had already outgrown the aesthetics of *The Modernist*. Most of it was garbage, he complained to Munson, "a confused, indiscriminate jelly-like mass."[5] Even *The Little Review* had sunk in his estimation. At night, back in his hotel room, he read by the light of a small desklamp pale titillations like Sir James Barrie ("subtle satire par excellence")[6] and, a treat, Mark Twain's underground scatological pamphlet *1601*. But he also read—at Munson's prompting—Waldo Frank's *Our America*, a just published analysis of the American national consciousness. The grim picture Frank had drawn was accurate enough, Crane could see, but it was too damn dark, and his midwestern optimism balked. Could Dreiser, Anderson, and Frost "have gone so far creatively" had they been given this analysis when they had started out? he wondered.[7] Those men had written as well as they had precisely because they'd not allowed themselves to overanalyze everything. Instead, they'd followed their natural inclinations and written of what they knew. Still, Frank had hit a nerve. He'd been right to question where the country was going.

So, when Bill Wright wrote Crane that after three months of it he was fed up with Columbia University and was thinking of leaving, Crane wrote back urging him to stick it out. Most Americans, he explained, were "mad fanatics on pragmatism." How much was a thing worth? How much did one make in a year? What was the bottom line? What was missing in Americans was a "seasoning of culture." Even the colleges had turned into "business institutions run by successful-business-men-trustees." He promised to send Wright his copy of *Our America*, which would make it clearer why Wright had to get an education: not for some job, but for the sake of knowledge itself. He urged Wright to read what he himself was reading: Rabelais, Twain, Conrad.[8] In turn, Anderson urged Crane on. Read Van Wyck Brooks's *Ordeal of Mark Twain*, he told him, for the "vague, intangible hunger" to express the inchoate that seemed to eat at Twain was eating at Anderson as well, as he sensed it was also eating at Crane. It wasn't so much a "hunger to defeat the materialism of the world," Anderson believed, as it was finding "brothers buried away beneath all this roaring, modern insanity of life. You in Akron, another man in California," another "shivering in some cold room in New York." America was vast, vast, and no single voice could "carry across the spaces." But together, think of what such a visionary company might achieve.[9]

Such thoughts were much on Crane's mind when he consented to an interview with a reporter from the *Akron Sunday Times*. The reporter, one Alice Chamberlain, learning that Crane was working in a local drugstore and that his father was the owner of Akron's premier drugstore, interviewed him for a double-columned article that appeared on December 21st. "Millionaire's Son Is a Clerk in an Akron Drug Store," the headline read, under which was a photograph of Crane staring into space. The interview, Crane told Munson afterward, had been "silly enough, but forced" upon him, misquotations and all. He'd taken the whole thing as "an agreeable joke and an anachronism in Akron." But his father had been "furious, at the headlines in particular," and Crane had spent the day after Christmas trying to shrug the whole thing off as a joke. C.A. was not amused.[10]

Yet what Crane had to say about the poet in America was worth listening to. "The modern American artist must generally go into business life," he'd told Chamberlain—something the artist was often forced to do out of necessity. The difficult balance was between being a viable part of society and yet keeping enough distance to be able to view that society objectively in order to write about it well enough to convince others of the truth of what you had to say. Too many American novels, he knew, had been written merely to serve as "whilers-away of evenings in Pullmans." How much better to read something that might help one understand oneself. The work of Sandburg, say, or Dreiser, or Edgar Lee Masters, or Sherwood Anderson. These writers understood their world, and the nation could ill "afford to ignore them."[11]

Nor could Crane any longer ignore other realities. A month into his job, with the full impact of the Christmas rush finally upon him, he began feeling the strain of standing at a candy counter fourteen hours a day, only to have to return to the loneliness of a hotel room. Nor could he ignore the reality that he was suddenly in the midst of a love affair with a shy, nondescript young man—an affair that kept Crane fluctuating between exhilaration and despair, with no time left for poetry. All this, he complained to Munson, without revealing the gender of his lover, had left him feeling "quite barbarous." Worse, there was nothing for it but to "recognize the situation and temporarily bow to it."[12] Soon he was telling Anderson more about the affair, though as yet only in the vaguest of terms. Anderson wrote back. He'd sensed something was going on, he told Crane, because he could feel a new vitality in his friend's letters.

It took two weeks before Crane could summon the courage to tell anyone that the affair he was having was with another man. When at last he broke the news, it was first of all to Munson. Sitting in his hotel room two days after Christmas, as he prepared to leave Akron now that the holiday rush was over, Crane explained that the affair had turned out to be "the most intense and satisfactory one of my whole life" and that he was "all broken up at the thought of leaving him." *Him.* That last word, he knew, would jolt Munson, but there it was. He had never in his life had "devotion returned before like this, nor ever found a soul, mind, and body so worthy of devotion." He was hoping to see his lover in Cleveland, if his father didn't send him too far away on his next assignment. He swore Munson to keep what he'd just told him "as unmentionable to anyone else."[13]

On the same Sunday that the newspaper interview had appeared—the 21st—Crane spent the afternoon with another new friend, Harry Candee, whom he'd met through his Akron book dealer. Candee was another "Akron exile from N.Y." like himself, but older and more sophisticated. He was well-read, part of the established gay community in Akron and elsewhere, and made his living as secretary to—as Crane phrased it—some "wheezing Philanthropist." Crane and Candee began that Sunday by drinking Prohibition wine in the kitchen of an immigrant Romanian family; and then, as the afternoon wore on, they walked over to Candee's boardinghouse room with bottles of wine under their overcoats. After those gave out, they polished off some "dreadful raisin brew" Candee had squirreled away.

It turned out to be Crane's "one purple evening" in Akron, and it ended with a reading from two ribald classics—Catullus and Edgar Saltus—while Crane and Candee each smoked "one of the cigars made especially" for the assassinated czar Nicholas. The evening culminated in Crane staggering down the dimly lit hallway of Candee's apartment and gloriously puking. "You will believe me an ox," he crowed meekly to Munson, "when I tell you that I was on the job again next morning, and carried the day through with flying colors."[14]

"I remember one Sunday noon," Crane would write six months later in "Porphyro in Akron," recalling that winter solstice spent in Akron:

Harry and I, "the gentlemen,"—seated around
A table of raisin-jack and wine, our host
Setting down a glass and saying,—

*   "One month,—I go back rich.*
I ride black horse . . . Have many sheep."
And his wife, like a mountain, coming in
With four tiny black-eyed girls around her
Twinkling like little Christmas trees.

And some Sunday fiddlers,
Roumanian business men,
Played ragtime and dances before the door,
And we overpayed them because we felt like it.[15]

The few evenings Crane had left in Akron he spent with Candee, sometimes joined by their mutual friend, the Akron bookseller, and meeting either in Candee's or Crane's room to drink and talk literature. A week before he returned to Cleveland, Crane discovered yet another friend, a brilliant photographer named Hervey Minns. "A filthy old man," Crane called him, and the only American "to hold the Dresden and Munich awards." Here he was, this old anarchist, living in a ramshackle house in Akron. It delighted Crane that Minns had refused to photograph F. H. Seiberling, the powerful king of rubber, because he'd found the man's face uninteresting. In the summer of 1920, Crane would write Minns up for *The Little Review,* noting particularly that in his photographic portraits one found the same "ethical curiosity and sympathy" one found in Henry James.[16]

As his love affair moderated, Crane went back to his reading. He was a voracious reader, and for a time he'd been able to steal an hour here and there reading behind his candy counter. Then he was told by the manager to stop reading and pay more attention to his customers, so that he had only a few hours each night now for books. On the job, time hung heavy on his hands. He was not asked to serve at the soda fountain and he did not volunteer. The other workers stayed away from him. Still, his two months in Akron turned out better than all the time he'd spent in New York. After all, he had room and board, a job, a little security, books, friends, even a lover. By 11 January 1920, he was back in Cleveland, living in a cramped room in a boardinghouse on Euclid Avenue (No. 11431) for the winter, Grace having closed the house while she and her mother left to winter on the Isle of Pines. If he thought his father was about to advance him in the business, he was wrong. Instead, he was transferred to the Cleveland factory and told to empty boxcars filled with cases of chocolate and barrels of sugar. This he did from five-thirty each morning until three-thirty in the afternoon, six days a week—and all for what he called starvation wages.

By the end of February, he was once again fed up. "It's the old bunko stuff about 'working from the bottom up' and 'earning an honest dollar,'" he told Bill Wright, who knew C.A.'s fondness for old saws. Somewhere in Catullus, Crane had come across the phrase "fucked flat." Well, that was just how he felt now. After four months of it, he was tired of hotel and boardinghouse life, tired of winter, tired of having to grab "hasty and inadequate meals" at "chance lunch counters." If there weren't some changes—and soon—he was going to walk into his father's office "and tell the amused and comfortable and rich and thriving spectator that 'the joke's up.'"[17]

At least evenings were his, when he could come and go as he wished. Sometimes on a lark he took the rapid transit Interurban trolley down to Akron for an overnight binge with Harry Candee. He spent Holy Saturday with Candee, drinking two bottles of Prohibition dago red he'd brought with him, which Candee followed up with a quart of raisin jack, so that Easter "was spent very quietly, watered and Bromo-Seltzered, with amusing anecdotes occasionally sprouting from toweled head to toweled head." This "bath in the unconscious" had done him a hell of a lot of good, he told Munson afterwards.[18] It was certainly better than watching the annual Easter parade in Cleveland, followed by a heavy dinner.

There was also his lover to amuse him. At first he'd come up to Cleveland as they'd arranged, providing Crane with "new treasures," so that for a while that winter Crane had lived for Saturdays. If nothing like this "realization of one's dreams in flesh, form, laughter and intelligence" ever came his way again, he swore, at least he would have "a pool of wonderful memories."[19] He wanted it to go on forever, this once-a-week affair, but forty miles was forty miles, and soon the visits grew fewer and the excuses longer as love turned to lust and then to bored indifference. By early March, Crane had to accept the fact that his lover was gone.

But there was good news, too. In late January, he received a check for ten dollars from *The Dial* for "My Grandmother's Love Letters." It was the first time he'd ever been paid for a poem and he was beside himself with happiness. This was the very poem he'd begun in New York, and he'd worked and reworked it during his time in Akron, satisfied with what he'd caught in the opening lines, but not sure where to go with it after that. Finally, he'd pared it back and sent it on its appointed rounds. "She [i.e., his poem] would get very fretful and peevish at times," he told Munson early on, "and at other times, hysterical and sentimental, and I have been obliged to handle her in the rather discouraging way that my words attest."[20] He had not said all he'd wanted to on the subject, but he'd said all he was prepared at the moment to say.

It was the only thing he'd yet done, he would later tell Munson, that satisfied him at all, and already Crane was worrying if he would ever again equal what he'd caught there. The mood—ironic, detached, poignant in its lost innocence—was the mood he'd found in reading both Vildrac (in translation) and the poems of Wallace Stevens he'd seen in *Poetry*. *There* was "a man whose work makes most of the rest of us quail," he told Munson. "His technical subtleties alone provide a great amount of interest." Crane noted for his friend's delectation "the novel rhyme and rhythm effects" in his own poem,[21] the chiming of *hair* and *air*, of *hand* and *understand*, the half-rhymes of *enough, roof, soft, self,* and *laughter*, refrain lines like "There is even room enough" faintly echoed twelve lines later in "Are your fingers long enough" and again in "Is the silence strong enough," the play of short lines against long.

His use of oblique metaphor was no less dazzling. The poem seemed to be about his grandmother's love letters, hidden now in some corner of the attic, evanescent, their secrets lost, fragments of a love affair that—except in the recesses of his grandmother Elizabeth's failing memory—would have long ago turned to dust. Could he recapture something as tremblingly delicate as that beautiful old music fast disappearing down the corridors of lost time? But where were last year's snows? Crane the Romantic, Crane hearing fragments of some lost melody, light falling through sepia shadow. To hold, to somehow hold in words, in faint phrasings, the echo of a music lost:

> Are your fingers long enough to play
> Old keys that are but echoes:
> Is the silence strong enough
> To carry back the music to its source
> And back to you again
> As though to her?

The poem might have ended with these lines; and if it did, it would have been merely an elegy to a lost world. But Crane upped the ante in the final four lines by offering to lead his grandmother—gently, gently—into a world of love of which she would have no understanding, the world of homoeroticism into which her grandson had been initiated:

> Yet I would lead my grandmother by the hand
> Through much of what she would not understand . . .

But now the poet faltered. If he could not recover her world of love and courtship, marriage and family (and divorce and sundered parentage as well), how could he expect her (or her daughter) to understand his world, the world where one man loved another? And so the poem breaks off, and the rain which has fallen throughout—obliterating the snow and all traces of his grandmother's world along with it—continues pattering on the roof, mocking anyone who would try to understand another's desires and hopes and needs, all of it falling away now, as the poet at last understands, "With such a sound of gently pitying laughter." All of these gradations Crane had somehow managed at twenty.[22]

First it had been *The Modernist* he'd outgrown. Now it was "that fetid corpse," Joe Kling's *The Pagan*. Like Keats, Crane's critical faculties were beginning to develop with quicksilver speed. He read Baudelaire's *Fleurs du mal,* and refused to "brook anything healthful or cheery" just now. He parted with two hard-earned dollars to purchase a copy of H. L. Mencken's *Heliogabolus,* a drama based on the life of the "most dissolute minion of decadent Rome." But Candee—who subsequently put Crane on to the Roman historian Dio Cassius, as well as Edgar Saltus's *Imperial Purple*—had known at once what a farce Mencken's *Heliogabolus* really was. To play to their ignorant American audiences, Mencken and his collaborator had created some "senile Al Jolson, farting the usual bedroom-farce calamities." Candee had written Crane eloquently in Beardsleyan tones of the image he himself carried of Heliogabolus as a "slim child of seventeen . . . hair powdered with diamond dust and gold, half oriental eyes all but closed, dressed in the costume of a priest of Baal, offering his hand covered with jewels" to a gladiator who had "fallen at his feet with the words, —'Hail, Lord,' and the boy answering him,— 'Call me not Lord, for I am thy Lady.'" Put *that* against "the senile, doddering creature with twelve wives as he is pictured by the joint authors," Crane closed, and all one could do was laugh.[23]

All winter Crane had waited for his mother to get back to Cleveland, for he had come to believe he'd finally shaped her into a suitable companion for himself: someone bright, witty, vivacious, electric in her conversation. But within days of her returning home at the beginning of March, he was near despair. She'd left Cleveland two months ago, he wrote Munson on the 6th, "a rather (for her) ductile and seductive woman with a certain aura of romance about her." And here she was back, self-satisfied, "shallow, unemotional, insistent on talking food receipts and household details during meals."[24] On her own for the first time in her life, she chattered on for hours about business matters of which she knew nothing, and smugly used her Christian Science to demonstrate that all was right with the world. Worse, he was expected to amuse her nightly with banalities, and be rewarded with a pat on the back and a goodnight kiss. If, stupid with exhaustion after lifting crates and barrels for ten hours a day, he showed the least ill humor, she burst into tears. And then there was his grandmother, whom he loved, but who only added to the household noise with her doddering confusion.

To amuse himself, he hung his walls with Gauguin reproductions and Japanese prints, played Russian records on his Victrola, read Djuna Barnes, Ida Rauh, Stendhal's *Chartreuse de Parme*, Samuel Butler's *Way of All Flesh*, Walter Savage Landor's *Conversations. The Moon and Sixpence*, Somerset Maugham's biographical novel about Gauguin, he read straight through in "a single sitting."[25] He read Rabelais, Villon, and Apuleius, along with Williams, Stevens, and Marianne Moore, in whose "extremity of detachment" he found "a kind of inspiration."[26] But mostly now he turned to Pound and Eliot and the Elizabethans for what he needed.

Still, there were times when there was nothing for it but to take in a good amateur prize fight at the local gym, and watch two men, stripped and muscular, stalk each other in a ring for dominance: feinting, jabbing, dodging (as he could not seem to do with his parents), before landing a crumpling blow that settled the matter one way or the other. Usually he went accompanied by one of the tenants from the boardinghouse who worked for the newspaper. He loved it, this Ashcan realism brought vividly to life. Yes, there were stretches of boredom, where the boxers simply danced around each other. But sometimes one was blessed with the spectacle of "two sublime machines of human muscle-play in the vivid light of a 'ring,'—stark darkness all around with yells from all sides and countless eyes gleaming, centered on the circle."[27] When that happened, he could feel himself becoming aroused, as he jumped up from his seat and roared with the best of them.

He wanted that for his own poems too—a "patent leather gloss," he called it, "an extreme freshness" that eschewed the traditional "dew-on the-grass" garden-variety lyric he had written as well as anyone in "My Grandmother's Love Letters." He was after something else now, something of Eliot's hard, metallic quatrains, something his Apeneck Sweeney seemed to evoke. Sherwood Anderson in "I Want to Know Why"—one of the greatest short stories he'd ever read—had just captured something of this quality.[28] He was tired of Yellow Decade stuff, with its servile French and Latin titles. He needed to go his own way, to earn a certain hardness and distance in his work.

In part this was because Crane at once feared, loved, and hated his father. He had to half beg, half wheedle him into giving him a five-dollar raise. Worse, he felt like a hypocrite for having to ask for what he felt he'd earned. He felt powerless. Was he, he wondered, "strong and hardened or not"?[29] Crane was learning the hard way to play the chameleon to get what he needed. Nor did it help matters when, at the end of April 1920, he hurt himself lifting his father's goddamn crates and had to spend a week in bed. He had not ruptured himself, he was relieved to hear, but he might have, and he was furious with his father and the foreman who had pushed him—the owner's son—into working so hard for nothing.

Did his father really believe he would ever win him over by forcing him to become a slave to a miserable job? To survive, he began affecting a certain hale bonhomie, acting like one of the boys, when in truth he did not feel at all like one of the boys. In time he came to like "the slippery scales-of-the-fish, continual escape, attitude" he'd affected.[30] But what he really wanted was not the company of factory workers standing at their stations on the assembly lines among whirring belts and wheels, but rather the company of the select few, men like Candee and Munson, with whom he could really talk, or the consolations of his lover, who had by then abandoned him.

But an accident at the factory changed all that. One of the workers gashed his hand on a machine, and like Whitman nursing soldiers
after Fredericksburg, Crane found himself coming to the young man's
assistance:

> *The unexpected interest made him flush,*
> *Suddenly he seemed to forget the pain,—*
> *Consented,—and held out*
> *One finger from the other . . .*

As the "fingers of the factory owner's son" tenderly bandaged
the young man's wound, and the broken sunlight settled on the hands
of the two men, the world of the factory—its maddening sounds and
noises—seemed suddenly to recede, so that the worker saw his fingers
transformed into "butterflies/Flickering in sunlight over summer
fields," his callused hand metamorphosed first into "wild ponies' play,"
and then to "Bunches of new green breaking a hard turf" as the two
men for a blessed moment smiled "into each other's eyes."[31]

Crane called the "mood" piece "Episode of Hands," and he sent
it on to Munson in mid-April, at the same time confessing that he was
still "much at sea about its qualities and faults." By then he was not even
sure what the poem's real drift was. So mind-numbing in fact did he
find the daily routine at the factory that he actually felt "an infantile
awe before any attempt whatever" to write. Within weeks, believing
that the poem lacked sufficient fire and form, he abandoned it.

That spring he endured two "terrible occasions." The first was
his paternal grandparents' golden anniversary—an event saved for him
because he was treated to real and not bootleg champagne. The second was his attendance at a collegiate ball, after which the car he was
driving broke down at 3:00 A.M., leaving him with "two hysterical,
extremely young and innocent females."[32]

Through May and June he slogged on at his job, and was finally
rewarded by C.A. with a paid vacation and a cash bonus, both of which
he spent in New York. He arrived in the city on the morning of the
Fourth of July, found himself a suite of rooms with a parlor at the
Prince George Hotel on 28th Street, and for the next two weeks
immersed himself in theaters, concerts, speakeasies, restaurants, parks,
bookshops, and art galleries. He went everywhere, visiting the offices of
The Dial and *The Little Review*, roaming the waterfronts, and lying in

the sun on the nearby beaches. Mornings he spent writing; afternoons shopping and sightseeing; evenings renewing old friendships: Gorham Munson, Charmion von Wiegand, Alex Baltzly, Joe Kling, among others. Then it was back to his miserable job at the factory.

Long days he worked, lifting cases and kegs, sweeping floors, taking inventory. His evenings he spent reading: Aldous Huxley's "Limbo," the Noh plays of Fenollosa and Pound, Conrad's *Nigger of the Narcissus* ("all polyphonic prose, plus the usual quality of Conrad characterization"),[33] and Henry James's *The American* and his letters. He even managed to work on an "uncouth trifle" he'd begun in June about his time in Akron, a poem he called "Porphyro in Akron."[34] By thus titling the poem, Crane signaled that he was evoking Keats's "Eve of St. Agnes," identifying with Keats's Porphyro, like himself nearly paralyzed by a world of ice relieved only by an occasional erotic interlude. Akron was history now, all except for a few images of Greeks and Swedes on their way to work on a winter's morning, or a drunken afternoon spent with Harry Candee and a family of Romanians, or nights alone in his hotel room reading poetry, while "a hash of noises" was "slung up from the street."[35] That, and some memories too private as yet for his poetry.

He managed to send out only one new poem, a twelve-line "highly concentrated piece of symbolism,"[36] only to have it rejected in turn by *The Freeman*, *The New Republic*, and *The Dial*. It was called "Garden Abstract," and it was—by his own admission—extremely phallic in nature. Ostensibly about Eve's temptation in the Garden, the poem was actually about his own homoerotic drive ("The apple on its bough is her desire"). It was a drive so intense, he felt, that it erased all time and reason as well as all clear moral judgment, leaving him speechless, with only the breathless moment of the encounter itself, no before or after, "no memory, nor fear, nor hope/Beyond the grass and shadows at her feet."[37]

Shortly after his twenty-first birthday that July, Crane was called into his father's office and told that he was being sent to Washington, D.C., in September to serve as sales representative for Mary Garden Chocolates for the Washington-Norfolk-Richmond area. The move pleased him even more than a return to New York would have, for he felt he knew New York, whereas Washington would be virgin territory. He would be able to come and go pretty much as he pleased; he would have a bank account at his disposal; and he would make a decent commission on whatever he sold. In fact, he'd been chosen to go to Washington, C.A. told him, because of the classier business types the capital attracted, as well as for the city's "literary and journalistic associations."[38]

He arrived in Woodrow Wilson's Washington on September 10th and three days later moved into what he described as an "unexceptional maison" at 1310 L Street NW, "situated among a row of other rooming houses." There was, he found, an openness and ease about the capital that reminded him of what he'd heard of Paris, with its tree-lined streets and endless parks and public monuments. It was certainly "more elegant than any other American city" he knew of and certainly unlike anything Cleveland, Akron, or even New York had offered.[39] Still, he dreaded the thought of tramping around the city trying to sell chocolates, a situation exacerbated by the sample boxes of candy that arrived in Washington already gray and sweaty with the late summer heat. Worse was "talking, talking, talking and waiting for the proper persons to arrive at their offices."[40] After two weeks of it, he managed to open up a total of two new accounts. The upside was that, since most offices didn't open for business until ten, he could sleep mornings. But Washington also proved deadly to his Muse. He'd now been without a creative impulse for so long, he complained, that he no longer even missed it.

Both times when he'd gone to New York, he'd gone armed with introductions from his parents and relatives. This time it was Harry Candee who had supplied the introductions. One was to Wilbur Underwood, a forty-four-year-old minor career officer who had been working for the State Department for as long as Crane had been alive. A decade and more earlier, Underwood had published two volumes of poetry in England in total obscurity. By 1920, enmeshed in the gray life of a bureaucrat, he had given up hope of ever publishing another book. But Crane took to Underwood at once, finding him charming, urbane, worldweary—one of the few people he'd ever met who seemed to know what was going on in world politics, including the "greedy tactics" of the new nations "freshly hatched" by the Treaty of Versailles.[41] And yet here he was, trapped in the world of official Washington, "the beauty and promise of his life all dried and withered" in him by "the daily grind" of work. Crane could not help but think of Pound's lines: "O helpless few in my country. . . . / You who cannot wear yourselves out by persisting to successes."[42]

Like Candee, Underwood owned a fine collection of ribald classics in translation, many of which he willingly lent Crane: Apuleius' *The Golden Ass* and Petronius' *Satyricon*, the latter in "a rare and completely unexpurgated Paris edition . . . purported to have been translated by Oscar Wilde," though Crane doubted that.[43] Soon Underwood was introducing him to various members of the Washington diplomatic corps, filling Crane in afterwards on the sexual scandals clinging to each. Each evening, thousands of clerks emptied out of the marmoreal government buildings and dined in the surrounding restaurants or fled to the movies. Crane himself took in several theatrical productions, among them Emily Stevens in *Foot-Loose*, and Walter Hampden in *The Merchant of Venice*, which, with its cast of burlesque queens and assorted other "bitches," had the audience clapping wildly, but which left him cold.[44] Washington, he'd by then decided, was indeed the city of the dead.

Besides, what he was really after more than anything else were the soldiers and sailors he found roaming the capital's streets. They had, he told Munson, "a strange psychology of their own that is new to me," and that would draw him to them for the rest of his life. The very air of Washington seemed to him to radiate America's "new vice": homosexuality. Every other bureaucrat and diplomat here seemed to be an enlarged edition of Lord Douglas, Oscar Wilde's old lover. And what of this "new VICE-president, Franklin Roosevelt," whose name and scandalous example already "scented the air of Washington," as he'd just learned from Underwood?[45] Although he was at first merely an observer at several of the homosexual orgies he attended with Underwood, Crane finally consented to enter the fray, joking about what he'd done, but disgusted with himself afterwards for his lack of discrimination. Still, most nights he spent at the boardinghouse alone, his imagination charged with homoerotic fantasies that remained unacted on because he feared inviting potential psychotics up to his room.

"I would like a walk again with you among the ghostly facades of Washington," Crane would write Underwood months after returning to Cleveland, remembering his time in the capital. Among his memories: evenings at the home of Underwood's friend, Madame Cooke, a male transvestite with a penchant for flowery evening gowns, whose housekeeper supplied her guests with a "delicious and potent home-brew"; *nuits au balcon*, the falling stars as the group read and commented on Beardsley's decadent novel, *Under the Hill*; "shameless anecdotes and half-sad and half-gay confessions." Crane joked about this "aged enchantress," this silly "baboon," whose tender flesh had been nourished by "the flesh of a thousand lovers," and whose parlors were open to all comers, especially sailors, most with assumed names. And yet there was something, Crane had to admit, "desperate, pitiful and grotesque" about the whole spectacle.[46]

Whatever else he learned during his Washington Satyricon, he knew after just five weeks that he'd struck out as a candy salesman, and it was only a matter of time before his father summoned him back home to Cleveland. Still, he'd worked hard and dutifully, seeing as many clients as he could, sometimes sitting for hours in waiting rooms for businessmen who either refused to see him or who kept him waiting, only to grant him a cursory interview or a promise that they would think about buying something before some secretary showed him the door. Anything, he gasped, had to be better than this "maddening experience . . . of clawing the air day after day" without having a thing to show for it. He was relieved to hear his father say that his failure to find new clients was due to the stifling heat of the city in September and October as well as to a general lack of business. It was certainly not his son's "personal inadequacy."[47]

In any event, by late October Crane was back in Cleveland again, working fourteen-hour days in the shipping department at his old job, with no advance in either salary or position, and with another Christmas rush about to descend on him. Still, it was better than being in Washington—"the most elegantly restricted and bigoted community" he'd ever seen. He was actually glad to be back among the factory whistles and smoke-laden air and "tawdry thoroughfares" of blue-collar Cleveland.[48] Once again he rose at five each morning to begin the crush of a new day, until he grew morose and irritable. "Our age tries hard enough to kill us," he complained to Munson, "but I begin to feel a pleasure in sheer stubbornness."[49]

He still read when he could: Suetonius' *History of the Caesars,* Sherwood Anderson's *Poor White,* and—at Munson's suggestion—Dostoyevsky's *The Possessed* and *The Brothers Karamazov.* The "greatest of novelists," Crane was soon calling the Russian.[50] But when he himself tried to write now, he felt rusty and awkward. Worse, he had no idea any more where his life was going. He knew he might be sent out on the road again after the New Year, or he might stay on in Cleveland. He felt humiliated being bossed about by his father as if he were just another hired hand, and began to speak now of "a clean and final break." He would save what he could for two years, and then go off to Italy, France, or Russia. "Literature and art be hanged!" he raged. Ordinary existence wasn't "worth the candle in these States now."[51]

Then, suddenly and unexpectedly, he found himself in love again. This time it was a young truck driver who worked at the warehouse where he himself worked, and he had the pleasure—as he would phrase it in a letter to Underwood two years later—of educating the young man into a world of new thresholds, new anatomies. As his mother prepared to close up house again and head south for the Isle of Pines with her mother, Crane moved into rooms in the Del Prado Apartment complex at Euclid and 40th. "I've been blind with happiness and beauty for the last full week!" he wrote Underwood three days before Christmas. He was so overcome by what was happening to him that he found himself sometimes weeping for joy. This time he was sure he'd found God. This was more than sex, which was—after all—a "brief and limited" thing. No, what he was experiencing was "something infinitely more thrilling and inclusive," and he wanted more than anything to be able to hold onto it even as he knew it too would inevitably be swept out to sea.[52]

Just after New Year's, 1921, C.A. had him in for a talk. He'd been watching Harold for the past fourteen months now, had calculated the miserable results of his sojourn in Washington, had remarked the desultory way he worked his fourteen-hour shifts on the factory floor, filling orders and juggling supplies. Finally he had had to accept the fact that Harold really did seem to have his heart set on writing and was never going to follow him in the business. Realizing this, C.A. was now transferring him to the main warehouse as supervisor of bulk storage and inventories, until Harold could find something more to his liking in the way of writing. The new job would be less rushed and Harold would be his own boss. Was there something more? Had he heard something about Harold or seen him in a less than flattering light? If he did, he said nothing. For his part, Crane swallowed hard and accepted his father's directive. At least now, he hoped, he might "get a little reading and writing done . . . in some sort of tranquility."[53]

Throughout January 1921, his love affair continued. He knew he paid for these affairs in blood, for he was terrified that his mother and even worse his father would learn about his real orientation. Still, he needed the feeling of being in love for the heightened sense of life it offered. They gave "the ego a rest," these affairs, he explained to Munson, and though he might "sound like an utter profligate," there was "much sincerity, too painfully much," in what he was telling him to laugh about it.[54] After all, as he confided to Underwood, even hell could "be turned into Paradise with the proper company." At the moment he was very much within the golden halo of this new affair—a metaphor he had learned from his Washington experience, which defined the first rapture of homoerotic love. *This* lover, he added, had "the head and eyes of Pierrot."[55] He was a mixture of grace and sadness, and his every movement was for Crane nothing less than a poem.

As for poetry, he'd managed two lines in three months, and these had come out of his reading of Rabelais, Rimbaud, Laforgue, and Vildrac in editions he'd ordered from Paris. They had also come out of his obsession with his lover:

> *The everlasting eyes of Pierrot*
> *And of Gargantua,—the laughter.*

The lines were certainly "contradictory and wide enough," he knew, to serve as his own epitaph. He hoped to build a poem on that beginning and thus, "like Lazarus, return" to the world of poetry. But the difficulty with writing now was not only the absence of good company in this God-forsaken province, but the higher critical standards he had set himself that did not allow him "the expression of the old asininities."[56] If he could not yet go forward, he was certainly not going to go back.

Nor was the literary news coming out of New York of much help, for it all seemed gripped by the madness of Dada. He'd heard that Man Ray and Marcel Duchamp were planning "a most exotic and worthless" review: "billets in a bag printed backwards, on rubber deluxe." But what Dadaism was, "beyond an insane jumble of the four winds, the six senses, and plum pudding," he had no idea.[57] And if, as had been reported, the Baroness was the incarnation of the movement, New York could have it. So, when he went down to Akron on the last Sunday in January to see his friend, the photographer Hervey Minns, he told him what Man Ray (himself a photographer) had said about art: that it was nothing more than a series of random accidents. Hearing that, Minns had flown "into a holy rage," Crane reported to Munson. Which was how he himself felt. Art demanded effort, it demanded form and design, and if Man Ray wasn't careful, Dada "and other flamdoodle" ideas were going to "run him off his track."[58]

Crane's job as warehouse supervisor lasted only until mid-February, when he was transferred to the basement storeroom of his father's large store and tearoom at 13th and Euclid. C.A. had just discharged a black handyman and now Crane would take the man's place. Whatever C.A. meant by ordering his own son into a basement room without windows, where exposed steampipes along the ceiling made the place a sauna, it certainly seemed to make Harold out to be a buffoon of some kind. Then he was told he would no longer be allowed to read on the job. It was clear to him that his father was at last writing him off. If Harold insisted on being a goddamned artist, let him see what an artist's life was really like. But Crane had one of those quicksilver personalities—a survivor's instinct, really—which allowed him to get along with almost anyone and besides, he genuinely liked people. Soon—to his father's horror—he was hobnobbing and clowning around with the black cooks and waiters in the kitchen across from his storeroom.

Whatever else the job did, it provided Crane with a poem: "Black Tambourine." In it he read his own condition: a poet caught like so many marginalized human beings, including the black handyman who'd been let go, his only companions in that basement hell gnats, roaches, and flies. He would later describe the poem as "Baudelairesque,"[59] but the more immediate influence on him was the hard, dry Eliot of the Sweeney poems that employed the same quatrains he used here. Crane had promised himself to avoid Eliot's influence as too negative, too despairing, but that was before he'd found himself banished to a basement and treated "like a dog."[60] C.A.'s world, he knew, was being closed to him, and—as time and exhaustion were amply demonstrating—the world of the imagination was now in danger of disappearing as well. He was the outcast singer, fate's exile, whose poems had been nailed to the wall, while he contemplated what lay ahead for him: the death of the poet, his "carcass quick with flies."[61]

When Grace and her mother returned to Cleveland at the beginning of April, Crane was allowed to move back into his tower. Again the pattern repeated itself: a day or two of relative peace, before Grace was at him, feeding his own misgivings about his new job. What did C.A. mean by giving Hart some "nigger's" job to do? Clearly, his father had meant to humiliate *her*, and that she would not tolerate. Finally, on the 19th, the storm that had been gathering for months broke.

That noon, as usual, Crane had gone across the hall to the kitchen to eat with the black staff. He was joking with them when he looked up to see his father walk through the swinging doors, looking for all the world like some red-faced gargoyle. For his part, C.A. was incredulous at what he was witnessing. Silence descended on the room, the waiters began dispersing, and suddenly Crane could hear himself being reprimanded and ordered back to the storeroom. From now on, his father told him, since he was back living with her, he could eat with his mother.

That was the last straw. Crane threw the storeroom keys at his father's feet and told him he was through. C.A.'s face turned beet red. To be spoken to, the boss, by a weak son in front of his "niggers"! He began swearing at Harold, threatening to disinherit him unless he apologized. His face swelling with welts, Harold yelled back at his father that he could take his money and go to hell.

So there it was: after eighteen months in his father's employ, with the promise of great things long since gone, to end up like this. Shaking with rage, Crane stormed out, leaving his father standing there likewise shaking, and went home. When Grace saw her son walk through the door that day, she knew something terrible had happened. But Crane was in no condition to talk. He stumbled up to his room, shut the door, drew the blinds, and stayed there for two days. He would have to make other plans now, find other work, perhaps relocate, he wrote Munson the day after the blowup. Who knew, especially with jobs so hard to come by now? But of one thing he was certain: never again would he work for his father. He knew now that nothing he did would ever please that man. "*Bridges burnt behind!*" he closed his letter.[62] It would be two and a half years before father and son so much as spoke to one another again.

4 / BREAKTHROUGH

CLEVELAND
MAY 1921–JUNE 1922

As BAD AS THINGS HAD BEEN with his father, at least Crane had had a salary he could count on, and with it a certain amount of independence. Now, suddenly, here he was, all communication with his father broken off, living at home, having to take whatever handouts his mother and grandmother could afford to give him. It was a situation he found more and more intolerable as the months wore on. The promise of a job with a Cleveland advertising house beginning in June or July shimmered on the horizon like an oasis and then evaporated. Friends offered vague hopes of jobs, then those jobs disappeared. Two years, he complained to Munson on 16 May 1921, two years "thrown away at the feet of my father without the gain of a jot of experience at anything but peon duties in a shipping room!"[1] What a fool he'd been to trust that sonofabitch. Worse, he had lost the peace of mind necessary to get on with his writing. His reading was reduced now mostly to poring over job ads.

Still, he did find moments when he could read *The Dial*, *The Freeman*, and a new magazine out of New Orleans called *The Double Dealer*, which blessedly began publishing him, beginning with "Black Tambourine" in June. He also read Williams's *Contact* (though he hated the wet-dream drivelings of Robert McAlmon and Virgil Jordan, whose work he found there), and bought Williams's *Kora in Hell: Impro-*

visations, "a book for poets alone," he noted, which, though "meaningless to a large extent to most people," he found "stimulating."[2] What he did not like reading about was politics, including *The New Republic,* which always seemed to talk about poetry in political terms, as if politics were in a "perpetual ferment." Nor did he much care for such burning issues as breast feeding and birth control, essays that stirred up a kind of intellectual unrest in him without ever settling anything one way or the other. And as for Washington politics, he knew too much about what went on there. No matter what the commentators said, the capital seemed to just keep on going along the same "old rotten paths." Not that he—the most apolitical of poets—gave a damn about what went on in the larger world beyond. It was only when these "political gentlemen (Irish potatobeds)" obstructed the view of his petunias and hollyhocks that he became irritated.[3]

Washington existed for other purposes. Washington was there to stimulate his secret life. Now that he was no longer working, he wrote Underwood, he was "tempted to spring to a Washington train and rush into your office with 'vine leaves in my hair.'" By then, Crane's latest lover had gone the way of all the others, including one with the codename "Ibsen," who'd spent a week with him in April before disappearing. All the excitement he could muster around Cleveland was "a person of ravenous appetites who entertains me with exceptional wines and gets drunk and silly about once a week."[4] Except for a note from Harry Candee saying he was on his way to some physical training camp with an intimate of his up on the Hudson, even that indefatigable source had disappeared.

But there were other friends. An artist named Bill Sommer, married and the father of three grown-up sons. Sommer, Crane was convinced, was a neglected genius who at fifty-four was still forced to work long hours in a lithograph factory to earn his living. Seven years earlier, Sommer had been just another run-of-the-mill painter. But after studying the work of Gauguin, Van Gogh, Picasso, and Wyndham Lewis, he'd decided to go and do likewise, and Crane found much to admire in the new work. By late June, he was spending one evening a week with the man at his studio farm (an old converted schoolhouse) in Brandywine, twenty miles south of Cleveland. There Crane could drink, bang away at an old piano—Chopin Ballades and Heine lyrics—or spar with his boyhood boxing gloves. Soon Sommer was showing Crane how to sketch and use watercolors, an exercise that—Crane believed—

was teaching him actually how to *see* what he was looking at. His drawings, especially of faces, Sommer found particularly original.

Their talks covered everything, but above all aesthetics. In truth, Crane saw something of himself in the older man—the provincial suddenly taking fire from the modern revolution in the arts—and he went to work at once to try to get Sommer the wider audience he deserved. But unlike Crane, Sommer proved indifferent to public opinion, refusing to exhibit even in Cleveland, much less caring about a place as far away as New York. So, at his own expense, Crane sent a number of Sommer's watercolors to *The Dial*, which was in the habit of publishing avant-garde artwork. The effort went nowhere. By July, he'd sent twenty-six of Sommer's paintings to New York, using Gorham Munson as his middleman. He'd also asked Bill DeZayas, whose own work had appeared in *The Dial,* to feature some of Sommer's paintings in his gallery. Again no luck, and Munson was left with the sorry task of shipping the paintings back to Cleveland before he sailed for Europe.

It was through Sommer that Crane was introduced to another painter, Willy Lescaze, a French-Swiss artist Crane's own age recently arrived from Paris. Lescaze had just been shown along with Charles Burchfield in Cleveland and had managed to create "a terrible furor" there. His work was striking, Crane told Munson, and had about it an edge of "diabolism" that reminded him of Baudelaire.[5] Now he sent some of Lescaze's drawings off to *The Little Review*, hoping they at least might publish something; but again nothing. Returning the interest, Lescaze began educating Crane in the subtleties of Nietzsche, Proust, Gide, and de Gourmont, as well as Joyce, Pound, Eliot, and John Donne. Come fall, he would sketch Crane, revealing a face with the right eye enlarged and riveted—as Crane phrased it—as if focused on some great unspoken mystery. Crane loved the portrait, though his friends did not think he looked quite as insane as the drawing suggested. Still, Lescaze had caught something there, and no one in Cleveland, Crane insisted, understood him better than this man.

In June, he wrote a laudatory essay on Sherwood Anderson for *The Double Dealer*, for which he was paid twenty dollars. The truth was that he felt uncomfortable writing reviews, he told Munson, because it was his way "to blindly enthuse or refute some ridiculous criticism" of a particular writer.[6] But writing this one—besides giving him some badly needed cash for cigars and booze—had helped get his mind going again. Lescaze dismissed the piece, saying it reminded him of someone playing with a bunch of colored balloons "in the boredom of his chambre," a criticism that Crane thought had gone right to the heart of the matter.[7] But that did not stop him from writing another in July, this one on George Bernard Shaw's *Back to Methuselah* for the same magazine. Then he tried a third, this one on Ezra Pound for a glitzy magazine called *Shadowland*, only to abandon it. For a while that summer he considered doing a play about John Brown and making a small fortune, but that too came to nothing.

On July 22nd, the day after his twenty-second birthday, he suffered through Cleveland's public celebrations marking its one hundred and twenty-fifth anniversary. The city's self-congratulatory theme was the March of Events, hideously enacted on the thoroughfares with all the attendant "inanities and advertisements" Cleveland could dream up. For two hours an exasperated Crane had been "obliged to wait while the initial 'peerade'" snaked its way past his house. America, he sighed. The only country in the world that could actually "relish & applaud anything so stupid & drab as that parade—led by the most notable and richest grafter of the place decked out in Colonial rags as the founder of the city Moses C." Here indeed was American Gothic. Perhaps the Baroness had been right after all. Americans really did seem to have "no *atom* of a conception of beauty," and—worse—didn't want it.[8]

The only thing that had given the miserable spectacle a shred of dignity had been a tiny contingent of Chinese in their "native and antique vestments & liveries," who had in fact prostituted themselves by trying to blend with the trash around them. "To see them passing the (inevitable) Soldier's Monument ablaze with their aristocratic barbarity of silk, gold and embroideries," Crane sighed, "*was* an anachronism that could occur *only* in America." Unbelievably, the last of their "section" had passed by in a float with a large "'melting pot'—its significance . . . blazoned in letters *on* it!!" And for what? Because it was good for business? America was becoming impossible. How he envied Munson taking off for France and Italy. Perhaps the way to go was to swim out with the tide and prostitute himself by writing "flattering biographies of rich businessmen," and then with his millions join Munson on Capri, where they would "rejuvenate the baths and temple there of Tiberius," waited on "by the only fair and unsullied youths & maidens then procurable in Europe."[9]

But as July turned to August and then September without his being able to find a job, and as his mother grew more and more agitated by his being around the house so much, and his hay fever returned with a vengeance, Crane became more and more restless. "I learn a Scriabin Prelude," he wrote Munson in August, "make a drawing, stroke my black cat . . . and read intermittently."[10] The cat, a stray he'd found in an alley and taken in, he'd named Agrippina, until he'd discovered that Agrippina was a male, when he changed its name to Agripenis. He managed to sell three poems to the little magazines: the slight "Pastorale"—written in July—to *The Dial*; "Persuasion" to *The Measure*; and "Porphyro in Akron" to *The Double Dealer,* so that for once he was sold out. He worked desultorily on a translation of de Gourmont's marginalia on Poe and Baudelaire for *The Double Dealer* and reworked a few poems.

Then, in late September, he saw Charlie Chaplin in *The Kid*. It was, he reported afterwards to Munson, "the greatest dramatic treat since seeing [Mary] Garden in *The Love of Three Kings* two winters ago." Never had comedy reached a higher level in America, and Chaplin was its genius. It had taken a year for the film even to make it to Cleveland, simply because of difficulties with the censors, though those same censors had no problem passing on a good deal of "sickening and false melodrama of high life and sex" or the usual crap about "lost virginities."

As a result of seeing *The Kid*, Crane wrote his strongest poem to date—"Chaplinesque"—an attempt "to put in words some of the Chaplin pantomime, so beautiful, and so full of eloquence, and so modern."[11] "We make our meek adjustments," Crane's poem begins, evoking Chaplin's slippery evasions before the authorities, an analog to what he himself had had to do to please his own father until the inevitable kick in the pants had come:

> Contented with such random consolations
> As the wind deposits
> In slithered and too ample pockets.
>
> For we can still love the world, who find
> A famished kitten on the step, and know
> Recesses for it from the fury of the street,
> Or warm torn elbow coverts.[12]

"I am moved to put Chaplin with the poets (of today), hence the 'we,'" he wrote Bill Wright, explaining what he'd tried to do in the poem. After all, he and Chaplin's character were in the same boat, weren't they? "Poetry, the human feelings, 'the kitten,' is so crowded out of the humdrum, rushing, mechanical scramble of today, that the man who would preserve them must duck and camouflage for dear life to keep them or keep himself from annihilation."[13] Crane was not alone in seeing Chaplin as a tragic figure, despite the buffos and guffaws one heard from the crowd. In fact, in the pages of the *Literary Digest* he'd read similar analyses of the comedian by the London and Paris critics. He confessed to stealing Eliot's lines about that "infinitely gentle/Infinitely suffering thing," turning the abstraction into the figure of the abandoned kitten that closed his poem. Chaplin's hilariously evasive gestures before the cop—standing in for a puritanical America—caught precisely what Crane felt were his own futile gestures as a poet (and as a homosexual) who was simply trying to survive. In spite of which, he insisted, the heart—the Hart—would somehow survive:

> We will sidestep, and to the final smirk
> Dally the doom of that inevitable thumb
> That slowly chafes its puckered index toward us,
> Facing the dull squint with what innocence
> And what surprise!
>
> And yet these fine collapses are not lies
> More than the pirouettes of any pliant cane;
> Our obsequies are, in a way, no enterprise.
> We can evade you, and all else but the heart:
> What blame to us if the heart live on.
>
> The game enforces smirks; but we have seen
> The moon in lonely alleys make
> A grail of laughter of an empty ash can,
> And through all sound of gaiety and quest
> Have heard a kitten in the wilderness.[14]

He'd written the poem, he confessed to Munson, because he felt "so particularly futile just now."[15] When Munson wrote back, accusing Chaplin of playing the sentimentalist, Crane answered by noting that Chaplin carried the theme of the outsider "with such power and universal portent" that sentimentality transcended itself "into a new kind of tragedy, eccentric, homely and yet brilliant."[16] Change "homely" to domestic, and the string of words described what Crane himself was doing in his own poetry.

He must surely have felt like Chaplin when he spent all one November Saturday as a foreman directing three men in distributing ads around the city. It wasn't much of a job, he knew, this trudging Cleveland's streets from early morning until nightfall, looking after a motley crew, but it was the only work he'd been able to find in seven months. The day after, he woke stiff and sore and went back down to the distribution center to see if they could use him again, only to be turned away. He put the best face on the situation he could: he'd been made foreman over three day workers, he'd gotten some good, hard exercise, he was $2.50 richer. If he worked hard enough, with planned increases he stood to make as much as thirty dollars a week. He returned to the site again on Monday and on Tuesday, only to be turned away each time. Finally he gave up. The job had lasted one day.

At least it was still possible to feed the heart. There was, for example, Willy Lescaze's salon, which met on Thursdays somewhere in Cleveland, sometimes in the ballroom of the New Amsterdam Hotel, sometimes at Klein's restaurant on Prospect Street, sometimes in Crane's own rooms. It was at one such meeting that Crane met two young Cleveland writers, Sam Loveman and Charles Harris, as well as the painter Richard Rychtarik and his wife Charlotte, with all of whom he would make long-lasting friendships. But often he shunned the meetings, especially when younger women were invited. He hated empty chatter and women who seemed always to expect "little compliments" and concessions, who were always insisting on "being the center of attention irrespective of their ability to take part in any argument." All these "interminable innuendoes and clucking and puffings," Crane complained, none of which ever led to anything.[17]

The truth was that he did not have very much to say in favor of either women or women artists. When Bill Wright wrote saying he'd been swept up by Edna St. Vincent Millay's poetry, Crane offered a far more restrained appraisal. He would go halfway with Wright, but no more. Millay had genius, perhaps, but a limited genius. Yes, she was better than Sara Teasdale and Marguerite Wilkinson, "to mention a few drops in the bucket of feminine lushness that forms a kind of milky way in the poetic firmament of the time (likewise all times)," and, yes, Millay was probably Elizabeth Browning's equal. But then he didn't much care for Mrs. Browning, either. To be fair, he did not much care for Tennyson or James Thompson or Chatterton or Byron or—for that matter—the great Milton. And yet, he joked, he had "the apparent brassiness" to call himself catholic in his tastes. Still, he did care—deeply—for Poe, Whitman, Keats, Shelley, Coleridge, and especially the Elizabethans (Marlowe, Shakespeare, Donne, and Webster), as well as Baudelaire, Laforgue, Dante, Cavalcanti, and Li Po. It was a veritable pantheon in itself.

Crane cared for these men, he told Wright, because they had all added something to the available stock of reality, and that, after all, was what he himself was after. "Unless one has some new, intensely personal viewpoint to record, say on the eternal feelings of love, and the suitable personal idiom to employ in the act," he insisted, "why write about it? Nine chances out of ten, if you know where in the past to look, you will find words already written in the moreorless exact tongue of your soul." For most poets, one could no doubt "find their sentiments much better expressed perhaps four hundred years past." The trouble with Millay, for instance, was that, for all her modest successes, she was simply too derivative. But since most readers couldn't tell the derivative from the new, they were content to crow her up as "a creditable heroine." Well, he already knew too much about poetry to buy into the popular assessment. If his own tastes were too esoteric, at least he was not after common table wine, but a vintage of "great fragility," such as Donne, for one, represented: "a dark, musky, brooding, speculative vintage, at once sensual and spiritual and singing rather the beauty of experience than innocence."[18]

By Thanksgiving, he had added Ben Jonson to his list of vintage Elizabethans. The truth was that he could find nothing among the moderns to match "the verbal richness, irony and emotion of these folks," and—as with Eliot and Eliot's followers—he was ready to let them influence him "as much as they can in the interpretation of modern moods." This was precisely why Eliot was the poet to watch now, for Eliot's poems had been nourished not only by Laforgue but by the great Elizabethans as well, and Eliot had in turn led Crane to them. Of course he did not want to end up merely imitating Eliot, but he was certainly ready to cultivate Eliot's "most congenial influences."

After all, it was getting harder and harder for modern poets to find satisfactory forms with which to express themselves. Was it not the case in fact that everything he had so far written was but a shadow of what he was after? Not once had he yet presented "a vital, living and tangible,—a positive emotion" to his own satisfaction. More and more now he abandoned poems as soon as he'd begun them, because they seemed either obvious or uninteresting to his own more discerning tastes. How hard to write what he wanted to write. One had to be "drenched in words, literally soaked with them to have the right ones form themselves into the proper pattern at the right moment." In the long run, it had nothing to do either with one's intentions or even one's emotions. When all was said and done, poetry was a matter of design, "felicitous juggling," and wordplay.[19]

But wasn't it always the case that the avant garde rejected current formulas in favor of originality, typographical innovation, and radical line breaks, the sort of thing Jean Cocteau was doing now in the pages of *The Little Review*? And yet for Crane personally, a radical movement like Dadaism was really little more than the death rattle of impressionism. Take the brilliant Matty Josephson, who seemed "afraid to use any emotion in his poetry," and so had had to resort to a poetry of mere "observation and sensation." Work like that was too thin, too cerebral. What Josephson was really doing was merely reacting to the outworn symbolism of a Mallarmé or a Huysmans. In Paris—where Josephson and Munson were now living—it was easy enough to do as the Parisians did. But from where he stood—in "Cleveland, Cuyhoga County, God's country"—such work seemed too easy.[20]

Better to work to recover an older, more authentic music, the cadences of Jonson, Drayton, and Donne, their rhymes and their rhythms, carrying these deftly and unself-consciously. What the old masters could provide was an interior form, "a form so thorough and intense as to dye the words themselves with a peculiarity of meaning, slightly different maybe from the ordinary definition of them separate from the poem."[21] Only once had he himself even approached a form like that, and that had been in "Black Tambourine." Well, he wanted that elusive form, and he was willing to wait for it to show itself rather than write something that did not satisfy him. If only he could find the money to get to Europe and breathe the air of the old masters, he might still find what he was looking for.

Instead, in September, he had to settle for a course in advertising at Western Reserve in Cleveland. It was a year-long class that met twice a week, and at the end of it he hoped to be able to land a job in copywriting. In mid-November, an agency offered him a week's trial—without pay—to sell real estate, and once again he failed gloriously. Then, as the Christmas rush picked up, he found work in the book department of Korner & Woods. By then there was "nothing but gall and disgust" left in him, especially at the thought of his father laughing at him for failing to find a decent job.[22] A week into December, Crane picked up a Frenchman and was "entertained," as he phrased it, in the usual way. This particular "breaker of the spell" had been a habitué of La Rotonde, he informed Munson, so that he'd been able to "enjoy a few Parisian sophistications" right there in dear old Cleveland.

With a modest salary coming in, and access to a storeful of books, he'd snatched up Aldous Huxley's translation of Rémy de Gourmont's *Un Coeur virginal* before the book could be removed from the shelves for indecency. How he hated to see it lying there alongside Zane Grey and the rush of Christmas gift books. If he had had any lingering fantasies of becoming a popular author, two weeks at Korner & Woods had changed that. So, while "poor dear Emerson" and Walt Whitman slumbered on their shelves unread, the public pawed over glitzy gift books in "tooled leather bindings," unable to get enough of the day's popular—and transient—writers.[23]

Then, just after New Year's, 1922, he began work as a copywriter at the direct-mail advertising firm of Corday & Gross at a salary of twenty-five dollars a week. He'd found the job because his instructor at Western Reserve had been impressed enough with Crane's work to set up the interview. "One year of this," he wrote Munson with characteristic optimism, "and I shall probably be trained in a profitable vocation that can be practiced anywhere."[24] He did not like having to take unfinished work home with him—he'd hoped to keep his nights free for his own work—but he liked the job and liked being treated for once as a human being. His boss had even taken the time to tell him how pleased he was with his work. Never once had his own father done that, and it delighted him now to be able to pass his "goggle-eyed father on the streets . . . without a tremor," knowing he was finally free of him.[25]

Things began looking up. There was another season of concerts at the Cleveland Institute of Music, under the brilliant directorship of Ernest Bloch. The previous winter, Crane had heard Bloch conduct his own Symphony in C# Minor and been deeply moved. Bloch seemed to be bringing in "interesting folks from all over everywhere," he wrote Munson.[26] In the fall it had been Jean Binet—a friend of Willy Lescaze's—performing Satie and Ravel. In January, a Beethoven concerto. In March, a performance of Bloch's *Trois poèmes juifs*, music Crane found "magnificent enough for Solomon to have marched & sung to."[27] He saw a performance of Eugene O'Neill's *The Emperor Jones* with the black thespian, John Gilpin, in the lead. He went with Bill Sommer on "mad carouses," beginning "with pigs' feet and sauerkraut" and ending with Debussy's *Gradus ad Parnassum* back in Crane's ivory tower. He dined at a nearby French restaurant where the proprietress actually stood "at the cashier's desk reading *La Nouvelle Revue Française*."[28] There one could enjoy steak and mushrooms and everything but the wine, outlawed now, alas, by Prohibition.

Early in February, Bill Wright came to visit. He was having a rocky relationship with a woman just now, and was anxious to seek out Crane's advice. Crane had never told Wright about his own homosexuality, and so the advice he offered him remained ambiguous. He advised Wright "not to let the caprices of any unmellow ladies result in your unbalance or extreme discomfiture." Even the best of them had the uncanny "faculty of producing very debilitating and thoroughly unprofitable effects on gentlemen who put themselves too much in their hands," and women, he was convinced, were not meant to occupy such a role. It had been the Catholic Church—blamed for everything under the sun—which had given woman her exalted position. The older civilizations—the Greeks, Romans, Egyptians—had known "better how to handle her." Get hold of de Gourmont, he suggested, that "adept scientist of the emotions." For even if the suffering Wright was going through over love had its romantic and beautiful side, he was still paying "a stupid price for it." Crane himself had been through "two or three of these cataclysms" (he did not mention that they'd been with men), and relations there had been even more difficult "because of their unusual and unsympathetic situations."[29] Crane did not know if he'd gained anything by suffering for love. But he did know he'd lost a great deal.

For months he'd had little time for poetry. But on Monday, February 13th, he joined Bill Sommer for lunch at a restaurant around the corner from the offices of Corday & Gross. One of the things they spoke of over their meal was the death of their friend, Ernest Nelson, who'd been killed by a car at Christmas. Sommer and Crane had both been pallbearers at the funeral, attended by almost no one, and Crane had been transfixed as he watched Nelson's body reduced to ashes at the crematorium. Something, he was convinced, some word had been given him from the face lying on the white pillow in the casket as he'd paid his last respects, though it would take several months to say just what that word was. As for the funeral itself, it had been "one of the few beautiful things" to happen to him in his long stay in Cleveland, and it had left him feeling "emotionally bankrupt" afterwards.[30]

In Nelson, he no doubt saw where his own life might lead if he ever settled down to a regular job and family. He'd met Nelson, a lithographer in his fifties, through Sommer, for they had been co-workers. A "Nietzschean and thorough appreciator of all the best," Crane summed up Nelson, a man who'd "pursued his lonely way in America since the age of fifteen," when he'd left his home in Norway over religious differences with his family. From there he'd gone on to art school in Washington, D.C., distinguishing himself, only to have his aunt suddenly withdraw "all her help and force him into the prostitution of all his ideals" by making him earn his living at "cheap lithographic work."[31] Years earlier, before he'd married, Nelson had published some of his poetry. Then he'd settled down, married, and lived out a quiet, nondescript life. And now even that was over.

Wilbur Underwood winked. Had there been anything more there, he wanted to know. But Crane set him straight at once. It had all been quite "platonic," his relationship with Nelson. The attraction had been with Nelson's extraordinary mind, a mind "broken against the stupidity of American life."[32] But now, on a Monday in mid-February, having returned to his desk after lunch, Crane began an elegy, "Praise for an Urn," in honor of his lost friend. At last he'd found a place for the lines that had haunted him for the past two years:

> It was a kind and northern face
> That mingled in such exile guise
> The everlasting eyes of Pierrot
> And, of Gargantua, the laughter.

His thoughts, delivered to me
From the white coverlet and pillow,
I see now, were inheritances—
Delicate riders of the storm. . . .

The slant moon on the slanting hill
Once moved us toward presentiments
Of what the dead keep, living still,
And such assessments of the soul

As, perched in the crematory lobby,
The insistent clock commented on . . .

Time had taken Nelson as it took everyone, Crane understood. Finally, it annihilated thought itself, which death reduced to the "dry sound of bees/Stretching across a lucid space," the self scattered as one day his own remains would be scattered, even the "well-meant idioms" of his poems melting into the "smoky spring that fills/The suburbs."[33]

But no sooner had the Muse returned than she too melted away. By March, financial problems for both his mother and himself had reached the point where he could concentrate on nothing but his job. Grace's alimony, according to the settlement, was about to end, and—at forty-three—she was going to have to join the work force for the first time in her life. Crane would not only have to take care of himself but also help out now at home, and he made precious little money as it was. Worse, his millionaire father was "too much of a cad to really do anything for his former wife" except what was in the agreement. Life had splintered again, he told Munson, not only because of money but because his job demanded "the most frequent jerks of the imagination from one thing to another."[34] He knew he was too much the gregarious, fun-loving creature ever to be satisfied with an ad job. And now, "with the banal arrival of spring," here he was in love again.[35] Yes, he knew he sounded like a profligate, he confessed, but something had to be conceded to eros to make Cleveland livable.

Though he'd already cautioned Munson against spending his money to bring out one more little magazine, Munson had gone ahead and published one in Paris with the improbable name of *The Gargoyle.* When the first issue reached Crane in late February, he had to admit he found it not altogether bad, though he was just then "hopelessly tired of Art and theories about Art."[36] Two months later, Munson was in Vienna, this time putting together yet another little magazine called *Secession.* Most of what Crane found there he disliked—Matty Josephson, Tristan Tzara, Malcolm Cowley—though he did like Louis Aragon's writing. What especially irked him was Josephson's going gaga over Apollinaire's celebration of the new: "the telegraph, the locomotive, the automat, the wireless, the street cars and electric lamp post." In Paris, such quotidian conveniences might be novelties, to be praised for their abstract design. But in Cleveland, such things were mere practicalities for getting things done or for getting from one point to another. God, he hated manifestoes. Why couldn't he just write what he wanted to without having to fit into some school? "I'm afraid I don't fit in your group," he told Munson. "Or any group, for all that."[37]

But then he had a change of heart. He found the second issue of *Secession* "filled with quite ultra things by E. E. Cummings, Marianne Moore, Slater Brown, Matthew Josephson, Malcolm Cowley, etc.," all of whom had been in Paris when Munson had conceived his magazine. Crane was still "skeptical about all such dear, darling and courageous and brief attempts," but he would do what he could to make the magazine a success. He knew what the French scene offered, he told his friend Charmion Wiegand. It offered Gide, Rimbaud, Laforgue (his favorite, though "very acid" and very hard to bring over into English, as he himself had just done), Apollinaire, and that "wild bird," Cocteau, "the present king of les boulevards." Just now, it seemed, everyone—the young Americans included—was bent on trying to be very clever.

For his part, he meant to stick with the Brits and the Americans, and that meant Yeats, Edward Thomas, Stevens, Eliot, Pound, and of course those "dear great Elizabethans like Marlowe, Webster, Donne and Drayton."[38] And now he was adding a "new" voice to his pantheon: Herman Melville. He'd discovered a new book, published seventy years earlier, but which he and others had just learned about: *Moby-Dick,* a great *American* classic. ("That delightful 'Moby Dick,'" he wrote Underwood, with its homoerotic portrayal "of dear Queequeg.")[39] To hell with France. The real action was in America. Who knew "but what our American scene will be the most intricate and absorbing one in fifty years or so." Munson had to understand that "Some kind of aristocracy of taste" was being established, and it was happening right here.[40] He urged his friend to get back to the States as soon as possible, where he belonged.

The Laforgue Crane had just translated into English consisted of three "Locutions," thirty-six lines altogether, published in the May issue of *The Double Dealer*. Some yellow nineties, then, thirty years later:

> *Ah! the divine infatuation*
> *That I nurse for Cydalise*
> *Now that she has fled the capture*
> *Of my lunar sensibility . . .*[41]

"My affection for Laforgue is none the less genuine for being led to him through Pound and T. S. Eliot than it would have been through Baudelaire," he explained to a new correspondent. And though he had to use a French dictionary to translate, "a certain sympathy with Laforgue's attitude" had made it easier for him to render the poet than it would have been, he believed, for a professional translator.[42] He'd done them for fun, though he hadn't minded getting paid for them.

The new correspondent was Allen Tate, Crane's exact contemporary, and Crane had written him after reading Tate's poem, "Euthanasia," in the same issue of *The Double Dealer* in which his own translations had appeared. Here was a contemporary interested in the same things as himself: Pound, Eliot, the Elizabethans. He'd felt an instant rapport with Tate, and, when Tate wrote back, Crane began at once to unburden himself. He knew the poetry of negation and despair, of "damnations and prostrations," knew it perhaps too well, and now he felt himself recoiling from it. For four years he'd analyzed the poetry of negation's foremost champion, T. S. Eliot, looking for a "weak spot . . . in his armor," without finding one. Only recently had he "discovered a safe tangent to strike" at him. He would arm himself with as many of Eliot's poetic techniques as he could master, but he would use them toward a more positive end. After all, one did have joys, and he meant to restore that balance to American poetry, light and darkness dancing in proper measure. Jazz, he now believed, would be the link. "Let us invent an idiom for the proper transposition of jazz into words!" he closed. "Something clean, sparkling, elusive!"[43]

It was precisely what he was trying to do in his own poetry at that very moment. And so in mid-May he began a long "metaphysical" poem in three parts entitled "For the Marriage of Faustus and Helen." He'd started with what would eventually become the second part of the poem, which—because he had so little time to devote to it— remained "hopelessly fragmentary" for weeks.[44] Still, he worked on, obsessed with the new idiom he was trying to get down on the page. "I have been at it for the last 24 hours," he wrote Munson on June 4th. It seemed like "a work of youth and magic."[45] Within days Crane was calling it "the most ambitious thing" he'd ever done: "a conscious pseudo-symphonic construction toward an abstract beauty" unheard of in English.[46]

There were jazz rhythms he'd caught in the opening movement that he'd been after for a long time, and now he was getting them down on the page, actually creating an idiom approaching the condition of music. Not Debussy, but an American jazz idiom, the equivalent of Louis Armstrong's brazen trumpet tonalities:

> Brazen hypnotics glitter here;
> Glee shifts from foot to foot,
> Magnetic to their tremulo.
> This crashing opéra bouffe,
> Blest excursion! this ricochet
> From roof to roof—
> Know, Olympians, we are breathless
> While nigger cupids scour the stars![47]

"Life is awful in Cleveland." Thus a by-now too familiar lament to Underwood in mid-June. The little magazines had said so. Willy Lescaze had said so. Now Crane was saying so. He would "write a play or something" and make a lot of money and then head for Long Island or the Jersey woods, as he had in 1917. He was growing more and more isolated even as he grew surer of his poetic powers. Each day he worked at his job, then, at five, rushed back to his room "hung with the creations of Sommer and Lescaze" and lined with his collection of rare art books—Derain, Vlaminck, Toulouse-Lautrec, Grosz, Gauguin, de Chirico—to begin writing with the help of three or four drinks. The only "bright spot ahead" for the summer was the promise of a visit from Munson, who would bring with him the copy of Ulysses he'd smuggled past the customs inspectors on his return to America.[48]

Nights Crane sometimes strolled over to Little Italy, a Sicilian community only a few blocks from his house, to get drunk on three-year-old Chianti. That was the place to enjoy oneself, he wrote Munson one night when he was still feeling high from drinking too much wine. That evening he'd found himself "in the family parlour of a pick-slinger's family with chromos on the walls that are right in style of Derain and Vlaminck. Bitch dogs and the rest of the family wander in while the bottle is still half empty and some of the family offspring. *Tristram Shandy* read to a friend"—this was Sam Loveman—"with a Spanish Bolero going on the Victrola sounds good in such a milieu!"[49] A record played over and over on his Victrola—that siren calling to him of sweet eros and guilty song on the black seventy-eight disk, the "incandescent wax/Striated with nuances, nervosities/That we are heir to."[50] Ah, to hear that music through the blessèd fumes of wine! For years now he'd enjoyed his booze, but by the summer of 1922 he was coming to believe he could never live without it. "When you come here," he promised Munson, "we shall make many visits to this charming family."

Munson would like his "classic, puritan, inhibited friend," Sam Loveman, who translated Baudelaire "charmingly." Sam lived totally in the world of the imagination, and—though part of Cleveland's gay community—had just innocently given Crane a book on Greek vases, "in which satyrs with great erections prance to the ceremonies of Dionysios with all the fervour of de Gourmont's descriptions of sexual sacrifice in *Physique de L'Amour*." Crane was warming to it now. "At times, dear Gorham," he went on, "I feel an enormous power in me— that seems almost supernatural." If he could just keep this new power from souring into discouragement, he believed he really might "amount to something sometime." There. He could say it now "with perfect equanimity" because he was drunk, "notoriously drunk," and the Victrola was still going "with that glorious 'Bolero.'"

How he loved what alcohol and drugs could do for one. "Did I tell you of that thrilling experience this last winter in the dentist's chair when under the influence of aether and amnesia my mind spiraled to a kind of seventh heaven of consciousness and egoistic dance among the seven spheres—and something like an objective voice kept saying to me—'You have the higher consciousness—you have the higher consciousness? This is something that very few have. This is what is called genius.'" So he was after all to be counted among the elect. Such a sense of happiness had come over him then as he'd felt only twice before in his life. And both those had been moments when poetic "inspirations" had been granted him.[51]

There in a dentist's chair, in quotidian Cleveland, amid the world of ad writing and snow and boredom, he had touched on the world of infinite consanguinities. And as the bore had drilled into his tooth, he followed its every spiral as if he were already dead and watching a body—his body?—at a funeral. Was this then the meaning behind the lines he'd written in February, thinking of Nelson's corpse lying there before it had been transformed by fire?

> *His thoughts, delivered to me*
> *From the white coverlet and pillow*
> *I see now, were inheritances—*
> *Delicate riders of the storm*[52]

"O Gorham," he closed, "I have known moments in eternity. I tell you this as one who is a brother. I want you to know me as I feel myself to be sometimes."

Crane was not bragging or giving himself airs when he said this; ever since that day in the dentist's chair, he'd felt a new confidence in himself. This was not some ordinary hallucination such as anyone might experience who took an anesthetic prior to having work done on their teeth. No, this was something altogether different, for with the voice had come a renewed sense of his poetic mission. And the imagination, after all, was "the only thing worth a damn." He would work and work, as he had with the elusive jazz rhythms he'd finally netted in his new poem, and he would arrive at last at his best work, he miscalculated, around the time he hit "35 or 40."[53]

5 / THE HIGHER CONSCIOUSNESS

CLEVELAND
JULY 1922–MARCH 1923

"AND YOU MAY FALL DOWNSTAIRS with me/With perfect grace and equanimity"[1]—Crane's words, written in mid-June 1922. On the evening of July 2nd he picked up a young man in Cleveland Park and seduced him "strenuously," he boasted afterward to Underwood. The evening had ended with his handling "the largest instrument" he'd ever had the pleasure of handling. Europa pursued by the Bull, bested right here in America by some anonymous Clevelander. Crane's fear now was that the rest of his days would be spent in a series of "anticlimaxes" after this one vigorous night. Oh, how he yearned for "new worlds to conquer," not only in his poems, but in his night wanderings as well, and bemoaned the fact that there were "only a few insignificant peninsulas and archipelagoes left" for him to discover.[2] He enclosed a letter from a former lover of his, the anonymous truck driver who had worked for his father and who had left at the same time he had. Now there, Crane sighed, was a genial soul it had been a pleasure to educate.

By then, however, his sexual indiscretions had become known to someone, and soon he had to face the threat that his father was about to find out about his nocturnal activities unless he came up with the money to keep his blackmailer quiet. All that summer, at regular intervals, he forked over ten dollars out of his weekly twenty-five to buy his blackmailer's silence. He had already suspected the risks involved in living on the edge as he did, had already written of it in a poem he'd composed ten months earlier, "The Bottom of the Sea Is Cruel." It was a threshold poem, really, in which he imagined himself watching a group of boys in striped bathing suits (unwitting prisoners of the human condition, like Crane himself?) as they played on the beach. Off to one side, he observed them, like some recording angel, as they threw sand at one another, frisked with their dog, collected the seashells and sticks "bleached/By time and the elements."

The lines of the poem are charged with a blend of voyeurism and sexual innocence, rather like Satan spying on Adam and Eve in the Garden. For this speaker knows what the young do not: that beyond their shouts, sun and time continue to beat "lightning on the waves," and the waves—like fate—keep crashing in. The children have yet to learn what the poet has learned: the two-edged knowledge that comes with sexual experience, and only to those who have dared the deeper waters of eros and betrayal to learn firsthand that "the bottom of the sea is cruel."[3] Crane was delighted to learn that Munson and his friend, Kenneth Burke—that astute reader, poet, essayist, budding editor, and fellow Ohioan transplanted now to New York—both liked the poem, but it was not one of his own favorites. In fact, he dismissed it as no more than an experiment spawned by the long days spent at his desk. "A kind of poster," he called it, with "nothing more profound in it than a 'stop, look and listen' sign," its final line "bold and unambitious like a skull & cross-bones insignia."[4] But though he shrugged the poem off, in time it would become the proem to "Voyages," Crane's brilliant sequence on the rise and fall of love.

"Bosses brush near my shoulder," he wrote Tate in mid-July, taking a break in the midst of his ad work. And poetry was not encouraged around the office. For weeks he'd been suffering from his annual bout with hay fever, and only now could he finally "peer again on the world with subsiding eyes." Tate had just written to say he was getting married—to another writer, the novelist Caroline Gordon. Marriage? Crane wrote back quizzically, with the same dismissive tone he'd used in advising Bill Wright; *that* certainly sounded ominous. "Think well, beforehand," he advised Tate.[5] Would he really be satisfied to settle down with just one person? Who, after all, could really do that?

Bearing with him the copy of *Ulysses* he'd smuggled into the

States for Crane, Gorham Munson arrived in Cleveland on July 12th for his planned two-week visit. Both men were prepared to catch up on several years' conversation. As he'd promised, Crane took Munson over to Little Italy to meet Dominic, the man who made the fine Prohibition Chianti he so enjoyed. Later, over many bottles, he composed scurrilous limericks on Bodenheim, Millay, and Pound. For his part, Munson told Crane he was now over his infatuation with Dadaism and deep into writing a book about his friend, Waldo Frank, the New York novelist, essayist, and commentator on the American scene, a man consumed with the question of the spiritual dimensions of modernity. It was a discussion that had been going on among American writers for the past decade, but Frank had brought a new urgency to it, especially now that the dead-end cynicism of Dadaism and the shock of the late war were beginning to recede.

During the two weeks Munson stayed with Crane, the discussions kept coming back to the question of how American poetry might incorporate the world around them into itself. How, in short, it was going to get typewriters into its lines, as well as jazz, the Charleston, Isadora Duncan, the Woolworth Building, Ford flivvers, steamships, electricity, airplanes, as well as the open vista provided by hundreds of new highways and tunnels and bridges opening all over the country, from New York City to San Francisco. Who would write of the still inchoate forces turning America into a literary and spiritual vortex? How would the poet be able to make others see the city and the machine as extensions of the higher consciousness pushing back the limits of the possible? How would he create the new trinity that would fuse together nature, man and the imagination?

Simultaneously, Harry Candee had been urging Crane to read P. D. Ouspensky's *Tertium Organum*, a book that spoke eloquently, mystically, and enthusiastically of the possibility of this higher consciousness. In Ouspensky's reading of the new order, it would be the artist who would prove the real superman, someone motivated not by power or money or fame but rather by love. The new poem, then, would have as one of its characteristics the ability to lead others to this new higher consciousness, where the limitations of time and space would themselves finally be transcended. All of this Crane mulled over, absorbed, and sought to translate into a living Word.

Toward the end of Munson's visit, in fact, Crane was as preoccupied with the second part of "For the Marriage of Faustus and Helen" (what would become Part I) as he had been the month before with the first part (which would in turn become Part II). Night after night, work and dinner over, he sat down to his Corona typewriter, rewinding his Victrola whenever it wound down, listening to the same record over and over, until Munson must have been driven to distraction. Split apart, split apart like the columns in the daily newspaper: that was the apt metaphor for the modern mind. A mind divided, as Crane found himself divided each day by his job at Corday & Gross, his day "partitioned" into chronometrical units, daily "memoranda, baseball scores,/The stenographic smiles and stock quotations." Each day he passed the divided streets, the "druggist, barber and tobacconist," on the yellow trolley that took him down Euclid Avenue to his office, catching as he could snatches of life's rapid flutterings, like sparrow wings brushing the gutters of Cleveland's crowded streets, or the gutters of his mind.

And then there was that other world, the world of night, with its "graduate opacities of evening" taking all that bustle away, leaving him with something "Virginal perhaps, less fragmentary, cool." It was then that he—the modern Faustus, the poet, the visionary, the alchemist whose mind had been "Too much the baked and labeled dough/Divided by accepted multitudes"—might begin again to build (in Ben Jonson's words, which served as head note) "Helen's house," in spite of these quotidian mercantile forces that seemed bent on destroying his peace. Now, inside his poem, he could imagine himself riding the trolley as he traveled home from work, suddenly looking up to gaze on the "pink and green" neon advertising lights stippling Helen's hands as she sat across from him, her eyes "prodigal" and "half-riant before the jerky window frame."

And the poet, expecting nothing, suddenly beholding now a presentiment of that eternal beauty he hungered after, of which Helen was the incarnated sign, the rainbow colors of the neon lights prefiguring the transubstantiated reality of the white city of the imagination, "That world which comes to each of us alone." Hart Crane there in his tower room, looking above his desk at the sketch Lescaze had done of him, the right eye mystical and brilliant and inturned, in love with eternity. Then ending his poem with a fervent prayer:

> *Accept a lone eye riveted to your plane,*
> *Bent axle of devotion along companion ways*
> *That beat, continuous, to hourless days—*
> *One inconspicuous, glowing orb of praise.*[6]

"I have been very quiet while Munson has been here," Crane wrote Underwood on July 27th, the day after Munson had left. "Tonight however, I break out into fresh violences." He'd been savoring his copy of *Ulysses*, which was probably one of only "two or three copies west of New York." It had been printed in Paris, "a huge tome"—800 pages— "on Verge d'arche paper," and now he wanted it properly bound. But because it was filled with "marvelous oaths and blasphemies," he was afraid of letting it out of his sight. Yes, Joyce had written the "epic of the age," as "great a thing as Goethe's *Faust*"—also very much on his mind just then.[7] He wished somehow he could talk face-to-face with the Irishman about modern literature.

One person he wished afterward he had *not* talked to was his steady correspondent for the past three years, Sherwood Anderson. Toward the end of Munson's stay, Anderson, who was in Cleveland at the time, finally came out to Crane's house to meet the poet. Crane in turn introduced Anderson to Munson, and things seemed to go well. But after dinner, when the three went upstairs to Crane's room, the topic of Paul Rosenfeld, the New York critic, came up, and things suddenly took a turn for the worse. Rosenfeld had, alas, just attacked Frank in print, and Munson had taken umbrage. Anderson, as fate would have it, happened to be a friend of Rosenfeld's, and, being twenty years Munson's senior, let him know in no uncertain terms exactly where he stood. Soon Munson and Anderson were hurling barbs at each other, barbs that Crane seemed unable to deflect.

When Anderson abruptly left Crane's house that night, he was clearly upset, and for the rest of his stay in Cleveland he refused to see Crane again, though he did send a note saying he was sorry about the argument. For three years Crane had followed Anderson's work assiduously, praising it warmly in print, even if privately he'd begun to think Anderson had already "like a diver, touched bottom."[8] Now, on their very first meeting, Crane had lost Anderson as a friend. Nor did it help matters that Munson would soon retaliate by going after both Rosenfeld and Anderson in the pages of *Secession*. On the other hand, Anderson had promised Crane to try to act as Bill Sommer's agent when he reached New York. So, despite the way things had turned out, Crane went ahead and sent Anderson twenty-seven drawings and paintings in care of *The Dial*.

Nevertheless, he wrote Munson afterwards, he could not help feeling uneasy, as if he'd delivered "Plato into the hands of the Philistines."[9] Anderson had turned out to be a nasty fool, adding insult to injury by refusing to see him again. So it came as no surprise when, after stirring up "a petty rumpus" at *The Dial* by repeating what Munson had said about Rosenfeld, Anderson then sent all of Sommer's things back to Crane. Rosenfeld had not been impressed by Sommer's work, Anderson explained. The work was a mere hodgepodge of French and German influences and—worse—Sommer seemed unable to "draw a head on man, woman or animal." This was not his own view, Anderson wanted Crane to know, but that was how matters stood.

The whole affair showed Anderson up in a "petty and malignant" light, Crane told his friend, Charmion von Weigand, afterwards.[10] True, he still liked some of Anderson's work, though most of his friends no longer did. But months later he was still smarting at Rosenfeld's rejection of his friend's paintings as derivative and old-fashioned. "God DAMN this constant nostalgia for something always 'new,'" he would tell Munson. "This disdain for anything with a trace of the past in it!!!" Criticism of that kind was like the newspapers, always shouting the latest headline and forgetting everything else. It was the very thing he hated about Matty Josephson, this forever commenting on the latest fad, a strategy that bred "its own swift decay." He would always enjoy old masters like El Greco and Goya. And so with Bill Sommer's canvases, filled as they were "with a solid and clear beauty" that was timeless.[11] But by then he must have known that his attempts to get a hearing for Sommer had failed completely.

In early August, Crane was given a week's vacation. He'd hoped to get to Washington or New York again, but he lacked the money to do either. He did, however, get down to see Sommer. On Sunday morning, August 6th, he wrote out the lines for "Sunday Morning Apples." A "homely and gay thing," he called it, written out of "sheer joy" in celebration of Sommer's spirit.[12] In the poem's lines he managed to catch the manner in which the returning seasons underwrote Sommer's own strong lines, the way in which an apple, surrounded by leaf and shadow, became for the painter a "ripe nude/reared/Into a realm of swords." He recalled the innocence of a boy—one of Sommer's own boys, or himself—running "with a dog before the sun," boy and dog each forming its own independent orbit. But he also saw that nature, observed that intently, could offer a counterresponse of its own. Apples, he saw,

might finally toss the artist who lived among them their own innermost
secrets, and be transformed by both the winepress and the press of the
imagination into wine and art, and so feed the spirit twice:

> Beloved apples of seasonable madness
> That feed your inquiries with aerial wine.
> Put them again beside a pitcher with a knife,
> And poise them full and ready for explosion—
> The apples, Bill, the apples![13]

But by August, in spite of his vacation, Crane's spirit was tired,
deeply tired. The pace, the steamy weather, hay fever, "the infinite and
distasteful detail work" of his job at Corday & Gross, and now the energy he needed to find a new job: all had conspired to empty him. He
could not eat and he actually feared he was on the verge of a nervous
breakdown. He had not felt this "dangerous" since the break with his
father two years before. Then, as luck would have it, he found a new
job, and had the pleasure of telling his old boss, who had been about
to hand him a "series of gentle reprimands," not to bother, since he
was quitting.[14] Amusing, he thought, to watch the man suddenly do an
about-face and ask him to stay on . . . with a raise. But Crane was firm.
He'd already been turned down for a raise, thank you. Come September, he would go to work for Patno's, a direct mail-order firm, at a salary
twice the twenty-five dollars he'd been making. Moreover, he would be
in complete charge of his own department. Patno's was a new agency,
and it needed someone with Crane's experience. Better still was the fact
that his writing poetry was actually considered a plus.

Had he not found a job, he would probably have left that September for New York. As it was, even with the new job, Cleveland was
finally wearing thin. He was feeling "doubly desolate," he confessed to
Underwood, especially after hearing from both Underwood and Candee. There was Harry, off in England, happy in the love of some gold-
en English lad, with whom he'd frolicked for four glorious days, "easy
and bored, careening from Buckingham Palace to the lanes of Limehouse," Harry's "glorious outburst after 18 months of celibacy!" How
he wished just now he could see Underwood. He'd tried calling him in
Washington and wasted half the night in the failed effort. How goddamned "stalked" he was "these dog days" by lust. Everywhere he
looked, he saw someone he wanted to be with. If only he could free

himself from family responsibilities, he confessed, he would gladly sacrifice himself "to passion to the final cinders." Sex and poetry: the only things life seemed to hold for him any more.

For Washington had by then faded into a mirage. True, when he'd actually been there, he confessed, he'd been miserable selling his father's goddamned chocolates. But he yearned to be back in Washington now, after a two-year hiatus, "for a few more evenings on that narrow balcony off that dreadful room," where the two of them could talk again "about Beardsley, Rabelais, aphrodisiacs, poetry and lust." Instead, he spent his days pumping up "enthusiasms . . . for various products from thermometers to gas ranges," turning out "written arguments in their praise as fast as possible."[15] Nothing, he knew from hard experience, *nothing* killed the imagination as fast as copywriting. To have to write each damned day of Fox furnaces and Pittsburgh hot-water heaters and Seiberling Tires just to make ends meet. No wonder he drank, drank whatever the hell he could get hold of, even communion wine and rabbinical wine ("Rabbi Crane! What strange conversions there are," he wrote one night after polishing off a gallon of rabbinical sherry).[16] Each day he tried to focus his energies by turning his ads into imagist poems—a lit cigarette on a mahogany desk, protected by a glass covering manufactured by the Pittsburgh Plate Glass Company. Properly presented, the image spoke for itself.

Then he struck gold with his love life. "Yesterday night I at last was taken into the arms of love again," he wrote ecstatically to Underwood. Seldom had he had affection like this offered him. This fellow was "an athlete—very strong—20 only—dark haired—distantly Bohemian." Oh, how he hoped it might last a bit longer this time. After all, he deserved "a little kindness," and this boy had been *so* kind.[17] For better or worse, Crane confessed to Munson, he'd "almost fallen in love" with the guy.[18] Love and Simoni's restaurant and a couple of bottles of dago red: Life was worth living after all, though being under the same roof with his mother and grandmother certainly could put the brakes on one's ardor. If only he could get back to New York.

How he missed the city and those long talks he used to have with Munson and Matty Josephson about everything under the sun: Blake, the quarterly wars—*Secession, The Little Review, The Dial, The Double Dealer.* He was anxious too to meet the new batch of New York writers. Lescaze had already gone from Cleveland, shaking the dust of the city from his sandals. That left the Rychtariks—Richard and Char-

lotte—and Sam Loveman, and Loveman was turning "more incoher-
ent every day." Crane had read about the "half-baked" gang of writers
who made up the in-group at the Algonquin Club in New York, and
hated them roundly for their habit of leveling everyone, so that Ben
Hecht and T. S. Eliot somehow got "equal honors." The only good news
was that the anthologist Stanley Braithwaite had written asking to
reprint "Praise for an Urn" in his new anthology. "At last," Crane
mocked, "I shall rub shoulders with Florence Wilkinson!"[19]

That September, he finally managed to sell one of Bill Sommer's
paintings: a small watercolor that William Carlos Williams himself
bought for twenty-five dollars. The picture—three figures against a
vibrant background—wound up in Williams's second-floor bedroom
next to his Demuths and Scheelers. "I wish you could meet old Sommer," Crane wrote Williams on the 19th. "We want to get him out of
that union labor hell-hole lithography factory before it's too late. Make
any noise you can about your picture to the right people." There was
"nobody in this country" who had the "line qualities" Sommer had,
he insisted, which he'd as much as said in "Sunday Morning Apples."[20]

Williams loved the painting, and wrote Sommer to say—in his
characteristic idiom—that Sommer's work had got under his under-
drawers. Such praise, coming from Williams, Crane knew, would mean
everything to Sommer, "more than the plaudits of a hundred Rosen-
felds."[21] How he wished he could finally meet Williams, whom he loved
for his clean directness. But Sommer himself seemed to take no interest whatever in the sale. Nor did he even bother to send Williams a
thank-you note. How peculiar the man was, Crane confessed to Munson on Thanksgiving Day. "Never looks you up, never phones or man-
ifests the slightest interest." Well, he was tired now of this "ever-lastingly
tagging after him." Next time he'd wait until he had "some important
news" before he tried crashing into the man's hermetically sealed world
again.[22] You did not win fame by acting the way Sommer acted. That
much was certain.

A slew of art books ordered months before from Germany had
finally reached Crane in October. Because of the country's postwar
inflation, he'd managed to buy the whole lot of them—monographs on
Chinese landscape painters, Egyptian sculpture, African art, Japanese

art—for the sum of three dollars. He also had a new coat, thanks to his mother, who'd bought it during a recent trip to New York. "Light brown with wide cross-stripes in orange! My progress down the avenue is attended with awesome gazes, to say the least,"[23] he told Munson. He even managed to see Harry Candee for the first time in three years, though it had meant getting up at 5:00 A.M. to meet him at the train station in Cleveland where Harry had a ninety-minute stopover. Harry was on his way to Chicago, and from there to the West Coast and China, where he meant to float down the Yangtze "under the dragon stars."[24] The man's life seemed golden.

Underwood, on the other hand, had not fared nearly as well when—at Crane's suggestion—he'd looked up Munson in New York. His Washington contact would be delightful company, Crane had promised Munson, "whether he goes in for post-Beardsley attitudes or not. The episodes of the *Satyricon* are mild as compared to his usual exploits in N.Y. during vacations."[25] But Munson was not impressed. "Poor Underwood," Crane wrote Munson afterwards. He'd been afraid the two would not hit it off. Crane's own affection for Underwood was "based on a certain community of taste and pursuit," which he'd hoped Munson would sympathize with. The trouble was that his old friend had been crushed by too much bureaucratic humdrum in the city of the dead, and he'd had to find whatever amusements he could in ways that over the years had become obsessions. Yes, Underwood was at best only a mediocre poet, but get him talking on his favorite topic—sex— and one got "as strong a satire as Petronius."[26] Still, Crane knew, these were his proclivities, not Munson's. Like Candee, Underwood was a product of the nineties, not the twenties, and so a sharp clash between Munson's group (which included Burke, Cummings, and Frank) and Underwood's was probably to be expected. Crane himself was pliant enough to bridge both worlds, as well as a host of others.

Whatever boredom Bill Wright was finding back in Warren, Crane wrote his friend that December, it couldn't be as boring as the ad campaign he'd been working on day and night for the past three weeks for the Pittsburgh Water Heater Company. "I am growing bald trying to scratch up new ideas in housekeeping and personal hygiene," he lamented. And all for what? To try and convince people that they need-ed more hot water? The night before he'd gotten drunk on rabbinical sherry again, but even then he'd been unable to rid himself of his "hot water complex" and had "sat down and reeled off the best lines written so far" in his handling of the campaign. Whatever poems he wrote from now on would no doubt "attest this sterilizing influence of HOT WATER!" Wine he had; lovers and song he did not. He pined for New York and summer weather. But it wasn't just Cleveland that was the problem. It was something about the times themselves, which felt directionless. What an age to be living in, "appalling and dull at the same time."[27]

Almost nightly now the drinking was repeated, until finally Grace put her foot down. No more wine in the house, she told him, and with that Crane exploded, slamming the door behind him and taking a room at a cheap hotel in downtown Cleveland. "I am thinking seriously of moving into permanent private quarters where one need not be questioned about every detail of life and where one can be free of the description of one's food and its contents and manner of preparation while it is eaten at the table," he wrote Underwood on December 10th. At the moment, he was sitting in his office, and since it was Sunday night and the place was empty, he'd looked in various cabinets until he'd found a gallon of delicious sherry someone had inadvertently left behind. He'd already had two glasses of it and he meant to have two more before he went with Sam Loveman to see Isadora Duncan dance that evening, after which he would trudge back to his boring hotel room.

He was going to stay away from the house for the next few days and see if *that* didn't make his mother change her mind. But he did miss his tower with its pictures and books and the Victrola enveloping him with the strains of Ravel, Debussy, Strauss, and Wagner. He hated having to abandon his mother because he knew how much she depended on him. But she had to let him have a little wine. After all, he'd never actually embarrassed her with his behavior. Life was hard enough "without having to put up with a hundred extra restrictions" just for a room and bed.[28] These family fusses had taken their toll on him from the time he was eight, which was when his parents had begun their incessant quarreling, quarreling that had led to estrangement, separation, and finally divorce. Amazing how the slightest disturbance now could bring back the whole wretched past, destroying his fragile equilibrium.

At least at the office he had people he could talk to, people who had actually heard of Joyce and Pater. Otherwise, life in Cleveland had become gruel-thin for him. "I cannot remember a more hectic month than the last," he complained, "unless I recall some of the old bivouacs of New York days, when I ricocheted 'from roof to roof' without intermission." This to Munson, five days into the new year of 1923, when the flood of work had for the moment subsided, leaving him exhausted and irritable. "Two rush campaigns to write, gifts and remembrances to buy and send to far too many people—suppers, parties and evenings—much tossing of the pot,—'prison, palace and reverberation'!" And here was one Dr. Coué, with his latest self-help book, telling Americans to say to themselves each day that they were "growing better and better in every way."[29] Maybe so, but he personally was being sacrificed at the stake of business, pieces of his burnt body flaking off with each passing day.

It may in fact have been Dr. Coué's insipid advice that served as the germ for Crane's send-up of America's obsession with how-to remedies for everything under the sun, including regularity. America, which could outlaw the taking of a simple glass of wine, could also spend millions advertising laxatives. "America's Plutonic Ecstasies" turned out to be Crane's Cummingsesque satire on the country's love affair with regularity:

> preferring laxatives to wine
> all america is saying
> "how are my bowels today?" and
> feeling them in every way . . .

Puritan, bourgeois America, thin-lipped and "fast/with righteousness," grown ecstatic over emetics. The only catharsis it seemed to care about was not what Aristotle and the Greek tragedians had offered or what Crane himself was searching for as he struggled toward the tragic resolution of his "Faustus and Helen," but what gin-daisies and maidenhair ferns picked fresh from the Bronx countryside might provide. This was not Whitman's call for a mystic "Passage to India," no, but a "FREE-ER PASSAGE" for a little "BACK DOOR DIGNITY."[30] A little magazine called S4N (the name borrowed from the insignia for a World War I mosquito fleet) would publish his comic offering the following spring.

So, when he went with Sam Loveman to see Isadora Duncan perform on the night of December 10th, he was both electrified by her swirling, unworldly dance movements and dismayed to see her treated with disdain by the audience. She was dancing an all-Tchaikowsky program that night, much like the one for which she'd received standing ovations in both Moscow and New York. To Crane, she was "glorious beyond words." How sad, then, to see the "rude and careless reception" afforded her in his city. In her scanty red dress (which had shocked Boston), she'd appeared a "flaming gale," "a wave of life," swirling and wavering above the heads of nine thousand spectators. And yet all her performance had evoked was a silence broken only by "maddening catcalls." Crane, incensed at the stupidity of the audience, began clapping furiously, his the only sound, he was convinced, as she disappeared behind the curtains.

When a few minutes later she came back on stage, it was to continue her performance "with utter indifference for the audience and with such intensity of gesture and such plastique grace" as Crane had never seen. And though catcalls had persisted, when it was all over, she walked to the front of the stage once more, this time to tell the audience "to go home and take from the bookshelf the works of Walt Whitman, and turn to the section called 'Calamus.'" Crane was sure most of that audience had never even heard of Whitman, which had been the point of her gesture. How "glorious to see her there with her right breast and nipple quite exposed, telling the audience that the truth was not pretty, that it was really indecent, and telling them (boobs!) about Beethoven, Tchaikowsky, and Scriabin." Well, she was now on her "way back to Moscow," where someone would surely "give her some roses for her pains."[31] In Duncan Crane had found his first heroine, to be joined later by Emily Dickinson. Given his complex and ambivalent feelings toward his mother, there would not be many other female heroes, but these two became beacons for him, and he would place them side by side in what was as yet still an inchoate dream: *The Bridge.*

By Christmas, a compromise had been worked out with Grace that allowed him the freedom to drink as long as he did so in the privacy of his own room. Grace tried to patch the rift between them by bearing gifts of puce-colored gloves to match the coat she'd given him two months earlier, as well as a spiffy new walking stick. The Muse too arrived bearing gifts, and on New Year's Eve, after getting properly drunk, Crane at last began work on the long-deferred third and final part of "Faustus and Helen." When work on the sequence had come to a halt that September, he'd reworked the first two parts and sent them out to make some much-needed cash. Part I he'd sent off to

Munson at *Secession*, Part II first to *The Dial* (which returned it) and then on to *Broom*. But Part III, which he envisioned as enacting the Faustian capabilities of the airplane for the conquest of space (spiritual or imperial, the choice remained open), had yet to be written, and would need to be "developed under a different sky."[32]

Back in August, he'd told Munson he was looking for a sense of speed for the conclusion of his poem, and had sent him four lines of the stil-unformed Part III. But he was struggling to come up with the language he felt the poem would need. Three weeks later, he'd changed his mind again. The theme of speed was not enough to convey all that he was after. The new poem would need "more sheer weight" than that; but what would provide that weight Crane did not yet know, except that it would touch on the war just concluded "and be Promethean in mood."[33] Finally, two weeks into January 1923, he sent Munson a tentative draft of the poem, underscoring its Dionysian splendor. It also caught some of their evenings drinking Chianti together the summer before. Still, the poem—on which he'd spent three nights running—was so "packed with tangential slants" and "interwoven symbolisms" that he was unsure if it would be understood, though he did believe it fit now with the first two sections of the poem. Part I, Crane summed up, would represent "Meditation, Evocation, Love, Beauty"; Part II, "Dance, Humor, Satisfaction"; Part III, "Tragedy, War (the eternal soldier), Resume, Ecstasy, Final Declaration." At last, after all these months, he'd found "an organization and symphonic rhythm" for the new section that surprised even him.[34]

"What do you think of Eliot's *The Waste Land*," Crane had asked Munson in late November 1922, soon after the poem made its American appearance in the pages of *The Dial*. He himself had been disappointed. "It was good, of course," he was quick to add, "but so damned dead." Nor did it, he miscalculated, "add anything important to Eliot's achievement."[35] Crane's initial and surprising evaluation of *The Waste Land* would in time come to be modified, though not substantially changed. In fact, the third section of "Faustus and Helen" would attempt to answer Eliot's worldweariness and despair with its own Nietzschean tragic gaiety. It would be Crane's final yes to life and love in spite of death and the mass destruction of modern war.

"My work for the past two years (those meagre drops) has been more influenced by Eliot than any other modern," he confessed to Munson in January, even as he was finishing Part III. No one writing in English could command as much respect as that man, for Eliot had turned out to be the touchstone against which modern English poetry had to be measured. Still, that could not deter him from trying to answer Eliot's negative assessment of modern life. Given Eliot's phlegmatic temperament and the subjects that he chose to write about, Crane could understand why the man was so damned pessimistic. But, having made Eliot's sources his own—Laforgue, Donne, Webster—he meant to "apply as much of [Eliot's] erudition and technique" as he could muster and direct these toward a more positive and, yes, ecstatic goal.

He needed to do this because in his own life—"at odd moments," unattended and rare—he'd experienced just such positive feelings himself, a music of a very real order, and now he was after some ineffable Word that he needed to somehow articulate. As fine a poet as Eliot was, Crane believed he'd "ignored certain spiritual events and possibilities as real and powerful now as, say, in the time of Blake." In doing so, he'd managed to bury hope "as deep and direfully as it can ever be done," out-Baudelairing Baudelaire, and doing so with "a devastating humor" Baudelaire had lacked.

What *The Waste Land* offered the age was, alas, a "perfection of death," to which the only adequate response would have to be "a resurrection of some kind." Not a Christian resurrection, for Crane had no way of personally gauging that, but an affirmation of some sort in the face of death and annihilation. All the philosophers seemed now to be writing on the death of Western civilization, a civilization whose fruits had long been harvested, leaving behind only gleanings here and there. "Everyone, of course, wants to die as soon and as painlessly as possible," he snapped, and Eliot, as poetry's current spokesman, had made his an age of ironies symbolized by "the Dance of Death." And yet Crane, in spite of his own humdrum existence, was prepared to "affirm certain things." That, he told Munson, was "the persisting theme" of Part III of his "Faustus and Helen."[36]

For years now he'd been fascinated by the possibilities of airpower, the Promethean hubris of it, canvas and gasoline and metal and wood somehow hurling into the air to climb the heavens' "nimble blue plateaus." To hear the awesome, terrifying drone of those staggered, flowerlike squadrons, those "corymbulous formations of mechanics," as they took possession of the heavens, machine guns "spouting malice/Plangent over meadows." What lexical treasures of language, Crane wondered, would it take to capture the awe of such a vision if not the language that Shakespeare and Marlowe and Jonson had bequeathed us? The sheer terror and splendor of tracers and bullets shaking down "vertical/repeated play of fire," against which no one was really safe, least of all the Faustian pilots at the controls. What language, what language to describe such destruction, and yet move the mind beyond despair toward awe and even acceptance of the savage beauty and sublimity of modern violence?

Yes, the war had killed many, but many too had survived, to await Death's coming another day. For no one escaped Death, that eternal and religious gunman, who was also—in his other guise—capped arbiter of beauty and "delicate ambassador" of those "intricate slain numbers" whose ghosts haunted the living. Let the dead bury the dead. Life went on, Crane insisted, life with all its richness and delights—"A goose, tobacco and cologne"—and in time these realities which daily fed the "lavish heart" ameliorated one's shame and guilt as the dead finally drifted off into the shadows. Anchises had died and his body had been offered to the sea, while his son Aeneas had gone on to found the Roman Empire. And two thousand years later, Erasmus would read the mythos that had underwritten both the classical age and medieval Catholicism, "Gathered the voltage of blown blood and vine"—all that energy—and would transubstantiate it into a new vision of Christian humanism. The new, then, finding its transubstantiated form flowing out of the old.

"Laugh out the meager penance of their days," Crane urged, rejecting Eliot's despair at the loss of Erasmus's vision, white cities become—in an image that echoed Eliot's *Gerontion*—a jumble "of torn and empty houses/Like old women with teeth unjubilant." Life was for the living, to be grasped at and enjoyed, even if the prize remained always just out of reach like some shadow fruit:

> *Laugh out the meager penance of their days*
> *Who dare not share with us the breath released,*
> *The substance drilled and spent beyond repair*
> *For golden, or the shadow of gold hair.*

Only the imagination is real, Williams had said. A sentiment shared by Crane. Consider the imagination, which had given humankind the miracle of the aeroplane, conquering time and space as it lifted humans into those Faustian "nimble blue plateaus" where none had ever been before, to reveal a reality beyond what desire, logic, or even prayer seemed to him to offer:

> *Distinctly praise the years, whose volatile*
> *Blamed bleeding hands extend and thresh the height*
> *The imagination spans beyond despair,*
> *Outpacing bargain, vocable and prayer.*

All this the poem offered, all this and a homosexual subtext as well—a text hinted at in the image of Crane's Faustian self beside the shadowy other, not Helen, but the "gunman" of the "saddled sky" with his "vertical/Repeated play of fire," Crane's flesh remembering those nights of repeated ecstasies and small deaths, those "tensile boughs" and "nimble blue plateaus" and the "mounted, yielding cities of the air."[37] In spite of moments of nearly impenetrable opacity, Crane had moved in this poem to a new plateau, employing a language which would challenge even his friendliest readers, but which brushed against a new sense of reality and therefore new thresholds, new anatomies, for American poetry.

In *The New Republic* for 6 December 1922, Crane found his name bunched together with the names of Munson, E. E. Cummings, Edmund Wilson, Kenneth Burke, Malcolm Cowley, and John Dos Passos—the group that loosely made up the magazine *Secession*—in an essay-review by Louis Untermeyer entitled "The New Patricians." Untermeyer, perhaps the most influential anthologist of modern poetry at the time, and something of a minor power broker among writers, saw these men as all holding to a new intellectual discipline in America whose signature was a "severity of structure" and a high degree of formal design. All seemed to Untermeyer to possess a "patrician attitude," which placed emphasis on "strangeness" of material and complexity of design. In the group he saw a turning away from the naturalism of Dreiser and a return to the French Symbolists.

It was a perceptive comment, and it naturally caught Crane's attention. "Untermeyer's article was at least decent," Crane reported to Munson on the 7th, "a non-insulting sort of bulletin and one of the better sort of things that could happen to *Secession* and its group." And because he did not have a high estimate of Untermeyer, that "parodist and facile assessor," he'd been all the more surprised that the man had found something useful to say about the movement with which Crane had come loosely to ally himself.[38] He knew Untermeyer's word carried weight, and he was so delighted to find his name in print that he wrote Underwood now to say that, though he himself would "probably never amount to anything," some of the others would.[39]

Five weeks later, in a piece called "Disillusion as Dogma" that appeared in *The Freeman* for 17 January 1923, Untermeyer reviewed Eliot's *The Waste Land,* noting that, while the poem had "documentary" value as a record of the times, its sentiments were misleading and inaccurate. "Man may be desperately insecure," Untermeyer intoned, "but he has not yet lost the greatest of his emotional needs, the need to believe in something—even in his disbelief. For an ideal-demanding race, there is always one more God—and Mr. Eliot is not his prophet." *An ideal-demanding race.* Crane's sentiments exactly, and he lost no time now in writing Untermeyer to tell him so, sending along Part III of "Faustus and Helen" for his perusal.

"I know I am running the risk of the conventional accusation of petuosity always accorded poets," Crane wrote Untermeyer on January 19th. But since he had been good enough to name him among the New Patricians, Crane was now sending him his poem. Yes, he admired Eliot, he admitted, had in fact admired him now for years, and felt that Untermeyer had perhaps underrated him. Still, since he too felt that Eliot was overly pessimistic, he wanted Untermeyer to see his own poetic response to Eliot. Ecstasy and beauty were after all both "possible to the active imagination" as much now as they had been in earlier times, and it was for this reason he'd written his poem. As with Joyce and Eliot, so too Crane's own modern images—streetcar and plane and jazz on a hot roof—had their classical counterparts while simultaneously retaining their contemporary forms. This "mystical fusion of beauty" *was* in fact Crane's religion, and "Faustus and Helen" a "kind of bridge" between the present moment and the eternal verities, "a more creative and stimulating thing"—Nietzschean, Dionysian—"than the settled formula of Mr. Eliot, superior technician" though he might be. He hoped Untermeyer would feel the same way about his poem.[40]

Untermeyer sent back a friendly note, commenting on Crane's

unusual poetic rhetoric, and asking if he might see him when he came out to Cleveland in March. There were other responses to Crane's poem as well. One was from Waldo Frank, with whom Crane had begun a correspondence in November, who praised Crane now as "a genuine poet" with "a genuine vision, and an amazingly honest form for it." In fact, Crane had made him see "the very stuffs of our beloved hated life . . . take on glittering and parabolic significances." "Faustus and Helen" was nothing less than a "modern Blakean marriage of heaven & hell," Frank rhapsodized, "the hell of our modern mechanized world suddenly bearing as its essence an antique beauty which certain Elizabethans glimpsed for our language."[41] Who could ask for a more penetrating analysis than that? Munson too was lavish with his praise, and Allen Tate, in his disciple's role, judged the twenty-three-year-old Crane to be "the greatest contemporary American poet" writing.[42]

Such praise helped spur Crane on to new thresholds, and for two days in late January he went to work on a new poem, using a rhetoric quite different from that he'd employed in the final movement of "Faustus and Helen." He called the new poem, "Stark Major," a "strange psychoanalytic thing."[43] An elegy in six rhymed quatrains on the theme of sundered love, it appeared to be an aubade. A young man leaving his beloved, "Her mound of undelivered life" still "cool upon her," as he walked down the stairs of some tenement and out into the lonely streets. But again, the subtext of the lyric was Crane's feeling of isolation, leading a double life as a gay poet: the brief encounter, the early morning departure with the other calling out the lover's name, the pain that followed each fated separation.[44]

Early that February, he began work on yet another long poem. This one he saw as carrying out tendencies begun in "Faustus and Helen." He called it *The Bridge*. In a letter to Tate dated February 12th, he quoted the opening lines, which in another form would find their way into one of the poem's interior sections:

> *Macadam, gun grey as the tunny's pelt,*
> *Leaps from Far Rockaway to Golden Gate,*
> *For first it was the road, the road only*
> *We heeded in joint piracy and pushed.*

He had made a beginning, but already he sensed that the poem would have to be a long time coming because of the formal difficulties he envisioned for it. To complicate matters, Crane now found himself in love again, a condition that always made writing heady, depressing, and sporadic for him. "I am in a very unfavorable mood," he told Munson on the 9th, "and just after having congratulated myself strongly on security against future outbreaks of the affections." For several years now he'd guarded against succumbing to his emotions. But at an evening concert the week before, a young man had sent him "some glances of such a very stirring response and beauty" that he'd been thrown once more into sweet agony. Sex he could handle, he insisted, but he seemed powerless before these "higher and certainly hopeless manifestations of the flesh." Worse was to feel this eruption and then remember that he was living in America, "where one cannot whisper a word" nor even "exchange a few words."[45] It might, he thought, almost have been enough. When he was like this, he knew now too well, writing was out of the question.

Eleven days after writing Munson, Crane found himself more than ever obsessed with his young satyr. A face "with faun precision of line and feature. Crisp ears, a little pointed, fine and docile hair almost golden, yet darker, —eyes that are a little heavy—but wide apart and usually a little narrowed, —aristocratic (English) jaws," and a mouth "just mobile enough to suggest voluptuousness. A strong rather slender figure, negligently carried, that is perfect from flanks that hold an easy persistence to shoulders that are soft yet full and hard. A smooth and rather olive skin that is cool—at first." Thus Crane, deep in his Dionysian cups, to Underwood as spring began. By then he was deeply in love. "Those who have wept in the darkness sometimes are rewarded with stray leaves blown inadvertently," he wrote in an outworn idiom dear to Underwood. It was an experience, incomplete as yet, but fine, fine, for all that. Always before there had been glances, "half-hinted speech," an electric stray touch. Always before his hopes had been quashed by the presence of the young faun's older brother standing watch like a sentinel. That is, until the previous night.

Then something had transpired, something of value. Well, he would see his Pan again. Soon enough, the climax would be "too easily reached" and the inevitable conquest made, and then the golden halo would once again begin to fade. Although not his "gratitude" that such happiness had been his, for another bridge would have been built. Once again, something beautiful had approached, enclosing Crane in its lover's arms and pulling him in, as if it were the most natural thing in the world. "And we who create must endure, must hold to spirit not by the mind, the intellect alone." No, the flesh too had its needs, and must be satisfied, if he was ever to touch life's "mystic possibilities." "O flesh damned to hate and scorn," he closed, "I have felt my cheek pressed on the desert these days and months too much."

Only twenty-three, and, he confessed to Underwood, how old he already felt. What he was going through of course he'd already been through before, many times, in fact. He knew too well by now love's opening gambits, its arc, its unique, one-time-only flowering, its inevitable blasting. Again he thought of Whitman's "Passage to India," of going "to India" with another, of living always in the imagination, of meditating always on the obliterating sun out of which all life had sprung and with which it would end. How he hated "the work of the workaday world," especially now that he was "bringing much into contemporary verse that is new," including what he thought of as nothing less than "a synthesis of America and its structural identity" in his still-forming poem, *The Bridge*.[46]

The problem was to have to work each damned day at a job writing ads, when what he should be doing was contemplating the higher synthesis he was searching for in *The Bridge*. Almost in spite of himself, Crane began staying away from work, saying he had back problems. To help him settle into the dreamlike mood he needed, he began drinking more and more heavily and indiscriminately, whatever came his way. He stopped writing even most letters now in order to concentrate on his "mystical synthesis of 'America.'" History, he realized, would have to be "transfigured into [an] abstract form," capable of functioning "independently of its subject matter." Filled as he was now with the poem's "mystic possibilities," he knew the "marshalling of . . . forces," would take many months.[47] That is, if he didn't simply abandon the whole project, overwhelmed by what it was he was attempting to do. Like "Faustus and Helen," *The Bridge* would be symphonic, and would run about the same length. Once he'd written it, there would be time enough to think about publishing a book.

He had at last his visionary company. Not only the great dead like Donne and Blake and his beloved Whitman, but Gorham Munson and Waldo Frank as well, both of whom shared with him a community of interest that was more than just another literary clique. What they shared went deeper, further. It was a vision of what America might be. *Ulysses* and *The Waste Land* were dead ends, portraits of the final decline of Western civilization, visions of hell, really. But the visionary possibilities Crane saw at work in Frank and Munson and himself might, just might, reverse that downward spiral and in the process revitalize the entire country.

In spite of the odd glances he'd gotten for writing in the elevated Elizabethan diction as well as the novel combinations he called his "natural idiom,"[48] and which he meant to stick to in spite of everything, Crane had reached one man at least. That man was Frank, who seemed to understand "the very blood and bone" of what he was about. "There is only one way of saying what comes to one in ecstasy," Crane confided to his friend,[49] and that was utterance that strained or even subverted logical discourse in order to touch the heart of the mystery. Now, having glimpsed that mystery, he could work and rework the long poem he had in mind until all the pieces fell perfectly into place. The trouble was that while he waited for the vision to coalesce, he would have to find a way to make a living. "The last several days have been equally among the most intense in my life," he wrote Munson at the beginning of March. "To be stimulated to the nth degree with your head burgeoning with ideas and conceptions of the most baffling interest and lure—and then to have to munch ideas on water heaters (I am writing another book for house fraus!) has been a real cruelty this time, however temporary." Pure poetry such as he was after was another thing altogether. Pure poetry aspired to the condition of music, as Mallarmé had said, and nothing killed the spirit faster than using language to make a buck.

One night, listening to d'Indy's Second Symphony, he told Munson, he had felt his hair stand "on end at its revelations." To have revealed the mystery at the heart of a Strauss, a Ravel, a Scriabin, a Bloch, and then find a verbal equivalent for that mystery, he had needed "to ransack the vocabularies of Shakespeare, Jonson, Webster (for theirs were the richest) and add our scientific, street and counter, and psychological terms." One needed "gigantic assimilative capacities, emotion,—and the greatest of all—vision," Crane insisted.[50] A multifoliate language, "Striated with nuances, nervosities,/That we are heir to." That was what he was after, that and nothing less.[51]

For all its complexities, the poetic vein he'd struck in "Faustus and

Helen" had been only a beginning, for each new day now revealed "new timbres," images and words chiming with dozens of others, each "unique, yet poignant and expressive of our epoch." What Pindar had done in publicly celebrating the ancient world, he would do for "the dawn of the machine age, so called." In the past few months he'd managed to leave behind "the last shreds of philosophical pessimism" as he moved into unmapped territory. Of course there was still the "background of life," all those forces that had shaped him. But all that was "three-dimensional" stuff, realities which, whatever else they did, still bound him to time and space. *His* vision would center instead on "the pulse of a greater dynamism," a higher consciousness, a sublimity both "terribly fierce and yet gentle."[52] All that stood between him and his spiritual "Passage to India" was his job selling hot-water heaters. And because that job interfered with the real work at hand, he had come at last to hate it.

Perhaps the gods heard him, for in mid-March 1923, Crane was fired. The reason Patno's gave was a lack of work, but someone in the office must have noticed that, as good as Crane was at copywriting, he was also taking more and more time off from his job and seemed more and more preoccupied with other things. But the abrupt termination turned out to be a blessing. For two years now he'd wanted to get back to New York. Cleveland had long ago outlasted its usefulness, and the people he needed most to talk to were all in New York. Then Munson, who'd recently married and moved with his wife, Lisa, to a small apartment in Greenwich Village, offered to put Crane up if he ever came east. Now, jobless in Cleveland once more, he was ready to take Munson up on that offer.

Since Crane was about to descend on the New York scene, Munson wondered how he wanted to deal with his homosexuality. In short, was Crane out or not? Better not to pass "the good word along" just yet, Crane wrote back. He'd been perhaps "all-too-easy" in telling too many people about his "sexual predilections." Not, he equivocated, that there'd been any repercussions yet, but he did find that having the word out allowed those in the know a power over him which he hated and feared. "After all," he added, "when you're dead it doesn't matter," and the fact that he was saying all this in a letter proved he had no shame about his orientation. Still, "the ordinary business of earning a living" was difficult enough, without serving that kind of information into the hands of "publicans and sinners." Better for now for Munson to keep what he knew to himself. New York was going to be tough enough without having to deal with that issue, too.[53]

Beyond that, the one thing he could not bear was having his father find out that he hadn't been able to hold on to a job. His paternal grandparents still lived across the street from him, and word had a way of getting around Cleveland anyway. On the eve of his departure for New York, Crane swore his mother, grandmother, and friends to secrecy while he worked out a strategy. He was going to New York on business for Patno's, they were to tell anyone who asked. Once he'd found work, he would "resign" from the firm. His last night in Cleveland—Saturday, March 24th—he spent with his mother, grandmother, and the Rychtariks, who gave him a box of cakes—a gift to the Munsons—and saw him off at the train station. If he needed a sign that the Fates were smiling upon his decision to return to New York—and he desperately did—it came with a start when he realized that the Pullman he had just boarded for the trip back east was emblazoned "The High Bridge."

PART II

6 / WHITE BUILDINGS

NEW YORK/WOODSTOCK
MARCH 1923–FEBRUARY 1924

PALM SUNDAY, 25 MARCH 1923. After a three years' absence, Crane found himself once more walking among New York's white canyons, this time into spring weather. By nightfall he had settled in with the Munsons in their two-room Village apartment in a small pre–Civil War flat at 4 Grove Street. A quiet, sycamore-lined street, residential, brownstones and two-story brick structures that would have been familiar not only to Henry James but to Melville, Poe, and Whitman. He was quite happy, he wrote the Rychtariks. That first afternoon he'd taken a long walk in the salt air and clear spring sunlight around lower New York. Close-cropped hair, filled out, experienced in the ways of the world as he had not been during his earlier sojourn in Manhattan, and sporting his dapper striped coat and nifty walking cane, Crane smiled on everything he saw. Munson seemed genuinely happy to have him, and the apartment itself he found fresh and roomy and charming. He would lunch with Frank the following day and so finally get to talk to the man whose work he'd been poring over for the past several months. How beautiful the Rychtariks were. How beautiful life was when one had such friends.

"I don't need to mention that it was great to shake hands and talk with you," he wrote Frank after their meeting. They'd spoken of great things, of Crane's admiration for Frank's short story collection,

City Block (he found Frank "the most vital consciousness in America"), and of Frank's take on the current state of the nation as he'd written of it in his essay for *Our America*.[1] Frank, taken with Crane, promised him that when the book was reissued in a year's time, his name would be among the up-and-coming luminaries mentioned there. Within days Crane had visited the Habichts in their well-furnished apartment, and been treated to sherry and Benedictine. Even the elusive Harry Candee, passing through New York on his way back to China, showed up, selling Crane a Chinese smock that Crane sent on to Charlotte Rychtarik in thanks for looking in on his mother and grandmother in his absence.

Once again he sought out the teeming life of the city: its vital immigrant populations, Wall Street, the art galleries (including a showing of Picasso), the docks along South Street, an omnibus up Fifth Avenue. Since his last visit, New York had become "a really stupendous place," tense with vitality and life. Overnight it seemed to have become a world center, a modern Alexandria. He admired the wealthier sections of the city—Fifth, Park, Madison—but he preferred the Lower East Side, "crowded with life, packed with movement and drama, children, kind and drab-looking women, elbows braced on window ledges, and rows of vegetables lining the streets."[2] The food he found rich and plentiful, especially in the Italian restaurants, where he could get a decent bottle of wine, spaghetti, meat and vegetables, and European-style service, all for a dollar.

He was not writing yet, had not in fact written since the dizzying flurry of activity in Cleveland, being too busy adjusting to the city. But listening in his room to the children down on the street laughing and skipping rope, he composed a six-line fragment:

> *Where gables pack the rainless*
> *fulsome sky*
> *permit a song as comes into the street*
>
> *permit a song that swings with ropes*
> *and skipping feet*
> *above the laughter that rebounds below.*

"The children in springtime come out and dance on the streets of the crowded city," he noted on the scrap of poetry, as he waited by the telephone for a job offer after three jobless weeks in New York.

"Why in hell can't we older people have the same freedom, to join the rhythm of life?"[3]

Each day he trudged the streets to speak with someone at one of the city's many ad agencies, or waited in some anteroom, being told by some secretary that Mr. So-and-So was out, or that Miss So-and-So was too busy to see him. If only he could find "a quiet room with plenty of quiet to work," he confessed to the Rychtariks.[4] He had to find a way to get back to his Bridge poem before the thing disappeared on him. On the evening of April 12th he read "For the Marriage of Faustus and Helen" to a small group of the Village's older poets and writers whom the Munsons had managed to squeeze into their apartment, only to be met with stares and puzzlements. He was not surprised. What, after all, did these people know about Modernism and the higher consciousness anyway? "If it weren't for the praise and understanding I have received from people like Frank and Munson and Allen Tate, etc.," he confessed, "I would begin to feel that I might be to blame."[5]

Then, two days later, by chance, he found his ideal audience when Munson took him to meet the eminent photographer Alfred Stieglitz, in his gallery at 291 Fifth Avenue. Crane was so taken by the photographs lining the walls that he could hardly contain himself, and soon he was praising the work so loudly and with such brilliance that Stieglitz, white-haired, mustached, approaching sixty, walked out from his office at the back of the gallery to see who this animated young man was. Within minutes the two men were involved in a spirited conversation over aesthetics. Standing before Stieglitz's *Apples and Gable*, Crane began extolling the metaphysical realities Stieglitz's camera had somehow managed to capture. Never, Stieglitz at last exclaimed, had anyone come this close to seeing what he'd wanted others to see.

The following day, he received a letter from Crane: "Dear great and good man," it began. Now that Crane had seen in the photographs a vision that he himself shared, he was eager to write a "comprehensive essay" about Stieglitz's work. Everything he was looking for in his own poetry, he confessed, he found paralleled in Stieglitz's photographs. The essay would take time to write, but for now he was including a few words to indicate a glimpse of what he thought Stieglitz had managed to capture with his camera. "The eerie speed of the shutter is more adequate than the human eye to remember," he wrote now. What the trained eye could catch on paper was something as evanescent as the mistmote as it was transformed into cloud, like thought itself, "jetted from the eye to leave it instantly forever." Somehow Stieglitz had found a way to frieze not only the motion but the very emotion of things. In fact, the lens allowed nature to "mirror itself so intimately and so unexpectedly" that one felt an ultimate harmony with what was—like God—both static and continually in motion.

It was precisely this paradox of motion in stillness that Crane was attempting to capture in *The Bridge* by employing the music of language. "If the essences of things were in their mass and bulk," Crane had come to understand, "we should not need the clairvoyance of Stieglitz's photography to arrest them for examination and appreciation." But things moved, kept constantly moving, and one moved with them, hardly ever taking the time to note the transcendent beauty of things except in unattended moments. All about us was a world suspended in an "invisible dimension whose vibrance has been denied the human eye at all times save in the intuition of ecstasy."[6]

"And Thee, across the harbor," Crane would write three years later, superimposing Stieglitz's silver spheres and cloud-flown sky against his image of the Brooklyn Bridge, forever reaching into the distances of Brooklyn or Manhattan, yet unmoving in its majesty:

> *silver-paced*
> *As though the sun took step of thee, yet left*
> *Some motion ever unspent in thy stride, —*
> *Implicitly thy freedom staying thee!*[7]

But Crane was also learning that nothing stayed forever. In early May 1923, his mother wrote him that his father's parents' house across the street from where he had grown up was in the process of being demolished. And though it would be a welcome change "to have them off of the street," Grace wrote, she felt awful seeing old Mrs. Crane weeping openly as the house was made "roofless, doorless, windowless and nearly sideless" in three short days. Then Crane's grandparents and the house were gone.[8]

But even as one reality evaporated, another began to coalesce. In mid-April, Crane met Slater Brown, E. E. Cummings's fellow ambulance driver in France during the war, and the "B" of Cummings's popular novel, *The Enormous Room*. Crane and Brown hit it off at once, and, when grippe soon after wracked the Munson household, it was Brown who invited Crane to stay with him in his Minetta Lane apartment, just a few blocks away. In the coming months it was Brown who often slipped Crane some much-needed cash, kept him in wine, gave him a key to his apartment, and even insisted on sleeping on the floor so Crane could have his bed. It was Brown too who introduced Crane to "the greatest burlesque shows down on the Lower East Side." On May 8th, in fact, Brown took him to a show that truly amazed him. They did "everything but the Act itself right on the stage," Crane told Bill Sommer afterwards, still staggered by what he'd witnessed. In all of New York there was nothing like it.[9] By then he was already in love with Brown, he confessed to Underwood, in love with his "beauty of manner, face, body and attitude," as well as with his generosity and wit. He was in fact ready to be the man's "most willing slave," if Brown would have let him.[10] But Brown was straight and so Crane had refrained from making advances. Still, the affection the two men felt for each other turned out to be genuine and lasting.

Then, at last, came a nibble for a job. It was from a prestigious advertising agency, J. Walter Thompson. To look more impressive, Crane invented a college degree for his résumé. He'd graduated two years before from Western Reserve, he lied, and had in addition taken several extension courses. He listed as references Hal Smith; Harry Candee (then sailing down the Yangtze); and Gorham Munson. Thompson let it be known that they were interested in his credentials, but as the weeks passed and no job was forthcoming, he began to despair of ever finding work. His behavior became more and more outrageous. "Policemen here don't mind if you step up and occasionally use their tummys as tom-toms," he wrote his Cleveland friend, Charles Harris, "neither do neighbors mind your 'early' shouts from windows hailing far from gently all the dawn. Or if you care to you can suspend yourself outside, feet raking up the clapboards and nothing is felt to be amiss." He'd slept everywhere and "on everything but walls and danced the gotzotzsky so much" his calves now refused to function.[11] Worse, his Muse had disappeared into the shadowy canyons of the city, knocking elsewhere. He tried putting the whole thing in perspective on the back of a postcard he sent Charlotte Rychtarik. It was virtually the only poetry he wrote that unsettling, frustrating spring and it read:

WELL/WELL/NOT-AT-ALL
Yakka-hoola-hikki-doola
Pico-della-miran-dohhh-la
leonarda-della-itchy-vinci
es braust ein ruhf Wie
   DONNERHALL
pffffff![12]

The blessèd break came in late May, when he was offered not one but two jobs: one with *Machinery*, a trade journal; the other with J. Walter Thompson, who gave him the nod now (thanks to Waldo Frank's intercession) and told him to report to the agency's statistical department at 244 Madison Avenue. As soon as an opening occurred in the copywriting department, he was assured, he would be reassigned there. His salary would be thirty-five dollars a week, fifteen dollars less than he'd made at Patno's, take it or leave it. Broke, and having long worn out his welcome with the Munsons, Crane accepted the position. The first thing he did was take a room at the Hotel Albert on 11th Street. Then he wrote Richard Rychtarik, asking for a ten-dollar loan to see him through to his first paycheck. He needed a place to live, he explained, needed his shoes resoled, clothes cleaned, hair cut. Next he wrote Bill Sommer, asking if he could repay him the twenty he'd forked out to get Sommer's paintings an audience. Reluctantly, Sommer sent him five dollars.

It had been hard living in a tiny apartment with two people who didn't know the first thing about housekeeping, Crane was soon complaining to his mother. Then the Munsons had had the audacity to get sick, which had meant his moving from one place to another, "clothes here, there and everywhere and not knowing where the next meal was coming from."[13] Besides, Munson needed the guest bed now for a young black writer named Jean Toomer, just up from Washington. Toomer was the author of a novel, *Cane*, about to be published and destined to become a classic, for which Frank had written the introduction. Now Toomer was coming to New York for much the same reason Crane had come: to make contacts.

At the beginning of June, Crane moved into an apartment at 45 Grove Street, sublet from a friend of Slater Brown's, a newspaper reporter who would be on assignment in Europe until the fall. The room was part of a nineteenth-century town house, a cold-water flat without central heating, but terrific for the summer months: large-windowed, airy, high-ceilinged, second-storied; black floor, black furniture, and a bath out in the hall. The place had just been repainted gray and white, and came furnished; Crane's friends pooled their money to buy him a Victrola and a set of records. The rent was thirty dollars a month, less than half what the Munsons were paying for their place just down the street. He was just as "happy 'as they make 'em'" to have a room of his own, he wrote his mother.[14] How fine to have a place to hang one's Lescazes, Sommers, and Rychtariks, as well as a new oil by a new friend, Edward Nagle.

Soon he was shopping all over Little Italy with Slater and Sue Jenkins, the woman Slater would shortly marry. They joked, laughed, clowned as they went from store to store, carrying pots and pans and vegetables, jostling with the crowds. A few weeks later, Crane was spending a weekend at Rye Beach as the guest of Willy Lescaze. He met Kenneth Burke, now one of the editors at *The Dial*. He met the sculptor Gaston Lachaise, and the writer Malcolm Cowley, just back from Europe. On the strength of "Faustus and Helen," Crane's reputation around New York began to grow rapidly. That poem alone made him, Frank insisted, "the greatest contemporary American poet."[15] Now he promised Crane to ask Boni & Liveright, his own publishers, to do Crane's poems when they were ready.

Finally settled in, despite blazing summer heat, Crane began working again on the overarching structure of *The Bridge*. For three months the poem had lain dormant while he'd made his meek adjustments. Now, however, he began by turning to the final section of the poem: "Atlantis." Willy Lescaze had just returned from Paris, and the two men spent several evenings deep in talk about how architecture and engineering might be used as metaphors for the Machine Age. For weeks Crane pounded at his typewriter, addressing the bridge that spanned his brown or gray-blue river, gulls rising above its double Gothic arches, wind playing its miles of bound cables like some massive harp, while headlights skimmed its surface nightly, the headlights through the cables replicating the zodiac with the *click-click-click* precision of the projectionist's camera, still moments fanning into the illusion of motion:

To be, Great Bridge, in vision bound of thee,
So widely straight and turning, ribbon-wound,
Multi-colored, river-harbored and upbourne
Through the bright drench and fabric of our veins . . .

He wrote draft after draft of the poem that June and July in a kind of ecstasy that all but dissolved time for him. By the end of July he had a presentable draft ready to show. The poem had been "written verse by verse in the most tremendous emotional exaltations I have ever felt," Crane told Charlotte Rychtarik, and he was now "perfectly sure" *The Bridge* would be finished in a year's time and would come to "about four or five times" the size of "Atlantis."[16] On the Fourth of July he wrote Stieglitz, apologizing for not having finished the essay he'd promised him. The reason, he explained, was simply that he'd been "neck high in writing some climacterics" for *The Bridge*, which had carried him out of himself evening after evening from the moment he got home from work until two in the morning. The whole "ordeal," he added, had left him exhausted but happy. But by then the jet of inspiration was gone. It would take another two years to get the poem jump-started once more.

Though New York was a city broken by conflicting visions, where everyone seemed at odds with everyone else, he and Stieglitz at least shared this: that they had both seen beyond that brokenness to a "kind of timeless vision." He'd just spent an evening with Matty Josephson, during which Josephson had slandered Munson in such a way that it had taken all Crane's self-control not to tell "the little clown" what he really thought of him. Yet every day he came in contact with people like Josephson: "sincere people, but limited, who deny the superior logic of metaphor in favor of their perfect sums, divisions and subtractions." Still, he knew, as Stieglitz knew, that there was an energy about them all that could never be tapped by reason alone. It was left to visionaries like Stieglitz and himself who, "by perfecting our sensibilities," would raise consciousness to the new level necessary.

When little people questioned what it was he saw in his vision, Crane told Stieglitz now, he always answered "a little vaguely." And this for two reasons: "first, because our ends are forever unaccomplished"; and secondly because his work, like Stieglitz's, was "self-explanatory enough," if only others could *see* it. Sometimes, when he had a glimpse of that "intense but always misty realization" of what was possible, he could feel his imperfect self turning into a more perfect through his poems.[17] Which was why he was now sending Stieglitz a draft of some lines from "Atlantis" instead of the essay he'd promised. Even in its unfinished state, "Atlantis" already symbolized *The Bridge*'s main intentions. In the mesh of its lines he hoped he'd caught something of what he had been trying to say to Stieglitz all these months.

Noises infiltrated his room through two windows, side and back, opened to allow cross-ventilation through the room: the sounds of neighbors' Victrolas vying with each other, couples arguing, street traffic, the clatter of garbage cans, the *click-clack* of his own typewriter in counterresponse. In the cool of the evenings, bootleg wine and electric conversation with friends there in his apartment, the visionary impulse of *The Bridge* punctuated by sharp arguments with the Munsons, Toomer, Burke, Brown, Frank, and Josephson on the possibility or impossibility of a mystical synthesis of America. Sometimes he grew tired of it all, Josephson in particular signaling all he disliked about the too-brassy aspects of the contemporary poetry scene. Comic moments too, as with Brown, with his champion bladder, "winning all endurance tests and in altitude rivaling" the city's five-story fire ladders, as he took on all challengers in pissing contests, Crane marveling at the awesome arc of Brown's stream arcing through the open window against the glow of lights from the surrounding apartments.[18]

But by the third week of July, most of his friends had left New York "for places more cool and green and watery." Crane celebrated his twenty-fourth birthday alone, dining at an Italian restaurant on Prince Street before returning to his apartment to listen to Ravel's "Faery Garden" on his Victrola. Sprawled out on his worktable were objects his mother had sent him preparatory to selling the family home: an ivory Chinese box, a jade buddha from Harry Candee. Now that the Cleveland house was on the market, he felt a particularly keen nostalgia for his old tower room. It had been "the center and beginning of all that I am and ever will be," he confessed to Charlotte Rychtarik, "the center of such pain as would tear me to pieces to tell you about, and equally the center of great joys!"[19] In that room, *The Bridge,* like so many of his poems, had been conceived.

A week before his twenty-fourth birthday, Crane had been transferred to Thompson's copywriting department. Now he had an office on the fourteenth floor overlooking the Murray Hill section of Manhattan and the East River. It was nothing less than a view from the empyrean. Then, within two weeks, he found himself on a Pullman bound for Buffalo and Chicago to do field work for the company's "Barreled Sunlight" account with the Gutta Percha Paint Company. The trip itself turned out to be a disaster. Rain was followed by muggy weather, followed in turn by yet more rain. There was the difficulty of getting from one hardware dealer to the next without a car in cities he had no way of negotiating. At night he was exiled to hotel accommodations so grand he felt swallowed up. "The imagination dwells on frangible boughs!" he wrote Stieglitz on August 11th, when back at last in New York.[20] The "frangible boughs" he recalled were those in Stieglitz's black and white photo of apples and a gable, an image that had consoled him through so much quotidian tedium. Ten days on the road, ten days too many, trying to sell house paint to hardware dealers.

All the trip had done in fact was turn his mind into that "baked and labeled dough" he'd written of in "Faustus and Helen." The upshot was that *The Bridge* seemed to have drifted further away than ever from him. Nor were things much better in New York that August. "Your little note was on the table when I came roistering in with Burke and the Cowleys after much to drink," he wrote Toomer on the morning of the 19th. The trip out to Buffalo and Chicago had so shattered him that he was only now able to put himself together. But something else had happened, though he could only bring himself to refer to it as the mysterious siren "beckonings and all that draws you into doorways, subways, sympathies, rapports and the City's complicated devastations."[21] Perhaps he'd picked someone up, perhaps in the 14th Street men's room had had sex, both men departing, leaving no forwarding addresses. "The phonographs of hades in the brain," he would write three years later in "The Tunnel," the scene played out like some "burnt match skating in a urinal."[22] It was too dangerous, that sort of thing, as he had had to learn the hard way, terrified now that he'd picked something up, though what it finally turned out to be was acidosis from too much alcohol in the bloodstream.

"I came near a collapse near the middle of the week—the trip, hot weather," he complained to his mother.[23] He had not been able to sleep, and now the city was sapping him of his strength and giving him nothing in return. If he could only get a decent bed, like the little brass one back home, he pleaded with her. To make matters worse, he was convinced that Willy Lescaze of all people had lifted his copy of *Ulysses* from his room in Cleveland. When he'd had lunch with Lescaze in New York he'd quietly asked him for the book back, no questions asked. Confusion and stammerings had followed, but no book. No doubt, Crane could not help feeling, Lescaze had already sold it for several hundred dollars. And what legal recourse did he have, with *Ulysses* banned by the U.S. mails? The incident marked the end of the friendship.

By August 25th he had to tell Stieglitz that not only had he failed to deliver on the essay he'd promised, but now he could not even see his way into the "Ave Maria," the opening section of *The Bridge*. He had the close, but as yet no way over to the other side, and no time now—with the heavy work of copywriting on him—to figure out how to get there. If only there were some way to take care of family obligations and find a simple job that would pay for room and board without occupying his every waking moment. As it was, streams of ad copy kept coursing through his head all through the night until he felt "like a thread singed and twisted in the morning."[24]

In September, it was ads for O'Sullivan's leather shoe heels, before Thompson began switching him to other accounts as he was needed. He was being treated decently enough, he had to admit, but how maddening to have to plot where every penny of his miserable salary was going. No money for shows, no money for clothes. What a waste the year was turning out to be. Perhaps with winter, when his noisy neighbors shut their windows once again, and the rumbling of trucks in the street diminished, and cats no longer spit and wailed in heat through half the night, and the "insidious impurity in the air that seems to seep from sweaty walls and subways" dissipated, and his hay fever left, and the weather braced one again, perhaps then the words—the sacred words—would return.[25]

Much to his relief, the sale of the family home was put on hold for the winter months. Uprooted and on the move constantly, he needed to believe that somewhere was a place he could still call home. "I never want to have any of us without some property of our own—land and building—whether we live in it or not, but just so that 'we have it' and are not entirely subject to the whims of fortune," he wrote his mother.[26] Indeed, if ever he came into money, the first thing he was going to buy was a house. Finally, with the return of his friends from the country and the advent of cooler weather, Crane's spirits revived. One evening, returning from work, he found Harry Candee waiting for him in his hallway. He liked Harry, but too much had happened over the past four years in which his friend had played no role. Harry was part of some earlier world, the world of Cleveland, not the more vivid world Crane had found for himself in New York.

He kept expecting to hear from his father, whom he knew was periodically in New York on business. But when he didn't hear from him, he was actually relieved, for reasons, he told his mother, "better explained in the science of psychoanalysis than in common language." Besides, he had his friends to think about now. Munson had been diagnosed with tuberculosis, brought on by exhaustion, and had gone up to Woodstock, New York, with Toomer to recuperate, leaving his wife Lisa to hunt for a new apartment for them. Months earlier, Toomer had begun an affair with Frank's wife, Margaret Naumburg, which had resulted in the Franks separating. Crane had listened to Frank's side of the story and then to Margaret's, and had come to the conclusion that it was better not to take sides, though Frank was just then so crazed by the breakup he seemed to Crane suicidal. That there was a baby to consider only made the separation all the more difficult. Life just now, Crane concluded, seemed to be "doing hard things to almost everyone."[27]

As winter came on, he realized he would have to move to heated quarters. He began looking for the right moment to ask his boss for a raise, and believed he would get one, especially given the added responsibilities the firm had put on him. In October, he was kept busy trying to sell Naugahyde, an imitation leather, to the public. Here he was, he complained to the Rychtariks, spilling out his brains on paper, while the high muckymucks at the agency acted as if money were beneath their notice. Could the Rychtariks, he wondered, lend him fifteen dollars so he could move? It drove him crazy to think he was making $1,800 a year when at least one of the art directors he knew was pulling in over $30,000.

The situation of the artist in America was growing harder and harder, he was finding, and just now most of his New York friends seemed worn out with the struggle to make a living and still find time to write. All the city really had to offer him any more were friends, most of whom, like the Munsons, themselves lived hand to mouth in crowded apartments. Really, it was "one of the most stupid places in the world to live in." He wanted, he told his mother, "to keep saying 'YES' to everything and never be beaten a moment."[28] He even believed that at some level he never would be beaten. And yet . . .

Then, on the evening of October 4th, just after Crane had gotten into his pajamas, there was a knock at his door. He was astounded to find Waldo Frank standing there and, behind him, a man in his mid-thirties, hair already graying, a twinkle in his eye, a black derby cocked to one side. It was Charlie Chaplin. Eighteen months earlier, he'd sent Chaplin a copy of "Chaplinesque," and Chaplin had responded warmly. "You know I worship Chaplin's work," Crane had written Charmion von Wiegand at the time, for Chaplin was undoubtedly "the greatest living actor" he'd ever seen, and even more, "the prime interpreter of the soul imposed upon by modern civilization."[29] And now here he was, the man himself.

Crane quickly dressed and the three men walked arm-in-arm over to Frank's apartment on Irving Place, wide-eyed kids following in their wake even at this hour. Late into the night Chaplin entertained them, speaking of his five-acre studio set in Berkeley, of his writing, producing, and directing *A Woman of Paris*, of his romance with Pola Negri, of his loneliness in Hollywood. For hours he pulled stories out of thin air, doing the policeman in different voices until Crane was holding his sides with laughter. Chaplin himself would remember other things. "We discussed the purpose of poetry," he recalled forty years later in his autobiography, long after Crane was gone. Poetry, Chaplin had ventured, was "a love letter to the world," to which Crane had countered with, "A very small world." And Crane, thinking of *The Kid*, commenting that Chaplin's comedy was very much in the tradition of the Greeks. And Chaplin, misunderstanding, answering that he'd tried once to read Aristophanes (in translation) and had failed.[30] Finally, at five in the morning, Chaplin deposited Crane back at his own doorstep. "It's been so nice," he heard Chaplin saying, as the taxi swung round to take the actor uptown to his own rooms at the Ritz.[31] A man of wit and grace and intelligence, Crane would write his mother later that day, after he'd slept, a man possessed of a spiritual honesty such as he too hoped one day to possess.

Chaplin had mentioned treating Crane to dinner, but the meeting was not to be, Chaplin being too much "under the weather . . . with too much champagne, parties and a bad cold" to go anywhere.[32] On the other hand, Crane did see a good deal of Toomer, who'd just presented him with a copy of *Cane*, inscribed: "For Hart,/instrument of the highest beauty, whose art,/four-conscinal, rich in symbols and ecstasy,/is great—/whose touch, deep and warm, is a sheer illuminant/with love, Jean." The sentiments chimed with Crane's own belief that his visionary company were "going on in the regular course of things toward a higher consciousness of life." True, there was no reason to believe that things would necessarily turn out well in the end, yet he did expect in the larger scheme of things to find some "great happiness."[33]

But already new trouble was brewing in Eden. When Josephson and Munson finally split over opposing ideologies, Cowley and Josephson called a meeting to determine just what the differences were. On the one hand, there was Munson's *Secession*, for which Josephson had served as associate editor, and then there was *Broom*, edited by Harold Loeb. (Hemingway would satirize him in the figure of Robert Cohn in *The Sun Also Rises*.) Ironically, both Munson and Josephson had contributed to both magazines. Word went out to—among others—Brown, Burke, Frank, Toomer, Wescott, Williams, and Crane—to meet on the evening of 19 October 1923 —a Friday—at an Italian restaurant on Prince Street under the shadow of the El to talk over the direction American literature would now take.

It was the sort of self-important gathering Crane personally loathed, but he'd promised Munson, still up in Woodstock recuperating, that he'd be there to represent the *Secession* side of things (Munson, Frank, and Toomer) in the absence of all three. "I seem to be the only delegate from the higher spaces at the *Broom* conclave," he complained. And if the wives were out in force, you could depend on it that nothing would get done. He didn't like meetings becoming "feministic," and he'd already told Cowley the whole damn affair meant less than nothing to him. What mattered was the work itself. He would attend the meeting, but only to keep things sweet and reasonable, though he knew himself well enough to realize that before things were over he would probably wind up getting drunk and making a scene.[34]

It was as he predicted. Thirty men and women showed up at the restaurant that night. Munson insisted on having a statement read which accused Josephson of being an intellectual faker. Cowley, delegated to read the statement aloud, began seriously enough. But soon he was declaiming its sentiments in mock heroics. Jeers, applause, boos, accusations on all sides. Jimmy Light, the founding force behind the

Provincetown Players, drunk, muttered something about Munson's side being trampled under by the *Broom* bastards. Crane joined him, and began wagging his finger at Josephson.

As the prohibition wine flowed, chaos ensued. Burke began wisecracking. Glenway Wescott, trying to rise above the factions, called for some semblance of decorum, then stormed out. Crane, meanwhile, kept pacing up and down, mocking Wescott's call for order. Fuck that. The proceedings were interrupted when a group of local hoods, uninterested in the cause of American literature, suddenly showed up at the back door of the restaurant and told everyone to shut the hell up. Then they were at the front door, blocking anyone from leaving.

"A most likable boy," that Crane, Josephson wrote to a friend afterwards, though Crane had made "great speeches" against him. "He is intensely loyal to Munson," he mused, "blindly so, and I like him for it."[35] But outside the restaurant, he and Crane had nearly come to blows when Josephson called Munson a liar to Crane's face. It was Jimmy Light, also drunk, who pushed ahead of Crane, looking for a fight with Josephson and swinging wildly at him. Josephson, who still thought of Crane as an old friend, was sure Crane himself hadn't been able to bring himself to take a swing at him. By then, however, the locals were also looking for a fight, or a quarter to hail a cab—they didn't much care which—and soon the literati picked themselves up and went home. A month later, with Munson still recovering from his bout with tuberculosis, Josephson would drive up to Woodstock to have it out with him, the two of them swinging wildly at each other on the edge of a cold swamp while a small crowd of spectators, including Crane, looked on.

A final irony of the *Secession/Broom* feud was the botched job John Wheelwright, managing editor of *Secession*, did in printing "For the Marriage of Faustus and Helen," copies of which arrived from Italy a week after the Prince Street brouhaha. Eight months earlier Crane had learned that *Broom*, having agreed to publish Parts I and II, had had to return the poem because the magazine was about to go under. Munson had come to the rescue then, promising to publish the entire poem that summer. Even now Crane was philosophical. "Cheero, Old bird," he consoled Munson in late October. He'd just read his botched poem in *Secession* and had to agree with Munson that the thing should probably have been suppressed, though it was really too late for that now. "A beautiful bit of business—'blues in your breasts,' and the two lines that our hero [Wheelwright] decided were inessential to the poem!" There it was. His beautiful poem "at last completely slain," and nothing to be done about it.[36] Within months, both *Broom* and *Secession* ceased publication altogether, *Broom* that January, *Secession* in April.

Shortly after the Prince Street meeting, Crane wrote his father what C.A. himself would dub his son's "six line challenge."[37] It was the first time since Crane had stormed out on his father thirty months before that he'd screwed up the courage to write him. C.A.'s answer arrived a week later. "It is now almost three years since you left my store with strange words and strong determination to never again be associated with me," C.A. wrote, weighing his words carefully. Still, he had always believed in his son, believed he had "sterling qualities, a good mind, and good morals."[38] He too was willing to let bygones be bygones, but he didn't like being challenged, and he wasn't jumping through hoops for anybody, especially his own son.

The same day Crane wrote his father he'd also written his mother, begging her to let him ship down to the Isle of Pines for the winter and recuperate. New York was killing him with overwork and noise, until he was in danger now of having a breakdown if he didn't get away. It was impossible to live in New York on thirty-five dollars a week, whereas in Cuba he could get by on a fraction of that. Besides, he could be a real help there, overseeing things, learning what marketing opportunities were available "in the way of cooperative fruit markets, etc."[39] The Isle of Pines was out of the question, Grace wrote back, because the plantation was now on the market. It would be better if he returned home. She enclosed enough money for a one-way ticket. But there was no way Crane was going back to Cleveland if he could help it.

Worse, even before he heard back from either parent, he quit his job at J. Walter Thompson. "It simply had to be," he told Munson afterwards. "It got so I gagged every time I sat down here."[40] The finishing touch was being assigned to write an ad for a cosmetic company. To help inspire him, Crane's boss had lined up bottles of perfume on Crane's desk, vials unstopped. These Crane found one morning when he also happened to be suffering from one of his hangovers. Nauseated by the sight and the scents, he proceeded to open his window and throw the bottles out. The gesture sent an unmistakable message to his boss. A week later, as November began, Crane sublet his apartment, wrote his mother for a loan of fifteen dollars, insisting that he knew "damned well" what he was doing, and left for Woodstock to join his friends, Slater Brown and Ed Nagle.[41] The week before, he'd met Eugene O'Neill at a party in the Village and the two had taken an immediate liking to each other. It was O'Neill's friend, Jimmy Light, who had put O'Neill on to Crane's poetry, and O'Neill took the opportunity to praise Crane for what he'd found there. Now, hearing that Crane was heading upstate in the company of Malcolm and Peggy Cowley, O'Neill invited them all to stay with him and his wife for the weekend at their Ridgefield, Connecticut, estate. He would personally see to it that Crane made it up to Woodstock—three hours away by car—on Sunday.

On the evening of November 1st, as Crane prepared to leave New York, his friends threw a farewell party for him, and soon he was drunk with visions of impending freedom. After he left the gathering, he hit the docks, picking up a sailor from the SS *Antwerp*, first name Jerry. What happened that night remains clouded, but the following day Crane wrote Underwood that the evening had ended in an "appalling tragedy" filled with a strange sort of illumination for him.[42] The next night, from Woodstock, he wrote Toomer, whom he'd also taken into his confidence, that the night with Jerry had turned out to be both "sad and wondrous." It was an experience that kept flashing back on him with "a kind of terrific rawness." Once more he spoke of the events in a kind of code, as if there were no other way his mind could deal with what had happened. In any case, the outcome of that evening he believed had been beyond his control, the affair itself turning into "a broken thing."

Still, what had happened, Crane told Toomer, cried out for expression, if only he could find language "equal to such an occasion, such beauty and anguish, all in one."[43] He tried getting the experience into a poem he called "White Buildings," but the poem refused to reveal itself. Perhaps it was just as well, for—given the times—he was well aware that even if the poem did get written, it would never be printed. "Certainly it is one of the most consciously written things I have ever attempted," he confided to Toomer three weeks later, from Woodstock, "whether or not it has any sense, direction or interest to anyone but myself."[44] But all he could ever get down on paper were some lines about a misty November night with autumn leaves falling, the felt sense of his inability to transform the experience, and the weight of an illumination flashing on his mind. He remembered an early morning part-ing with a washerwoman already whistling at her tubs, laundry hanging from the dingy court behind his apartment, early sunlight filling the stairwell. This and the enigmatic line, "These are thy misused deeds." And that was all, except that the name of the aborted poem would become the title for his first book of poems.[45]

Two other poems emerged from the detritus of the "White Build-ings" experience, however, both the results of two months' meditation on that evening: "Possessions" and "Recitative," both of almost identi-cal length, one in four irregular stanzas, the other made up of seven quatrains, and both unrhymed except as they resolved themselves in their final lines. The first enacted what Crane must have experienced on many nights: the deep, troubling, only partly understood drives that urged him out onto the city's streets by night on the prowl for some-one as lonely and desperate as himself. Rain, heat lightning, the black foam of an indifferent night smothering everything, a prospect glimpsed on Bleecker Street, in shadow, desired, unknown. Then a key turning in a lock, the anticipation, the suppressed lightning of it all, the daydreams and fantasies flooding his brain while he wrote ads for goddamn tires and water heaters and books on cheeses, that suppressed eros released now in the hour of "this fixed stone of lust." The knowl-edge too that this hour, anticipated for months, years perhaps, would so shortly disappear with morning on "distant flying taps."

What Crane described here in metaphorical terms was anal inter-course—the speaker "turning on smoked forking spires," the sum of many lovers, one as nameless as the next, until the city itself became a landscape of desire. It was he who was "Tossed on these horns," who bleeding died. But why spill out these confessions, these "all but piteous admissions," here "Upon the page" of the poem, where the elusive "blind sum" of his burning words finally burned "Record of rage and partial appetites"? For the sake of rage, the poet insists. Rage against a possessive mother, rage too against a demanding father. That and the fact that his lust had at least been quenched for the moment, leaving him both satisfied and dissatisfied, no matter how many times this night and others like it were reenacted.

No matter, the poem ends, no matter, since at least for one brief moment the poet had come into "pure possession" of the vision, a communion, the divine in him and the other glimpsed as God's cho-sen ones glimpsed Him in the desert, "the inclusive cloud/Whose heart is fire" visiting him now, on a fall night in a world of fall—the dark night, the rage, and the loss for at least this one moment transformed as the "white wind" of sex burned everything away, alchemizing his stone of lust, leaving the "bright stones" (the words of this poem) behind, "wherein our smiling plays."[46]

If "Possessions" mapped the terrain of distance and desire, "Recitative" addressed the terrible cost to the self of the fractured psyche, of a man unable to say just what had happened—or why. "Recitative," Crane told Munson, was a "more metaphysical and restrained" thing than the confessional "White Buildings" would have been.[47] And it is true that these seven quatrains are in Crane's more elliptical style, rising out of their metaphorical darkness by slow degrees to reveal a man coming to an understanding of his doubleness. Two Cranes: the Marlowevian overreacher prowling the docks and alleys of lower Manhattan and Brooklyn by night, and the visionary, the nine-to-five man, the solitary alone on his mountaintop. The eyes alternately searching and at rest, the voice of suffering, the voice of ecstasy, the face itself and the shattered face in the mirror, Crane's features reflected in the face of some shadow other—as for instance a sailor from the SS *Antwerp*—a face changing minute by minute, like Crane's identity, become for the night Mike Drayton or Jack Donne or Kit Marlowe, mercurial as any changing face in any mirror. Love and need, lust's shiver. Tears and smiles, laughter and tears.

And then the darkness gradually falling away like some ape's face to reveal the white buildings of New York, reflected in the white structures of Crane's poems, his buildings—stanza by stanza, room by room, and those across the chained bay waters, both "Built floor by floor." Absalom, that other lost son, suspended helplessly over the abyss, his eyes watching the "highest tower"—the Woolworth Building across from his apartment—but also the tower of the imagination and the covenant of the bridge swinging over the wreck of one's life, all time condensed, "All hours clapped dense into a single stride," the shattered self restored. All of this, Crane the secret queer and Crane the public visionary, containing all shadow figures—lovers picked up, flesh groped, discarded with the dawn, leaving no name and no forwarding address—the whole forked, bifurcated, necessary thing.[48]

Later, he would send both poems to Jean Toomer and Allen Tate for their comments. Both apparently "got" "Possessions," Toomer praising it as "a deep, thrusting, dense, organized, strong, passionate, luminous, and ecstatic poem."[49] But Tate had to admit that even on rereading it later, "Recitative" remained elusive. Crane understood. Given the nature of the poem's disclosures, it was bound, he admitted, to remain "complex, exceedingly." He'd worked and reworked it for weeks, "trying to simplify the presentation of the ideas in it, the conception." He asked Tate to "imagine the poet . . . on a platform speaking it. The audience is one half of Humanity, Man (in the sense of Blake) and the poet the other. ALSO, the poet sees himself in the audience as in a mirror. ALSO, the audience sees itself, in part, in the poet. Against this paradoxical DUALITY is posed the UNITY, or the conception of it (as you got it) in the last verse. In another sense, the poet is talking to himself all the way through the poem."

At most, that was only the half of it, for he was anxious to conceal the deeper homoerotic elements of the poem, saying simply that there were, "as too often in my poems, other reflexes and symbolisms . . . which it would be silly to write here—at least for the present." Still, it pleased him to know that people got—or at least said they got—"some kind of impact" from his poems, "even when they are honest in admitting considerable mystification." Donne's prayer, he added, had long since become his own: "Make my dark poem light, and light." He strove always, he believed, "for a more perfect lucidity," and hated being thought of as either "willfully obscure or esoteric," even when—writing about what mattered most to him—he was both obscure and esoteric.[50]

The stay at the O'Neills that first weekend in November had turned out splendidly. A noisy, happy affair, Crane summed it up, with enough hard cider to keep him drunk and smiling for the two days he was there. The first night, the O'Neills had thrown a party featuring cakewalks and belly dances that had lasted until dawn. Breakfast on Sunday had been served in bed. He liked O'Neill very much and he found O'Neill's wife, Agnes, charming and deliciously flirtatious. Then he was up in Woodstock, staying with Slater Brown and Ed Nagle, taking long walks into the surrounding hills or into town to get the mail, often with Munson, who was living with William Fisher, Ed Nagle's uncle and a New York art dealer, half a mile away, until Munson finally returned to New York in November. Crane was in heaven, out in nature for the first time in years, felling trees, chopping and sawing wood, building up an enormous appetite, checking his swelling biceps every few hours, and finally getting back into the best shape he'd been in in years. Soon the laid-back Slater and the fastidious Nagle were urging him to stay on with them through the winter. It sounded like a terrific idea, Crane thought, if he could only make some money with his writing. Villanelles, for instance, which Sue Jenkins had asked him to write for her magazine, *Telling Tales,* though the "joyful little s-s of b-tches"—he indexed the words him-self—remained like so many other promises he'd made in his more ebul-lient moments "in an orphaned purgatory."[51]

He donned his new woolen army shirt, woolen socks, and cor-duroy trousers, and worked to his heart's content. It took time—and he took it—to adjust to the deafening silence after the roar of the city. The house, surrounded by delicious woods, had four bedrooms, a bath, a kitchen (heated by an oil stove), a dining room, and a large studio with a huge open fireplace. Everything was plainly but adequately fur-nished. A week into his stay came the first intrusion, when the owner of the cabin arrived to work on a flivver he kept on the property. An amateur inventor, he tried for several days to run the car with kerosene, but after much smoke and combustious noise Crane was praying the guy would either get the goddamned thing going or blow himself to hell and get it over with. The owner did neither, but he did—merci-fully—depart.

Nights, Crane rolled up his sleeves and joined in the cooking: a luscious gravy one night, apples fried in pork sausage fat another, both just the way his mother had taught him. Friends visited: Gaston Lachaise and his wife, staying at a local boardinghouse; and the recov-ering Munson and his host, Bill Fisher. After dinner each night, Crane and his two housemates sat down to an evening of talk—joke-filled, heated, no-holds-barred—on every topic under the sun. One night it was a defense of the modern machine (Brown was pro on that one, Crane and Nagle against), which segued into a discussion of Marinet-ti's aesthetics, John Brown, the KKK, and Jesus Christ. A vat of elder-berry wine was "discovered" in the cellar and secretly tapped thereafter nightly. It all added to the zest of Crane's retreat. Mostly, though, he was happy just to wake up to see the mountains misted in rain or covered with the white radiance of sunshine on snow. Sometimes, he looked up from chopping wood simply to listen to the wind sloughing through the birches, pines, and maples. On rainy days, he read James Frazer's *Golden Bough* and stroked the two house cats who negotiated his lap: black Jazz, and the tiger, Chauncey Depew, named in mock honor of one of Jean Toomer's characters in *Cane*.

For Thanksgiving it was turkey and trimmings, with fresh pine boughs strewn liberally about the studio and dining room. There were eight for dinner—John Dos Passos and the Lachaises and two women friends up from New York: a freshly killed turkey, roasted slowly in the fireplace, onion soup, mashed potatoes, squash, cranberry and apple sauces, cider, and a stuffing offered up by Crane, concocted without benefit of cookbook. Then mince and pumpkin pie, and a fruitcake from McNally's in Cleveland, a gift from Crane's mother. Since Brown and Nagle both had women friends up for the holiday, Crane spent the day happily cooking in the kitchen. After dinner they danced to jazz records on the wind-up Victrola, courtesy of the Lachaises, Crane spinning "fat Mme. Lachaise around" until she sat down exhausted, then Crane—alone—doing the gotzotzsky with one of the girls from New York until he could dance no more.[52]

It was decided. He would stay on until after New Year's, then return to New York to find whatever work he could. How delicious it was to be "irresponsible and purely bovine" for the first time in five years, he sighed.[53] He even began growing a mustache, a patchy blond thing that looked vaguely Breton, but that (alas) refused to fill out. He wrote his father—a more relaxed letter this time—explaining how much he needed this change. It was a month before C.A. could write back, blaming the delay on the press of holiday orders. In a few weeks he would be moving to a new factory and changing the location of two stores. Being so busy, he had to admit, made it difficult for him to understand this "fresh air impulse" of Harold's, but if Harold could find a way to live in the woods and still carry on with his writing, he'd solved the problem of living better than most.[54] If Crane expected something in the way of monetary aid from his father, he was disappointed, for his father sent him nothing. As for his mother, she was working now as a hostess in an antique shop, and had nothing to spare.

Early in December, Crane climbed to the top of Mount Overlook, the 2,500-foot mountain behind the house where he was staying. From the summit he could see the Hudson Valley and—to his right and left—the majestic river, which emptied a hundred miles south into the Atlantic. He'd been told of the fire that had destroyed the old hotel that had dominated the summit until just a few months before. A caretaker still lived nearby in a small house, his only company a cow, two horses, and a few chickens. The man had been up there since the spring thaws, he told Crane, and was eager to leave before the winter snows came. How much did the job pay? Crane wondered. Forty a month. Hell, Crane thought, he could make do on that. The winter would be tough, but he pined for the simplicity of a life lived apart from others, where he could write poems to his heart's content. He wrote the owner, a man from Brooklyn, asking about the job, and while he waited to hear back busied himself taking long walks through the silence of the mountain woods and meadows, "quite alone by one-self," catching—as Stieglitz's photographs had taught him—cloud for-mations "floating over the edge of the mountains like white chariots in the sunshine."[55]

A week before Christmas, over at Bill Fisher's cabin, he read the manuscript poems of a young poet named Samuel Greenberg who'd died seven years earlier of tuberculosis. Fisher had nursed his friend through his last illness at the hospital on Ward's Island, looming out in the East River, and when Greenberg had died (he was just twenty-three), Fisher had gathered his poems for safekeeping. In them Crane found elements of Rimbaud and Laforgue, as well as recurrent images of sea, rainbow, and flower: the same images he himself had begun assembling for *The Bridge*. "Did you ever see some of the hobbling yet really gorgeous attempts that boy made without any education or time except when he became confined to a cot?" Crane wrote Munson. He was so taken by what he'd read of Greenberg's that he copied out as many of the poems as he could. There was little in the way of gram-mar in them, and the spelling was even worse than Crane's. But there was about the poems a "most convincing gusto."[56] Eventually, elements of Greenberg's diction and images, like so many other influences, would wind themselves into the steel cables that would hold together *The Bridge*.

More problematic was the lyric Crane composed that winter which borrowed phrases from Greenberg's manuscripts and arranged them collage-wise into Crane's seventeen-line "Emblems of Conduct." It was a dreamlike poem, uncharacteristic of Crane, really, through which two quasi-allegorical figures, the wanderer and the apostle, moved in a Poussin-like landscape of marble clouds, valley graves, volcanoes, and—weirdly enough—airwaves filled with the voices of radio evangelists. More characteristic of Crane himself was the tension between the spiritual and the sensual, the cataclysmic passage of time, and the enigmatic close in which dolphins arched across the sea's horizon, evoking the image of pathways to a spiritual world. Crane's attempt to take by eminent domain the scattered remains of a dead young poet was not, finally, one of his best efforts, and he may have included the poem in his first collection merely as an accent mark to eke out the requisite number of pages he needed for a book.[57]

For Christmas, he cut down a fir and lugged it back to the house, decorating it on Christmas Eve with toys and candles the Lachaises had supplied. Christmas Day, Crane, Brown, and Nagle trekked over to the Lachaises' boardinghouse for dinner, then on to another party where the hostess put on the liveliest dance Crane could remember. He danced and danced with all the women, until even the hostess, he couldn't help but notice, seemed to be falling for him. The first heavy snowfall came several days later, transforming the countryside into a winter paradise. Then some much-needed cash arrived from Grace, which got him back down to New York just after the New Year. Once more he settled into the Grove Street apartment, seeing old friends again: Burke, Toomer, the Munsons, the Cowleys, Paul Rosenfeld, O'Neill, Jimmy Light, and even Matty Josephson. He also made sure he saw Stieglitz's new series of cloudscapes at 291.

He began pounding the sidewalks again, looking for work in retail or editing. In the meantime, C.A., hearing from Grace that his son still did not have a job, wrote offering him one. He did not wish to make Harold over into something he wasn't, C.A. explained, but if he was ever going to assume the family business, now was the time to start. "Along comes a letter from my father this morning offering me a position with him as traveling salesman!" Crane wrote Munson on 9 January 1924. It was too bad he couldn't accept it, for he certainly needed the money. But he couldn't work for his father, he explained to his mother, because he knew C.A. still wanted to turn him into "a mere tool," when what Crane wanted more than anything was to be a poet.[58]

In a letter to his father on January 12th, Crane was more circumspect. He was writing as a son to a father, he told C.A., "without prej-

udices or worldly issues interfering on either side." He'd already proven
that he could succeed in advertising, if that was what he'd wanted. After
all, he'd landed a job with "the largest agency in the world." Had he
stayed on there, he was sure he would have eventually found "a highly
paid and rather distinguished position" with the company. But he'd
left to do the one thing needful: find the time "to do some real thinking and writing." And if so far he had little to show for his labors, if he
was now down to his last two dollars and still without a job, it was also
true that "many distinguished people" admired his poems and believed
he had already made "a real contribution to American literature."

He counted them off: Eugene O'Neill (who thought Crane "the
most important writer of all in the group of younger men with whom
I am generally classed"); the internationally acclaimed actor Charlie
Chaplin; Waldo Frank; Alfred Stieglitz; and Gaston Lachaise, "the sculptor who did the famous Rockefeller tomb at Tarrytown and the stone
frescoes in the Telephone Building." These were not, he wanted C.A.
to realize, your typical Village bohemians. If he could only keep on with
his dream, he closed, even C.A. might live "to see the name 'Crane'
stand for something where literature is talked about, not only in New
York but in London and abroad." Try "to imagine working for the
pure love of simply making something beautiful," he begged his father,
"something that maybe can't be sold or used to help sell anything else,
but that is simply a communication between man and man, a bond of
understanding and human enlightenment—which is what a real work
of art is." That was all he was trying to do.[59]

The letter was a masterpiece, and in it Crane showed himself to be
every bit the salesman his father was, except that *he* had opted for the
things of the spirit. C.A. wrote back at once, this time enclosing a check
and the promise of a steady allowance to help Harold make his dream
come true. He really did understand his boy, he insisted, and could see
many similarities between them. After all, he himself wasn't in this
candy business simply to make a buck. There were other things in life as
well, including the things Harold himself had mentioned. C.A.'s reply,
Crane told his mother afterwards, was a "sincere and cordial document"
and the finest letter he'd ever received from his father.[60] A bridge of
sorts had finally been built between the two men.

The foot-slogging, cobblestone-pounding treks about New York
in search of work paid off finally when Crane was hired—thanks in part
to Munson—by the advertising firm of Pratt & Lindsay. Crane began

work bright and early Monday morning, January 28th. His starting salary was fifty dollars a week; that was what he'd made working in Cleveland two years earlier, and fifteen dollars more than Thompson had paid him. He'd been "pretty blue for awhile and poor," he wrote his mother, but even that hadn't prevented his "meeting new people and revisiting the old, dining here and there and enjoying free tickets to modern concerts, plays and exhibitions of modern painters." And, he added coyly, it didn't hurt personally knowing just about all "the most interesting and vital people in New York" there were to know.[61]

Then he was in the midst of it again, "working like a tiger" alongside two stenographers, an office boy, and the one other copywriter in the firm, another friend of Munson's. He had "the nicest niche" he'd ever had: fifteen stories up in a corner office, looking out on two angles of the city he both loved and hated. It was exciting to press a button and have an office boy come running. And all this so that he might put together a book on cheese: "how happy it makes you and how good it is for tissues, stomach, and bowels, etc."[62] He liked his bosses; his bosses liked him. And things went swimmingly. He was tickled to have his father telephone him at his office one week into his new job. C.A., it happened, was in town on business, staying at the Waldorf, and had called to invite Harold to meet him after work for a chat.

The chat began stiffly, C.A. not really knowing how to speak to his son except about business, so that Crane had to be careful not to get up and begin screaming that his old man still didn't get it. Finally, C.A. found some common ground. He had a new product he wanted to market. What should he call it? How best to advertise it? Perhaps he could send Harold some data about it and have him write some ads? Crane was delighted. His father was actually asking him for advice about a business matter. When, at five that afternoon, Crane left for another appointment, C.A. slipped him a greenback to show how pleased he was with his boy, a successful businessman with his own office in the great city of Manhattan.

Then, suddenly, everything changed again. On Monday, February 11th—two weeks into his job and down with the "grippe"—Crane staggered into his office to learn that he was being terminated at once. He called it the grippe, but the truth is he may simply have been hungover again. In any event, he was told there was no work for him. Next, he heard from the man from whom he was subletting that he would need the Grove Street apartment back on March 1st. Crane had fifty dollars to his name, thirty of which he owed for rent. He tried finding work as a journalist, trolling for commissions to do feature articles of some sort. Nothing. He wrote his father, asking for a hundred-dollar loan (at 6 percent) to tide him over. Nothing. He began borrowing from friends, trusting that their respect for his genius might translate into a few bucks or a meal. Again nothing. "Hart Crane—lost job—losing room—disgusted with New York and thinks of returning to Cleveland," Cowley informed Burke a week after Crane's firing. "It is disquieting to find a man more episodic [fragmented] than myself."[63] But Crane wasn't leaving New York that easily. Like Chaplin, he meant to pick himself up, brush himself off, and go on whistling into the teeth of fate.

7 / IN THE SHADOW OF
THE BRIDGE

BROOKLYN
MARCH 1924–JUNE 1925

A T THE BEGINNING OF MARCH 1924, Crane found himself in a furnished room on Van Nest Place (No. 15), a room Waldo Frank had told him about. For two weeks, Crane wrote Tate afterward, he'd been scrambling like hell for a place to move his "few clothes, books, knickknacks and pictures," and now he was dead tired.[1] The upside was that at last he had a comfortable bed and a landlady to clean up after him, a marked improvement on Grove Street, which had somehow degenerated into chaos. What had made the downturn in his fortunes palatable was Eugene O'Neill's inviting him up to his Connecticut estate for a week in late February. That and the flurry in the arts around New York. Besides the Europeans—Maillol, Rousseau, Picasso, Braque, Duchamp—there were the Americans: Stieglitz and Georgia O'Keeffe at the Anderson Galleries, a show by the Independents at the Waldorf, an exhibition of John Marin's watercolors.

He took in several concerts: "a miserable performance by [Josef] Hofmann of his own feeble compositions," together with two rousing concerts featuring the work of Bartók, Varèse, Casella, Szymanowski, and Schoenberg. He took Sue Jenkins to the opening of "an old play written seriously in 1840, but the funniest thing in the world to see now," put on at the Provincetown Theatre.[2] He also saw O'Neill's new offering, *All God's Chillun Got Wings*, which had caused a stir in the newspapers because it featured a black man married to a white woman. O'Neill himself, in fact, had received death threats from the Ku Klux Klan. Why in hell didn't America grow up? Crane raged. If there was any trouble when the play opened, he promised himself, he would be there with his cane, ready to lay into the troublemakers.

Once again he was broke and trying to be philosophical about it. "We may realize that we are always losing," he lectured his mother on March 23rd. "But it means a lot to realize that, also, all the while you are losing you are also gaining!"[3] A week later he was talking about living off the oats the sparrows left behind if things didn't change, and soon. He dreamed of finding work on some "West Indian cruiser,—United Fruit, Munson line or some such."[4] In April, he moved his things over to Jimmy Light and Sue Jenkins's apartment on Jones Street (No. 30) until he could find another apartment. Once again his mother offered to send him the money to come back home, but he warned her that if she sent him anything, he would use it to buy food. He did not like having to live off his friends, but he was not going to pull up anchor and leave New York now. "The poorer I get, the prouder I get," he told her, and this in "reaction to the damnably unjust mechanics of business everywhere prevalent."[5] Missing a few meals was no big deal. He'd done that before.

Worse, he had yet to hear from his father and couldn't puzzle out the reason for the silence. The man was surely "the strangest animal" he'd ever heard of.[6] If only he could get down to the Isle of Pines and write. Why let strangers work the place, he pleaded with his mother, when he could live there instead of slogging it out in New York? Both sides of his family seemed always to ball things up, he lamented, so why should he go on worrying. If he turned out to be a bum, he promised her, she would never see him again. "Suffering is a real purification," he'd written her back in December, "and the worst thing I have always had to say against Christian Science is that it willfully avoided suffering, without a certain measure of which any true happiness cannot be fully realized."[7] Now he could feel the spikes driving into his wrists, and knew what it meant to suffer for one's art. In fact, the shadow of the suffering Christ had already played over several of his poems, including "Possessions" and "Recitative," but now the crucified Nazarene took the foreground in a poem begun as the cold light of spring and the season of Lent returned.

"Lachrymae Christi": Latin for Christ's tears, but also the name of a delicate white wine. The suffering Christ, then, transformed into the ecstatic Dionysus, the necessary crush of grapes before the ecstatic wine could be distilled and gathered. So too the poet, Christ *and* Dionysus, their pain transformed to song:

> *Names peeling from Thine eyes*
> *And their undimming lattices of flame,*
> *Spell out in palm and pain*
> *Compulsion of the year, O Nazarene . . .*

It is a poem of linguistic transubstantiations: the wine become the blood (and tears) of Christ, signaling too the changes wine brings to the human spirit, liberating the poet, his suffering turned to joy with its help. Even for Crane this was a complex piece of work, setting out to enact the transformation of one thing into another, as if the poet realized via the enactment of the poem itself the alchemical mystery whereby suffering became joy.

"Whitely," the poem opens, the way the moon—the imagination—will transform even some drab mill factory at night, purifying the scene, dissolving all but the windows which reflect back the light. But those windows seem also the windows of a face in repose, the eyes the eyes of the poet who sees and smiles. Does he smile because of the wine he has drunk or because he has seen into the mystery? And yet, for all the "red perfidies" and "perjuries" that have galvanized his vision and turned his life into a Calvary, he hears beneath the crush of things "distilling clemencies" and the grave's worms "tunneling/Not penitence/But song." The eyes of the poet, then, become here the Nazarene's, no longer sorrowful but blazing like tinder with new revelations.

For years Crane had been in love with Egyptian art, which, he believed, underwrote Greek art and therefore all Western art. Older than the Nazarene, he implies here, older even than Dionysus, are the pyramid (symbol of death and rebirth) and the sphinx (the mystery of the riddle of life at last articulated). The poet has looked into the abyss and has come back to tell us what he has seen. And what he has seen is that death and the life of self-sacrifice must no longer hold humankind in bondage. In this, Crane's *esthetique du mal*, he has looked upon the face of Dionysus as it forms itself out of the face of the sacrificed Christ, joy rising out of suffering, poetry out of pain. It is on this, the reconstituted, "Unmangled target smile" of the accomplished poem, that the poet has chosen to fix his eye and ours.[8]

Then, just as suddenly, Crane's fortunes were on the upswing again. A letter from Waldo Frank, posted from Madrid, arrived to buck him up. Crane was truly a man of genius, Frank assured him. Of this Frank had not the slightest doubt. Crane clearly possessed the necessary spark of that "divine force, more immediately, more intensely, more consciously, above all more articulately than is the usual case of men." Of course there would be vagaries and dislocations on the "personal human plane," Frank understood. That was life. He was all too aware of Crane's excesses and he took the time now to warn him that he had to take better care of himself (code for cutting back on his drinking), for no one could "articulate God . . . without a well functioning personal body, any more than we could write a poem with a punk pen or typewriter."[9] He had just come from Paris, where he had talked with Valéry Larbaud, the French scholar of American letters. Could Crane send Larbaud a copy of "For the Marriage of Faustus and Helen," which the final issue of *Secession* had at last printed in its correct form? Crane had needed a word of encouragement, and mercifully it had come.

Next came a job. Cowley, employed as a copywriter for Sweet's Catalogue Service off Times Square, found Crane work there writing scientific catalogues. The pay would be forty dollars a week, ten less than Crane's last job, and he would have to sweat to get down the scientific jargon, but at least he could hold up his head again. As soon as he collected his first paycheck, he moved out of Jimmy Light's apartment and into the Hotel Albert until he could find something for himself. By Easter—April 20th—he had it: a front-room apartment at 110 Columbia Heights in Brooklyn, just across the East River and in plain view of the Brooklyn Bridge. The building faced onto a quiet, sycamore-lined street of mid-nineteenth-century houses, the back onto a breathtaking panorama of the river and the white buildings of the Manhattan skyline.

"Just imagine looking out your window directly on the East River with nothing intervening between your view of the statue of Liberty, way down the harbor, and the marvelous beauty of Brooklyn

Bridge close above you on your right," he wrote his mother that Easter. "All of the great new skyscrapers of lower Manhattan are marshaled directly across from you, and there is a constant stream of tugs, liners, sail boats, etc. in procession before you on the river!" Best, he was only twenty minutes from Times Square on the subway. What a place to read and write, and all for only six dollars a week! It was the Opffers, father and sons—translated Danes—who already had rooms in the building, who'd been responsible for his move. The building, he would learn only years later, had also been the home of Washington Roebling, the man who'd designed the Brooklyn Bridge.

He'd meant to attend Easter Mass at St. Patrick's, instead of which he'd got uproariously drunk the night before at Squarcialupi's on Perry Street off West Houston where he'd gone with the Opffers: Emil Senior, "an old man but very distinguished as an editor [of the Danish weekly *Nordlyset*] and an anarchist," and two of Opffer's sons: Ivan and Emil Junior, twenty-seven.[10] In fact, Crane was already head over heels in love with Emil. "For many days, now," he wrote Frank the following day, "I have gone about quite dumb with something for which 'happiness' must be too mild a term." At last he had actually seen the very Word made Flesh and witnessed the "indestructibility" of love, "where flesh became transformed through intensity of response to counter-response, where sex was beaten out, where a purity of joy was reached that included tears." No matter what happened from this moment on, for once at least he'd found real happiness in "walking hand in hand across the most beautiful bridge in the world, the cables enclosing us and pulling us upward in such a dance as I have never walked and never can walk with another."

It was like the moment of communion with the "religious gunman" in "Faustus and Helen," where the edge of the bridge suddenly leaped over the edge of the street and then rose high above the chained bay waters of the river. In fact, he'd set the last part of that poem in the evening shadows of this very bridge. Blond, blue-eyed, stolid in appearance, Emil Opffer was three years older than Crane, and had first arrived in the States with his family nearly twenty years before. His brother, Ivan, worked with the Provincetown Players as a musician, and Emil had called on Sue Jenkins while Crane was living over on Van Nest Place. He'd already been introduced to Crane and Sue had told him that Crane had some pictures he was anxious to share with him. When he knocked on the door to Crane's apartment, a radio—

he could hear music from inside—or perhaps Crane's ubiquitous phonograph was playing loudly. They talked, they had a drink, and then another, moves were made, and the two men spent the night together on Crane's too-narrow bed. For all its difficulties, its separations, reunions, betrayals, and Sargasso Seas of disappointment, it was to be the most satisfying emotional relationship of Crane's life.[11]

At first it seemed more dream than reality. Walking hand-in-hand across the Brooklyn Bridge, then over to Emil's apartment at 110 Columbia Heights, then looking back under the shadow of that bridge, its granite mass and shadow, the gulls wheeling, the heft of the river riding seaward, the spindrift waves. To witness then the very bridge that had become for Crane "more familiar than a hundred factual previsions could have rendered it." And to be at that window, looking out on the river. *That* was where he wanted most of all to be remembered, along with "the ships, the harbor, and the skyline of Manhattan, midnight, morning or evening—rain, snow or sun." It was his Jerusalem, his Nineveh, his holy city "in actual contact with the changelessness of the many waters that surround it." The sea had thrown itself upon him, altering him "as anyone is who has asked a question and been answered." His eyes had now been "kissed with a speech . . . beyond words entirely." Once again, as in the weeks and months before he'd left Cleveland, he could feel the flood tide of inspiration rising within him.[12]

"The bottom of the sea is cruel," Crane had written three years before, closing what would become the first of his six "Voyages" poems. Now, in the second of the "Voyages," he picked up on that thought again, this time with a qualifying "And yet":

> —And yet this great wink of eternity,
> Of rimless floods, unfettered leewardings,
> Samite sheeted and processioned where
> Her undinal vast belly moonward bends,
> Laughing the wrapt inflections of our love . . .

Yes, the sea—out into which only a relative handful ever ventured—could be cruel. But it could also offer something to those willing to give themselves to it. For even the terrifying awe-filling sublimity of the sea, viewed from the perspective of eternity, was circumscribed.

From that height it seemed no more than "a great wink of eternity,/Of rimless floods, unfettered leewardings . . ." Love, he had come to understand, was greater than death, greater than the annihilating sea, for it was love alone that allowed us to open ourselves to life's greatest mysteries. At this point even the syntax of the poem began to unfold scroll-like, revealing with each new phrase new mysteries as it rehearsed something of the orphic music the poet had been privileged to hear.

This sea, this sea of love, this "Samite sheeted and processioned" sea, unfolding like some majestic silk scroll laced with moon-reflected silver tracing across its surface, went on and on, even as the voyager traveled deeper and deeper into uncharted waters, touching the expanse of love's vastness for the first time. It was a sea whose surface was like the belly of some sea nymph beckoning in the rise and fall of waves, some undine, bending and turning before the forces of the moon, regulating and charting the ageless seasons of the sea, until even the moonlight seemed to join in the laughter before the wrapt and rapt "inflections" of two lovers. At this height, Crane underscored, language itself fell away. It was no longer even a matter of will or ego, he knew, for he had been summoned by forces far beyond his ability to withstand, and all he could do now was to move as the sea itself gestured. Such love compels and terrifies, for even in love's orgasmic completion he tasted his own mortality. After all, what timebound creature could look upon the face of rapture such as this and live?

In this transport he has heard the diapason knell—orphic music so exquisite it contains within itself its own sure annihilation. For what Ishmael has ever brought back word of what was glimpsed in those latitudes? Who would believe, except those who have voyaged out into those depths themselves? As soon cup and hold the snow as it writes itself upon those "scrolls of silver" we call the motions of the sea. This sea, which can kill as quickly as it can be kind, the poet has come to understand, at last erases everything but the memory of those "pieties of lovers' hands." For to discover another inch by inch, span by span, can be as daunting and yet as exalting as Columbus setting out into uncharted waters to find a New World he once heard was there, and then—the quest at last completed—to hear those faint "bells off San Salvador" growing louder as carillon after carillon of unheard melody salutes the eternal stars. "Crocus lustres," "poinsettia meadows": springtime in the New World, as now the lover coasts among the inlets and islands of the beloved in a prodigality of expectation and discovery.

Yes, we know, this too will end, as everything bound by time must end, for we are wrapped in time, fit only to taste the ecstasy of such love before we must turn back to shore again.

But not yet, the lover pleads. Not yet. Not until we have spent ourselves, not until we have died into one another. Not until, like seals—accustomed to living out in those unfathomed depths—we have found the answer to their "wide spindrift gaze toward paradise." The answer that returns to us is, of course, news of our own death, a death we will pay out at some undisclosed date. Still, the reward for this journey out into the depths, this Faustian overreaching, is to have brushed against such intimations of an all-consuming love as must make the whole transaction worth it.[13] All this Crane has given us in a language of such orphic intensity and musicality as he would touch on only once or twice again. And never would he surpass what he gifts us with here.

"Permit me voyage, love, into your hands." Thus ends the third movement of "Voyages," as now dawn breaks over the sleeping lover upon whom the poet gazes in awe and thanksgiving, as the seal—that other warm-blooded creature, merman, consanguineous with ourselves, and adapted to these depths—might watch dawn break over the waves. Death and eros, those "black swollen gates/That must arrest all distance" unless the lover be admitted. And the lover rocking his beloved until in an ecstasy of self-emptying the "silken skilled transmemberment of song" is glimpsed again and yes again.[14]

At the end of April, Crane's father was in New York once more. Crane saw him on several occasions, though always on his father's turf. Once it was the Hotel Commodore for lunch, followed by a matinée, dinner, and another show. The time passed agreeably, Crane told his mother, with C.A. regaling his son with stories about his prospering business and going on about New York being a splendid market for his products. Alternately, C.A. complained about how much he was losing because most people in Cleveland refused to pay for quality chocolate. Crane was therefore at a loss to explain C.A.'s silence afterwards, though he knew his father well enough by now not to try to account for these shifts between intimacy and indifference. There had also been Cleveland cousins to squire about and the Rychtariks to entertain. These, plus the demands of his job, left him feeling exhausted.

On the other hand, there was the new freedom of living in Brooklyn Heights and of being very much in love. Walking home from breakfast one Sunday morning that May, he noticed rows of tulips "dotting the edge of one of the several beautiful garden patches that edge the embankment that leads down to the river." Even better was Emil Senior letting him use his apartment—the one with the magnificent view of the river—whenever he was away. Every time Crane looked out over the harbor and the Manhattan skyline, he seemed to look on a new world, depending on the time of day, the time of year, the light, the weather, the moods of the city.

One evening, there was fog over the whole river, and the vision nearly transported him. "Gradually the lights in the enormously tall buildings begin to flicker through the mist," he wrote his mother. "There was a great cloud enveloping the top of the Woolworth tower, while below, in the river, were streaming reflections of myriad lights, continually being crossed by the twinkling mast and deck lights of little tugs scudding along, freight rafts, and occasional liners starting outward." To his left he could make out the Statue of Liberty, "with that remarkable lamp of hers that makes her seen for miles." And up to his right: "the most superb piece of construction in the modern world," the Brooklyn Bridge, "with strings of light crossing it like glowing worms as the L's and surface cars pass each other going and coming." How good "to feel the greatest city in the world from enough distance" to see it laid out before one in all its recumbent majesty, as Wordsworth in a similar mood had looked upon the sleeping city of London just over a century earlier and found it very good.[15]

People were still congratulating him on his "Faustus and Helen," which Munson had called the greatest poem written by an American since Walt Whitman. But as his affair with his sailor-lover intensified, and with it his sequence of love poems, Crane went into a kind of hiding. One sign of this was that his usually voluble correspondence fell off dramatically. When Jean Toomer, miffed that he hadn't heard from Crane in over a month, wrote him in early June asking if their correspondence was now a thing of the past, Crane broke his silence to explain. He was with Emil again, who was home on a ten-day shore leave before he would have to go away for another six weeks. When Emil was home or was expected, he wrote no one. He was sorry, but there it was. In fact, he could barely stay afloat, much less write these days. It was another two weeks before he wrote Toomer again, and this time he enclosed a draft of the poem he was then working on: the fourth of the six "Voyages."

What he'd been through that spring with Emil, Crane tried explaining now to Toomer, had hit him with the force of a typhoon smashing into an island. It had been a time of "unbelievable promises . . . fulfilled," but of unforeseen complications as well. The love he felt for this man, he was sure, would never come again, at least not with this intensity. In fact, the initial exaltation—which he'd mapped out in the second and third "Voyages"—had by mid-June long passed. Yet the peace, the God-like peace, which had, in spite of anxieties and fears, replaced it, was something new and nearly as satisfying in its own way. So much agony and so much joy, one emotion following the next in swift alternation, until he was "almost a shadow" of himself.[16]

But through it all there was "a conviction of love," which he believed he and Emil both shared. Words could never capture what he felt now. Which was why—paradoxically—he'd been driven to write the "Voyages" sequence in the first place. Language was bound to fall short of what he felt; but then, language was all he had to report back what he had been through. Hence these poems, meant to capture love's arc rising to a pitch and then falling of necessity away. Somehow to summon the halo of the thing itself, and do so in song, transmembered song, a song that touched one, if not soul to soul, then surely membrane to vibrant membrane.

Eternity, and its finite counterpart, the sea. Consider the wide spectrum of love's possibilities, south to north, "from palms to the severe/Chilled albatross's white immutability"—an image gleaned from *Moby-Dick*, white death erasing time. To cry out in an agony of ecstasy, to merge with the other for all time, as the East River flowed forever out into the vast Atlantic waiting just beyond, to merge with it and be lost in it. It was a reality that, once experienced, forever after altered one's perception of reality. Not argument, then, not logic, but a reality evanescent as a fragrance, yet beyond refutation, this glimpse of love itself. A music, a mystical rose, "bright staves of flowers," something beyond words, which the poet was nevertheless compelled to celebrate in words. A new world of love as transforming to the poet as that New World Columbus had once happened upon, calling it the most beautiful thing he had ever seen. To have entered on the immense chill deep of the unknown to find, then, Cathay. "Voyages IV" turns out to be also a mimesis of the sexual act itself, evoking those "secret oar and petals," the ship's prow entering the harbor of the beloved, the moment of expectation, the cry as lover is received by beloved, the voyager reaching at last his destination, this sacred altar, this "chancel port and portion of our June."[17]

Still, part of the agony Crane was feeling that June came from the panic he was thrown into believing he'd contracted some venereal disease. Not from Emil, but from a casual partner he seems to have picked up while Emil was at sea. In mid-June, he confessed to Toomer that for the past several weeks he'd been in "a state of almost hysterical despair," and would not rest until the doctor gave him a clean bill of health.[18] The problem turned out, finally, to be too much alcohol, which had led to urethritis—"very painful and nerve-wracking"—he told his mother, but which was at least treatable with "a steady diet of buttermilk."[19] Still, the possibility that he'd contacted syphilis or gonorrhea by his dangerous behavior had nearly paralyzed him with fear. Relieved to learn what the problem was, he retreated to his poems with renewed oaths of fidelity sworn to Emil, at least for the moment. It was a pattern—this wandering eye even in the midst of a serious relationship—that would dog Crane until his death.

On the other hand, part of the joy he felt now came from being in the midst of his visionary company of pals. Allen Tate was back in New York again; on the evening of June 24th—in company with Malcolm Cowley—he went out to Brooklyn Heights to visit Crane. Late that night, the three men walked down to the edge of the East River under the shadow of the bridge facing New York, all the while Cowley reciting lines from Poe. At the river's edge, the three stepped out onto the far end of a scow moored to one of the piers, listening to the black waters lapping beneath them. From there they watched as the SS *Shenandoah* sailed downriver past them, its shadow outlined against the damascene backdrop of the Manhattan skyline and, foregrounding it all, a huge neon sign heralding—perhaps fortuitously—WATERMAN'S FOUNTAIN PENS.

A few days later, Crane and Tate visited the Munsons in their Village apartment. For Crane, it was a rekindling of those "earlier Munson-Burke-Toomer-etc. engagements" he'd so loved when he'd first come to New York two years earlier. That was before "the grand dissolution" had begun: a slow, smoldering falling out effected by Munson and Toomer becoming disciples that winter of 1924, disciples of one G. I. Gurdjieff, Russian expatriate and sometime mystic, now in New York, now at his Institute outside Paris, who was propounding what Crane dubbed that "birth control, re-swaddling and new-synthesizing, grandma-confusion movement."[20] Back in February, Crane too, struck by the "astonishing dances and psychic feats" of Gurdjieff's disciples,[21] had flirted with the idea of following Gurdjieff's advice for living. But Gurdjieff was after disciples, and that was where Crane, as always, drew the line. So, as Munson and Toomer began to fade from the scene, Cowley and Frank and Tate loomed brighter. As did of course Emil Opffer.

And then there was Crane's job in Manhattan to think about each damned day. Pressures at the office and the "anvil weather" of July made him more and more irritable,[22] his one consolation Emil's presence for the short time he was home on shore leave. Letters home, letters to anyone, again shrank to the occasional postcard. But now Crane's inspiration likewise fizzled. His twenty-fifth birthday came and went. "Three more hellishly hot days," he wrote his mother in mid-August, "and at 4 this morning it began to rain. I hope it pours for days." Nights he tossed and turned, shaking, disoriented, unable to sleep. "If you were once to pile into a steaming, rushing mob in the subway where the stinks of millions accumulate from day to day," he complained, "you'd see how I feel about the next day's work after a sleepless night. And when one goes to one's room afterward, believe me, it isn't to write letters!"

There was nothing for it but to "work & complain," and he contributed his share of both. When he thought of his father these days—and he did, he admitted, far too often—it was of some "poisonous and unnatural" creature whose continued silence left him stunned and baffled.[23] Maybe if "the chocolate maggot" lost his wealth, he told his mother, he might finally assume some human shape.[24] What good did it do him to have a millionaire father when he was still slogging it out in New York in this unbearable heat writing inane catalogue copy? "When people like Gorham & Waldo Frank ask me why I don't write more," he snapped, "it fairly makes me rage. They—with money supplied them and their time all their own!"[25]

When Frank wrote him again to say he still thought Crane one of the finest poets writing in America, book or no book, Crane flinched. In spite of the poems he'd written that spring and summer, he could see little but failure. In fact, he told Frank, he feared he was already used up as a poet. But two weeks later, fearing he had disturbed Frank by his despairing tone, Crane wrote again to clarify what he'd meant. He'd been in real despair and torture all summer, and was still experiencing bouts of black depression, though these had finally abated. Then, as he had with Toomer, he included a draft of "Voyages IV." The poem, Crane said, might reveal better than anything else could something of what he'd been through, especially now, when the initial ecstasy had given way to something more like wistful acceptance.

Which was what the fifth movement of the poem was attempting to chart: Ice, midnight, rime. Not the open sea now, but the "bay estuaries," as he returned from his dream of love to find "the cables of our sleep so swiftly filed" and his beloved drawing in his head and shrugging off the intensity of what Crane knew they had both been through. To have felt that, and then to hear his beloved sum it up in a phrase like, "There's/Nothing like this in the world"! At last the full tyranny of time had returned to reveal "dead sands flashing," the lover robbed by the quiet despair of the beloved's comment that he would never "quite understand" what the lover was feeling, as he turned once more to drift off into the oblivion of sleep and distance, to join there the ghosts of other loves. Well, there it was, Crane was forced to admit. There really was nothing for it but to acknowledge the fact that his dream of love had been dreamed only by himself:

> But now
> Draw in your head, alone and too tall here.
> Your eyes already in the slant of drifting foam;
> Your breath sealed by the ghosts I do not know:
> Draw in your head and sleep the long way home.[26]

But if the relationship had fallen short of what Crane had dreamed it might be—he and Emil both having damaged it by taking other lovers—still there was the *idea* of love. And so the final movement of the "Voyages" sequence (written in fact the year before) proceeds in stately tetrameter rhyming quatrains. The scene is much like that which Crane would repeat later in "At Melville's Tomb": swimmers out far and in deep who lift their "lost morning eyes" now to mourn their

The young Harold Hart Crane, 1906.

Harold Hart Crane with family and relatives, around 1915.
At top: Hart's father, C.A. Crane. *Second row from top:* a local dentist; Arthur Crane, C.A.'s father; Fred Crane, C.A.'s brother; Byron and Bess Madden's maid; Ella Crane, C.A.'s mother; Lotta Crane, Fred's wife; Grace Crane, C.A.'s wife.
Bottom row: Harold Hart Crane, Fredrica Crane, Fred's daughter; Byron Madden (holding Betty Madden); Bess Madden, C.A.'s sister; Jack Madden, Bess's son; and Margery Crane, Fred's daughter.

Grace Crane, 1915.

C. A. Crane with bowler, about 1910.

Harold Hart Crane on train tracks, age 17, summer 1916, shortly before leaving for New York.

Portrait of Hart Crane by Willy Lescaze, fall 1921. "Accept a lone eye riveted to your plane," Crane would write in "For the Marriage of Faustus and Helen," recalling this portrait with its mystical eye turned upward and inward:

Bent axle of devotion along companion ways
That beat, continuous, to hourless days—
One inconspicuous, glowing orb of praise.

Gorham Munson, 1932.

Sherwood Anderson, mid-1920s.

Waldo Frank, early 1920s.

Jean Toomer, 1923, at the time of the publication of *Cane*.

Emil Opffer, the muse of Crane's *Voyager* sequence, summer 1924, from the roof of 110 Columbia Heights.

Photo of lower Manhattan from Crane's window at 110 Columbia Heights, Brooklyn, taken by Hart Crane, 1924.

Hart Crane in woodsman's clothing and Chinese mustache, Woodstock, late 1924.

Marianne Moore, 1926.

William Carlos Williams, 1926.

Malcolm Cowley, late 1920s.

Hart Crane's patron, the banker Otto Kahn, mid-1920s.

Caroline Gordon, Allen Tate, and Gordon's close friend Sally Wood, in Paris, 1932.

Hart Crane, Allen Tate, and William Slater Brown, acting the toughs in a photo arcade in Times Square, winter 1925.

Grace Crane with Charles Curtis, 1926.

lost innocence—the morning/mourning of their love. The pilgrim lover: like some ship's keel pressed against uncharted waters, a "derelict and blinded guest" not unlike Coleridge's Ancient Mariner or Melville's Ishmael alone returned. And now the lover cries out to make some sense of it all. He needs some answer, some "blithe and petaled word" beyond language as one commonly understands it, some smile offered in the new dawn. Perhaps a covenant marked by a rainbow twining above the dark waters he has traversed, the promised rainbow glinting in his lover's hair.

Not the oar, then, the phallic thrust alone, but some "white echo of the oar," the memory of what such lovemaking points to and signifies. Is it the unutterable Word of Love the poet wishes to celebrate, "the imaged Word," holding in its glow a figure that meant everything to Crane, those "hushed willows," which he would evoke again in "Repose of Rivers": childhood, innocence, elegy, loss? Not the death of love, then, but rather the death of the death of love. Lovers may and do betray each other, Crane too well knew. But that did not mean that the sacred idea of love need be compromised. Love remained unbetrayable because . . . because he needed it to be so. Love was a phoenix, dying and being continually reborn in the imagination, rising from its own spent ashes. It is a yes and a yes, "Whose accent no farewell can know," that "know" punning on the negation of "no." Let that be the last word not only of "Voyages" but of Crane's credo as well. In two years' time, it would come to stand as the final yes of his first book, *White Buildings*.[27]

By now his mother was also, if not exactly undergoing a belated "Voyages" of her own, at least enjoying the attentions of one Charles Curtis, sixty-four (sixteen years older than Grace), a gentleman of the old school, a Cleveland insurance adjuster, poker player, ballroom dancer, and genial escort who'd begun pursuing Grace with something approaching ardor. Crane learned of the love interest from Sam Loveman, who was in New York that summer of 1924 and bunking in the back room of Crane's apartment. When he wrote home, Crane fairly shouted with happiness about the courtship. In truth, he wanted his mother married and cared for, in part for her own happiness, in part so that her obsessive attentions might be deflected and he could at last get on with his own life. If she was happy with Mr. Curtis, he told her, he was happy. Money was secondary. What mattered, what really mattered, was that the heart be fed and the mind be at peace. "As the years go on," he warned her, "I am quite apt to be away for long periods, for I admit that the freedom of my imagination is the most precious thing that life holds for me—and the only reason I can see for living."[28]

By September, besides the work he'd done on "Voyages," he'd managed three other new poems and published four: two in *The Little Review*, two in a little magazine published out of Woodstock called *1924*. He was still anxious to get on with *The Bridge*, which would complete the manuscript for his first book of poems; but that would need "unbroken time and extensive concentration," neither of which his work at Sweet's Catalogue Service allowed. "There are days when I simply have to 'sit on myself' at my desk to shut out rhythms and melodies that belong to that poem and have never been written because I have succeeded only too well during the course of the day's work in excluding and stifling such a train of thoughts," he complained to his mother. But there were also times when not even his job could "shut out the plans and beauties of that work," and he was able to get something of the poem's music down on paper.[29] It was at such times that he was most happy.

When the catalogue he'd slaved over for the past six months was at last readied for press, he feared he had just worked himself out of a job. Instead, he was kept on and told he could have a week's paid vacation in October. He still missed Emil, who was away for six weeks, home for ten days, then away for another six-week stretch. "He is so much more to me than anyone I have ever met that I miss him terribly," he confessed to his mother, without explaining the intimate nature of the relationship.[30] Worst, in September, Emil's father died on the operating table and it was left to Crane and Ivan to meet Emil's ship when it anchored in New York harbor on October 1st. Emil took the news hard—so hard that for the ten days he was in New York, he remained quiet and withdrawn, "almost transformed," Crane told his mother, by the realization that his father was gone for good.[31]

This time Emil's presence turned out to be difficult for Crane, for there was little he seemed able to do to assuage the loss. Then Emil was gone once more, bound for South America, and Crane had the back room overlooking the river and his beloved bridge, though under circumstances he had never imagined.

It was most likely in response to Emil's father's death that he wrote "Paraphrase," and probably that October. Four unrhymed quatrains imagining death overtaking him there in his apartment, the last thing seen as the self entered the "antarctic blaze" of death those "bruised roses on the papered wall." ("Either I or the wallpaper goes": thus Oscar Wilde's final words.) The "steady winking beat" of the pumping heart (systole, diastole), what we take for granted, as one rises from one's bed in the dead of night. One moves, the feet move, the toes at the end of the feet move, the hand reaches out to touch the toes. If we can do that, we know at least we are still alive. But what will it be like on that last morning, when the light returns again, as it has for the last million million years, and floods the pillow where the still head, "hollowed" now, lies unmoved and unmoving, and the "crow's cavil" grows faint and fainter, and language goes, and all that remains is the final "white paraphrase" of death?[32]

News that the house in which he had grown up, the house where he'd written so many of his early poems, was once again on the market hit Crane hard. His room there had been one of the few fixed points in his tumultuous life, and he hated the thought of its soon becoming someone else's, or—worse—torn down. "It's so deep in my consciousness and so much the frame of the past," he tried to explain to his mother. He begged her to at least save some of his books—the ones in the "glass-doored bookcase"—and put them in the drawers of his desk, the desk where he'd composed his first poems. It was the one piece of furniture he hoped might still be saved. Please, would she pack his books, along with his letters, clippings, and photos, and send them on to him? He'd moved so many times in the past few years he was afraid now of keeping so much as "an extra sheet of paper" because he might lose that as well. He knew his request reeked of self-pity. "I should rise above such feelings," he confessed, "but I haven't been able to thus far."[33]

In mid-October, Crane took his well-earned week's vacation. "The last day of my vacation," he wrote his mother on the 21st, "and somehow the best!" By then the weather had turned "cold and sharp." Thanksgiving weather, really, with a delicious edge to the "glorious light" overlooking the harbor. And the East River, "so very blue, the foam and steam from the tugs so dazzlingly white," the white liners with their "red and black funnels like those United Fruit boats across the river, standing at rest" along the South Street piers. And above the river on the Manhattan side "lovely plumes of steam" rising from his white skyscrapers. How happy he was just to be here overlooking the harbor, feet warmed by a small electric stove, the bay off to his right, his books on their shelves, his writing table before him. There was "a kind of keen sensual bliss" in the mere being of it all that was "in itself something like action." So much excitement, so much pure pleasure in the vista and the dream.[34]

He even managed a poem during his week's respite from Sweet's. It was the lyric that would eventually open his first book of poems. "As silent as a mirror is believed"—"Legend" begins—"Realities plunge in silence by." Silence, the silence before a single word is uttered, the silence too into which all words must finally return. Knowledge and belief, reality and the mirror image of reality we call the poem. Love and its mirror image, desire. Desire, and the forms desire takes in its incessant, mocking demands. "Legend," a word rooted in the Word, the Logos, though a word that had dwindled in Crane's own time to suggest mere possibility, a story told, a glimmer of some original vision, the way in which a legend is said to hold a whisper of the truth. But legend too as a listing, an explanation of the symbols on a map, as the poem he was writing held within itself a shadow only of the themes of love and death, illusion and reality, time and memory, which each white building in *White Buildings* would announce, "drop by caustic drop," until "a perfect cry" should "string some constant harmony." Drops on a line, a line of poetry, lights too across the bridge by night, all like white seed pearls laid out on a string.

The search for language and the search for love: were they not part of the same visionary endeavor? A mouth for kissing, for speaking, eating, exploring with, until the human voice uttered itself in trembling ecstasy, a cry costing not less than everything, the body spent time and time again, the body rocking and coming, hoping each time for that elusive perfect ecstasy. *Not* an intimation of the thing, but the thing itself, caught tremulously in the act of language, a coming back and back again to the burning flame, which in turn leaned out to us, beseeching until at last it consumed us:

Twice and twice
(Again the smoking souvenir,
Bleeding eidolon!) and yet again.
Until the bright logic is won
Unwhispering as a mirror
Is believed.

The vision like a moth drawn to a flame, until the self lay shattered by the vision. To approach the flame, to immolate oneself, attempting the impossible brilliance of the poem again and yet again, refusing to regret the inevitable failures and the growing losses. To spend oneself, to burn always with a hard gemlike flame until the self was but a "smoking souvenir," burnt ash leaving behind hints only of the vision seized. What was this but "relentless caper," frolic, theft, the signature of the overreacher, the whole endeavor perhaps only a delusion for all those like Crane, Rimbaud, Blake, or Whitman, "who step/The legend of their youth" into the ecstatic, self-obliterating "bright logic" of that noon.[35]

Legend: the very thing into which Hart Crane was already turning. H. P. Lovecraft, a Cleveland native, writer of horror stories and Gothic tales, fastidious friend of Sam Loveman's—that "queer Lovecraft person," Crane called him[36]—had his own assessment of Crane. He'd known Hart Crane in Cleveland back in 1923, and—seeing him here in New York—noted that he seemed now "a little ruddier, a little puffier, and slightly more moustached." Neither man really cared for the other, and Crane, with his bristling hair, brawling strength, and fox-glint eyes, no doubt frightened Lovecraft as he frightened others. "An egotistical young aesthete," Lovecraft noted condescendingly, "who has attained some real recognition in *The Dial* and other modernist organs, and who has an unfortunate predilection for the wine when it is red."[37]

And five weeks later, in early November, on another visit to 110 Columbia Heights to see Sam Loveman, Lovecraft was surprised to find Crane the legend actually sober, but "boasting over the two-day spree he had just slept off, during which he'd been picked up dead drunk off a street in Greenwich Village by the eminent modernist E. E. Cummings—whom he knows well—and put in a homeward taxi." Poor

Crane, Lovecraft summed up, "I hope he'll sober up with the years, for there's really good stuff & a bit of genius in him."[38] "Who asks for me, the Shelley of my age,/Must lay his heart out for my bed and board." The words, meant for Crane, are Robert Lowell's, written thirty years later, and give a better sense than Lovecraft's of who Crane was, this *Catullus redivivus,* this stalker of sailors, seducing his prey, then scattering "Uncle Sam's/phony gold-plated laurels to the birds."[39]

Crane's two-day spree, if it happened, would have taken place in late October. After all, he had a way of telling the most outrageous stories on himself deadpan for the sake of people like Lovecraft. In any case, he did not record this spree in the letters he sent home. In early November, he went with the Munsons to visit Kenneth Burke and his family at their Andover farmstead in the New Jersey hills. That afternoon, Crane watched with drunken fascination as the Burkes' collie and tomcat ate, slept, and played together. Within hours he'd managed to polish off the better part of a gallon and a half "of fine home made blackberry wine" before going out and making the empty roads and hillsides "resound with songs and merriment." At one point he "sat down in the wrong place" and managed to whack his head against a tree in the darkness. The bump was still there the following morning.[40]

Late that afternoon, he and the Munsons taxied down to the train station and returned to New York in time for dinner with Waldo Frank. Afterwards it was a lecture by A. R. Orage, editor of the recently defunct *New Age* (London), a socialist weekly review of politics, literature, and the arts, and a follower of P. D. Ouspensky and Gurdjieff. Orage's lecture was about the year he'd just spent at the Gurdjieff Institute, Le Prieure, in Fontainebleau, outside Paris. Jean Toomer—who had also been at Le Prieure—had just returned too, much to Crane's delight, and the two men caught up on old times, though Crane could not help noticing that Toomer had somehow changed, and—as far as he was concerned—not necessarily for the better.

The following day, Tate arrived in New York, just up from Washington to begin a job in publishing that Sue Jenkins had found for him. Then it was Underwood, also up from Washington after a two-year hiatus and ready for some fun. The elusive Harry Candee was in New York for several weeks that fall, this time back from a trip to Italy with his mother, but then he was off again—this time for England—before Crane had a chance to see him. Perhaps it was just as well, Crane may have figured, for the Cleveland crowd surely belonged now to another epoch. On November 5th he attended a performance at the Province-town Theatre of *S.S. Glencairn,* a cycle of four of O'Neill's one-acters focusing on the sea: *Bound East for Cardiff, Moon of the Caribbees, In the Zone,* and *The Long Voyage Home.* O'Neill's decision to string these four plays together may have suggested to Crane his own stringing of the "Voyages" together into a sequence, for in a letter to his mother shortly after seeing the O'Neill plays, he mentioned for the first time that the sea poems he had been working on for the past six months would form a six-part structure.

Later that month, he took in a performance of O'Neill's new play, *Desire Under the Elms,* at the Greenwich Village Theatre. It was, he thought, nothing less than "the most astonishing play ever written by an American."[41] Why was it, he wondered, that America's best writers were more highly valued abroad than in America? Take O'Neill, for instance, who had a dozen plays being produced in Europe's great cities: Berlin, Munich, Vienna, Paris, Copenhagen, Budapest. "The American pub-lic," Crane lamented, was "still strangely unprepared for its men of high-er talents," even as Europe itself looked more and more to the New World "for the renascence of a creative spirit."[42]

On November 8th he celebrated "a wild jubilee" with Tate and a few of Underwood's friends.[43] The following week, it was more of the same. Only at night, often into the early hours of morning, did he find time to work on his poems, spending hours polishing just "one or two stubborn lines." His work, he knew, was already "becoming known for its formal perfection and hard glowing polish."[44] But those qualities had been won one way only: not by giving vent to an exuberant spirit, which he did often enough, but rather by dint of hard work, work salted with patience, while he pored over each line until it sang in per-fect pitch with every other.

For if there was the wild Crane, the roaring boy, there was also the poet who could spend hours staring out his window at his beloved East River. Sundays, his one day off from work, he loved to hole up and write. One Sunday he watched the river for hours as it turned slowly dark in the autumn afternoon, "the wind's onslaught across the bay" turning up whitecaps in the river's mouth, prelude to a cold rain. And the gulls: those "chillylooking creatures," who wheeled constantly about "in search of food here in the river as they do hundreds of miles out at sea in the wakes of liners." The week before it had been fog: eigh-teen hours of it. Fog so thick he could not even see the gardens below that led to the river. "All night long," he wrote his mother, there'd been "distant tinklings, buoy bells and siren warnings from river craft. It was like wakening into a dreamland in the early dawn—one wondered where one was with only a milky light in the window and that vague music from a hidden world." Then, rising the next morning, he'd found the air "clear and glittering as usual. Like champagne, or a cold bath to look [at] it. Such a world!"[45]

"Insistently through sleep," he would write a year later in "The Harbor Dawn," recalling this scene, this dreamlike passage from one world into another. Dawn into daylight, the past turning into a present four and a half centuries on, the New World of San Salvador's royal palms Columbus had witnessed become the New Atlantis of the Manhattan skyline across the river, a vague music from a hidden world:

> —a tide of voices—
> They meet you listening midway in your dream.
> The long, tired sounds, fog-insulated noises:
> Gongs in white surplices, beshrouded wails,
> Far strum of foghorns . . . signals dispersed in veils . . .

And then the window slowly going blond and the benzine-rinsed white buildings of Manhattan in the morning sun, those

> Cyclopean towers across Manhattan waters
> —Two—three—bright window-eyes aglitter, disk
> The sun, released—aloft with cold gulls hither.[46]

All this he saw, and it was good.

When his cousin, Helen Hart Hurlbert (Aunt Zell's daughter), had visited Crane in New York in the summer of 1924, she could see that Harold was very much in love. Back in Cleveland, she reported what she'd seen to his mother. Helen "says you are in love," Grace twitted her son in mid-November. "I will address you in that connection when you come home." After all, he hadn't been very "confidential" with her about his affairs of the heart. Well, what he did was up to him, as long as he didn't do something foolish like getting married. Marriage, she feared, would end not only his writing career but all his ambitions.

Keep your head, she advised him. Love was, she knew from her own hard experience, a sickness only.[47] She sent him a new suit as an early Christmas present, something he badly needed. Now, at least when he came home for Christmas, he confessed, he wouldn't look like some Prodigal Son, "returning in woeful tatters."[48] But he had to warn her that since, even after seven months at Sweet's, he'd yet to receive a raise, he would be coming back empty-handed, unable to give her anything except himself.

On the last Saturday night in November, Crane was asked to give a reading. Except for the closet reading he'd done in Munson's tiny living room two years earlier, it was to be his first public appearance. Paul Rosenfeld, who in the past had snubbed both Bill Sommer and Munson, was not on the list of Crane's best friends. Nevertheless, when Rosenfeld phoned Crane inviting him to a reception for Jean Catel, the former French literary critic for the *Mercure de France*, he asked Crane if he would read. "When Rosenfeld gives this sort of party," Crane reported back to his mother, "whatever you may feel about it—you at least know that everybody (spelled with a capital E) in modern American painting, letters and art . . . will be there."[49] But, as fate would have it, he nearly missed his own reading.

The night before the gathering, he came down with ptomaine poisoning from eating something at a local restaurant. Walking home afterwards, he began "to swell up and burn like fire." At first he thought it was a case of hives, brought on by the sheer nervousness of reading before Rosenfeld's distinguished crowd. But back at 110 Columbia Heights he crawled into bed, and then—his pulse pounding—just made it to the sink before he vomited. Afterwards, as he tried to drink a glass of bicarbonate of soda, he lost his "sight and hearing in a kind of rushing and smothering of the blood" and nearly passed out. The attack subsided, but later, "lying rigidly still" in bed, it began all over again. He spent the rest of the night on the toilet, evacuating "in both directions," though he somehow managed to get himself over to the office on Saturday for his half day of work. Then back to bed until it was time to go to Rosenfeld's. What alkalithia and Milk of Magnesia and hot baths could not accomplish, five whiskies and sodas did, and he finally revived, looking in no time the "picture of health."[50]

The effort turned out to be worth it. As Crane had thought, the New York literary crowd had turned out in force, and they seemed genuinely pleased to hear him. Alfred Stieglitz was there, and Georgia

O'Keeffe, along with Jean Toomer, the photographer Paul Strand, Van Wyck Brooks, Edmund Wilson, Lewis Mumford, and the composer Aaron Copland, who provided music for the evening. Two other poets also gave readings: Alfred Kreymborg and Marianne Moore. Moore read first in her "tiny" voice and seemed—to Crane's eyes—no less nervous than he had been. Then it was his turn. Then the more self-assured Kreymborg. Finally, Jean Catel got up and read for what seemed forever a poem, all in French, by Paul Valéry. Crane listened, half mystified, half bored.

Reading as "deliberately and distinctly" as he could manage, Crane himself began with three lyrics: "Chaplinesque," "Sunday Morning Apples," and his new poem, "Paraphrase." Then, urged on by the others, he read the whole of "For the Marriage of Faustus and Helen." Afterwards, Kreymborg told him that the last poem was magnificent, and Toomer came up to him and whispered that even the conservative Van Wyck Brooks had clapped. Until that point, Crane had turned down all invitations to read in public. "I am no vocalist," he told his mother, and—besides—he too easily got stage fright. But he was determined not to be "a wall flower" before such an audience.[51] He knew his poems were good—no one had to convince him of that—but to have been asked to read before he even had a book out, and to have won the applause of that distinguished company. *That* was something.

There was another side to this world of poetry, however. No matter how he'd tried to extricate himself from the literary wars raging between the Munson and Josephson factions, he seemed unable to do so. Then, in late November, the issue came to a boil when he attended a meeting at the offices of *1924*. Someone present proposed that the neo-Romantic aesthetics which Frank and Munson had been advocating be attacked in the pages of the magazine. Crane had already given several poems to the issue, but now he offered to withdraw them, out of loyalty to his two friends. On December 3rd, over lunch with Munson, he explained what had happened. Yet, while he was temperamentally aligned to Munson and Frank's response to literature, he was also catholic enough to be attracted by the gritty toughness he found in Josephson, Cowley, and Burke.

Munson refused to be appeased. Later that same day, he wrote Crane, demanding a fuller explanation. Was Crane with him in this or wasn't he? Crane wrote back. Yes, he was behind Munson, but he was not blind to the fact that much of what the other side had to say also made sense. Perhaps Munson was becoming a bit too rigid in his think-ing. After all, there were parts of Munson's platform that he personally found "unnecessarily unwieldy, limited and stolid."[52] Munson's blast-ing Josephson in absentia the year before, for instance, or Gurdjieff's "birth control, re-swaddling and new-synthesizing . . . movement," which Munson had swallowed whole.[53]

Munson demanded too much in the way of loyalty, and Crane's own temperament was too easygoing to get caught up in such battles. One had to "be broken up to live," he insisted, "confused" enough to be able to see both sides of an issue. It was Keats's negative capability he was defending, this ability to remain in doubts without tidying every-thing up into one overarching theory. "I am growing more and more sick of factions, gossip, jealousies, recriminations, excoriations and the whole literary shee-bang right now," he ended. What he really wanted was "a little more solitude."[54] Besides, Munson had a high-paying job as editor of one of those more mainstream magazines, *Psychology,* and with money and position was becoming duller and more entrenched. Screw that. That was his father's way.

When Munson met Crane for lunch again five days later, he was more dissatisfied than ever with what he saw now as Crane's "oppor-tunism" in trying to remain friendly with both sides. If he wasn't care-ful, Munson told Crane half jokingly, he might get himself "excommunicated" from Munson's circle. Crane smiled, but the barb stuck. That evening, still brooding over the remark, he shot off a short note telling Munson to go ahead and excommunicate him. "I am not prepared to welcome threats," he added, "from any quarters that I know of—which are based on assumptions of my literary ambitions in rela-tion to one group, faction, 'opportunity,' or another."[55] And with that letter the long friendship that had spanned the past seven years, during much of which Munson had been Crane's closest literary confidant, came to a jarring close.

Three months later, Crane would hear through Toomer and Frank just how much Munson had come to regret what had happened. But it was too late; the break was final. He and Munson were still friends, Crane reassured his mother, but it was time that each went his own way now. The truth was that Munson had long ago begun to bore him with his politicizing of every agenda. There would be letters from time to time between the two, but the closeness, the sense of a shared vision: that was gone forever.

For the next two weeks, Crane worked at the new catalogue each day and late into the evenings. Only on Christmas Eve was he able to get away, taking the night train out to Cleveland and arriving home on Christmas morning. He had not been back in twenty months, but even so he could stay only a day and a half before he was on the train heading for New York and the office to make up for lost time.

New Year's Eve he spent at Squarcialupi's on Perry Street in the Village. There was booze and dancing to the Victrola, which began scratching its way through the stack of records shortly before midnight, so that Crane was out searching for needles when the whistles signaling the beginning of 1925 began blowing. By then the streets were nearly empty, but those who were out hugged each other, dancing and singing. Caught up in the moment, he began singing an ersatz version of Gregorian chant in what Latin he could muster. Then back to the restaurant, where he drank until five in the morning. By six, he was back in his apartment and asleep, only to be awakened a few hours later by the telephone: it was a telegram from his mother wishing him a Happy New Year. Hours later, refreshed and on his way to breakfast, he stopped off at a Western Union office to send his mother and grand-mother best wishes by return.

That first Sunday in January Crane slept in again, then walked out into the winter air to have a hearty breakfast at the local diner. On his way back, he stopped to buy a quarter's worth of marigolds and nar-cissi from the local florist, a funny old woman with a pockmarked face and a rat's nest of hair who liked to flirt with him. She'd caught him going by her window and had beckoned him in. It was the usual refrain:"Well my handsome Good Looking again!" or, "How's my big boy?" and, "Ain't he a dandy!"[56] Flowers and Christmas decorations and strong January sunshine reflecting off the snow-covered roofs of the piers below him. And Tate due over with Sue Jenkins and Slater Brown for tea in the afternoon. Life could be grand.

One afternoon that January, Crane, Brown, Jenkins, and the Tates strolled about the Village, pausing before Number 3 Washington Square, one of the elegant brick row houses facing the park, and the residence of Edmund Wilson. Having met the eminence two months before, Crane took it on himself to pay him homage now by dancing an Irish jig before his door. He was just warming up when he was whisked away by the others, before Wilson (if he was home) was aware of Crane's clowning. Later that afternoon, Crane and his friends found themselves at a shooting gallery on Times Square, where they had their photos taken. One showed Crane, Brown, and Tate posing as tough detectives—"Dead-Eye Dicks"—leaning against the bar of a Wild West saloon. "Lodging by Night, Week, or Hour," a sign in the background read. And: "This is No Man's Land—Come in and START Something." That sign caught more of Crane's secret life, and of what his life would soon become, than anyone could have realized at the time.

On the evening of the 24th, standing on the fire escape at Sweet's Catalogue, twenty stories above Bryant Park and the New York Public Library, he watched the strange green light of a lunar eclipse begin spreading over the city, until everything was plunged into an eerie darkness. Below: antlike crowds scurrying out of subway exits, curious to watch as the paper moon high above them disappeared. In early February, it was fog, fog everywhere, day after day of it. "What with the bedlam of bells, grunts, whistles, screams and groans of all the river and harbor buoys, which have kept up an incessant grinding program as noisome as the midnight passing into new year," he wrote his mother, he hadn't managed six hours of sleep in three days. It was like living in "the mouth of hell, not being able to see six feet from the window and yet hearing all that weird jargon constantly."[57]

Then, on the evening of February 28th, in the midst of writing the Rychtariks, he felt the apartment begin swaying back and forth. It was, he wrote when he resumed his letter the following day, "the most sickening and helpless feeling I hope to ever have."[58] When the quake had struck, he'd raced downstairs and out into the street, which was already crowded with neighbors as nervous as himself. Finally, when things seemed to quiet down, he returned to his apartment and began drinking to steady himself.

But Brooklyn had its compensations, among them good, cheap food. With the help of Frank, Crane discovered a Spanish restaurant in the neighborhood that served "the finest ruby-colored and rose-scented wine in N.Y. besides delicious smoky tasting sardines and hidalgo-esque chicken."[59] They'd been able to tap into the wine supply there, it turned out, only because Frank, who spoke Spanish fluently, had first convinced the owners that he and Crane were not revenue officers.

By the winter of '25 he at last had enough poems for a book. All that was left to do was put the finishing touches on the "Voyages" sequence and rework a few poems until they matched the finish of the rest. *The Bridge*, he had decided, would make a book by itself. He would call his first book *White Buildings*, a title he told his mother he'd taken from the work of the Italian painter, di Chirico, though the words carried a great many private echoes for him as well. They were after all what he saw when he looked out his window. They were also the impossible condition to which all his poems aspired. A book, he felt, would at last give him "some credit in the world."[60]

A small-time printer named Sam Jacobs, owner of the Polytype Press—located at 39 West 8th Street—offered to publish the book in a modest private edition for next to nothing. Not only was Jacobs willing to set and design the book free of charge; he even volunteered to pay for the paper and the binding. Because his was not a commercial press, he explained, he would not be able to distribute copies, but at least Crane would have his book. Crane accepted, without realizing just how strapped for money Jacobs was. Jacobs would have to print the book page by stubborn page whenever he could find a free moment between jobs. Yet, with all the goodwill in the world, *White Buildings* was soon hopelessly stalled. Then work on the new Sweet's Catalogue began picking up again and once again Crane found himself working long hours overtime without compensation.

He grew edgy and tired, resenting all this "going around and around,"[61] pounding the streets on errands, until he felt his legs or nerves would give out at any moment. Emil had broached the possibility of the two of them sailing to Norway with the money Emil expected from his late father's estate, but soon enough the lawyers had tied up the money and the trip had to be scrapped. Once again Crane considered taking a job as ship's writer, a soft job disseminating shipboard news on the journey out to and back from South America. In fact, it was only the thought of getting *White Buildings* into final shape that kept him in New York. For, if there was the "usual bacchanale of life" around the city, the place was finally beginning to seem like more of the same. He needed to escape to some quieter place "to do the work, the *real* work."[62] Though, looking back, even he had to admit he'd managed a good deal of exceptional verse in the past two years.

By mid-April, realizing that Jacobs would never get the book printed, Crane gave the manuscript to Frank, hoping he could get Boni & Liveright to publish it. He knew that almost all commercial publishers viewed poetry—especially poetry like his own—as "a dead financial loss," since the audience for it was pitiably small. Still, a few were willing to publish the odd volume if they thought it might flatter "their literary judgment before the public" and prove them "to be more interested in literature than in the so-called 'best-sellers.'" The problem was, as Frank had explained to Crane, that with radio and the craze for crossword puzzles "and other such baby-rattles for the great American public" expanding, sales of serious books in the past year had plummeted and most publishers now shied "at such philanthropic interests as good poetry."[63] If Liveright turned down the book, at least Crane would understand why.

When several weeks had passed and Frank had still not found the right opportunity to show the manuscript to Liveright, Crane decided to try elsewhere. At Jacobs's recommendation, he sent it off to the publishing house of Thomas Seltzer. Jacobs, who had done the composition work for Cummings's *Tulips and Chimneys*, was still willing to do the composition for *White Buildings* gratis. Crane wanted an edition of five hundred. Including stock, makeup, lockup and presswork, casing, shipping, and binding, he figured the cost would come to a modest $200. He was sure, he told Seltzer, that there were five hundred admirers of good poetry out there somewhere, and he personally guaranteed the sale of one hundred and fifty copies through mailing lists and friends. Frank and O'Neill had promised blurbs for the jacket, and most reviewers, he emphasized, would treat the book well. ("There won't be any explosions of praise when the book appears," he told his mother more frankly, but having a book out would at least make him *feel* like a poet.)[64]

In the midst of all this Crane had a call from Aunt Zell, in New York on business, inviting him out to dinner. Good old Zell, who seemed to "grow mellower and more jovial, generous and pleasant" with time. Of all his relatives—with the exception of his mother and grandmother—she was about his "only pride or satisfaction." When he arrived at the restaurant, he was surprised to find his old friend, Carl Schmitt, with her. Ten years almost since the two men had seen each other, and here was Schmitt, married now and living at an artists' colony in Norwalk, Connecticut, at the moment doing church frescoes up in Mamaroneck. "I certainly was glad to see him again," Crane reported to his mother afterwards. "More than I had thought I would be. He was as always, looked and acted exactly the same as we remember him."[65] After dinner and a show, the two men walked down to 14th Street together, where Crane hugged his old friend, then disappeared into the subway for the trip back to Brooklyn.

As the specter of another hot, sticky summer working overtime to prepare yet another catalogue loomed before him, Crane seriously considered quitting. He'd been with the company a year now and had yet to receive a single raise. Two more years of this and he would surely see his imagination permanently muzzled. At Christmas, during his flying trip to Cleveland, he'd run into his former bosses from Corday & Gross, who'd told him he was the best copywriter they'd ever had and that they'd made a big mistake in letting him go. If he ever came back to Cleveland, he could rest assured a job would be waiting for him. And though he had no intention of going back, it was enough to give him the courage to ask Sweet's for a raise. The request, he was informed, would be taken into consideration. At the same time, his father, in New York on business, offered him a position that sounded so good he almost took it on the spot, until C.A. made the mistake of telling his son he would have to shave off his wispy-looking moustache. That ended both the conversation and the job offer.

A month later, having still heard nothing from Sweet's, Crane went in to see his boss, demanding to know where he stood. There would be no raise, he was informed, at least for the present. Nothing for it then but to hand in his two weeks' notice. June began inauspiciously enough, with a heat wave that laid him low. Then his urethritis returned, and with it intense headaches and difficulty urinating. Once again he was reduced to a diet of buttermilk and crackers. Sleep too eluded him. Then toothaches so severe he feared abscesses. On top of which he was broke. On Saturday, June 6th, he picked up his final paycheck and walked out the door of Sweet's Catalogue for the last time, then went over to Grand Central and boarded the New York–Albany train for Pawling, New York, seventy miles north of the city.

Slater Brown and Sue Jenkins—newly married—had just bought a farm in Patterson, an old settlement southeast of Pawling, and had invited him to spend a month with them. There he might loaf at his ease, or help with the chores as he wished. A chance for fresh air, then, for exercise, for "relaxation from the tension of the desk," which had nearly crushed the spirit out of him.[66] Emil would take over the apartment until he returned. On the eve of his departure, Crane got the news that Seltzer had decided to pass on his poems. There was nothing he could do now but send the manuscript out into the world in search of another publisher. This time it was Harcourt, where his old friend Hal Smith might have some clout. Why couldn't some patron of the arts give him enough cash to live on for six months and let him write the poems he knew he had it in him to write, if only he could find the time?

8 / THE HAWK'S
FAR STEMMING VIEW

PATTERSON, CLEVELAND, NEW YORK
JUNE 1925–APRIL 1926

LATE ON THE AFTERNOON of 6 June 1925, Slater Brown and Sue Jenkins picked Crane up at the Pawling train depot for the seven-mile ride back to the farm they'd recently bought for a song. The couple had married following Sue Jenkins's divorce from Jim Light, and had decided to leave New York and start a new life for themselves in upstate New York. The farm itself dated back to the early 1770s and still lacked insulation and indoor plumbing. Situated off a country road between rural Pawling and even more rural Sherman, Connecticut, the house sat surrounded by a hundred acres of old, untended apple orchards, one of many farms abandoned by farmers who had died or moved elsewhere, tired of struggling with glacial rock and glacial weather. The Browns had christened their home "Robber Rocks" after a cave used for contraband stolen by Tory sympathizers from Washington's supply trains as they shifted supplies in the war against British troops.

As they had at Woodstock a year and a half earlier, Crane's spirits soared in the summer outdoors. He felt terrific, he assured his grandmother after a week and a half of it. Guernsey milk, fresh butter, fresh eggs, fresh vegetables, all supplied by a local farmer. "And so much outdoors exercise that I am brown as a nut already with the sun and all greased up at the joints." With his new regimen, his urethritis had disappeared almost overnight and he was sleeping now "like a top" on a mattress Slater had laid over an old rope bed.[1] There was work to do, naturally, and he pitched in, clearing tons of wood and rubbish and old plaster from the house, building bookcases, shelves, screens, and tables, as well as scrubbing and rubbing old wide-board floors, or painting the weathered and dilapidated exterior clapboards of the house a gleaming white.

Mornings the three rose at half past five, the sun already up, the birds up, the air crisp and sweet. Brown had bought an old Tin Lizzie for thirty-five dollars, and every few days he and Crane drove into Pawling for supplies and the local news. It was exactly the kind of place Crane wanted for himself when he came into some money, he told his mother and grandmother. "Perfect quiet and rolling hills" all round and blueberries galore, "great patches of bushes laden to bending with the beautiful milky-blue fruit that looks the freshest thing on earth."[2] Better, there would be huckleberries, raspberries, blackberries, currants, gooseberries, even elderberries, as the season unfolded.

Caught up in the fever of the Florida real estate boom, Grace too was seriously considering buying property, in Miami. Crane tried to caution her not to make that mistake. "Everyone—even the farmers around here," he advised her, were "scraping their coins together and rushing down to Miami to buy little lots." True, some speculators had made fortunes. But the boom was just too uncertain. This was a fool's gold rush, he was sure, one more wild Wall Street speculation, something for suckers to invest in. One of these days the land speculation thing would overheat and blow up, and when it did, it would take her investment with it. It was one giant hallucination, as if everyone—winners and losers alike—had "all sat down together at a great mass meeting and agreed to swear they each saw Jesus bathing on the beach." Besides, she already had the Isle of Pines plantation, only a day and a half further away than Miami, where she could live far more cheaply than in Florida. Or what about buying land around Patterson, which was still cheap and plentiful? Slater, in fact, had already offered him a lot along with cut timber if he would only build himself a cabin and settle down.

The problem was that all the money Crane had to his name was barely enough for a one-way ticket back to New York. Still, for the moment he was "content to drift a little, let things take care of themselves," reduce his needs to a minimum, and avail himself of "as much time for free breathing and meditation as possible."[3] Once back in New York, he told himself, he was bound to find work, though he still dreamed of voyages. A job like Emil's as ship's writer or even as night-watchman on the South American line paid sixty-five dollars a month, but his expenses would be taken care of and he would have New York at one end of the journey and Buenos Aires at the other, with twelve thousand miles of ocean to contemplate and three weeks out of every eight to devote to his writing.

Only the July Fourth celebrations broke the country quiet, when a busload of New Yorkers—Malcolm and Peggy Cowley, Allen Tate and Caroline Gordon, among them—arrived with a case of contraband gin, supplemented by a stash of hard cider from one of the local farms. After a month of solitude, Crane was ready to party. He dressed up as a twenties Hollywood version of an African cannibal, decorating himself in red and brown house paint, placing a small keg atop his head, and donning a pair of cerise drawers. For three days the party ebbed and flowed, with midnight swims, tree climbing, blindman's buff, rides in wheelbarrows over the old corduroy fields. Whatever whim possessed the revelers they pursued—and none more so than Crane. But aside from that one "blowout," he drank nothing. If he drank in the city, he rationalized to himself, it was because of the pressures of office work, and now that pressure was gone.

It was during his three-day celebration that he conceived two more poems: "Passage" and "The Wine Menagerie." After he'd performed his cannibal dance on Saturday afternoon, still dressed in his costume du jour, he sat down under some lilac bushes near the doorway to Robber Rocks and began pouring a box of salt onto the Victrola as if he were pouring sand. Now and again he would look up into an overhanging cedar, repeating over and over, "Where the cedar leaf divides the sky . . . Where the cedar leaf divides the sky . . . I was promised an improved infancy." These lines would become—had already become—the opening of "Passage":

Where the cedar leaf divides the sky
I heard the sea.
In sapphire arenas of the hills
I was promised an improved infancy.

To leave behind in the ravine with all the other garbage one's memory and one's past: all that baggage, that "casual louse" which killed even as it recalled, wakening what awful "alleys with a hidden cough"? Crane as noble savage here in the deep woods of Patterson, where the surrounding sapphire hills reminded him of the rise and trough of the open sea, without a care in the world, the summer sun at its apogee. And then to realize in the "shadows of boulders"—time itself lengthening down one's back—that one could never lose one's past. Wherever you went, there you were. *Sunt lacrimae rerum*. Tears, useless tears, like rain down "the bronze gongs of my cheeks" for the "chimney-sooted heart of man." Black Pierrot in cerise drawers. The fire within, signaled by the soot of Crane's outlandish costume: the grotesque image of the comic exile assembling "a too well known biography."

And then, beneath the "opening laurel" of his infant fame as poet, to be aware of death the thief with Crane's "stolen book in hand." Death, time, rumor, a book rejected for publication. Why continue? the thief taunts him. Why try? Because Crane still had somehow to justify his few years on earth, to hold death at arm's length. And yet it was death, Crane knew, that always held the winning hand. Death, yawning and already beginning to close the book on him. It was how all human endeavor ended, with time swallowing not only the poet but all achievement "in a glittering abyss" of sand—time's undecipherable voice crashing against those "unpaced beaches" where no mortal could long walk, as he strolled unerringly into the annihilating center of the setting sun.

For once, then, he had seen into the heart of the mystery, the salt taste of truth's cold springs with their "icy speeches," but a truth too which, "committed to the page," was inevitably lost. He knew that, while the others danced and joked, in the midst of so much music, booze, and friendship, he alone had once again been granted the ecstatic salt bitterness of truth. And how bring back to them the vision so that they too might see what he had seen? Even to ask that question was to swim back into time and memory, the woods about Patterson, a cedar tree, and the lengthening shadows of late afternoon edging now toward darkness, the *ticktock* of each gasping hour passing across the clock's round face in its "dozen particular decimals." One. Two. Three. Four.[4]

A week after he drafted "Passage," Crane received the manuscript of *White Buildings* back from fame's thief, this time in the guise of the publishing firm of Harcourt. "It came back . . . yesterday," he wrote Waldo Frank on July 14th. So Harcourt too had been unable to "make anything out of most of the poems." But why his poems should remain obscure puzzled him. Was he any more obscure than Sir John Davies or Donne or Baudelaire or Rimbaud or Valéry or Emily Dickinson? He sent Frank a copy of the manuscript to look over and comment on, forced now to try Liveright once again. Even he was unhappy with "at least half the poems," he had to admit, but what was he to do with a book that contained work going back eight years?[5] What he'd written in the past two years he felt strongly about, but if he kept the manuscript until he was happy with every goddamn poem, he'd never publish a book.

Then "Passage" was rejected. He'd sent the poem, which he thought "the most interesting and conjectural thing" he'd yet written, on to Marianne Moore at *The Dial*, only to have it returned, tail between its legs. Yes, she'd been moved by the poem's imagination and sensibility, the fastidious Moore had to admit, but the thing was simply too complicated, its "multiform content" revealing "a lack of simplicity and cumulative force."[6] Was she really talking of *his* poetry, he complained to Frank, or of her own?

In mid-July, he heard from his mother that the house was at last going to be sold. It would be just a matter of time before he was summoned back to Cleveland to help close the place, something he welcomed as much as death itself. Always, it seemed, always there was some "immediate duty or requirement" other than writing to be performed.[7] Yet the truth was that, in his six weeks at Robber Rocks, he'd spent a total of five hours writing, and he was so broke now he didn't even have the three cents necessary to post a letter to Frank. He loved being up in the country, loved painting the house and gardening. And yet . . .

Crane celebrated his twenty-sixth birthday in New York, en route to Cleveland. There was a week of heavy drinking and a night with someone he'd picked up, before he set out for his old home. When his urethritis flared up again, he went back on a diet of buttermilk and swore to give up drinking for at least a year. The resolution would last ten weeks, itself a record. Finally, on the morning of July 27th, the day the house was sold, he reached Cleveland. His mother and grandmother would relocate to Miami, and Cleveland would begin its transformation into "a myth of remembrance."[8] Only his myth of a father would stay on, selling his chocolates.

Within a week, half the furniture had been sold and carted off, and the house itself reduced to a skeleton of its former self. "Minds are changed each day about what I am to have preserved for myself," he wrote the Browns. He was being translated out here into Hungarian by a friend of the Rychtariks (a member of the MA group based in Vienna), and had been invited "to reword into proper paraphrases" the young Hungarian's "rather hobbling translations of his own poems," which in truth rather embarrassed Crane. "Cannibal songs and Adam before the Cross, etc.—such titles and subjects."[9] Like all the young Europeans, this one was also mad about Whitman.

Two weeks later, Crane sent the Browns another report. The place was nearly empty now, though he still hoped to get away with another Indian rug. He was getting good at these petty heists—antiquities, portraits, stacks of books, knickknacks—as good as he'd been at stealing biscuits at the general store in Sherman. In late August, he sent everything he'd collected—his "assorted atrocities"[10]—by freight back to Patterson: his desk, chair, five crates of books (including a slightly battered set of the unreliable *Everyman's Encyclopaedia*), and his trunk, crammed with (among other things) his mother's old clothes. It was everything he'd managed to save from his past, and it wasn't much. Actually, his mother and grandmother had been so distraught by the move that he doubted if they would have noticed had the house itself "slid en masse for fifty feet."[11] He itched to get back east, but was so broke he had to wait for his mother to offer to pay his carfare, and she meant to keep him in Cleveland for as long as possible.

During his stay in Cleveland, he did manage to get down to Brandywine to see Bill Sommer for the first time in three years. His old friend had been sound asleep on a sofa when he'd shown up, his "great bulk in white undershirt and loose white duck pants" rising groggily to let Crane in through the battered screen door, his "black eyes revolving in the . . . dusty-white miller face like a sardonic Pierrot's." That afternoon, the two talked in Sommer's schoolhouse studio, "surrounded by a flower garden and filled with plentiful new wonders of line and color,"[12] Sommer chewing tobacco while Crane smoked cigars

amid the sound of crickets. The reason Sommer had never done anything about his fame, in spite of his best efforts on the man's behalf,
Crane had finally learned that afternoon, was that the man couldn't
bear to part with any of his paintings. In that case, of course, there was
no way he was ever going to have an audience, a fact that did not seem
particularly to trouble him. Crane could only scratch his head in wonder. How could anyone throw away fame like that?

Crane, strolling down the imitation marble corridor of an apart-
ment building in Cleveland to see his friend, Bert Ginther, shouting the
same mantra over and over: "Painted emulsion of snow, eggs, yarn,
coal, SHIT." Ah yes, "Painted emulsion of snow, eggs, yarn, coal, SHIT."[13]
The line, with modifications, would embed itself in "The Wine
Menagerie," a poem that owed some of its origins to the drunken
Fourth of July celebrations and some again to his drunken week in
New York:

> Against the imitation onyx wainscoting
> (Painted emulsion of snow, eggs, yarn, coal, manure)
> Regard the forceps of the smile that takes her . . .

Delusions, imitations: things pretending to be what they were not.
Imitation marble, imitation love, eros as the gate to entrapment.

All that summer he worked on "The Wine Menagerie," fascinated
with the idea behind the poem but dissatisfied with its execution. It was
a brilliant, complex poem (perhaps too complex) about the Dionysian
world of drink and delusion, a world where wine redeemed the sight
by cutting away the "mustard scansions of the eyes." A poem too about
the ways in which one censored oneself to live in what the world liked
to think of as the norm. But it was in the "slumbering gaze" of the
inebriate that a leopard—the cat attendant, according to the ancient
myth, on Bacchus, god of wine—ranged "always in the brow," stealth-
ily on the prowl, hunting its prey. Malcolm Cowley for one had seen
this foxlike glint in Crane's eye when Crane was drunk and on the
prowl, and even he had had to flinch before it.

"The Wine Menagerie" is set in a New York speakeasy in mid-
winter, the poet staring into rows of liquor bottles—those "glozening

decanters." (Old words these, words Kit Marlowe or Michael Drayton might have used as Crane used Marlowe and Drayton's names as covers when he was on the prowl. Like "glozening"—a word meaning to flatter or to lie to, as liquor changed one's perspective on things.) In any case, those brown, green, blue, opaque bottles lining the mirror behind the bar. The poet stares into those bottles and sees the street reflected rosily there—the traffic, people outside somewhere walking. But he sees himself as well, many times over, his face clownishly distorted, misshapen by the "crescents on their bellies," as though the bottles were sirens beckoning. He hears the bartender pouring shots into shot glasses, beer into beer glasses, whiskey, Scotch, wine, gin, rum, until the gurgling and plash sound to him like some "Slow applause" flowing into "liquid cynosures." Cynosure: dog's tail, the north star, light of the world, the point that guides us on, and holds our attention. A boozer's vision: blessèd liquor in a glass.

But if it is winter outside, inside his mind it is August, eternal summer. Percussive jazz plays on a nickelodeon as he watches a man smile at a woman, who smiles back, her forceps smile (the fear of children there), her large eyes mallets until time—that serpent—sheds its skin, unmaking "an instant of the world." And now those mallets strike softly the man's eyes: sweet lies, sweet guile, until one can almost hear the hammered bells of "some whispered carillon." An urchin enters the bar with a canister to be filled with beer for his father or his mother, the fruit of some momentary liaison perhaps, the boy himself—like Crane—the incarnation of love's entrapment. And now the poet's attention is focused back on the game of eros he has been watching. For it is a game, a game played by countless billions over the centuries.

"New thresholds, new anatomies!" the poet understands, "new thresholds" of sexual experience to be crossed, "new anatomies" in women's bodies to be explored, the ecstasy of being caught up in the smile of "another's will," like that man over there against the background lie of onyx wainscoting ("Painted emulsion of snow, eggs, yarn, coal, SHIT"). He himself, he thinks, might also win the dream of "a receptive smile," such as this woman has bestowed upon this lucky fellow. He too might snare "new purities," though he knows the lying bells he hears ringing in his head have been tolled many times before "by every tongue in hell." And now he catches himself. Eat and be eaten, he thinks, the rule of all such sexual encounters. The bondage of sex and offspring. "Ruddy, the tooth implicit of the world," a marriage, quarrels, recriminations, angers resolved in the hungers of the bed, an expulsion, a mother's interminable ruses and demands, until one's family home is put on the block. This, then, the savage cold reality, what awaits those who follow that lying smile somewhere down the line. It is what "Passage" had called the "glittering abyss" of death. It is sure oblivion; it is our "dim inheritance of sand."

The poet looks again at the woman, to whom he too is dangerously attracted—the moves, the smiles, the flashing eyes. Eyes such as those the classic mankillers have flashed: Judith, who made love to a drunken Holofernes before she cut off his head. Or Salome, who drove Herod half insane with her swaying and rippling body, until he gave her what she wanted: the lopped head of the prophet John. Images of castration, impotence, entrapment. Better to walk away from all this, Crane understands, the "frozen billows" of cold semen and cold reality having shaken him again. Better to remain apart, like Stravinsky's poor Petrushka, Pierrot's double, exile and sad clown pivoting and writhing back upon himself. Not voyager now but voyeur: a man and a woman in love, and Crane's understanding that that world is not for him. Nor is that world what it seems to be. Nor is he what he is not. "Painted emulsion of snow, eggs, yarn, coal, SHIT."[14]

By early September, he was back at 110 Columbia Heights. Having lost his childhood home, he was more desperate than ever to have some place he could call his own. He had the Browns out scouring the country around Patterson for something he could afford, whatever *that* meant. Sue Brown wrote him, urging him to buy eighty acres of land with a cellar hole sitting in the middle of it from their neighbor, Charlie Jennings. Five bucks an acre: two hundred down, two hundred later in cash. Too much. Then a better deal: ten acres on the top slopes of a mountain overlooking the valley, part of a parcel of one hundred and sixty acres with a Revolutionary War–era Dutch house that had just been bought by a friend of Slater's, Bina Flynn. The land was only half a mile from Robber Rocks, and "plenty to spread out in."[15] It could be his for two hundred.

It was the only way to live, Crane had convinced himself. He would buy the land and, the following summer, build himself a cabin there. Then he would roll in the lush grass of his ten acres and offer up prayers of thanksgiving. The only problem was that the land was heavily wooded and there were no access roads. That and the fact that he didn't have five cents, much less two hundred dollars to his name. But that was not going to stop him now. First he wrote his Aunt Zell for a loan at 6 percent, but the idea of her nephew buying inaccessible acreage made no sense and she turned him down. Then he tried the Rychtariks, explaining that if he didn't act soon, the land would slip away. When he'd seen them in Cleveland recently they'd offered to help, and now he was writing to take them up on their offer. Reluctantly they agreed, and Crane had his land.

On September 17th he went back up to Patterson. By then the Browns had turned the largest downstairs room of their house into "Hart's Room" where he soon had his collection of antiquities (gifts from Harry Candee, Wilbur Underwood, and others) spread out, Bill Sommer's pictures hung, and the Navajo rug from the house in Cleveland rolled out across the wide pine-board floor. From old oak lumber lying about he slapped together a table and some bookshelves. To finish it all off, he hung a Currier and Ives print that had come with the house: a colored lithograph of one of "Barnum's Gallery of Wonders" displaying the eighteen-year-old, 628-pound "Miss Jane Campbell, the Great Connecticut Giantess." Jane was family, for Jane had been a friend of Charlie Jennings's mother, Rosella, who'd lived at Robber Rocks until her death at eighty-seven the year before. Crane had fallen in love with the Connecticut Giantess, and now her picture had been bequeathed to him. His mother's garments he distributed among his women friends: a pair of black and white check riding breeches to Sue Brown; a brown hound's-tooth topcoat to Eleanor "Fitzi" Fitzgerald; a baby blue negligée to Caroline Gordon; and a girl's lace dress, white with pale pink ribbons, which would be passed about over the coming years for party games.

The late September weather was heaven. "Big fires in the evenings," he wrote the Rychtariks, "long walks, big meals almost entirely of lettuce, carrots, beets, turnips, squash . . . just taken from the garden." Sue had taken to country living with a vengeance, turning out jellies, jams, pickles. And the hills about were covered now with wild grapes, quince (with its "kid glove golden fruit"), elderberries, apples.[16] At the beginning of October, Crane and the Browns made six gallons of ale and set it out in a huge crock by the chimney to age. Then it was cider, which they brewed out in the distillery Brown had built in the shed, though Crane, still on the wagon after his July debacle, heroically refrained.

Refrained, that is, until he returned to Brooklyn on October 11th, where he rented a room for two weeks at 65 Columbia Heights, until his old apartment at 110 (which the Opffer brothers had sublet) could once again be turned over to him. At once he began celebrating his newfound sobriety by partying with old friends from his Woodstock sojourn and polishing off jugs of bad applejack, an experiment that nearly killed him. When an inebriated Crane stopped by Sam Loveman's apartment one night soon after arriving in New York, H. P. Lovecraft, who was there with Loveman, was shocked at Crane's appearance. How sad, he confided to his journal, to witness "a real poet and a man of taste, descendant of an ancient Connecticut family and a gentleman to his fingertips," becoming "the slave of dissipated habits," habits which were already beginning to "ruin both his constitution and his still striking handsomeness!"[17]

It was the start of two weeks of nonstop parties, mostly in the Village, mostly in the company of the "engrossing" young poet, Laura Riding Gottschalk, or "Rideshalk-Godding," as Crane dubbed her. For a while it looked as if the two were inseparable, and some (who did not know about Emil) began whispering that Crane and Riding were an item. At the end of October, Crane drove up with Riding and a second couple to Patterson for what turned out to be yet another wild weekend. From house to house they sailed, beginning with Robber Rocks and circling out from there in white rings of tumult, Crane dangling an omnipresent jug of hard cider over his shoulder while he recited poetry or shouted his opinion on the state of the art. For her part, Riding shouted back her own strong views, and the two danced and danced late into the night to jazz, grabbing rides as they glided from house to house, Faustus and his Helen, until toward dawn they staggered back up the dirt roads to Robber Rocks.

Back in New York, Crane kept searching for a job he could stomach. He just missed a dream, he told the Browns, as deck yeoman on a steamer bound for South America, "20 minutes work a day, all freedom of ship, mess with officers or any first class passengers that seemed colloquial, white uniform, brass buttons, cap; meditation on the sun deck all day long, and seventy-five dollars a month clear sailing!" In fact, he'd been given the nod by the chief officer aboard ship over in Brook-lyn and had taken the subway back over to the line's offices in Man-hattan for final approval, only to learn that the office had just sent someone else over to fill the job. If he would come back in two weeks when the next steamer arrived, perhaps then. "We must have passed under the river," he sighed. He also knew there was little chance of another plum like that becoming available any time soon. Barring that, Crane asked Kenneth Burke at *The Dial* if he could do some paid reviews for Marianne Moore, whom Crane had taken to referring to as "the Right Reverend Miss Mountjoy."[18]

In the meantime, he sent off "The Wine Menagerie," along with a copy of "Passage," to T. S. Eliot at *The Criterion* in London. Both were rejected. For several months he had been waiting for "Voyages" II–V (the four new poems in the sequence) to appear together in the *Guardian*, a Philadelphia publication, along with an introductory essay that Tate had written. Instead, the most recent issue of the magazine announced ("unforgivably," in Crane's eyes)[19] the appearance in the next issue of a suite of four remarkable "Voyages" by Allen Tate. Frank, still trying to interest Liveright in publishing *White Buildings*, was given an updated copy of the manuscript. Crane had been led to believe that Liveright had "practically agreed to bring it out" if O'Neill would only write a short foreword to help out a book certain to lose money otherwise. He wasn't sure if O'Neill would agree or not, but Frank had promised to try to "engineer the matter" through.[20] Then, on October 26th, Crane sent him yet another poem to be added to *White Buildings*. It was "At Melville's Tomb," and it was one of Crane's most haunting and memorable lyrics:

> *Often beneath the wave, wide from this ledge*
> *The dice of drowned men's bones he saw bequeath*
> *An embassy. Their numbers as he watched,*
> *Beat on the dusty shore and were obscured.*
>
> *And wrecks passed without sound of bells,*
> *The calyx of death's bounty giving back*
> *A scattered chapter, livid hieroglyph,*
> *The portent wound in corridors of shells.*

Then in the circuit calm of one vast coil,
Its lashings charmed and malice reconciled,
Frosted eyes there were that lifted altars;
And silent answers crept across the stars.

Compass, quadrant and sextant contrive
No farther tides . . . High in the azure steeps
Monody shall not wake the mariner.
This fabulous shadow only the sea keeps.[21]

As a token of appreciation for lending him the money to buy his ten acres, Crane had just sent the Rychtariks one of two masks Jimmy Light had created for a production of Coleridge's *The Ancient Mariner*, put on at the Provincetown Theatre the year before. The mask he sent them was that of one of the angels who stood on the deck of the doomed ship as it made its way into port. The other mask Crane kept for himself, proudly displaying it in his room in Patterson. It was the face of a drowned sailor and it would become in effect Crane's effigy and death mask, as "At Melville's Tomb" would become his epitaph.

In the poem, Crane calls upon the ghost of his beloved Melville, the lost voyager at the end of his journey, which has turned out to be not some distant shore but rather the bottom of the sea. From that perspective, "beneath the wave," the poet—like Melville—sees the bones of the drowned churned and diced by the sea, to be buried beneath the ocean floor or tossed up on some beach, there to be mixed in the general obscurity of shells and sand. The voyagers—that visionary company—who sought some answer to life's meaning have their answer now, Crane intimates, though—being dead—they can no more tell us what they have seen than a seashell, held up to the ear, can say what the sea means by its distant roar. Ghostly, silent, the drowned sailors watch now as the wrecks of thousands of ships pass by in silence on their way to their final resting place below. And as the scattered remains of the *Pequod* in *Moby-Dick's* closing lines are thrown up from the vortex created by the ship's spiraling down to death, paradoxically they become an unexpected horn of plenty, a "calyx of death's bounty giving back" its "scattered chapter," a scrambled text delivered out of the flotsam and jetsam of that lost ship.

The difficulty, though, is in reading the partial text given back, for if it is a sign, the meaning remains undecipherable, transcribed in a "livid hieroglyph" for which the living have no Rosetta stone. Only in death, Crane suggests, is the circuit of life calmed, all "lashings charmed and malice reconciled," so that now the drowned mariners, their struggles over, lift frosted eyes in death ("Those are pearls that were his eyes," as the eyes roll backward to reveal their whites). It is a gesture of awe and sacrifice and homage to the hidden Word, sought for daily in the long voyage out, and acknowledged even in death where, ironically, that Word at last provides the dead mariners with "silent answers" writ large in the circuit of the stars moving across the heavens. Or small, as in the ghostly movement of starfish as they sweep slowly across the ocean floor.

Compass, quadrant, sextant: three instruments devised to measure time and space. But how shall we measure eternity? Are they not all relative, these instruments, creating ever finer instruments to measure what must remain immeasurable? Nothing, certainly not the poet's elegy, will ever wake this mariner, either before he descends to his final resting place or wakes from his eternal sleep. "This fabulous shadow," Crane ends, this fabled shadow, this brilliant absence, this myth, this legend, "only the sea keeps." And that word "only," situated midway through the line, looks both before and after, back to the poet's shadow, forward to the sea. Is it the shadow only that the sea keeps? Or is the poet's shadow so tied to the sea now that only the sea is large enough and home enough to contain it? Or is it both? Let the hissing of the waves as they beat against death's dusty shore in the lyric's final line provide us with its sibylline prophecy, an answer that is no answer after all: *This fabulous shadow only the sea keeps.*

When Crane submitted the poem to Harriet Monroe at *Poetry* magazine the following spring, she answered that she would publish it if Crane provided an extensive prose paraphrase for her readers. Exasperated, but on his best behavior, he responded as best he could, in a spirited letter written in the late summer of 1926 from the Isle of Pines and published in *Poetry* that fall.[22] He would make his meaning as clear as possible, even if his "explanation" should meet with uncomprehending silence. Naturally, no prose paraphrase, he reminded her, could ever substitute for the "more essentialized form of the poem itself." That was because the poem operated not by way of logic, but by a logic of metaphor or, rather, the "illogical impingements of the connotations of words on the consciousness (and their combinations and interplay in metaphor on this basis)." Such an approach, the poet insisted, might free his subject matter and his perceptions to say more than mere logical discourse could ever do.

To deny the poet the ability to work in this way by insisting he follow the classical approach to poetry was to limit the possibilities of poetic language and negate what other Romantic precursors such as Blake, Rimbaud, and even Eliot had already achieved. The illogical approach meant going beyond the denotative definition of a word to include its connotative resonances. These of course depended on one's receptivity to such resonances. A reader therefore either responded to a word (or a phrase or an image) because it chimed with something in his or her own experience, or that reader did not. Had not the eminent critic I. A. Richards recently called the logic of metaphor a "pseudostatement"? And by that he'd meant writing that depended for its force not on logic but on the imagination to grasp the poet's linguistic and imagistic connections.

For those who read widely and who had experienced a good deal of what life had to offer, Crane insisted, it made no sense to keep returning to the basic ABCs of the already known. For more advanced readers there had to be an advanced calculus of sorts, a shorthand that went beyond "the usual description and dialectics" to move toward "fresh concepts" and "more inclusive evaluations" of experience. To underscore what he was doing in his poetry, he called on Einstein's theory of relativity as itself a metaphor borrowed by science to approach the nature of reality. "Hasn't it often occurred," he asked, "that instruments originally invented for record and computation have inadvertently so extended the concepts of the entity they were invented to measure (concepts of space, etc.) in the mind and imagination that employed them, that they may metaphorically be said to have extended the original boundaries of the entity measured?" And if science could speak in metaphor, why not poetry, the mother of metaphor? If a poem was to break through to "new thresholds, new anatomies," new configurations of reality, it would have to be through the "bright illogic" of metaphorical speech, a game plan the scientist, if not the literary critic, already understood.

At the same time that he was writing "At Melville's Tomb," pushing the limits of what human consciousness was capable of understanding intuitively, Crane wrote out some "notes" to help Eugene

O'Neill with the foreword he'd agreed to do for *White Buildings*. These notes—Crane called them his "General Aims and Theories"[23]—were meant to spell out what Crane was trying to accomplish in constructing a bridge out of words that would connect him with his audience. As it turned out, the notes also served as a response to the High Modernist moment signaled by Joyce's *Ulysses* and Eliot's *Waste Land*, as well as to Eliot's crucial essay on *Ulysses* and his "Tradition and the Individual Talent."

Crane began by focusing on the breakthrough moment in May 1922 when he'd started work on "For the Marriage of Faustus and Helen." It had been his intention there "to embody in modern terms (words, symbols, metaphors)"—as Yeats, Joyce, Pound, and Eliot had done—a parallel between his own historic moment and the ancient myths. This connection with a viable past had been "obscured rather than illumined," he believed, by the way the previous century had dealt with mythic material. Like Swinburne, Hardy, and Pound, Crane wanted to bypass the overwriting of these ancient myths that had occurred under Christianity. So, for instance, Helen was more than just a name to be evoked whenever the poet felt the need to call on the beautiful. What she really stood for, and what he had tried to evoke, was an emotional complex, a religious awe, really, similar to what the ancients had felt when they'd invoked her name, but to do this in modern terms.

To achieve this, Crane would have to build *a bridge* between the ancient world and the complex, fragmented "realities of our seething, confused cosmos of today," which did not yet have the terms by which it could apprehend what the ancients meant when they invoked the name of Helen. Homer's Helen sitting across from him in a Cleveland streetcar, modern jazz as a correlative for the sacred music invoked for the Eleusynian mysteries, modern trench warfare recalling the smoky ruins of Troy. All these were correspondences between two widely separated worlds that Crane had touched on in treating the eternal themes of love and beauty, death and rebirth. Even so, the early "grafting process" he'd used in "Faustus and Helen" had been only a first step in defining his own relation to tradition and the modern imagination.

Like Oswald Spengler and Yeats, that other last Romantic, Crane too believed he was living through a period of Western decadence, the end of one historical cycle and the beginning of a new. Words had become shells, bare husks, where vibrant myths had once lived but lived no longer. What words were there that could still ring "with any vibration or spiritual conviction," he wondered. All the great mythologies of the past—not only of the classical world but the Christian world as well—were hardly strong enough any more even to be effectively attacked. And yet elements of those traditions still lived in everyone's experience, "in millions of chance combinations of related and unrelated detail, psychological reference, figures of speech, precepts, etc.," for they were the terms by which one understood oneself. They were, in short, coins with a negotiable value. To attempt to break with the past in order to make everything new was simply a "sentimental fallacy" and unworkable. The modern poet had not only a right, he had an obligation to take from whatever material was available to him—including large chunks of the past. But only if what he found measured up against the "touchstone of experience." Better to discard as "useless archeology" whatever did not resonate with one's own experience. If, on the other hand, it did resonate with his own experience, then why not use it?

Of course, a poet had to reflect his own historical moment by reacting honestly and fully "to the states of passion, experience and rumination" that any life brought. Beyond that, he had "to know and experience enough to make his imagination selective and valuable." Then what he chose to portray of the world and his historic moment— the "by-product of his curiosity and the relation of his experience to a postulated 'eternity'"—would come to define a historical epoch. Here he was, an American poet living in the first half of the twentieth century. There was nothing of any absolute significance to that accident of fate, he realized, except that it was also the case that America was the new frontier, and that here if anywhere would "be discovered certain as yet undefined spiritual quantities," a reality "not to be developed so completely elsewhere." And though he could not quite bring himself to say it, in 1925 Crane firmly believed himself to be one of the high priests of this higher consciousness.

One did not reach this higher consciousness, however, merely by writing about such contemporary phenomena as "skyscrapers, radio antennae, steam whistles," Pullmans, Spads, auto racing, flappers, and on and on. To do that was merely "to paint a photograph." No, what he was after was something deeper. To come in genuine contact with one's historic moment meant submitting to what was new about the age and allowing that experience to enter oneself as fully as the air one breathed. It was also important to remember that one's own historical moment was shaped by the best of the past—"the vocabulary and blank verse of the Elizabethans," say— as well as by the brilliant typographical innovations and jazzy linguistic surface of "an impressionist like Cummings." Let all language of whatever sort—the new word at ease with the old—dance together in consort to give the reader as full a sense of reality—what he called the Word—as language was capable of reproducing. Not the "retinal registration" of surface phenomenon only—that was the job of the impressionist—but the metaphysical reality that lay beyond or beneath the surface of things.

Experience was the springboard that led to a higher state of consciousness and that might end in a glimpse of radical innocence, or absolute beauty, or spiritual illumination: a shining moment (moral at its core) alchemized out of the stuff of experience. The result—if the alchemical moment occurred—would be a poem that left the reader with "a single, new word, never before spoken and impossible to actually enunciate, but self-evident as an active principle in the reader's consciousness henceforward." Within each successful poem, then, lay an "implicit emotional dynamics" reflected in the associational meanings of each word revealed through a logic of metaphor or dreams, itself the genesis of all speech, and thus of human consciousness. Crane knew that such a logic of "inferential mention" often led to difficulties in others understanding his poems, but it was the way he had to proceed if he was ever to reach the higher consciousness he was after and bring news of it back into his poems. At the same time he needed to offer his readers some echo of that new music. Nothing for it, then, but to risk obscurity in "the conquest of consciousness." New conditions, new realities, necessarily generated new ways of speaking. Language had always built bridges to new levels of spiritual understanding, even as it remained—as it had to—a river in constant flux.

Though he was to continue working on it for another year, "Atlantis"—which would become the final section of *The Bridge*—perhaps best enacts Crane's multitudinous Word and his theory of logic. When he sent a draft of the poem to Frank, he took pains to explain that it was "symphonic in including the convergence of all the strands separately detailed in antecedent sections of the poem—Columbus, conquests of water, land, etc., Pocahontas, subways, offices, etc., etc." He was delighted to have found at last a form that could absorb his "condensed metaphorical habit" of speaking. Thus, in finding a way to transform his bridge into "a ship, a world, a woman [and] a tremendous harp," the poem had finally revealed itself to him. Somehow, he believed, he'd succeeded in inducing in the poem "the same feelings of elation, etc.—like being carried forward and upward simultaneous-ly . . . that one experiences in walking across" the Brooklyn Bridge.[24]

Whatever else it is, "Atlantis" is a poem whose words strain to the breaking point to enmesh in their netting the single multitudinous Verb containing all language. Call it the quest for the impossible white Anemone—that wind flower—the Word Itself. "Through the bound cable strands," the poem begins, pointing at once to the roped strands that hold up the bridge, as well as to the thousands of bound cable strands of the entire epic poem itself. These strands have become now at once a "flight of strings" and "Taut miles of shuttling moonlight," through which the winds of inspiration play. Most poetry resides some-where in the middle register, between the demotic on the one end and the orphic at the other. But "Atlantis" seems to begin two octaves above the higher end of the scale and to ascend from there. And indeed, the poet invites our eye upward, toward the stars and beyond, where deepest night becomes transparent day, and where "the arching path" of the bridge becomes the "One arc synoptic" of the rainbow, sign of the covenant between the Word and humankind.

The architecture of "Atlantis," on which Crane worked for three years—those twelve eight-line stanzas of blank verse with occasional rhyme—follows the architecture of his beloved bridge, across which he had walked hand-in-hand with his lover: the cable strands of the bridge, arching upward toward the cathedral-like granite stanchions, then the descent and rise of cable strand, then granite stanchion again, then the final descent to land. And the imitation of that motion in the poem itself: a rise through the first six stanzas, then a lull, followed by another rise, as the poet addresses the bridge, symbol of love itself. And then the final dying fall. Hundreds of earlier strands—images, words, motifs—recur and are bound up here: Tyre and Troy, those other lost Atlantises, resurrected again in the brilliant white buildings of modern New York. The quest for the holy city. Call it Babylon, Jerusalem, Athens, call it Rome, Paris, London, Kyoto, Benares, Atlantis, New York. The polis, that shimmering anemone: the quest of Ulysses and the Argonauts and of all visionary artists—Whitman and Poe and Dickin-son and Isadora Duncan and Crane among them—the shipwrecked among the rest.

And the music of the bridge—the rushed idiom of its traffic, the blare of tugs beneath, the "wrapping harness" of airplanes high above, the tympanum of waves, the mew of gulls in the winter storms hovering above the river, the buoy bells tolling out in the harbor, the wind caressing the strings along the bridge like some giant harp: discordancies creating a sound that now the poet must somehow balance and orchestrate into a modern symphony. And always the eyes of the poet half-blinded by those heady altitudes, lifting in blind reverence toward the empyrean beyond. At last, having willed the annihilation of time and space in that sidereal infinity, bleeding starlight as in some cosmic crucifixion of the world.

And yet to be left wondering whether the vision he has been vouchsafed holds any truth at all. To wonder if, like Columbus before him, he really has found a New World, or whether he has been left with nothing more than an indecipherable Sanskrit whisper, a ghostly music, shuttling back and forth in the void between some half-heard hint of authentic vision and mere self-willed self-delusion.[25]

By early November 1925, after a month of futile job searching, Crane was once again reduced to begging his father for a loan. The letter bristled with what C.A. took as Harold's usual contemptuous tone, and it was two weeks before he decided to answer his son's plea. When he did, it was only to say that he did not like being spoken to condescendingly, especially by someone with such impoverished prospects. He did, however, come to Harold's rescue once again with a check for fifty dollars. At wit's end, Crane wrote his father again. Couldn't C.A. see that he was hurting, that he needed him, that they were on each other's hands and would have to find some way out of the impasse between them before time itself ran out?

"Dear Father," the letter began, "I was very glad to hear from you and it was generous of you to thus come to my aid." But what a shame it was to let "artificial theories and principles" come between the two of them. It was the same charge he'd leveled against Munson and Toomer in speaking of their poetic differences, and he'd already lost both his friends. How much better it would be, Crane pleaded now with his father, to let the "natural relationship of confidence and affection" they both so much needed finally take root. He did not know what his father had been told by others about his feelings for him, but whatever those rumors were, he begged him not to trust them. "God knows," he added, "how much we all are secretly suffering from the alienations that have been somehow forced upon us."

If only they could both step back for a moment and see things as they would look once this life was over, he was sure they would both see "a lot of social defenses and disguises fall from each other, and we would begin from that instant onward to really know and love each other." Here they were, the tattered remnants of a family, the old house gone, his grandmother close to death and living alone in Florida, his mother likewise alone and living "somewhere in Cuba or the Isle of Pines," and with no word from either of them now for over a month. How few they were, just the four of them. How great a loss, then, that they didn't all "mean a little more to each other." There; he had said it. "Please," he begged his father, "let me hear from you when the spirit moves you."[26]

C.A.'s answer arrived just in time for Thanksgiving. He was *not* uninterested in his son, he explained defensively, and he did not believe fate had caused their estrangement. The fact was it was all Harold's fault. If his son would only listen to him and get a decent job and leave the writing to spare moments here and there . . . In short, if he would just use good commonsense, the two of them might still be friends some day. Crane could hardly believe what he was reading. Why was it, he answered, exhausted, that he always had to play the Prodigal Son returning to the largess of a forgiving father? Really, he insisted, there was nothing on his part to repent of. If he was sorry, it was only because his father could not see him "in a clearer light" for who he really was. And this blindness, he feared, would probably not change in either of their lifetimes. Wouldn't it be better, the son pleaded, simply to drop all these mutual recriminations, forget "all the unnatural and painful episodes that life has put between us via not only ourselves but other people during the last ten years," and work for a more natural father/son relationship?

For six weeks that fall he'd tramped the streets, "being questioned, smelled and refused in various offices." He'd tried everything—bookstores, ad agencies, ship companies—even jobs that offered as little as twenty-five dollars a week, and had still come up with nothing, and now his shoes leaked, he was in tatters, and broke. He'd borrowed until he could borrow no more. He was at his wits' end, with nowhere to turn. He was therefore going to do what he'd always been too proud to do: Beg for money. To that end, he was writing Otto Kahn, an internationally known banker with Kuhn, Lieb & Company, headquartered in New York, and a patron of the performing arts (especially the Metropolitan Opera and O'Neill's Provincetown Players), who'd just given a friend of Crane's $5,000 to study painting in Paris. Crane was going to ask for a large enough loan to get through the winter so he could finally get some work done without having to grind his brains "through six sausage machines a day" in some office job just to steal an hour at his typewriter in the evenings.

If that failed, he would try O'Neill, and if that failed, he would take to the sea. In any case, he was not going back to the old nine-to-five grind. He had ten acres of land in Connecticut and he meant to put up a cabin there and raise vegetables and a few chickens. No doubt his father would scoff at the thought of a son of his settling for so little, but what did it all mean if he wasn't happy? The truth was that he'd never yet been happy a single day of his life "cooped up in an office having to calculate everything" he said to please people he actually despised.[27]

So reduced was he by then that, when Marianne Moore wrote Crane accepting "The Wine Menagerie" for *The Dial* with the stipulation that he change the title to "Again" and allow her to rewrite the poem in the interests of clarity, he readily submitted. Later, however, when he saw what the Reverend Miss Mountjoy had done to his poem, he was appalled. What the poor thing now meant he had no idea whatever, he confessed to the Rychtariks, but he would "never have consented to such an outrageous joke" if he hadn't needed the twenty dollars so badly.[28] "Miss Moore's paces are stubborn," he would tell Yvor Winters a year later, "and once, in my case destructive. What she must have said with lifted brows and a ? mark when she opened the envelope" containing the poem! Alas, "Again" was merely "the wreck of a longer and entirely different poem" which readers would see "in its original nudity" only when *White Buildings* was finally published. When he saw the "senseless thing in print" Moore had made of "The Wine Menagerie," he confessed, "I almost wept."[29]

In fact, he *had* wept. After acceding to the changes, he'd gone to Matty Josephson's apartment, asking for help before falling asleep on Josephson's bed, exhausted from crying. Josephson, moved by his friend's plight, wrote Moore at once, offering to buy the poem back from her, only to have Crane in turn reject his overture. Moore herself could not for the life of her understand what all the fuss was about. Asked about the incident in a *Paris Review* interview thirty years after Crane's death, she could still bristle. "Hart Crane complains of me? Well, I complain of *him*. He liked *The Dial* and we liked him—friends, and with certain tastes in common. He was in dire need of money. . . . 'Well, if you would modify it a little,' I said, 'we would like it better.'"[30] But as Kenneth Burke, then working at *The Dial* (and accused by Moore of acting as Crane's spy) later wagged: Moore succeeded only in taking all the Wine out of the Menagerie.

Once again, Crane's fortunes were about to turn around. On the afternoon of 3 December 1925, he wrote Kahn as he'd told his father he would. He had a book of poems coming out in the spring with a foreword by Eugene O'Neill, he explained, and although he had published in the best little magazines, he had yet "to reap any substantial benefits" from his writing. He was twenty-six, and for the past seven years had made his living writing advertising copy. But the work had sapped him, and he'd had to resign to save his health. He'd looked all over New York for work without success, and now he was broke. In spite of which, Crane went on, he had managed to write part of a long poem, "the conception of which has been in my mind for some years." But he'd been forced by the exigencies of his job to work on this late at night and then only intermittently. He could write short lyrics that way, but it had turned out to be impossible to work on something as complicated as *The Bridge* in the same fashion. After all, the long poem aimed at nothing short of enunciating "a new cultural synthesis of values in terms of our America."

Perhaps, therefore, Mr. Kahn would consider lending him $1,000 "at any rate of interest within six percent," so that he could live in the country for the following year, finish *The Bridge*, and begin work on a drama he envisioned as his next major project.[31] As security, Crane offered to put up as collateral the $5,000 he would inherit from his grandfather's estate on the death of his grandmother. Finally, he appended statements from three men who believed in what he was doing: Frank, Tate, and Munson, and then for good measure added the names of O'Neill, Light, Eleanor Fitzgerald, Jane Heap, Hal Smith, Paul Rosenfeld, and Marianne Moore as further references. Five days later, Kahn came through with an outright gift of $2,000—half at once, the second half come May. The only stipulation was that Crane write as well as he could, regardless of whether or not he published a word.

The day after he received the award, Crane wrote his mother from the stately old Hotel St. George, a few blocks east of his old apartment on Columbia Heights. He'd heard nothing from her or his grandmother for six weeks, and he was worried, hurt, and upset that she could so easily forget him, especially now when he so deeply needed her. He knew he'd not made life easy for her when he'd been home the summer before, but she was after all still his mother. Then he broke the news. He'd been given $2,000 to write and would soon be settled back up in Patterson. Finally, Grace wrote back. She'd been too ill to write, she told him, too ill in fact even to leave Florida, and in her hour of need had called not on him but on the reliable Mr. Curtis to come down to help her and her poor mother. She ended by wishing her son joy and best wishes.

Then Crane wrote his father about the award. "Agreeable to your request," C.A. wrote back in mid-December, "I am not referring to any further differences of opinion."[32] He was happy Harold would at last be settled and doing what he had always wanted to do. He would try to be helpful and promised to send some chocolates to the Patterson address. He enclosed a generous check and promised to pay Harold's train fare if Harold would come out to Cleveland to visit his mother and grandmother for Christmas.

On the 18th, Crane was back in Patterson, where the Tates arranged for him to be given two large rooms in an old eight-room farmhouse belonging to Mrs. Addie Turner, ancient-looking at sixty-four, who lived there with her even more ancient aunt (eighty) and her cats. The rent came to an unbelievably low ten dollars a month. Seeing how desperate Crane had been earlier that fall, the Tates, who had moved from New York to Mrs. Turner's in November, had invited Crane to come up and share the house with them to help him through a difficult time. Now—like that—Crane was suddenly $2,000 richer, and wending his way back up into the countryside he loved so much.

Christmas Day he wrote his father thanking him for the chocolates and the Christmas check he'd sent. The day was almost over, and he was very happy. He'd settled into his east-facing rooms on the second floor, overlooking a moonlit snow-covered valley. He and the Tates had had a delicious midday Christmas dinner, after which he'd visited with Sue Jenkins and Slater Brown a mile away, taking a long walk over the hills through a light snow. He'd spent the past week settling in and getting provisions from Macy's in New York against the "strenuous cold weather and snow to come."[33] As for returning to Cleveland, he would do that come spring, after he got some real work on *The Bridge* done. If his father planned to be in Manhattan that winter, he would come down to see him, since both men were anxious to get back on something like an equal footing and make up for the lost years.

What "a godsend to get away from the rasping metropolis for awhile," he wrote Underwood later that same evening. Yes, he loved New York, but he'd been, he realized now, on the "edge of a serious sort of breakup," and he was exhausted. So much so, in fact, that he meant to do nothing for the next month but "vegetate, walk and read." For the first time he spoke of feeling old, and when he looked in the mirror he could already see strands of white hair among the gray. Things were on a better footing with his family, he added, especially now that he had the backing of a New York banker. "Shakespeare's own endorsement," he was quick to add, would have meant little next to Kahn's, as far as his mother and father were concerned.

Now, with snow on the ground and quiet all about him, he'd gone back to his Whitman again. No other American had bequeathed the country "so great a heritage" as that man had. And yet, thirty-five years after his death, Whitman was still being attacked. In fact, Crane had just read an editorial in *The Nation* on an exhibition of Whitman's writings at the New York Public Library that revealed just how unrelenting the attack on the gay artist in America could be. There were still critics in this country who had no difficulty charging Whitman with subverting an entire literary generation, both here and abroad. When Americans realized that the author of the *Calamus* poems was actually "abnormal," one open letter had insisted, people would at last stop reading him. Worse, there were actually librarians at prestigious eastern colleges who still warned students away from the poet. Crane could see he had his own battles lined up not only for the next few years, but for the next hundred.[34]

Here he was, he wrote the Rychtariks on New Year's Eve, sixty-six miles from his nearest drink, with absolutely no whistles or shouting as he was in the habit of doing in New York to greet the New Year. By midnight he would probably be snug in the old sleigh bed that Mrs. Turner had found for him. Crane had in fact quickly charmed the old woman, so that Gordon was convinced that Mrs. Turner was already falling in love with Crane, a sight Gordon found amusing at first, and later merely pathetic.

By then the weather had turned cold—minus zero—but he'd come prepared this time, wrapping himself each morning in "boots, woolens, and furs." His pictures and knickknacks had been hung about the study on the kalsomined walls and his books glistened from their makeshift shelves. He had two oil stoves to keep him warm. Downstairs, he and the Tates cooked and heated with wood-burning stoves, which meant chopping wood each day. The work toughened him up and kept him glowing. Tate got breakfast, Caroline Gordon fixed lunch and dinner, and Crane cleaned up after each meal. The rest of the day was his in which to write. Gordon was now into her second novel, and Tate was doing reviews, though in truth the staunch Tennessean spent most of his time with an old rifle he'd dubbed "The White Powder Wonder," ranging over the snow-covered hills, shooting at sparrows, and making an "exclamatory stew" from the one squirrel he'd so far managed to bag.[35]

Four days into 1926, Crane finally got down to work on *The Bridge*, picking up once more on the "Atlantis" section. "One really has to keep one's self in such a keyed-up mood for the thing that no predictions can be made ahead as to whether one is going to have the wit to work on it steadily or not," he wrote his grandmother.[36] But the Muse was with him this time, and for the next two days he worked steadily on the poem in an "almost ecstatic mood." Never, he wrote his mother, had he felt "such range and symphonic power before."[37] It bode well for his dream of the poem. Then, on January 12th, having earned a vacation, he returned to New York to play for a few days. "You know what the Governor of North Carolina said to the Governor of South Carolina," he joked to Cowley. "I'm such a rum-scallion that I never even planned to stay put anywhere very long in the woods."[38]

Crane's sentiments exactly, as he began a two-day drinking binge with an American sailor named Jack Fitzin he'd picked up on the Brooklyn docks. Pockets loaded with money, Crane flashed bills, commissioned a sculpture of a seagull from Gaston Lachaise, went on a shopping spree that included snowshoes and a hundred dollars' worth of authentic Congo wood carvings (wooden knives, a ceremonial spear, shield, headdress, libation cup, viol)[39] bought from a shop on Brooklyn's Fulton Street, all of which (except for the seagull) he lugged back to the white hills of Patterson when he returned on the 17th. By then he was glad to be away from the soot blowing everywhere in New York that winter from the soft coal the city had been forced to burn because of an anthracite strike. The spear, he figured, would look great the next time he did his cannibal dance.

He put the "Atlantis" aside again and began work on the "Ave Maria" section, the poem meant to hold up the other end of *The Bridge*. Columbus's quest for Cathay would stand in for "an attitude of spirit"[40] rather than for the conquest of the New World, forcible conquest being a subject anathema to him. He read Columbus's *Journal*. He read W. H. Prescott's *History of the Reign of Ferdinand and Isabella* and a bad book on Magellan. Then it was George Warr's wooden translation of the *Oresteia* for its compact metaphors and "density of image." He was amazed at the "soul-shivering economy" Aeschylus had achieved there, something no English writer he was aware of had ever matched. Next, he turned to Melville's *White Jacket* and George Francis Dow's illustrated *Whale Ships and Whaling*, Alfred North Whitehead's *Science and the Modern World* and Waldo Frank's study of colonial Mexico, *Virgin Spain*, a book whose depiction of that part of the New World Crane found so convincing he yearned to see it for himself. "As a document of the spirit," he wrote Munson after a year's silence, it was "one of the most lively testaments ever written," better even than Lawrence's portrait of the country in *Plumed Serpent*.[41]

And as winter pushed in and hunkered down for the duration, with ice and snow piling up and temperatures plummeting nightly to thirty below, he tried keeping warm by dreaming of the Isle of Pines with its "gorgeous palms, unexpected pines [and] balmy breezes."[42] By the end of the month, he was spending hours each day chopping wood and beginning to understand what roughing it really meant. Chilblains developed, then a cold. "My hands are so stiff from wood-cutting that my writing looks funny," he complained to his mother on the 26th. "It is very, very cold today, was yesterday and promises to continue. We all go about shivering most of the time and . . . get too little freedom for our writing."[43] He laid in a fifty-gallon drum of kerosene to keep the stoves in his study going through the winter, only to learn that the fuel he'd bought from the local supplier had been adulterated and refused to burn. He pined for spring, still three months off.

By mid-February, he was suffering from an advanced case of cabin fever. The snow he'd pined for at Christmas was now so deep that the roads around him went unplowed. Mail delivery to the outlying areas had ceased altogether at the end of January, not to be resumed for another two months. If Crane went anywhere, it was on snowshoes. Villon with his frozen inkwell in medieval Paris; Crane with his cold-to-the-touch typewriter in subzero upstate New York. Even indoors his every breath rose like some "steaming snort from a dragon."[44] By mid-February his fingers refused to do their bidding at the typewriter and his feet bloomed with chilblains from contact with the cold floors. Thirty years later, Caroline Gordon would remember Crane soaking his feet in pans of hot water while he invoked in mocking accents the tropic climes of "Voyages II": "Salute the crocus lustres of the stars,/In these poinsettia meadows of her tides." When he wasn't dreaming of the Caribbean, he dreamed of New York with its cocktails, taxis, and sailor boys. But he also knew he needed this isolation to get on with *The Bridge*. Here was where he had to be now, here in Patterson, with its "temperate living, good sleep and considerable outdoor exercise," and here he would stay "indefinitely and unregretfully" until a good chunk of his poem was there on the page in a form he could recognize as his.

By March, he looked upon "Atlantis" as all but finished, though he realized just how time-consuming the other parts of *The Bridge* were going to be. Sometimes, he told the Rychtariks, the project seemed "hopeless, horribly so."[45] And then something would happen and he would see extraordinary possibilities for his epic. If nothing else, he told Munson on March 5th, the poem would be "hugely and unforgivably, distinguishedly bad." Surely the project was worth it, surely there was more to life than Eliot's summation at the end of "The Hollow Men," that the world would end "Not with a bang but a whimper." Whatever happened, he would not—repeat *not*—give in to some "easy acceptance . . . of death," which most writers—including the New York crowd—seemed so intent these days on doing.[46] The silences of Patterson's woods with its moon-silvered hills, the vast reaches of the spindrift ocean, where deep called to deep—these too were part of the real, which he promised himself to listen to. Never again would he allow himself to live in a city for more than six months at a time.

On March 9th Crane returned to New York for the first time in six weeks. Once again he stayed at the Hotel Albert, visiting with the Cowleys and other New York friends, and then—on the 11th—took the overnight Pullman to Cleveland to visit his mother and grandmother. He stayed three days, just long enough to experience "a perfect spasm of sentiment and 'inspection,'" before he returned to Manhattan.[47] He stayed one night in the city to have a long "rummy conversation"[48] with Munson about Munson's essay on his poetry, due to appear shortly in *Destinations,* Munson's book of essays on the state of the arts in contemporary America. Much of what Munson had written about him Crane was in agreement with, and told him so, thanking Munson for the critical attention. But there were still things about himself he did not seem to be able to make Munson understand. What was this goddamn moral myopia and tunnel vision Munson suffered from, anyway? Finally Crane got up, shook hands with his old ex-friend, and staggered out of the bar, to spend the night on one of those wild "one-night sprees" of his along the docks. By midnight he had managed to pick up several "friends," whom he tried to sneak past the desk manager and up into his room at the Albert, without any luck. Defeated, he finally retired, as he phrased it, "tout seul."[49] The following morning, he took the train back up to Patterson.

He thought back to his talk with Munson of the night before, still bristling, still dissatisfied with Munson's summations. Now, settled into his room in Patterson, he wrote Munson to explain what he was really trying to do in his work. Perhaps if he took it one step at a time. What was a poem, after all, he tried enlightening Munson, but the "concrete evidence of the experience of a recognition," language capable of matching the poet's perceptions with the thing perceived? This was all a poem could ever give us, and it was useless to ask it to do more than that. He was sorry, but the poem could not give one God—whether one called that eminence Osiris, Zeus, or Indra—any more than philosophy could. On the other hand, what poetry *could* deliver was the sense of being in the presence of God, "the very 'sign manifest' on which rests the assumption of a godhead." Not God, then, but—given the limitations imposed upon us by our subjectivity—something like a sublime sense of God.

But to ask poetry to provide its readers with a map of eternity or furnish them with "ethical morality or moral classifications" was to subordinate poetry to science or philosophy. Munson had to understand that Crane was not out to discredit science, for science and poetry were both inspired, and both relied fundamentally on metaphor, or the ratio of one likeness to another. Munson also had to understand that Plato's philosophy lived, not because of the truth of his statements, but because of the "architecture of his logic," the "harmonious relationship" of idea to idea. This same relationship, Crane insisted, was true of poetry, and in fact—though he did not say so—formed the very foundation upon which the vastly intricate architecture of *The Bridge* was now being built. It was because Plato the rationalist understood that poets were out to reorganize the chaos of experience on their own grounds—different from Plato's but no less metaphoric for all that—that the philosopher had wanted to banish poets from his city.

It was important to understand that both Crane and Munson lived in a world in which moral, ethical, and philosophical language had all lost much of their value. Given the fact, therefore, that there was no underlying mythos to which he could subscribe, Crane had had to go his own way. If a "synthesis of reasonable laws" could have been discovered "which might provide a consistent philosophical and moral program" for the twentieth century, he was quick to add, he would have been happy subscribing to it. In fact, he would no doubt have already been writing under its "classic power of dictation." But (alas) no such system now existed, and Munson was asking too much if he expected the poet to provide that system. If he had written under such a system, he knew, Munson would no doubt have been happy; but only because Munson would have already understood the underlying plan of Crane's poetry, rather than having to grope blindly to find it, as Crane had been forced by necessity to do.

Even then, his poetry would still have to be treated as poetry and not philosophy, expressed in terms of how experience had affected the poet's psyche through the mediation of metaphorical language. Wasn't that, after all, the nature of poetry? Like life, something at the heart of poetry remained elusive to analysis. Naturally, he resented Munson's fumbling attempts to fit him into Procrustean categories where even he no longer recognized himself, and then criticized for not living up to those imposed categories. Crane was well aware that his poetry was open to criticism on many fronts, but what troubled him most was that Munson was still making so many "extra-literary" judgments about his work, including criticizing his subject matter and his psychological explorations of those subjects. For several years Munson had been one of his closest confidants, and now he had used that privileged knowledge to judge his poems on personal grounds, even where the poems called for no such judgments. Truth, he reminded Munson, would always avoid the names one tried to pin on her. For Truth had no name, but only names, Relativity being merely the latest.[50]

The following day, Crane sent off a progress report to Otto Kahn. *The Bridge* was under construction, he wrote, and he was just now playing the part of Columbus returning from his initial voyage to the New World. As he saw it, *The Bridge* would open with Columbus and end with "Atlantis," with the poet standing in the middle of the bridge at midnight. Because "Atlantis" was "the mystic consummation toward which all the other sections of the poem converge," the difficulties of actually realizing the rest of the work were growing more and more complex with each passing day, what with the thousands of interrelated details that would have to go into building a bridge commensurate with the complexities of modern life. But when it was at last completed, it would be a symphony celebrating "the conquest of space and knowledge." Thus, Columbus's search for what the explorer had originally imagined was the land of Cathay would transform itself by poem's end into nothing less than an enlargement of "consciousness, knowledge, [and] spiritual unity" coming down to his own protean moment.

At present, he saw *The Bridge* as containing six sections: Columbus and the conquest of space (the male of it); Pocahontas and the physical body of America (the female of it); the poet and the spiritual body of America (Whitman in Washington during the Civil War, nursing a dying soldier: death, disunity, immortality); the tragedy of the black experience (portrayed through a porter on the Canadian Calgary Express making up berths and singing a jazz tune to himself of love and the death of John Brown); the descent into hell via the New York subway; and—finally—the "Atlantis" section, where the Brooklyn Bridge would become "the symbol of consciousness spanning time and space."

Both the "Ave Maria" and "Atlantis" sections had been composed in blank verse with occasional rhyming lines. What form the other parts would take would depend on how the spirit moved him when he actually came to write them.[51] As with any living organism, the poem would change as the year stretched into years, bringing changes to

Crane himself he could not have then foreseen. But in the early spring of '26 he was content to see the world through the eyes of Columbus, "mid-channel" in his discovery, joyfully adrift in a music that was, he was beginning to realize, a burden in several senses of the word.

"'Be with me,'" Crane's Columbus prays in the opening lines of the "Ave Maria," addressing Luis de San Angel and Juan Perez, his absent advisers back in Spain who had advocated for him before Spain's king and queen. Then it had all been speculation and dream and possibility. But now he has actually seen his Cathay, witnessing with his own eyes a New World, the Word, San Salvador, the Holy Savior. Now, as he sails home with his one remaining ship, he is faced with a new difficulty, for he finds himself in the midst of a terrible storm at sea, which threatens to swamp his craft and drown him and his men, silencing all of them forever—drowned men's bones—so that he cries out, pleading that he may return with word of what he has seen. It is of course a paradigm for the visionary's crisis: to bring back word of a world he has been blessed to brush against, and which nothing—"no perjured breath/Of clown nor sage"—can ever "riddle or gainsay."

The sublime terror of having spent months out on those depths, where first his ships headed west into the "red caravel" of the sun dropping nightly into the yawning ocean, and where now that sun drops nightly behind him as his battered ship travels east and back toward Spain, even as giant

> waves climb into dusk on gleaming mail;
> Invisible valves of the sea,—locks, tendons
> Crested and creeping, troughing corridors
> That fall back yawning to another plunge . . .

It is an extraordinary gift that has been proffered to the world, Crane's Columbus sees. But "Rush down this plenitude," rape this New World, despoil it, he warns, "and you shall see/Isaiah counting famine on this lee!" Break *this* new covenant, and watch the incredible gift of the New World turn into one vast waste.

And now Columbus addresses God's Hand of Fire glimpsed in the lightning crashing about the ship, much as Crane will later address Whitman, extending his own hand across the chasm of death, to touch the living hand of Whitman extended to him in turn. Already there have been signs vouchsafed. Volcanic activity on Teneriffe on the outward voyage, reminding Columbus of the cloud that went before God's chosen ones as they wandered in the inhospitable desert. Then the corposant (holy body) Columbus's men call St. Elmo's Fire, turning the mast of the ship struck by lightning into a radiant, shimmering blue cross all along its breadth and length, becoming yet another sign (*In hoc signo vinces*), a sign Columbus would surely understand.

And now, at last, Columbus's prayer is answered, The storm passes, the clouds lift, and he can see signs that he is indeed approaching land—"a salty branch," "jellied weeds that drag the shore"—and then the stars again, and the Pleiades, "The kindled Crown," granting victory. The prayer of beseechment has become as well a prayer of praise to God, the great *Te Deum* sung, victory at last granted, and word of his return become the Word enfleshed in the reality of Cathay glimpsed. Kingdoms, Crane concludes, punning once more on his name, kingdoms for the asking, kingdoms lying there "naked in the/trembling heart": the Word made flesh in the chevroned palms of a New World naked.[52]

Then another word, this time from his mother. She was going to marry Mr. Curtis after all, and was busy just now orchestrating a modest ceremony in New York at The Little Church in the Bowery so that her Hart could be there to see her married. They'd both been through a great deal, hadn't they, he wrote her at the end of March. But suffering, he'd come to understand, if willingly accepted, was a "kingdom among those initiated, a kingdom that has the widest kind of communion." He loved her because she'd been willing to accept him for who he was, even when he himself had had misgivings. "I hope you never will turn your back on me," he begged her now, brushing up against his hidden life. "I do some awfully silly things sometimes—most of which you don't know about, but which I sometimes (not always) regret." He did not want to make her apprehensive, he added, and he was "in no particular pickle at present." But still, it was good to know that she would always be there for him.[53]

By early April, after a soul-killing winter that still hung on, Crane could feel the Tates and the Browns isolating themselves from him and from each other. Even his own mood, he confessed to Munson, had become more and more "North Labrador" until now he pined for "a little good company." He'd all but ceased writing, spending his days ambling about Addie Turner's place, "reading, eating and sleeping," amazed to discover that "a life of perfect virtue [and] redundant health" did not always encourage the Muse. He briefly considered moving back to New York and (God forbid) finding a job. Three months of nonstop work on *The Bridge* had led to so much systematic objectivizing of his theme and the multitude of details that were pouring into the construction that the "subjective lymph and sinew" necessary actually to build the poem had frozen, like everything else in Patterson. Theoretically, he knew what he had to do with his lyric epic, but fleshing it out was something else. The truth was that the whole goddamn undertaking was proving so "complex and difficult" it would take a great deal more than mere desire ever to see the poem into existence.[54] What he needed was to be possessed again, and that would happen only when it happened.

In mid-April, the sullen storm that had been brewing between the Tates and Crane finally broke. Crane would put the blame for the consequent rupture squarely on the Tates, especially Caroline Gordon. Somehow, over the winter months, the farmhouse had become an armed camp, and the easy come-and-go that had characterized Crane's and the Tates' movements for the first months of their living together was by now severely restricted. While all three had been busy at their writing, each had worked in his or her assigned quarters. But as Crane became more and more restless, he seemed always underfoot.

There was also, alas, the problem of sharing the outdoor pump, which meant he had to pass back and forth through the Tates' kitchen, where Gordon had had to set up a makeshift study. Instead of talking to Crane about this, however, she began bolting the door, so that he would have to go the long way round. From her point of view, Crane didn't take hints, and he hadn't learned that, just because he wasn't busy, other people might be. Besides, she'd had to send her infant daughter to live with her mother in Kentucky because she and her husband were desperately poor. And here was Crane with two thousand to spend. "I could take the hint without having to be knocked down by a hammer," Crane told his mother.[55] Stung by the Tates' rebuttal, he removed his razor and shaving brush, which he'd been in the habit of leaving out by the pump, and reorganized them in Addie Turner's kitchen. He also pointedly avoided the Tates' part of the house altogether, something that only irritated them further.

Then, on April 16th, just after breakfast, while Crane was talking with Addie Turner in her kitchen, Tate opened the door from his part of the kitchen and snapped out that if Crane had a criticism of Tate's work to make, he would appreciate it if Crane spoke directly to him about it. Having said this, he turned and slammed the door. Crane stared at Mrs. Turner, Mrs. Turner at Crane. He could feel himself becoming so upset he was afraid he might start hurling things against the door. Instead, he had Mrs. Turner walk into the Tates' kitchen with him, asking her to corroborate that he'd not been talking about the Tates. Tate had finally to admit that he hadn't actually heard what Crane was saying through the closed door.

But the following night Crane was awakened by the shuffle of the Tates moving about in their bedroom, followed by the *clackclack* of typewriters. Next morning he found two notes under his door, one from Tate, the other from Gordon. They had been there first, Gordon's note ran. And it was they who'd invited *him* when he was down on his luck. When—at the last—he'd come into his unexpected windfall and had money to burn, they'd reconsidered, but had let it go. And how had he repaid their kindness? By taking over two rooms instead of one, spreading his things all over the house, and expecting the Tates to act as his servants. Tate's letter, though "a little more gracefully phrased," was more of the same.

Crane could hardly believe what he was reading. His interpretation of events went something like this: Soon after his arrival, he'd decided to take his meals with Mrs. Turner to give the Tates some privacy; and though he got no benefit from their kitchen, he'd continued to help Tate chop and saw the huge stacks of wood needed to keep the fires going in there. More, he'd generously lent the Tates God knew how much to help them out, including slipping Tate train fare for two trips to New York as well as enough extra for the opera. He'd even given Gordon his old typewriter when he'd bought a new one, just so she wouldn't have to wait for her husband to free up the one they owned. For her part, Addie Turner took the quarrel hard, crying day and night, so devoted was she to her Hart.

But the problem ran deeper. By April, the Tates had come to dislike Crane and his ways. The man was an unbridled romantic, without morals or even steady work habits. Here they were, virtual prisoners in the same isolated farmhouse out in the woods, with a man in the next room who came and went as he pretty much damned pleased, so that, as Caroline Gordon phrased it, "any social life which we all might have enjoyed together has been prevented by the feeling that we have to protect ourselves from you." Tate went further. It had all come to a head the night he and Crane had discussed Eliot's "negativity," he reminded Crane.

The trouble with Crane, Tate had told him, was that Crane always saw things in terms of his own insatiable ego. Negativity therefore for Crane was simply the name Crane applied "to any force not directly sympathetic to your own personal aims." And those aims, Tate summed up, included his poetry *and* his morals. Crane did whatever he damned well pleased, forever excusing himself as being possessed by some demonic force, much as he believed Christopher Marlowe had done. Not that Tate was necessarily right, he was quick to add, but wasn't it interesting that he (Tate) always seemed to be able to get along with other people with whom he disagreed? No, the trouble with Crane wasn't with Crane's ideas. The trouble with Crane was Crane. Tate was not accusing Crane, then; merely challenging him. And though Tate had not said so, Crane knew he kept a gun and could use it.[56]

How did one answer accusations like these? And from people he considered close friends? Crane tried to answer point for point, but there were too many points, and the letter snaked on and on. Yes, he was a "barbarian in many ways," and not used to living in domestic arrangements. No, he did not dislike Tate's poetry, and was sure it would never (mercifully) replicate the "supine narcissism" of his mentor, Eliot. Then he put all this aside as too "long and tiresome" and wrote more briefly: "We should be able to agree to disagree about such [literary] matters without calling in dish pans, saws and slop jars." Well, he had no apologies to make; his "frequent vulgarities and assumptions" were not really what was troubling the Tates anyway, and they all knew that. It was his way of living. There was no use "being either defensive or ironic." Better to let the whole thing drop. He was sorry, he ended, sorry for his "failings wherever they have incurred your inconvenience and displeasure." He asked Tate now to forget both them and himself "as soon as possible." He was hurt—far more deeply than he expected the Tates would ever know—and it was time to go. Crane stored his belongings in an unused room and prepared to leave. There was nothing for it but to get away from these two as soon as possible.

His first $1,000, which was to have lasted until May, was gone by late March; much of it had been spent on making his rooms in Patterson hospitable and conducive to creativity. At that point, believing he had no other options open to him, he'd written Kahn, asking for an advance on the second $1,000. Kahn had replied by sending him $500. Now here it was, mid-April, with winter just about over and the whole spring and summer open to him for his work, and he was going to have to find another place to live. He wrote his mother, begging her to let him go down to the Isle of Pines and finish *The Bridge*. He still had enough money for passage, and once there, he would be able to live frugally and prudently. Yes, it would be hot come summer; and, yes, there would be the hurricane season to contend with. But those he would manage. Besides, better a summer down there than some railroad flat in New York, its brick walls baking him alive with the insane summer heat. He was in fact so desperate to get away from the Tates that he sent her an ultimatum. Either she let him go to the one place where he could work on his poem, or he would do something drastic, since he would no longer care "about life or any future efforts to live." He might even go off to the Far East, with "just enough to get there and no more." Or he might just end it all "with powder and bullet."[57]

Terrified by her son's threats, Grace at last capitulated. If that was what Hart wanted, he could have it. Two days later, he was in New York to book cabin space on the next available ship. He wrote Waldo Frank, asking him to accompany him on the trip down. He wrote the caretaker of the Hart plantation, Mrs. T. W. Simpson, widow of the former caretaker, informing her of his arrival. Then he took the train back to Patterson to collect his things. Six weeks earlier, the Rychtariks had written, asking him to repay the $225 they'd lent him for the property he'd bought. Now he wrote to say he could spare only $100, for he would need the rest of his capital to get through the next seven months. The night of the 26th, his bags packed, he stayed at Robber Rocks.

Early the next morning, the Browns prepared to drive him into Pawling in the flivver. Just as it was getting light, Sue went out to the pump to fetch water and saw fifteen deer drinking at a waterhole a hundred feet off. She signaled to Crane and Slater through the window to tiptoe quietly out, and the three watched until finally, sensing the intruders, all the deer turned and ran single-file back up the hill into the woods again, leaping one after the other over a low stone wall. Crane watched the spectacle in awed silence. Then, suddenly, he began to weep, hugging first Sue and then Slater, telling them how much he loved them both and always would, until his dying day.

"Hart is a fine poet," Gordon would write her friend, Sally Wood, a month after Crane's departure. "But God save me from ever having another romantic in the house with me." Within a day of Crane's departure, Gordon at last had the room of her own she'd pined for.[58]

Two days later, at The Little Church in lower Manhattan, Crane watched as his mother and Charles Curtis exchanged vows. The couple had come to New York early so that Hart could be there for the wedding before sailing for Cuba. Afterwards there was a small dinner party with Bina Flynn, the O'Neills, the Cowleys, and a few others. Crane would remember Cecil Fiske, Eugene O'Neill's sister-in-law, gnawing at his hand while he talked with Malcolm and Peggy Cowley. "I don't remember what it was all about," Crane confessed to the Browns a week later, "but I think we fell in love with each other."[59] The following day, he took his mother and stepfather to lunch with the Lachaises and gathered the bronze seagull he'd commissioned. In the evening he took his mother and Charles Curtis over to MacDougal Street to see O'Neill's *The Great God Brown*. Everyone seemed happy. But during the intermission Grace said something that sent Crane into a rage and there was a shouting match in the lobby, which effectively froze the evening. Crane could take his mother, but only in small doses.

As it turned out, C.A. also happened to be in New York on business. Since he'd been told nothing of either the marriage or Harold's departure, he missed seeing his son altogether, though he did manage "a very pleasant visit" with Grace and her new husband before they left New York. C.A. wrote Harold afterwards that his mother had "chosen very wisely."[60] As for Crane, he had three mad days of it in New York, much of it drunk, before the SS *Orizaba* pulled out of its berth on the East River early Saturday morning, May 1st, bound for Cuba. From Batabanó, he would take the boat for the Isle of Pines and the plantation he'd dreamed of so often, the same place where, eleven years before, he'd twice tried to kill himself.

9 / CLENCHED BEAKS COUGHING FOR THE SURGE AGAIN!

ISLE *of* PINES, CUBA
MAY–OCTOBER 1926

ORTY-EIGHT HOURS OUT, somewhere off the coast of Florida: smooth waters, smooth as glass, the ocean blue-green turning to deeper blue, Crane in a deck chair watching like Columbus before him as flying fish smacked the waves off starboard, appearing, disappearing. Fine meals, impeccable service, his mother's farewell flowers on his cabin table, Waldo Frank still asleep. French wines (a "genial" Saint-Julien,[1] a respectable Sauternes), cordials, real Corona-Coronas each evening in the smoking room. The boat only half filled with passengers, mostly Cubans bound for Havana. The lights of "Pam Bitch" and "My Ammy" (Palm Beach and Miami) "and other Coney islands" (New York still on his mind) passing in the middle of the night.[2] And the open sea, the pitch and trough of it, the "sceptered terror" of that "Samite sheeted and processioned," all-mastering sea, rending "as her demeanors motion well or ill."[3]

They reached Havana the following day, 4 May 1926, the city's pastel-tinted colonial buildings glistening like something out of de Chirico. Frank's fluent Spanish meant they could see something of the real Havana: bars, cafés, theaters, a world filled with "blacks, reds, browns, greys and every permutation and combination of southern bloods." Sherry, Cognac, vermouth, a local beer Crane couldn't get enough of called *Tropical*. Taxis for twenty cents. "Great black-bushed buxom Jamaican senoritas" laughing, old women hobbling crabwise, trying to sell him lottery tickets, Crane taking one on a hunch. Their one night in Cuba, he and Frank checked into the Isla de Cuba Hotel and sauntered off to the Alhambra, Havana's version of New York's National Winter Garden Burlesque on East Houston Street. And though most of the double entendres of the risqué Spanish exchange escaped Crane, the stripteases and the sexual gyrations were universal enough, and more forthright than anything he'd ever seen on the Lower East Side. Women in scanty clothing beckoning from wrought-iron balconies in noisy side streets. The whole city both "hypersensual and mad," without any "apparent direction, destiny, or purpose," the sort of anarchic city, he imagined, Cummings would have called paradise.[4] But when he wrote his father, he described the place as "more like a toy city than a real one," its people a "trashy bastard" lot, though he certainly enjoyed the tobacco and the Bacardi.[5] And the Cuban and Spanish sailors in impeccable, tight-fitting trousers. Someday, he promised himself, he would come back, without Frank, and really let loose.

On the evening of the 5th, as he and Frank prepared to sail from Batabanó for the Isle of Pines, the U.S. Fleet, made up mostly of destroyers, landed in Havana, and suddenly the darkening streets were filled with waves of white uniforms pressing everywhere. Crane noticed one sailor who had "exactly the Chinese mustache effect" he himself had hoped to cultivate,[6] though without much success. But his eye was especially out for Jack Fitzin, the sailor he'd spent two heady days with back in January. As it turned out, Jack had been on a destroyer that had sailed right past Cuba on its way up to Norfolk. Within days Crane would have a batch of letters from Jack, first from Norfolk, then Washington, then Passaic, all forwarded by a puzzled Addie Turner, wondering who this Jack could be who was so anxious to get in touch with Hart. Then Sue Brown, informing him that Jack had actually made it up to Patterson looking for him. Crane thought he might have to phone Jack at his home in Passaic to try to "save" his honor, Mrs. Turner having no inkling yet of Crane's other life. Instead, he wrote Jack before leaving Havana to explain where he was, and why. "I commend your control under the penetrating gazes of Mrs. T," Crane thanked Sue, noting that one letter from Jack had contained a closing greeting from the gob's sister, "written in a very elegant hand." He was sure to be "well introduced" if he ever made it over to Passaic.[7]

On the morning of May 6th, Crane and Frank reached the Isle of Pines, then went on to Villa Casas, the Hart plantation outside the village of Nueva Gerona. There they met a stunned Mrs. Simpson. The frail, elderly widow of the caretaker was living alone on the decaying estate with Attaboy her parrot, who, hearing there were visitors at the front door, began squawking, "Damned poor dinner! Damned poor dinner!"[8] Mrs. Simpson had seen none of the Cranes in five years now, Grace being the last to visit back in 1921. She'd expected Crane to arrive alone, and then not for another three days. Charmer that he was, Crane quickly put her at her ease. She was "very sociable and jolly," he wrote his mother, and didn't at all mind his cigars or pipe. Besides, he'd already fallen in love with the woman for "her wit . . . good sense and lack of all sentimentality," and soon she was his "Aunt Sally."[9] For her part, reassured that Crane only wanted to help and meant to pay his own board, Aunt Sally quickly relaxed.

He loved the spaciousness of the old house, and soon settled into his mother's old room on the front west corner, with Frank in the adjoining room. There was even an indoor bathroom now, added since his last visit eleven years before. Here was the house he'd dreamed of in all its decayed splendor, its ruined roof above him, tropical beauty all about him, "the mountains, strange greens, native thatched huts,"[10] the perfume of oleanders and mimosas filling the air, and the warm coastal waters to swim and lounge and bathe in. At Frank's suggestion, he bought a pair of hemp-soled shoes, the sort worn by the local peasants, and found them "the coolest thing" for hot, dusty roads he'd ever tried.[11]

Though it was now the rainy season, there had as yet been almost no rain. And hot as the sun was, it wasn't half as bad as "midsummer heat in a NY office building, not to mention subways!" The major problem was mosquitoes, out in force and nesting in the now-ruined fruit groves his grandfather had planted, as Crane had seen at a glance, far too close to the house, so that he was soon hacking away at them with a machete. He wandered through Nueva Gerona, buying fresh fish off the docks and trying all sorts of exotic fruits and vegetables: cassavas, guavas, breadfruit, limes, kumquats, cashew apples, coconuts, wild oranges, bananas, mulberries, avocados, papayas, tamarinds, pomegranates, grabanas, and especially mangoes. Soon he was writing his father with a scheme for importing mangoes. They were the most delicious fruit he'd ever tasted, he wrote, man to man, and though it would "take millions of dollars to advertise them" enough to make them acceptable, once Americans tasted them they were sure to "come back for them like wildfire!"[12]

Within days, he and Frank had made friends with a pygmy owl. "Pythagoras," Crane named him, amazed at how a creature not much bigger than a plump sparrow could swallow a lizard whole, blinking as it did so, much to Crane's delight. One evening at dinner, Pythagoras deposited a small turd in Frank's salad, which Crane found very funny—though the fastidious Frank did not. He loved the way the owl squeaked, reminding him of Peggy Cowley when she'd had too much to drink. He rented a car and drove Frank and Aunt Sally over to visit with the Joneses, Americans who had been on the island since 1903. Over the years the couple had built up a local attraction called Jones's Jungle, filled with all sorts of exotic flora and fauna. Crane liked the old couple—"by far the pleasantest and most cultured people" he'd met on the Isle of Pines—and was saddened to learn that, with the signing of the Cuban-American Treaty returning the island to Cuba, all the Jones's labor—"twenty-three years of unremitting toil"—was about to come to nothing.[13] At any moment, Crane had discovered, the Cuban bureaucracy might simply seize the plantation, offering Jones a mere five dollars an acre, and there would be nothing Jones could do about it. Many Americans were in the same boat, Crane knew, including his grandmother: Americans who could no longer even give their estates away. One could work and work, Crane understood anew, and this be the end of all one's toil.

On the night of the 18th, Frank left the island to return to the States. Crane and Aunt Sally saw him off on the boat that would take him to Batabanó, where he would embark for New York. A few days later Crane had a letter from Eugene O'Neill, saying that Liveright was waiting for the final manuscript of *White Buildings*. What the hell did that mean? Crane wondered. He'd already given him the final manuscript months before. Did Liveright want the book or not? And was O'Neill doing the foreword or not? It had been hard enough asking him to write it in the first place, but it was going to be "harder and more embarrassing still" to have to keep reminding him that the book was in limbo until O'Neill wrote something by way of a preface.[14]

Perhaps the news contributed to Crane's going on a bender. Perhaps by now he needed no excuse, though he had been the model of decorum in front of Aunt Sally for the past two weeks. In any event, on the 21st—Cuban Independence Day—he got uproariously drunk for the first time since his arrival. Staggering back from town to the plantation in the darkness, he found himself at one point surrounded by a flock of goats that had wandered up onto the road. He stumbled, got up, stumbled again, terrified at what Aunt Sally would say when she saw him, but helpless now to do anything about it. In fact, when he finally crashed into the house, there was a scene, the two of them having it out "fair and square." But when he reminded her that there were "a couple of murdering desperadoes" who'd recently escaped from the island's penitentiary and were still on the loose, she at last relented.[15] Besides, she liked having Crane around, drunk or no. Finally it was resolved that he would be allowed to drink as much as he damned please whenever he damned pleased and that Aunt Sally would look the other way. She was certainly more pliable and understanding than Grace had ever been about his peccadilloes.

The following morning, sitting down to work on the "Ave Maria" section, he wrote out instead "a little unconscious calligramme" called "The Mango Tree." In semicoherent fashion he managed to sing the mango's "old hypnotisms," which rippled along its golden boughs. The mango, he believed, was after all the original apple in the Garden of Eden, "being the first fruit tree to be mentioned in history with any accuracy of denomination." This and other such questionable esoterica he'd culled from *The Problem of Atlantis* by one Lewis Spence, "the last book out on the subject, and full of exciting suggestions." Forty or fifty thousand years back, he'd discovered, there had actually been a continent in the mid-Atlantic which, except for its highest points in the Antilles and West Indies, had sunk beneath the waves. Such a theory was "impossible forever to prove," of course, but it resonated beautifully with Crane's own idea that Atlantis and the New World were one and the same.[16]

Then came the rains, threatening to wash his own island under. He and Aunt Sally spent hours lugging whatever pots and pans they could find up into the attic to keep the water from crashing down into the rooms below. Already he could visualize the damaged tiles, the rotting main beams, the water washing into crevices through the ruined roof. Either it was repaired at once or the house would soon be gone, he wrote his mother and grandmother, begging them to have the work done before it was too late. The wooden water tank too, which had all but collapsed, would have to be replaced. He expected to hear by telegram, then by letter, but there was no answer. In the meantime, he set about trying to save the house in whatever way he could. He worked under a blazing sun, cutting down rotten orange trees in the front yard and replacing them with young royal palms, the "perfect . . . tree to have round a house," he wrote home again, perfect for "their ornamentation, stateliness and openairyness."[17] He put in rock and cement gateposts and repaired the fence along the front of the house as best he could. But he had to know, damn it, if his mother planned to keep the place or get rid of it as she'd gotten rid of his boyhood home in Cleveland.

Then, on June 3rd, a month into his stay, dulled by the intense heat of the island and unable to get any more work done on *The Bridge*, he booked passage on a sixty-foot schooner bound for Grand Cayman Island, a coral outcrop twenty-two miles long and about a third as wide. Having been told by some of the Americans on the Isle of Pines that Grand Cayman was incredibly beautiful, Crane was anxious to find out for himself. The 150-mile outward-bound trip should have taken two days, but the headwinds were so strong it took double that time to reach the island, on a crowded boat, under a tropical sun, "with thirty-five cackling, puking, farting Negroes (women and children first)." The deck was strewn with basins for catching vomit, as well as chamberpots, some of which dribbled their contents over onto the deck. Worse was the drinking water, passed about from mouth to mouth in a common can, and so contaminated, cloudy, and vile-tasting that he drank only when he was forced to by a driving thirst. For the entire, becalmed trip he listened to the passengers singing song after song, interspersed with the moans and weeping of a dozen seasick women, their cries rising from below deck, unseen except for the occasional hand passing up a bucket of human waste to be dumped overboard.

And then the descent into hell itself. On Grand Cayman, he encountered a flat and sandy desert, with black clouds of mosquitoes everywhere. The only place Crane could find to put up was a boardinghouse with babies and small children everywhere, making a constant racket, and—when that quieted down—hymn-singing pilgrims in the

next house shouting far into the night. Worse, he could find no netting anywhere, so that he was reduced to dusting himself with insect
powders and burning smudge pots in his room day and night, eyes
smarting and tearing, while he "lunged back and forth," half maddened
by the swarms of mosquitoes. By the end of his first day, the right side
of his face and neck was swollen with insect bites.

He spent an eternity of ten days on the island, never once seeing
any of the beautiful beaches he'd been told about, for "to walk more
than half a mile from your doorstep was almost to court madness, St.
Vitus dance, or death." Instead, he holed up in his room and read *Moby-
Dick* through for the third time, waiting for the schooner to take him
back to the Isle of Pines and his aunt Sally.

The trip back turned out to be no better than the trip out. Once
again he faced the same crowded, filthy decks, and a two-day trip that
stretched to four, two of those drifting, drifting on a becalmed Sargasso Sea, the waters glassy-smooth with the tropic sun beating down on
his hatless head, unable to go below deck without getting sick to his
stomach with the stench and moans. In those four days, without shade
on that deck, Crane felt himself turn darker and darker until he looked
like any of the other passengers, or, as he put it, "positively Ethiopian."
Worse, he developed a serious ear infection, so that even sounds began
to hurt. By the time he reached Villa Casas on the 18th, he was grateful for everything. Fresh water and mangoes and green thoughts in a
green shade. Seeing toothless old Aunt Sally, he said, was like catching
a glimpse of the Statue of Liberty as one sailed into New York.

At some deep level, he'd actually enjoyed the trip, lulled by the
hypnotic rhythm of the boat cutting through the waves when the wind
was up. It was like nothing he'd ever experienced, and it made him
feel closer to what he imagined Columbus's crew (or even Ahab's) must
have felt as they crossed the Atlantic in boats not much larger or better
outfitted than the one he was on. Infinite blue skies, an open sea, and
"acres of man-sized leaping porpoises (the 'Huzza Porpoises' so aptly
named in *Moby-Dick*) that greet you in tandems." Like the Lachaises out
walking, with Madame always a step behind her husband. Once, he
watched an enormous white fin shark as it swam alongside the
schooner before at last it disappeared from sight.

Still, the whole experience had left his brain baked and empty.
After what he'd been through, how would he ever return to *The Bridge*
now? Whatever had first spurred him to envision the possibility of map-

ping his New World vision, his "Atlantis," was gone, and pounding away at his typewriter felt like mental masturbation. Poetry had devolved into "mere wordpainting and juggling, however fastidious," and seemed worse than useless. Better, he confessed to Frank, if Kahn had never given him the money to write in the first place. At least then he might be sweating it out in some office in Manhattan in the summer heat, "nose to the grindstone," fooling himself that if he only had the freedom to write, the poem would be there. As it was, with all the time in the world he had written nothing, zero, and there was no hiding the fact. Having read Oswald Spengler's *Decline of the West*, he understood now that the philosopher's bleak vision of the inevitable end of Western civilization was true, after all. The modern visionary was merely a licker of his own bile and vomit, something he had mistaken for the common diet. The truth was that American culture was "without faith and convictions." Better to be an elf in "elfin land with a hop pipe" dangling from one's mouth than try to be a poet.[18]

He knew that the artist's vision had always to be checked against reality, and that the darkness had always to be taken into account in understanding the light. Heaven, yes, but the necessary concomitant of a hell as well. The trouble was this: in the past, whether for an ecstatic like Blake or a poet of luminous darkness like Rimbaud, at least the poet and his audience could assume that his intuitions were salutary and his vision represented those experiences shared with his readership. But now one could not even speak of a common idea of what constituted good or evil. How, then, speak of the transcendent when the idea of the transcendent was no longer something held in common? How lonely, how goddamn terrifyingly lonely, to inhabit a heaven where you were forever alone, singing in the void to yourself. He still wanted to write *The Bridge*. But he'd seen too much, including the whiteout of all values on that God-forsaken island, so that—barely three years after conceiving the work—he was afraid the whole idea now of a bridge linking the reader and the self was only a bad joke, and one at his expense.

Admittedly, there had been authentic enough "materials that would have been a pleasurable agony" to wrestle into some final form: themes and images and a music all making up a single unitary vision. Shared notions of space, time, love, and eternity. And foremost among those ideas had been the idea of a bridge, both as "an act of faith" and as a way of communicating across the void that separated each from the

other. He'd needed symbols—Cathay, Columbus, the Indian, the journey west, the river, the skyscraper, the airplane, the railroad, the subway, the voyager—to support that vision. But on Grand Cayman, Crane
had seen something that had shaken him to the core and that had made
him question himself and his grand project. He knew all of this was of
vast importance to him. But was it important to anyone else? Was it at
all important to those black women crying out in the hold of that
schooner? Would they have given a nickel for his vision? Really, did the
issues that Emerson and Whitman, Poe and Dickinson and Melville had
raised matter any more? He might "amuse and delight and flatter" himself as much as he liked, but wasn't he just fooling himself, playing the
part of some out-of-fashion Don Quixote tilting at windmills, wasting
his time and his reader's time, that is, if he even had a readership?

When he looked at the past—at Columbus sailing off into
uncharted waters after a vision, or the intrinsic nobility of the Indian,
or the westward march, or the classical age of American prose, or a
technology that had conquered space and time—and then looked at his
own moment—the age of the flapper, of the grisly war so recently concluded, of the Babbitts of the world out to make a buck while artists
like himself lived hand to mouth, of the repressive sexuality that could
boo Isadora Duncan off stage or force him to hide his own homosexuality—when he considered all this, he was simply at a loss to explain
how there could ever have existed anything between the past he'd
worked so feverishly to uncover "and a future destiny worthy of it."
Perhaps America had completed its manifest destiny with the opening
of the West, and the vision he'd tried to catch in the language mesh of
"Atlantis" was merely an empty echo of that earlier vision, a mock
vision, a bad dream, something suspended "in ether like an Absalom
by his hair," waiting to be put out of its misery.

The Bridge as a symbol in 1926? What a joke! What in God's name
was his bridge when all was said and done but some stone pile held
together by miles of baling wire? A way of getting from Brooklyn to
Manhattan faster and cheaper than by ferry, an "economical approach
to shorter hours, quicker lunches, behaviorism and toothpicks." Admit
it. His brand of Romantic poetry was dead. Better to go back to New
York, the bubble of his delusion at last burst, and get on with his life.
Which really did come down at last—as his father had been telling him
for years—to a steady job and a paycheck.

Rimbaud had been "the last great poet" Western civilization
would ever see, the man who'd "let off all the great cannon crackers in

Valhalla's parapets." How ironic then that just as American poets were beginning to be recognized, the vision Whitman's poems had announced for America fifty years before should bob up dead on the surface. Not of course that his countrymen had ever accepted Whitman's democratic, all-embracing vision of a brotherhood of the spirit. Which meant that all that was left for Whitman's heirs—himself included—were some elaborate word games for some inner circle of poets to admire or envy. At least that was how Crane felt in the summer of 1926, exiled to some far-off island, his skin peeling like old wallpaper and his ears humming with some infernal infection. Who knew? Perhaps tomorrow would find him tinkering with his poem again, for something would have to be written if he wasn't to be a total laughingstock, some sort of poem, even if it turned out to be no better than the goddamned ad copy he'd written so often in the past.[19]

Whether or not he yet realized it, Crane had hit bottom. He had just confessed to his own deepest misgivings for his poem. When he finally began writing again a month after his return from Grand Cayman, it was not *The Bridge* to which he turned, but a poem dealing with the hypnotic lure of the sea, "Repose of Rivers," a lyric he would publish that September in *The Dial* under the provisional title, "Tampa Schooner." It would turn out to be the final poem he would add to *White Buildings*, and it struck a note there of repose reached only after the hard-won experience recorded in so many of the book's other poems. It was a repose that would be heightened by his placing it just before "Paraphrase," the poem in which Crane had imagined the final "white paraphrase" of his own death.

"I have just now returned from a western trip and confidently hope that the Kansas City plant has been sold to my employees there," C.A. wrote his son in early July.[20] He'd opened two new wholesale outlets and was expanding his retail business as well. But he took a moment now to remember the comforting sound of rustling palms in the late afternoons when the trade winds came up the bay on the Isle of Pines. Crane was touched by his father's forgetting his business affairs long enough to share that memory with him. And in "Repose of Rivers" he would begin with the sound of that wind sloughing through the willows of his nearly obliterated boyhood: the slightly disturbing sibilants of the wind whispering across meadows, leveling marsh grass and wave, and the poet—at one now with the river, in fact, become the river—moving surely, inevitably, toward the open seas, the beginning remembered as the end came on:

The willows carried a slow sound,
A sarabande the wind mowed on the mead.
I could never remember
That seething, steady leveling of the marshes
Till age had brought me to the sea.

And other memories: cliffs, the hell-like "alcoves/Where cypresses shared the noon's/Tyranny." The image too of "mammoth turtles climbing sulphur dreams," as they swam in the sun-silt shallows, following their dreams as he had followed his. And further evocations: an early spring landscape not unlike the one he'd fled from in Patterson, a family of beavers (the Tates?) busy at their "stitch and tooth." The escape too from the feverish, erotic world of New York with its "scalding unguents spread and smoking darts." And then, "beyond the dykes," all that torment behind him now, sinking under its own weight, and the sound of wind again, sweeping across the massive green waves of the open sea, "wind flaking sapphire, like this summer," a music that had haunted him since childhood, caught now, understood, and—yes—at last embraced, like easeful death itself. What did anything finally matter, knowing as he did that out there the ocean waited patiently, whenever he was ready, to claim her own?[21]

Just as things were looking their darkest, he had a letter from Sue Brown and a telegram from Frank. At the very time he'd been fending off clouds of mosquitoes on Grand Cayman, it turned out, Jimmy Light and Horace Liveright had been talking with Otto Kahn in New York. Liveright had had Crane's manuscript with him at the time, and had already told Light he'd decided against publishing *White Buildings*. He did not like the poems, did not understand them, and was sure the book would lose him money. Besides, O'Neill had yet to produce the promised foreword and—knowing O'Neill—Liveright was sure he never would. Then, at the end of June, Light and O'Neill had been in Liveright's office on business and had noticed Crane's manuscript lying on Liveright's desk. Liveright was about to return the manuscript, he told them, but now Light and O'Neill—at the last moment—persuaded him to go ahead and publish it. Hart Crane was the real thing, they told him, and some day Liveright was going to be proud he'd published the book.

Okay, Liveright told them. He'd do the damn book, but only—and this he insisted on—when O'Neill came through with the foreword he'd promised months ago. Now it was O'Neill who demurred. He liked the poems, he said, though why he couldn't exactly say. Damn it, he was a dramatist, not a literary critic, and Liveright was putting him on the spot asking him to do what he couldn't do. But for Crane's sake he would write something. And with that, Liveright picked up the phone and called his printer. They were going to publish *White Buildings.*

This was the news awaiting Crane on his return from hell. In the meantime, he had other problems to contend with. Within forty-eight hours of his return, besides a terrible case of sunburn, he developed painful abscesses in both ears that left him disoriented and unable to sleep. Then his chest began hurting. When the symptoms persisted, he finally took the boat to Havana in early July to see a Dr. Agramento there, a man who'd trained at Columbia. What Agramento found was a slight throat infection, caused by Crane's drinking tainted water on the boat. That and an ear infection caused by the heat baking down on his head during the trip out and back from Grand Cayman, for which he was given medication. He stayed in Havana only one night, he told his mother, during which time he'd sipped *limonades* and taken a long walk around the harbor and the extensive seaside public park called the Malaçon.

What he did not tell her was that he'd picked up a Spanish sailor who turned out to be such an ardent lover Crane swore to get back to Havana as soon as God permitted. Give him the society of vagabonds and sailors any time, he wrote Underwood, perhaps that same day. *There* were men who didn't go in for idle "chit-chat" like his gossipy literary friends. "Immortally choice and funny and pathetic" his encounters with sailors had been, he confessed, unlike some to whom he had betrothed his faith only to be disappointed. But with sailors no faith was expected, "and how jolly and cordial and warm the touseling" (did he mean tousling or tonsilling?) could be, after all. When faith in *The Bridge,* faith in his friends, his family, even himself, proved "a fake and a mockery," there was still the electric thrill of uncomplicated sex. Long live lust. Let it be his ruin.[22]

After having lost contact with his old classmate, Bill Wright, for the past several years, Crane was now surprised and delighted to hear from him again. Bill was finally getting married, he wrote. In mid-July, Crane wrote to congratulate him, adding that he himself had "hovered on the brink" of getting married several times, but had decided finally that he was "too ridiculously romantic for marriage," a decision he thought showed him "to be cautious and wise in the extreme!" He bemoaned not being able yet to get back to *The Bridge*. "I get awfully exhausted sometimes," he confessed, "trying to achieve some kind of consistent vision of things." And though it did him no good to worry, what could he do?[23]

Two days later, the Muse mercifully, inexplicably returned. But only after Crane closed his copy of Spengler with its long lament for the death of Western civilization and turned instead to the epic, life-sustaining pages of *Don Quixote*. Cervantes's comic vision somehow allowed Crane once more to get on with his poem. Now, as the throbbing in his ear disappeared, his brain began teeming with images, themes, and lines, and suddenly he found himself writing "like mad."[24] In fact, for the next ten weeks he would exist in a prolonged ecstasy of creation such as he had never before experienced and would never experience again. "Hail Brother," he wrote Frank on July 24th, three days after his twenty-seventh birthday. "I feel an absolute music in the air again, and some tremendous rondure floating somewhere." For the past week he'd worked on his "little dedication"—his "prelude"—to *The Bridge*, the poem entitled "To Brooklyn Bridge." A "steady and uncompromising" piece of work, Crane called it, and "almost the best thing" he'd ever done.[25]

"How many dawns," he wrote, reimagining New York with its harbor and bridge as he sat in his room on a ruined plantation fifteen hundred miles away on the Isle of Pines. New York, blessèd New York, with its white buildings gleaming across the waters in the morning sun, the whole poem lifting now, like those gulls rising in "white rings of tumult" from their sleep to rise into the skies above them, unchained at last and free:

> *How many dawns, chill from his rippling rest*
> *The seagull's wings shall dip and pivot him,*
> *Shedding white rings of tumult, building high*
> *Over the chained bay waters Liberty . . .*

How many times had he glimpsed that promise, the incredible vision of a New World, the mystic's vision of a love so immense it saturated the world with light? New York and the Brooklyn Bridge seen from his window, unobstructed by the welter of subways or cramped office buildings facing onto other office buildings, or shadowed side streets with their cold-water flats, or the canyons created by Wall Street's skyscrapers. The bridge, his bridge, "across the harbor, silver-paced/as though the sun took step of thee," dawn and midmorning and noon and midafternoon and evening, the infinite play of light and shadow across its stone pilings and those harplike Aeolian cables. That bridge and his Bridge, each a harp, each a possibility invoking the real possibility of the divine. Each then an altar lifting its voice of praise to the idea of Love. Each fused in the white heat of the imagination. He too, like Columbus and Roebling before him, questioned, mocked, their visionary projects—like Don Quixote's—rejected as feverish dreams:

> Terrific threshold of the prophet's pledge,
> Prayer of pariah, and the lover's cry.[26]

In spite of the prostrating heat, Crane worked steadily. At last, on the evening of July 25th, he walked out through the ruined orange groves singing to the great moon, which seemed to bend down to listen to his serenade. Struts and cables, winches and cranes. Finally the poem was coming together. On the 22nd, he'd sent a copy of "To Brooklyn Bridge" to Marianne Moore at The Dial, begging her to forgive his not being able to supply return U.S. postage (impossible for him to get in Cuba) should she wish to send the poem back. Four days later, he sent Frank a copy of the "Ave Maria," explaining that accidents happened, and so he wanted Frank to have copies of those parts of The Bridge he'd completed. Each day now the poem seemed to reach after greater and greater heights. In the "Ave Maria," he'd somehow managed to get the sea itself, which had so haunted him on the trip back from Grand Cayman, into his poem. "Observe the water-swell rhythm that persists until the Palos reference," he whistled. "Then the more absolute and marked intimation of the great Te Deum of the court, later held,—here in the terms of Columbus's own cosmography."[27]

On the 29th, he wrote the Cowleys that the Columbus section had been cleared up and that the last ten days had seen the beginning of several other sections of the poem. After finishing Basil Lubbock's The China Clippers, he'd drafted "Cutty Sark," yet another sea section, enclosing that in his letter (in case something happened to him) and asking the Cowleys to show it to no one but the Browns and Allen Tate. "In the middle of *The Bridge* the old man of the sea (page [*pace*] Herr Freud) suddenly comes up," he explained. He also wanted Malcolm and Peggy to know that all the clippers mentioned in the poem had actually existed, with "extensive histories in the Tea trade." In fact, the two ships that ended the poem—he was thinking perhaps of Tate—had been "life-long rivals." Gone, all gone now, ghost ships sailing under the East River in the dead of night.[28]

Aunt Sally had proved a godsend. She was a mother who did not intrude, but allowed him to come and go as he wished. She never pried, delighted in his writing, and was ready to listen whenever he was ready to talk. "I'm lucky to have a decent female around here," he confided to Underwood, such women in his experience being rare enough. "She's old, wizened, has a parrot, and lets me alone; but this doesn't begin to do her justice."[29] He'd been reading Smollett's *Ferdinand Count Fathom,* and Aunt Sally had listened to him talk about the book for so long she'd even named one of her roosters after the hero. When he wasn't writing or reading, he sat in the ruined parlor and strummed away at the piano for hours at a time, soothing the two of them:

> *in the nickel-in-the-slot piano jogged*
> *"Stamboul Nights"—weaving somebody's nickel—sang . . .*[30]

Nights he tossed, troubled by the stifling heat pressing succubus-like against his chest. Or it was the hayhennies and crowing roosters in the first light of dawn, and soon he would be up and back at his desk writing once more. In ten days, he somehow managed to write ten pages of *The Bridge.* "Highly concentrated stuff, as you know it is with me," he wrote Grace on the 30th, "and more than I ever crammed into that period of time before." He was sure the poem would be "brightly finished" by the time he was ready to return to the States the following May. Then he would make "a magnificent bow to that magnificent structure, The Brooklyn Bridge, when I steam (almost under it) into dock!"[31]

He even began making "Notes" for *The Bridge,* in imitation of Eliot's for *The Waste Land.* He did not know if he would include them or not, but one—an angle chart lifted from a copy of *Scientific American*—seemed to embody for Crane "a complete symbolism of both Bridge and Star."[32] Perhaps he would use that for the cover. (He did not.) The reading continued as well: *Don Quixote,* Smollett, Proust, Fielding's *Jonathan Wild,* Nashe's *The Unfortunate Traveller,* the last two "full of marvelous prose and observations, satire and diamonds."[33] All of it was ballast, he explained, the necessary counterweight to the more transcendental flights of *The Bridge.*

And on it went. "Have been so fast at work the last two weeks— almost *possessed* in the Dostoyevskian sense," he wrote Underwood on August 3rd, when he came up for air again.[34] That same day he'd sent Kahn copies of "To Brooklyn Bridge" and the "Ave Maria." Then a note to Frank with a revised version of "Atlantis." He was "dancing on dynamite these days," he told his old confrere, "so absolute and elaborated has become the conception. All sections moving forward now at once!"[35] Not until then had he realized just why a bridge was built from both ends at once. Well, both ends were finished now, as well as the threshold proem and a draft of "Cutty Sark," which he meant to situate somewhere toward the end. Now he began working on "Powhatan's Daughter," the poem's central span: the necessary antecedent to the thematic conquest of time and space via the railroad and the airplane, which parts would surely follow.

In late July, word had reached him through Frank that Tate, in an effort to make up for his argument with Crane, had offered to write an introduction to *White Buildings.* By then, since it was clear that O'Neill was never going to do it, Tate went so far as to suggest that he write the introduction under O'Neill's name, if that would get the book published. It was a selfless gesture on Tate's part, this salvage operation, though of course Crane would insist that the introduction be published under Tate's own name. He wasn't really even upset with O'Neill, for he knew the man did not have "the necessary nerve to write what his honesty demanded—a thorough and accurate appraisal" of the book.[36] Tate set out at once to write the piece and a week later it was in Crane's hands, sent on by Munson. Crane loved it, finding it "clever, valiant, concise and beautiful."[37] Tate's gesture had completely erased Crane's anger toward the man, Crane wrote his mother, delighted with "so discriminating an estimate."[38] Then came the contract for *White Buildings,* along with a check for $100 as an advance against royalties. Other checks followed, from *The Dial* and *The Calendar* of London, for poems accepted. How bountiful, when they wished to be, the gods.

By August 12th he'd completed most of "Powhatan's Daughter," including "The Harbor Dawn," "Van Winkle," and "The Dance," and was now reading Carl Sandburg's *The Prairie Years*, hoping it might inspire him to finish "Indiana," the last part of the Indian sequence. This last part would, he hoped, round the entire section out with the '49 gold rush and the return of the Prodigal Son east to merge with the sea. By then he'd also written two of his "Three Songs," modeled loosely on Eliot's three songs from the third section of *The Waste Land*. Even the third Song, entitled "Virginia," spoofing America's obsession with the Saturday-Mary-Shredded-Wheat-golden-tressed girl seated in New York's tallest white building, the nickel-and-dime Woolworth Building, was well on its way to being finished. These songs would all follow "Cutty Sark," on the other side of the poem's divide. He toyed with the idea of including "The Mango Tree" in his epic, though he soon changed his mind on that score. Even the subway section ("The Tunnel") and the "Calgary Express" (probably an early version of "The River") were now under construction. Each day he skipped back and forth between sections, "like a sky-gack [sic] or girder-jack" working on one of those white buildings going up all the time in New York.[39] Truly, he was going to need all the inspiration he could muster to see through to completion the new experiments in form and meter he was working with in "Cutty Sark," "The Tunnel," and "Three Songs."

For this one brief moment he felt "happy, quite well, and living as never before." He even had enough money to see him through for the next few months, so that for once he did not have to worry about food or shelter at this most critical of junctures when all the "impressions and concepts" that had been ripening for the past three years seemed to be coming to fruition. Nothing but a form as large and as generous as *The Bridge*, Crane believed, could have held all his images and themes without the syntactic "violences" that had marred what he thought of now as the "more casual" poems of *White Buildings*.[40] Although only half finished, his poem was already longer than *The Waste Land*, the poem he had kept constantly in mind as the paradigm to work with and against. *The Bridge*, he told the Rychtariks, was not only alive and kicking, but actually "becoming divine."[41]

Even dismal Spengler had been important, he could see, for the philosopher's vision, dark as it was, had "conspired in a strangely symbolical way toward the present speed" of *The Bridge*. Hard experience had taught Crane that as soon as one understood that life was essentially tragic, "immediately every circumstance and incident in one's life" seemed to turn toward "a positive center of action, control and beauty." He was finally at the point where he was living *inside* his poem, allowing it to teach him what it had to teach. "To handle the beautiful skeins of this myth of America, to realize suddenly . . . how much of the past is living under only slightly altered forms, even in machinery and suchlike," was tremendously exciting. He was in very heaven now, and he was having the time of his life.[42]

But by then the Isle of Pines was in the midst of the equatorial storm season. Thunder rolled in across the mountains and deep into the cavernous cliffs facing into the Atlantic. "You can hear the very snakes rejoice," Crane wrote Frank on August 19th, "the long, shaken-out convulsions of rock and roots." At night he found himself lying half awake, listening to the rain and dreaming "the most speechless and glorious dreams." Words came and went, like wrecks passing without the sound of bells, or like a rose yielding "only its light, never its . . . form." Then, with first light, he would hear the cocks begin crowing again, and Aunt Sally's familiar cough as she began stirring, Attaboy imitating the cough in the other room until he could almost believe she was in two places at once. How he loved that "little wrinkled burnous wisp" of a woman, who seemed capable of doing anything and who seemed to remember everything.[43]

By late August he had completed "The Tunnel." It was "rather ghastly,"[44] he confessed to Frank, having to stitch together the hundreds of notes he'd written while swinging on the subway straps as he passed under the East River, the wheels screeching against the rails, the agate lights blinking in the midnight tunnel, the car deserted, as he rode back to his apartment after a night in Manhattan. Times Square (time squared), Columbus Circle (time circling back on itself), Broadway's "Performances, assortments, résumés." Columbus's dream of the New World versus the world Crane found himself in in the 1920s figured in a subway ride beneath the East River at the darkest hour. Not Whitman's Open Road now, but Poe's City of Hell: a night world, the world as bad theater, where the curtain lifted "in hell's despite." The finale, Columbus on his third journey to the New World, having committed

himself by then to Indian despoliation and murder, as well as to slavery, as Africans were brought in to replace the decimated native populations. Less than ten years after the discovery of the New World, and
already large-scale greed taking its toll, and Eden—that Garden in the
third act—dead. History reduced to a series of "tabloid crime-sheets"
one leafed through before turning in to sleep the long sleep home.

Winter. Midnight. The agony in the garden. The hour of the wolf.
The descent into hell. Rip, following his childhood dream of America, returning now, older and wiser at nightfall. And that nickel that he
had carried with him throughout his journey across the continent,
dropped into the subway turnstile now, as the gongs signaled the
incoming train rivering beneath the city. Other faces, other voices,
heard underground, like the hoboes in "The River" section, these
speaking of gambling, of "the/girls all shaping up." A whore haggling
with a john on 14th Street. "If/you don't like my gate why did
you/swing on it, why didja/swing on it/anyhow," the lines themselves
mocking the prophetic Blake's injunction "To Find the Western
path/Right thro' the Gates of Wrath." To swing, to "somehow anyhow
swing," as Crane had swung, sometimes with casual partners picked
up in places like this. Had he too visited the 14th Street men's room?
Had he picked up some stranger there two years earlier, with Emil out
to sea? The thought of having picked something up—syphilis, gonorrhea, whatever—terrifying him for weeks on end, the fear playing over
and over like some old phonograph record:

> The phonographs of hades in the brain
> Are tunnels that re-wind themselves, and love
> A burnt match skating in a urinal . . .

A voice demanding service. To be serviced, and "after/the show" crying
a little, crying a lot, the head and swollen gonads, the "riven stump far
out behind," the horror of unlove reflected now in the disembodied
head of Poe, the demon visionary's agate eyes swinging from a noose-
like strap on the subway car. Poe in Baltimore, Poe (so the story went)
being dragged drunk from poll to poll to vote as the mob dictated—ah,
democracy—then left alone to die.

Gravesend Manor, Chambers Street, dead stop. And the living
dead, as Eliot had them, echoing Dante's surprise that "death had
undone so many." Riding the subway escalator at 14th Street, each eye
downcast, avoiding direct contact with anyone, each staring intently at

his shoes. Then the gongs again, and the train bound for Brooklyn. And now another vision: some "Wop washerwoman," hair bandaged, going home after sweeping the endless corridors and emptying slime from the cuspidors in those same white buildings—those "gaunt sky barracks"—left behind. Columbus—the original Genoese—and his descendant: some nameless immigrant Italian woman at the bottom of the rung, struggling to hold her family together. And "do you bring mother eyes and hands/Back home to children and to golden hair," the poet asks, as Whitman would have, Crane's heart going out to her. And the laughter of the demon—Lucifer, eldest star—in the insane screech of metal on metal as the train descends now, laughing at what we who have fled the Garden have become, the visionary voice itself reduced to a heap of "shrill ganglia/Impassioned with some song we fail to keep."

And then, at the lowest point of the journey, to feel the train begin to rise again, like Lazarus. To feel the rising slope and hear the "sound of waters" once more—the waters of "the River that is East," and the sea beyond it—"bending astride the sky/Unceasing with some Word that will not die." To have touched bottom, to have tasted this Bosch-like hell, and yet to refuse to say he can no more. He can. Can watch a tugboat lunge like a stallion up the river, signaling its passage. And now, released, to stand there along the Brooklyn piers, looking out across the river as so often Crane had done, listening for signs, counting like Dante released from hell the stars:

> the echoes assembling, one after one,
> Searching, thumbing the midnight on the piers.
> Lights, coasting, left the oily tympanum of waters;
> The blackness somewhere gouged glass on a sky.
> And this thy harbor, O my City, I have driven under,
> Tossed from the coil of ticking towers . . . Tomorrow,
> And to be . . . Here by the River that is East—
> Here at the waters' edge the hands drop memory;
> Shadowless in that abyss they unaccounting lie.

But is it all a lie, for which there is no word, no language, nothing to hold the vision gracing the poet in some unifying moment? A city running on time and never sleeping. And the East River, rolling on like the great Mississippi, outside time, until the sea itself seems pooled again in the ancient star he has followed since dawn. The hands of a clock and the hands of lovers. But to whom addressed? The beloved? God? Lucifer? The Bridge?

> *Kiss of our agony Thou gatherest,*
> *O Hand of Fire*
> *gatherest . . .*[45]

There were other poems as well from the bounty of that summer of 1926. Poems that would one day go into a third book, made up—like *White Buildings*—of discrete lyrics. Among these, a group of poems he would come to call "Key West: An Island Sheaf," among this group a lyric called "Island Quarry," a landscape poem based on the marble quarry near Villa Casas. That August, he sent a picture postcard of the marble pit to his sculptor friend Gaston Lachaise with the note, "This quarry is in the mountains, near our place. There's plenty to work on anytime you come!"[46] His bronze seagull, he told its creator, he carried with him wherever he went to remind him of his own work on *The Bridge*, for both gull and bridge seemed to grow more divine with time, he thought, each producing its own sea music, each at times winking at him.

How many times had he walked the road past the quarried mountain, watching the sweating chain gangs from the island penitentiary sawing marble slabs into square sheets? Or again at dusk, palms chevroning the mountain, beyond which lay the vast and unforgiving sea? Other times it was neither mountain nor sea nor even the goat path quivering with its creaturely needs, its sex, tears, its urge to sleep, but something far more perdurable: the marble itself like some Grecian urn, like his own vision sculpted into words, he hoped—something hard, something lasting beyond the time of flesh and blood:

> *—It is at times as though the eyes burned and glad*
> *And did not take the goat path quivering to the right,*
> *Wide of the mountain—thence to tears and sleep—*
> *But went on into marble that does not weep.*[47]

And other walks, as on the road into Nueva Gerona to pick up his mail, when he would see the village idiot watching him from behind some bush. For weeks he'd passed the boy daily, saying hello or waving, without receiving as much as a nod in return. But by mid-August they'd struck up a guarded friendship, the boy even responding to his greetings. One day he'd heard screeching, and saw a group of children standing in a semicircle pointing toward a house. And there he was, the boy, "standing mostly hid behind the wooden shutters behind the grating; his huge limp phallus" waving at the children while he grinned back at them.

A few days later Crane caught sight of the boy again, this time "talking to a blue little kite high in the afternoon." How beautiful the boy could be at times, he told Frank, "rendingly beautiful," talking to himself "and examining pebbles and cinders and marble chips through the telescope of a twiceopened tomato can."[48] A boy staring through a tin can at a kite made of sticks and paper, flying high in the heavens, a song on his lips "Above all reason lifting." Then the boy grown suddenly quiet at the approach of the poet, and the poet's "trespass vision" shrinking as the boy stared intently at him. Crane would not complete "The Idiot" for another year, but the poem belongs to this period, its image consonant with the Bedlamite poet scaling the bridge in Crane's Prologue to his poem. In that broken boy, in fact, Crane had glimpsed his double, singing as he worked to lift his paper-built machine high into the cheering skies above.[49]

Six weeks of it, night and day. Time then to take a break from the insects and whatever was creating havoc with his hay fever and get back to Havana for a visit. On August 29th, he took the boat to Batabanó and then went up to Havana to see the sights and take in a "few bad shows" for a week before returning to The Bridge. He was tired now, he told his mother, tired "from doing more writing than all the last three years together," itself "a glorious triumph."[50] The trouble was that by the time he reached Havana, he was broke again. Kahn had yet to send him his last installment of $500, and he was reduced to asking his father to lend him $50 to help see him through. Strangely, there was no reply. Crane stayed at the Nuevo Hotel (it advertised the fact that it had big rooms, sanitary service, yes, even elevators). He purposely avoided "American" restaurants, sticking only to Cuban fare, and walked the "quaint old streets and alleys" of the city, or took long cool drives along the Malaçon as he had with his father years before.[51]

But he had not been alone in Havana, as he admitted to Frank his last night in the city, sitting in *La Diana* and downing one more glass of "Diamante" before taking the night boat back to the Isle of Pines. At the moment he was watching a little drama unfold between a pestulant (a neologism combining petulant and pestilent?) monk "gulping olives at the next table" and a Spanish waiter, who was becoming more and more impatient with the priest. "Fuck la Cubana," the waiter was muttering, and it was all Crane could do to keep from roaring out loud at the little comedy of manners he was witnessing.

Well, he had a right to be happy, he confessed to Frank, for he was in love again, this time with Alfredo, a young Cuban sailor of Spanish heritage he'd met one night in Park Central after attending a burlesque show at the Alhambra. Between them, both monoglots, they'd somehow managed a dozen words. How many more did one need to communicate one's feelings, anyway? "Immaculate, ardent and delicately restrained," was how he ticked off Alfredo's virtues. "I have learned much about love which I did not think existed. What delicate revelations may bloom from the humble." Three devoted evenings together, long walks, drives on the Malaçon, a change of hotels. He'd come for relaxation, and he'd found it, and now he was going back to work, armed with a fresh perspective and an "internal glow . . . hard to describe." Life could be so kind at times.[52]

"Caro Hermano," he began his next letter to Frank, back on the Isle of Pines. "Estoy en casa ayer de madrugada. No dormaba la noche a bordo mar. Mucha calor. . . ." He went on for a few more lines in his newly acquired Spanish, "the most beautiful language in the world," before switching back to English. This was what Alfredo had done for him; and just as one love affair had led to the conception of *The Bridge*, so now he began dreaming again of his next project. It would be "a blank verse tragedy of Aztec mythology," for which he would have to study "the obscure calendars of dead kings." Some time in the next five years he meant to get to Spain to learn the language.[53]

But on his return from Havana Crane also found two letters from his mother that yanked him hard out of his reverie. After just four months of marriage, Grace and Charles Curtis had separated. "I think you are very brave," he wrote her as soon as he could steel himself for what he now feared lay ahead for him and his mother. "I'm proud of your spirit, and you must not fail to maintain it steadily."[54] Privately, he was seething. Two years of courtship, followed by a la-de-da charade of a wedding in New York, and now this! It was absolutely imperative that his mother not rob him—now of all times—of the focus he needed to get *The Bridge* finished. For this reason he did not write her again for two weeks, and then only after she wrote accusing him of being indifferent to her plight. Stung, he tried to explain. "If I sometimes seem indifferent," he reminded her, "remember that I'm attempting a titanic job myself, and if anything of that is to be accomplished there must be some calm and detachment sought for." He begged her to brace up, and not to dwell so much on "melodramatic things like old ladies homes."[55]

As hurricane season approached, Crane reached back into memory to the feverish desolation of his Grand Cayman journey. Of the poems that came out of his experience in the tropics, none is more powerful than "O Carib Isle!" Like Whitman in his dark threshold poem, "As I Ebb'd with the Ocean of Life," "O Carib Isle!" asks whether the whole project of poetry, *The Bridge* included, can ever amount to anything more than a futile exhalation of air. "I'll never forget that trip," Crane would write to Yvor Winters the following January. "The . . . schooner had *only* 35 on it (myself the only white); the sun was practically 'equatorial' at that time and latitude; and we were becalmed—dead still—under that sun," until (quoting from Coleridge's *Rime of the Ancient Mariner*) "the very deep did rot." And still, he added, amazed, "nothing stopped the enchanted tongues of those niggers."[56]

Song, poetry, something to lift the human spirit in a time of extremity. Crane's poem begins with his standing before a graveyard scooped out of the marl and coral and questioning even the possibility of a link between nature and human meaning. In the feverish sibilants of the opening lines one hears the dominant key of a hostile and indifferent nature that kills and obliterates:

> *The tarantula rattling at the lily's foot*
> *Across the feet of the dead, laid in white sand*
> *Near the coral beach . . .*

They have the tradition of blank verse behind them, these lines, though they are more irregular and dissonant, as if even the sureties of the traditional line were breaking up. Likewise, if the lily remembers the resurrection of the dead, it is the tarantula that reigns in this kingdom. That and the white sand and coral beach made up of the remains of millions upon millions of once-living creatures reduced now to white death.

And there, crawling grotesquely across the landscape, fiddler crabs, mocking the poet's attempts to create an order out of words. For what the crabs leave behind are only illegible markings in the sand, as if they meant to "shift, subvert/And anagrammatize" the poet's very name and identity. In fact, they seem to mock his attempts to order his world, to call things by their living names, until even his name—his very identity—is transformed into white death, "Crane" anagrammatized to "nacre"—mother-of pearl. "Those are pearls that were his eyes," *The Waste Land* remembering Ariel's taunt from *The Tempest*, Crane meditating now on the transformations death accomplishes in us. "Nacreous frames of tropic death": the once living become limestone, coral, bone, shell, those "brutal necklaces of shells" that frame these tropic graves. The poet has stared into the face of death, only to discover an image of the ultimate entropy of poetry itself: a human being become at last a chalklike frame of words.

Worse is knowing that nothing mourns the passing of life here in the insane heat of the summer tropics. Beyond: the undifferentiating, unmanning sea always somewhere near, ready to erase any sign that one ever passed this way before. In his condensed Mallarméan syntax, "neither," it turns out, is actually the unspoken first word of Crane's poem, the stripped syntax, reconstituted, reading, "Neither" the tarantula . . . nor the zigzag crabs . . . mourn." Nothing mourns, and even the one health-giving eucalyptus—palsied now—"merely lifts/In wrinkled shadows" as its leaves are moved by the passing wind. This is hell, really, for the word "hell" is itself backformed on the Greek *kalyptos*: something hidden, concealed, much like its echo, "crypt," *kryptos*, which Crane also evokes here. The poet who had sought a vision of the truth of things has this time come up blank.

Against nature's gargantuan pressure to white out all human meaning and all human feeling, then, the poet can do nothing but surrender or try to answer the insistent rattle and cicadalike pressure of nature with the counterpressure of the human imagination. But how else do this except by ordering and naming? Like Adam in the Garden making the world in his own image, he too must name, though to be sure he no longer has Adam's assurance that there is any correspondence between the things he names and the words (and music) he has at his disposal. The human tongue, he has been warned by Spengler & Company, has become an utter stranger to nature. And yet to name—to utter "Tree names, flower names," and to do so in the face of an indifferent nature—is all the poet can do to "gainsay" for a little "death's brittle crypt," a phrase that echoes uncannily the phrasing "death's brittle script."

Crypt, kryptos: something hidden, something concealed. It is a key concept for Crane, as for all the Romantics. Bodies hidden, meanings concealed. The dead tell no secrets, Crane knows, though—as he had iterated earlier in "At Melville's Tomb"—they maddeningly intimate them, much as seashells, washed up on the beach, give us intimations of the secrets of the great sea, and so of our origins of ourselves and of our destinies. Against our feeble utterances, our little namings, our tiny exhalations of clicking syllables, our beating of the gums, Crane suddenly evokes the Carib hurricane, a version of the vast Sublime which advances and retreats as it pleases, as now "The wind that knots itself in one great death—/Coils and withdraws."

A great wind coiling like a snake, then striking, then withdrawing for a time. Ananke. Hurricane season in the tropics. And the force that first merely stirred the palsied eucalyptus returns with a vengeance. Crane actually began writing this poem in late August, when the hurricane that would strike the Hart plantation was still two months away. When it finally did strike, he spent the night under a bed with Aunt Sally and Attaboy, while above their heads the roof screamed as the winds clawed away at the house, intent on getting at the flesh inside:

> *Slagged of the hurricane—I, cast within its flow,*
> *Congeal by afternoons here, satin and vacant.*
> *You have given me the shell, Satan,—carbonic amulet*
> *Sere of the sun exploded in the sea . . .*

Somehow Crane has managed to hear and even to record something of nature's sublime terror. True, he is forced by what he has seen to admit that there does seem after all to be no "Captain," no God, no ordering principle on "this doubloon isle/Without a turnstile"; that there is no way in, and no possibility of a way in, to a deeper understanding of the nature of things. For this Carib isle, this isle of the crabs (another anagrammatization), he sees, belongs finally to those same "catchword crabs" scuttling about in the underbrush as they have for millennia, repeating their same unvarying sounds ad nauseam, until they have become metaphors for the experience of the place itself. In such a world, vision seems impossible. Indeed, Crane's senses have been "ambushed," his ideas of order, shaped by the civilized, coifed minor verities of Ohio and New York, rendered void in these tropics, his own eyes "webbed" and "baked."

Yet, in spite of the absence of any God he can name, there is a desperate vulnerability about Crane's prayer for meaning. And now, when it seems least expected, his cry is answered. For now he gives utterance to five of the most powerful lines found anywhere in modern poetry, lines (four of them rhyming on a single note) which are a cry chiming with the "enchanted tongues" of those black passengers on the schooner with Crane, whose songs he had listened to, mesmerized and dizzy, for four becalmed days on the baked and open sea. Call these lines a prayer, a petition, a striving for eloquence, a desire to hear the mighty strain of the Sublime again. They are lines stretched to six and seven stresses, made heavier by the strategic placement of stately spondees. Marlovian lines, perhaps, but necessary, as this last Romantic sees himself as one of those sea turtles here in the Tortugas, wrenched up from the ocean to be bound, spiked, eviscerated—crucified—along the wharves of the world's marketplace each morning, their eyes caked by the bitter salt that still reminds them of their lost first world:

> Let not the pilgrim see himself again
> For slow evisceration bound like those huge terrapin
> Each daybreak on the wharf, their brine caked eyes;
> —Spiked, overturned; such thunder in their strain!
> And clenched beaks coughing for the surge again!

"Such thunder in their strain," Crane marvels, as these otherworldly visionaries, hung upside down, attempt to sing of a world glimpsed and lost, "clenched beaks coughing for the surge again!" For tragically, although they cry out, all that the world hears are the hissings of these dying creatures who will soon be rendered into soup. There *is* another world, Crane has said, and in it there *is* a music he has heard, and which he has tried to make us hear as well, even if only by fits and starts, in coughs, in broken arcs and stifled orphic cries. And yet we too must feel something of his cry here in the majestic music he has rendered in these lines, in the slow evisceration of the speaker, in the trembling, electric surge and majesty of his words. A shadow music, then, of that unheard melody Crane somehow captured in the mesh of language, that "nacreous frame" of words, holding within its pliant lines an echo of that distant, thundering strain.[57]

By late September, he'd written Kahn twice, pleading for his last $500 so he could pay his bills and eat. "You can see the situation is a little harrowing," he explained, "especially as I am ill, entirely without funds, and need to get to a cooler locality." The summer he had just lived through had been "the hottest in twenty years" and, along with the insects and his work schedule, had left him exhausted.[58] But Kahn was away on business, and Crane was left to fend for himself as best he could. It was in the midst of these difficulties that he received a letter from a twenty-six-year-old poet, critic, and instructor of French and Spanish at Moscow University in Idaho, named Yvor Winters. He was delighted by Winters's interest. "It is just a 10-to-1 accident that I didn't write you first," Crane wrote Winters on October 5th. "What little of your work I have occasionally seen has stuck in my mind—as little else I see does." And being away from most magazines here on the island, he'd had to learn secondhand about Winters's spirited defense of his "For the Marriage of Faustus and Helen" in *Poetry*, which Winters had written to educate "Aunt" Harriet Monroe for her sorry treatment of Crane's Melville poem.

As for American poetry in general, Crane began by dismissing first the "scullery permutations of Amy Lowell," and then Carl Sandburg, whose life of Lincoln he'd tried reading. After all, what was Sandburg but a poet conceived "on a slab of sunburnt West" by the conjoining of old Elbert Hubbard and the ghost of Harriet Beecher Stowe? How one yearned for Poe and Whitman "and always my beloved Melville," Crane went on, thankful for what America could be at its best. He admired Frost ("a good, clean artist, however lean"), Cummings ("at times"), and even Moore. Like Winters, he too admired Williams, though he found the doctor "too much a quickchange artist," continually experimenting and never settling into a characteristic idiom or even a single approach to his subject. And why did the man keep swinging from one extreme to the next, "hair-shirting" one minute and "war-whooping" the next?

But it was Whitman who interested him most. *There* was the foundation stone for the new poetry being written today, including of course *The Bridge*. Which was why he was on this island, "fighting off miasmas, bugs, hay fever, bats and tropical squeks and birds," trying to complete "a very long poem for these days, extending from Columbus to Brooklyn Bridge and Atlantis." It was "threefourths done" now, though he was ready to get off the island and set up shop in New Orleans—a place Aunt Sally had recommended as conducive to writing—where he could finish the thing.[59] But, even as torrential rains poured down over the house again and again, Crane stayed on, working on *The Bridge*. On October 9th he sent Winters a carbon copy of "Cutty Sark" to show him that he too—like Williams and Cummings—knew how to experiment with the line. "The punctuation, or rather lack of it," he told Winters, mimicked "the endless continuum of water motion, with the rather 'grailish' Atlantis-Rose theme—

> *O Stamboul Rose—dreams weave the rose! . . .*
> *ATLANTIS ROSE dreams wreathe the rose,*
> *the star floats burning in a gulf of tears*
> *and sleep another thousand—*

acting as a kind of fugue counterpoint." And in case Winters missed the point, Crane was careful to point out that the poem employed a calligramme to imitate the clipper race between the *Ariel* and the *Taeping* (both wrecked half a century earlier). He'd had more fun writing this poem, Crane added, than anything else he'd ever done.[60]

A week later he was back at work on "The River," using whatever paper he could lay his hands on, including the back of a letter from Cowley that had just arrived. He'd wanted to get Aunt Sally and her memories of Louisiana into the poem, and now he did just that, using one of his hobo wanderers to recall her world:

> *That cricket never finishes, Uncle Stephen said*
> *—When Aunt Sally smiled it was almost Louisiana*
> *And afterwards (who had a colt's eyes) one said,*
> *"Jesus! Oh I remember watermelon days!" And sped*
> *High in a cloud of merriment, recalled*
> *"—And when my Aunt Sally Simpson smiled," he drawled—*
> *"It was almost Louisiana, long ago."*[61]

He was still at it when the hurricane the islanders had dreaded at last smashed into the Isle of Pines on October 18th. Villa Casas, along with so many other houses, was badly damaged and the sagging roof finally torn apart. He and Aunt Sally watched in disbelief as the walls of the house began collapsing around them and the plaster ceiling buckled and then came down in sections. Finally, having spent much of the night shifting from one room to another for safety, they crawled under a bed, taking Attaboy with them, covering their heads with soaked pillows in case the entire ceiling caved in. When at last the storm receded toward dawn, they crawled out from under the bed to survey the damage. Somehow they had made it through. And since there was nothing else they could do about the damage, Crane wound up his Victrola, put a recording of the "Valencia" on the turnstile, and began dancing a one-step with Aunt Sally, soaked pillows still on their heads in case the ceiling did go after all.

He would write about this when he'd had time to think about what they'd been through. Using a style as compact and as clear as Williams's, Crane, in a poem entitled "Eternity," brought to bear on the scene the reportorial skills he'd learned years before, in an unobtrusive rhyming iambic pentameter:

> After it was over, though still gusting balefully
> The old woman and I foraged some drier clothes
> And left the house, or what was left of it;
> Parts of the roof reached Yucatan, I suppose.
> She almost—even then—got blown across lots
> At the base of the mountain. But the town, the town!
> Wires in the streets and Chinamen up and down
> With arms in slings, plaster strewn dense with tiles,
> And Cuban doctors, troopers, trucks, loose hens . . .

The ferry boat for Batabanó had been ripped apart as it lay in dock, its massive funnel lying now on its side up on the grass; buildings had been brought to their knees; the quarry mountain stripped of its palm trees; and all communication with Havana (which itself lay under several feet of water) cut off. And then the sun was out again with a vengeance, burning the grass a patent leather brown. Everything was gone

> or strewn in ridfdled grace—
> Long tropic roots high in the air, like lace.
> And somebody's mule steamed, swaying right by the pump,
> Good God! as though his sinking carcass there
> Were death predestined! You held your nose already
> Along the roads, begging for buzzards, vultures . . .

He would remember beating a crazed mule to make it turn from the swamp and back up onto the high road, only to watch it stumble and lie there. The dead were buried quickly, without ceremony, roads cleared, and the sound of hammers in the town signaled the work of rebuilding. President Coolidge ordered the battleship USS *Milwaukee* (with thousands of delicious sailors and Marines!) to assist the residents on the island in getting back on their feet, the ship baking two thousand loaves of bread for the victims even as it sped toward the stricken island:

> *Doctors shot ahead from the deck in planes.*
> *The fever was checked. I stood a long time in Mack's talking*
> *New York with the gobs, Guantanamo, Norfolk,—*
> *Drinking Bacardi and talking U.S.A.*

After so much devastation, who could blame him for being delighted with the unexpected picnic Uncle Sam had provided?[62]

Nothing for it, then, but to get Aunt Sally settled somewhere and take the first available boat back to New York. Crane borrowed ship fare from her, promising to repay her as soon as Kahn came through with the final five hundred, and then left the island. It would be the last time he ever saw it or Aunt Sally, though he remained loyal to the memories of both. One of the casualties of the hurricane had been the sinking of the Cuban vessel *Gomez*, on which his friend Alfredo had been stationed, his whereabouts a source of concern for Crane. Passing through Havana he ran into a sailor who had been on the *Gomez* with Alfredo, and he surmised via the Spanish-speaking mariner's "signs and contortions" that Alfredo had been "laid up with a broken arm and a smashed shoulder."[63] It was only weeks later that he learned the truth: Alfredo had made it through the ordeal safely. Only his clothes had been drowned.

On October 28th Crane reached New York and booked into the Hotel Albert. Then he wired his mother to let her know he was safe and back on U.S. soil. Two days later, he had a telegram from her. The separation from Curtis had so prostrated her, she told him, that she'd been in a Cleveland hospital for the past two weeks, "in terrible shape."[64] She'd also gone ahead and actually approached Otto Kahn for money. Crane surely must have cringed at that bit of news. The following day he wrote his father, puzzled as to why he had not answered any of his letters. Perhaps his father had not cared to write. But since so much mail both coming and going had never reached its destination, thanks to the "corrupt manners of the Havana postoffice," he was writing again.[65] C.A. wrote back at once with a check for twenty-five dollars, along with the news that he'd not had the heart to write since he'd learned that his dear Frances was dying of cancer. "I am so nearly broken," he wrote his son, "that I don't know whether I can bear up through the valley that is ahead of me or not."[66] In the meantime it might be good for Harold to return to Cleveland to be with his mother.

But with one parent beside himself with grief and the other unable to get out of bed because her second husband had left her, Crane thought it best to avoid Cleveland altogether and return instead to Patterson. "I don't want to do anything to hurt *anyone's* feelings," he confessed to Charlotte Rychtarik. "But I think that unless I isolate myself somewhat (and pretty soon) from the avalanche of bitterness and wailing that has flooded me ever since I was seven years old, there won't be enough left of me to even breathe, not to mention writing."[67] After all, he had his own child—three-quarters to term—to feed and care for now.

PART III

10 / AFTERMATH

ENERVATING HEAT FOLLOWED BY a killer hurricane that had all but ripped the Isle of Pines plantation apart should have been bad enough. But now, back at Addie Turner's farmhouse in Patterson as winter closed in—just himself, the old woman, and her two cats— Crane had a new problem to deal with. Suddenly, with the stanchions up, the main cables bound and anchored, and the crosshatch netting nearly strung, work on *The Bridge* came to a halt.

At first he was not overly concerned. After all, he'd accomplished miracles in the past few months, and it was time to rest. Enough to walk among the hundred-year-old oaks and maples and the rock-tossed streams again, frost in the air, the promise of the season's first snowfall. And nights, crisp nights without "the overweening, obscene vitality of the tropics which never lets you (a northerner) rest." Weird how fate seemed to throw him "into sudden extremes," he remarked to Winters, so that he found himself spending "winters in polar regions and summers under the equator."[1] Still, if he could stay clear of Cleveland, he hoped soon to be back at work on his bridge again.

He also needed to find work, for the last of his money was quickly dribbling away. Winters wrote back, suggesting he might find a job teaching. But Crane knew better. He had no experience whatsoever teaching and hadn't even finished high school. When Tate had first mentioned the possibility of teaching, Crane had answered that, knowing Tate, he would not find standing on a platform and dispensing judgment and information so terrible, whatever "erosions and disgusts" the job might incidentally incur.[2] As for himself—whose work would one day be the subject of seminars and classes in hundreds of colleges and universities—Crane would never formally teach, never so much as lecture or read at a college or university forum, never once even visit a university. There is a story that he recorded his poems for a New York radio station, but that the wire was later erased to be used for another show. So much for Love & Fame, Time & Money.

Much of November was taken up answering Winters's questions about the state of poetry, a dialogue begun in the tropics and continued now in an isolated farmhouse in upstate New York beneath denuded maples. What, Winters was curious to know, had really been behind Harriet Monroe's insistence that Crane explain "At Melville's Tomb" in the pages of *Poetry* before she would print it? What had originally given *Poetry* its distinction, Crane wrote back, had been Pound. Once he was gone, Aunt Harriet had had to fall back on her old journalistic approach to poetry. And her midwestern self-confidence was never going to forsake her, that much was certain, for she was just "the kind of person who would run up to Newton, and in behalf of all good easy-going 'hopefuls' of the middle-west . . . query, 'But aren't you a little bit too mathematical, Sir Isaac?'"[3] So too with Crane's new poetic calculus as measured against the abacus of most modern poetry.

In 1926, Winters was still an ardent admirer of William Carlos Williams's poetry, rating him the equal of Hardy, Arnold, Dickinson, Browning, and Corbière, and far above Cummings. He'd spent five years trying to understand Williams's poetics on theoretical grounds, only to realize it couldn't be done. Yet what poetry Williams had written in that indefinable line! Crane listened, but he came nowhere close to sharing Winters's enthusiasm. On the other hand, he had to admit, he had not read as much of Williams as Winters had. Still, of what he had read, he liked particularly two lyrics: "Postlude" and "To Mark Antony in Heaven." He owned *Sour Grapes* and *had* owned *Spring and All*, until it had been blown across the Isle of Pines during the recent hurricane. He had not—*not*—read *In the American Grain*, Williams's poetic essays on American history published the year before, for the simple reason that he did not want it interfering with his own work on *The Bridge*.

Columbus, the Spanish Conquest, Pocahontas, the Puritans, the tragic Poe: *In the American Grain* and *The Bridge* shared all these subjects. Having learned this secondhand, Crane had promised himself to stay away from the book until he was finished with his own poem to avoid being influenced by a work so similar to his own. But only nine days later he was telling Frank that *In the American Grain* was an achievement he himself would have been proud of. He'd found the book "important and sincere," though he'd "put off reading it" until he'd felt his "own way cleared beyond chance of confusions incident to reading a book so intimate to my theme." He was especially interested to see that Williams had put Poe "in the same position" that he himself had symbolized for him in "The Tunnel."[4]

In the meantime, Winters wrote Crane an assessment of his work that delighted Crane. It was, Crane wrote back on the 15th, "the most intimate sort of critical sympathy—not only with my work, but my aims—that I've about ever been given." When Winters asked if *The Bridge* were some sort of modern epic, Crane answered that, while "new forms are never desirable" in themselves, sometimes they were "simply forced into being by new materials." Perhaps a new name was needed for what he was attempting, for this was *not* an epic in the classical sense, except in certain fundamentals. The use of myth was one. He was not, after all, writing a history of America, but a poem about the age's obsession with the relativity of space and time and the concomitant explorations into the interior universe of the mind, whose chiasmic shapers (outer and inner) had been Einstein and Freud. Such were his subjects: those, and—as always—"the eternal verities of sea, mountain and river."

But it was important to realize that no modern poet could afford to write narrative history in the old sense again. That time was over. Still, the myths which underlay the old epics and which cried out for embodiment could only "appear in their true, luminous reality" if they were presented as unfolding. And that of course meant some sort of "chronological and organic order." So he would have to treat the discovery of America, the crossing of the continent by ship, horse, wagon, train, and plane, as well as by telegraph, telephone, and radio. Underlying all these modes lay the idea of a bridge transcending time and space. It was in the conquest of these two dimensions—time and space—that Western civilization had attempted to reach God, and perhaps even to become God, as the myth of Faust (with which Crane had earlier wrestled) so amply demonstrated.

But how did one capture such luminous realities in a poem, of whatever length? The expenditure of labor involved "in locating the interrelations between sources, facts and appearances in all this" had already proven nearly overwhelming. Still, wasn't it better to fail at getting it right than to settle for some sort of half-success? So with his attempts to capture what was proving so frustratingly elusive: the persistence of the reality of Native American symbols in contemporary culture, "despite our really slight contact with that race." And yet it was a reality that continued to reveal itself in places where one least expected it.

Take the two lines he'd used to evoke the dance of the Indian warrior, Maquokeeta:

> *A cyclone threshes in the turbine crest,*
> *Swooping in eagle feathers down your back . . .*

Nature's cyclone and man's turbines—aircraft engines, for instance, or electrical generating plants—chiming with the warrior's eagle-feathered headdress whirling in ritual dance. Energy unleashed and space conquered in the same instant, presented as the mind apprehended such a synesthetic complex, without the drag of narrative time or logical exposition. This was what Crane was after in his poem: the same linguistic instantaneousness he saw in America's attempts to conquer space and time with theorem and dynamo. He delighted in this metaphysical condensation and density, and believed there was a correspondence between it and the life force at the spiritual core "of Indian design and ritual."

Consider, for instance, "Cutty Sark," the poem that came midway through *The Bridge* and not only touched on "the sea—and its presence under the center of the bridge," but also sank vertically into the mind, revealing the dark side of what it cost to kill time and space. He was "engrossed in a thousand problems of form and material all at once these days," and there was only so much he could explain. All the explaining in the world would never get the poem done. That would come only by dreaming, playing with words, and praying for the necessary fusion of forces. When that fusion finally occurred, the poem would stand up on its own legs, alive "with its own sudden life," as all successful poems finally did.[5]

Crane would return to the issue of the immense difficulties in being able always to find the exact word in a poem he wrote a year later and subsequently published in *The Dial* in the spring of 1929. It was called "A Name for All," and in it he said plainly what he'd labored to say in "The Wine Menagerie" and "Atlantis": that the names the poet used for things and experiences were always double-edged, covering over even as they sought to re-cover the experience itself. There was after all something corrupting about the naming of things: a wooing of the thing that too often led to domination over it once it had surrendered its name to the poet. What was it about us, Crane wondered, this need to sum everything up into some neat little ball, the perversity of always trying to pin the ineffable to the page. Impossible, of course, though that did not seem to stop us:

> *Moonmoth and grasshopper that flee our page*
> *And still wing on, untarnished of the name*
> *We pinion to your bodies to assuage*
> *Our envy of your freedom . . .*[6]

How marvelous to be able "to sleep again," he wrote Frank in late November, to be "buried under the sound of an autumn wind—and to wake with the sense of the faculties being on the mend."[7] On the 20th, he composed a fourteen-line poem in heroic couplets addressed to the spirit of Emily Dickinson, numbered now among his Visionary Company, though the poem was—inevitably—an address to himself as well. "You who desired so much," "To Emily Dickinson" begins, you who "fed your hunger like an endless task," you who—after a lifetime of struggling with the language—ended where all voyagers must end: by reaching "that stillness ultimately best." What he'd heard in her poems—as in his own—was something that went beyond words, something most people only brushed up against in isolate moments over a lifetime: the sweet silence of Eternity. This insight most rare, this presentiment, this harvest, took more than wit, more even than love. It took nothing less than the "reconcilement of remotest mind," the very sort of mystical synthesis Crane was struggling to achieve in *The Bridge*, where he too hoped to bring over from the sacred precincts of Silence some Word he could share as she had. Otherwise, his struggles, like his tears, were destined eventually to lie buried along with his rotting body in the clay-cold annihilating grave.[8]

In early December, winter settled in with a vengeance. "From hurricane to Blizzards—all in six weeks," he wrote Aunt Sally. It was "two below naught" outside, with "snowdrifts on the hills and windows," and not much warmer inside, so that even "tickling the typewriter keys" was proving once again to be "a stiff proposition." At night he tried burying himself under blankets, but often it was so cold he could not sleep, and he found himself spending the interminable hours of darkness listening to "the congealing water click into ice in the pitcher on the washstand, ticking, ticking—every few moments."[9] At least this time he'd learned his lesson and provided himself with good heating oil, so that his kerosene stoves were in working order. But there was ice elsewhere too to contend with: his mother's silence for not rushing to her side after she'd sent her telegram summoning him to Cleveland. Worse, he couldn't even point to work done on *The Bridge*, which still refused to inch forward.

Of all his old literary friends, he had only Winters now. What a scholar the man was, Crane marveled. Winters had Latin, he had Greek, he had "French and Spanish and Portuguese,"[10] none of which he himself possessed, so that he was glad (and embarrassed) to have Winters's corrections of his Latin and Spanish in the "Ave Maria" section he'd sent him. He even had to rely on Winters to check his Indian sources, including the authenticity of Maquokeeta, the name Crane had given his Indian warrior in "The Dance":

> *Know, Maquokeeta, greeting; know death's best;*
> *—Fall, Sachem, strictly as the tamarack!*

The name itself Crane had gotten from an American Indian taxi driver one night in New York, and he'd wondered afterwards what the hell it might mean. Winters had done what he could to learn the etymology but had come up with nothing definite. Better that way, Crane wrote back, "especially as Pocahontas had a thousand Indian lovers for the one white marriage license to the English planter." Actually, he'd come to depend on taxi drivers for much of his folklore. At least Winters's research had reassured him he wasn't using a name that meant Rosenphallus (Red Dick) or Hot Tomaly.[11]

Twice he heard from his sailor friend, Alfredo, the first time in Spanish, the second in a broken English Alfredo's niece had supplied him with ("*Maximo Gomez*, my ship—him sink in ciclon. All my clothes drowned"). Crane was still bent on learning Spanish, for with enough of the language under his belt, he joked, "and enough reputation as a poet," he just might "someday . . . be appointed to sell tires or toothpaste in Rio de Janeiro," where, he'd forgotten, it was actually Portuguese that was spoken. Aunt Sally he'd repaid as soon as he'd received his money from Kahn. "I'm eating like a horse," he wrote her now, "losing my becoming tan, and getting fat." He found himself daydreaming more and more of stepping "into a grove of royal palms," doffing his woolens, and having a glass of *cerveza* with her.[12] God, it was going to be a long, cold winter.

In mid-December, he came down with tonsillitis. "Nothing but illness and mental disorder in my family," he complained to Underwood. He was still feeling the pressure to hie him back to Cleveland and devote himself "interminably to nursing, sympathizing with woes" he had "no sympathy for because they are all unnecessary," and bolstering up his mother's and grandmother's faith in Christian Science, something he himself had "long ago discarded as crass and cheap."[13] Give him love any time—spontaneous love freely given and freely taken. And where was the goddamn fleet and what was he doing up here in the country freezing to death anyway? Finally, three days before Christmas, he composed the letter he could no longer postpone. It would be "a very melancholy Christmas for all of us," Crane wrote his mother, gritting his teeth and letting her know how miserable he too was feeling (though he was *not* going home, at least not yet).

Sleep still eluded him, and when he did doze off, he was "plagued by an endless reel of pictures, startling and unhappy—like some endless cinematograph." He was trying to free up his imagination so that he could work with the little time left him (that was the way he put it) on *The Bridge.* So much depended now on that poem that if he failed to deliver, he would become "a laughing stock" and his career would come to a crashing end. After all, if *he* didn't finish it, it would never get finished. It was as simple as that. He scolded his mother to stop being a martyr and get on with her life. "The only real martyrs the world ever worships," he added, were "those devoted exclusively to the worship of God, poverty and suffering," and Grace was hardly in that category.[14]

Christmas came, receded. No gifts from any of his family. Only Underwood troubled to send something: a book of poems. That and some old copies of *The Times* of London, which Crane especially welcomed since he could ill afford to subscribe to anything any more. Three days into the New Year he wrote to thank Underwood, congratulating him on the "brass-buttoned-tattooed vision" of a gob Underwood had bragged he'd carried back to Washington with him from New York. As for himself, he'd heard nothing from either Jack Fitzin or Alfredo for too long now. "O, the navies old and oaken,/O, the Téméraire no more!" he sighed, quoting himself, in turn quoting Melville on the loss of the old frigates. And now Harry Candee too was gone. Life surely had become "a frightful torture" to Harry by the end, Crane was coming to understand. But didn't everyone end up mad?[15]

Then came a "scrumptious New Year's card from Gibraltar—with verses! about waking up in the morning—dew and all that." The card was from Jack Fitzin, who had written his own name beneath the verses he'd obviously stolen, much to Crane's amusement. "Just a line to say I'm in the best of health and wish you the same," Jack had added. "Anything beyond that must demand too great an effort ever to be attempted," Crane quipped.[16] Well, it would have to do. After all, he hadn't written much more himself in the past few months. Instead, he turned his attention to the study of Spanish. How he wanted to live where Spanish was spoken: Spain, Mexico, Peru. Even the little he'd seen of the Spanish character in Cuba he'd liked, and he loved the language, though he could still manage only the barest of sentences. What he longed for was someplace where he could come and go as he pleased, take his time, drink. But the reality was that he was flat broke, so that he was going to have to return to New York and find some kind of job . . . and soon.

Then he learned that his father's wife, Frances, had just succumbed to cancer. He wrote C.A. at once, offering condolences, but heard nothing back. In fact, he'd heard nothing from his father since October, and with this turn of events didn't expect to hear anything more for a while. Instead, it was his mother he heard from now, telling him about the response among their relatives and friends in Cleveland to the news that his book was due out at any minute. "Wait until they see it," he warned her, "and try to read it!" Of course they would be befuddled by it, for the poetry he wrote was "farther from their grasp than the farthest planets."[17] But wasn't that to be expected of folks who never read anything more taxing than the *Saturday Evening Post* and *Success*? Later, when he learned that a friend of his mother's had read from the book to the Garrettsville Federated Women's Clubs, he rocked with laughter. "The poor dears will never," he sighed, "NEVER know what in hell to make of it all!"[18]

When Winters's copy of *White Buildings* arrived, Winters read through it at once, awed by what he found there. "I withdraw all minor objections I have ever made to your work," he wrote Crane. "I have never read anything greater and have read very little as great."[19] Waldo Frank, reviewing the book for *The New Republic*, would have ended (had the passage not been cut) by announcing to his audience that, as good as *White Buildings* was—and it really was—the book Crane was now writing was greater still. "Not since Whitman," he insisted, had "so original, so profound and—above all—so important a poetic promise come to the American scene."[20]

White Buildings was getting and was going to get even more terrific reviews, Crane confided to Frank in late January 1927. "Not to mention yours, there's a great explosion coming from Yvor Winters in *The Dial*; another from Mark Van Doren (of all the unexpected!) in *The Nation*," as well as "a sincere and just estimate in the *Sun*." Other raves were expected from Matty Josephson in the *New York Herald Tribune* and Archibald MacLeish in *Poetry*, though these did not—as it turned out—appear. Thirty poems, white buildings all, including the three-part "For the Marriage of Faustus and Helen," and the six-part "Voyages" that closed the book. Eight years of work condensed between two thin covers. That work, at least, was now behind him. Ahead of him lay his still unfinished bridge, taunting him in the glittering winter distance.

Sitting there in Addie Turner's kitchen near the stove to keep warm, with the temperature outside sixteen below even in bright January sunshine, Crane mentioned in a letter to Frank that one of the stipulations of the $2,000 grant Kahn had bestowed on him was that he would now have to pay sixty bucks a year for "the rest of my mortal term on life insurance to the Kahn estate." He did not particularly mind, he explained, nor did he feel he'd been taken. Especially since he'd just "discovered a new way to avoid income taxes and become heroic—both at once," if Frank caught his drift, his drift being that, by dropping out of the scene early and taking his own life, both problems would take care of themselves.[21]

By early February, Crane was back in New York again, looking for work. But as the days passed without anything turning up, he became more and more frantic. He scribbled off a quick note to Winters on the 9th from the Provincetown Playhouse on MacDougal Street, promising himself that if he didn't find something in the next couple of days, he was heading back up to Patterson again. Nor did it help his mood to learn that a span of *The Bridge* had just been rejected by *The Dial*. On the other hand, Paul Rosenfeld, one of the editors of *The American Caravan*, an annual of American letters recently begun by Alfred Kreymborg and Van Wyck Brooks, had called Crane saying he had to have a piece of *The Bridge* for the magazine.

Two nights later, *The Caravan's* publisher—Macauley & Company—threw a large party for all the annual's contributors at a posh apartment on West End Avenue. Everyone Crane had ever heard of was there, he wrote his mother, to be fêted with "enormous quantities of wine, cocktails and highballs." And, since he'd "just landed in town after three months with the bossy cows," he was definitely ready to party.[22] Party he did, becoming drunker and drunker that night, until finally he staggered off, taking the Christopher Street Ferry over to the Hoboken docks and then up along Front Street, on the prowl for sailors. "Good old beer and the old free-lunch counter and everything thrown in—for 15 cents a glass," he wrote the Browns afterwards. Plus whiskey and gin, much superior—and a lot cheaper—to what one could find in New York.

It was simply a matter of finding someone interested in a night of drinking and uncomplicated sex. When the fleet was in, he thumbed through his address book, filled with the names of gobs he knew and others whose names had been passed along to him. He even subscribed now to a navy bulletin that reported on the movements of the fleet, so that, whenever a battleship or cruiser anchored in the Hudson or at the Brooklyn Navy Yard, he got to a phone to check on the whereabouts of old friends. Otherwise he simply assumed an old alias—in this case the name of the long-dead Elizabethan playwright, Mike Drayton—and went off under cover of the night. His final night in New York—February 12th, Lincoln's Birthday—he left Hoboken "with a wild Irish red-headed sailor of the Coast Guard" and rushed back to the Brooklyn waterfront, where the redhead introduced him "to a lot of coffee dens and cousys" over on Sands Street, infamous for its seedy gay hangouts, then took Crane "to some kind of opium den way off, God knows where." But sex and booze were Crane's thing, not dope, and when he couldn't get the redhead to leave the den, Drayton got angry and stalked off. When he finally resurfaced the following morning in Grand Central, preparing to take the train back to Patterson, he found himself broke, depressed, and still without a job.[23]

Back home, there were six cards from "Jack the Incomparable," a few with more than their "usual brief greetings." He sent off at least two Valentine's Day cards, one to Emil, the other to Sam Loveman, each with one of his infamous limericks attached. "For the Memoires of a Man-Eater," the title went, its double entendre not lost on the recipients:

> There once was a cannibal nigger
> Who ate up his enemy's frigger;
> His dozens of wives
> Had the time of their lives;
> He grew bigger and Bigger and BIGGER.[24]

So excited was Addie Turner to have her Hart back that all Valentine's Day she lay in bed, "from an excess of oatmeal eaten at breakfast in celebration" of his return. The following day, he went to look over his property on Tory Hill and ran into the extraordinary Mrs. Porwitzki—all two hundred and fifty pounds of her—at Farmer Jennings's place. She'd had sixteen children, all without the help of a doctor, and Crane could only marvel at this vital mound of a woman. What locutions, he wrote the Browns. "I should love to tickle her." When he came to compose the "Quaker Hill" section of *The Bridge* three years later, he would find a place for her too, as he'd found places for Aunt Sally and other characters to whom he'd taken an instant liking.

A few years earlier, he'd read Ernest Hemingway's first book, a small collection of short stories, soon after its publication. Now, back in Patterson, he swept through *The Sun Also Rises*, renaming it *The Cock Also Rises*. Just reading it, he told the Browns, had given him "a perfect case of acidosis." No wonder the book had sold, he marveled, for there wasn't "a sentence without a highball or a martini in it to satisfy all the suppressed desires of the public" in a time of alcoholic drought. It was, he had to admit, "a brilliant and a terrible book," though without a hint of warmth or charm, which—he understood—was just how Hemingway wanted it.[25] Here was a book that gave one "a slant at one aspect of the age," though without the "ingratiating qualities" that made *Ulysses* "that bitter book, a thing to keep and enjoy many times."[26]

By mid-February the snows were once again so high that the mailman had stopped delivering to Birch Hill. "They may get the roads cleared out before Easter," Crane grumbled. "I don't know."[27] Just now he would give anything for a little sun and warmth again. By late February, he was stir-crazy. Nothing seemed to be going right. His relations with his parents were really still in tatters, and *The Bridge* was going nowhere fast. If something didn't happen soon he was going to lose his mind, as had happened the year before, culminating in the blowup with the Tates. He was so broke, in fact, that he wrote Tate asking if he could see his way clear to sending him some postage stamps.

As for Winters, Crane was surprised at just how rigid the man could be when it came to questions of theory and traditional forms. Theory, ideology, formalized religion: they all gave Crane the creeps, and it was his refusal to side with Munson's view of the world that had led to their break. When Winters sent him an essay on "Dynamism" outlining his theory of poetry, Crane dismissed it as "hugger-mugger." If Winters's theoretical grid helped him write poems, all well and good. Otherwise, Crane thought, the best thing Winters could do was get rid of "Dynamism" altogether. Certainly as theory it had no absolute value in and of itself. "No such incantation can lay life bare," he insisted, "or bring it a bit nearer—for me."[28]

The truth was that he was finding Winters's own poems too full of "moral zeal—a preoccupation with the gauntness and bareness of things"—and something that got in the way of his enjoying the poems for themselves. "Laying Life bare is all very well," Crane tried to explain to Winters, but the Muse was "best approached with a less obvious or deliberate signal than an upraised ax." Winters's poems were becoming too intellectual, too rigid, too limited. Perhaps he and Winters really did see poetry differently. "You want to strike directly inward," Crane summed up, "whereas I never consciously premeditate striking at all." What *he* was after was creating an autonomous construction, whose semblance to life was "dependent on organic correspondences to Nature." So the title of *White Buildings*, for instance, had slowly come to have "two symbolic meanings." One was the "Woolworthian," the literal, in the sense of New York's skyscrapers glistening in the distance. The other, and more important, was the "metaphysic-mechanical" meaning: white buildings as poetic constructs that reached ineluctably after some sort of snow-white transcendence.[29]

"A vague roar of snow water streaming the valley," he wrote the Browns at the beginning of March. Spring was still two weeks away, but if the warm weather kept up, the roads would soon be open to cars again. It was late, and he'd just returned from a moonlight tour of Tory Hill to check out the Browns' place. Their old Ford flivver was still up there, looking forlorn with "its ditty box and rear parts quite gone," so that he'd been "tempted to steal the shovel lying in the coal pile," though he'd refrained.[30] Mrs. Turner had put on weight over the winter, but he insisted that he'd not been to blame there, recalling a limerick he thought appropriate for the occasion:

> There was a young lady from Thrace
> Who attempted her corset to lace.
> Her mother said: "Nelly,
> There's more in your belly
> Than ever came in through your face."[31]

It was about the only poetry he could summon, for he was "too addled these days," he told Tate, "to have any ideas." It was now five months since he'd written anything of worth, and still the writing refused to come. All he could do was polish those parts of *The Bridge* that seemed "to lack a final sense of conviction," though he knew that no poem he wrote would ever fully satisfy him. Then even his reading stopped when he came down with conjunctivitis—due in part, he believed, to his inability to get on with his poem, and in part to the hard sun glare off the frozen snow—and soon his eyes were swelled shut.

Worse, sections of *The Bridge* kept being returned—first by Marianne Moore at *The Dial* and then by Ridgely Torrence at *The New Republic*. What was the matter with these people—the fastidious Moore, who blanched at the word "breasts," and the awful "male Miss" at *The New Republic*, who refused even tea because he found the experience too stimulating. Such people were "always in a flutter," Crane complained to Tate, "for fear bowels will be mentioned, forever carrying on a tradition that both Poe and Whitman spent half their lives railing against."[32] How could these people call themselves liberals? How he envied the old "buck-and-wing dancers and the Al Jolsons of the world."[33] At least they didn't have to deal with milksops. They even did some good for people, and when they laughed, at least people knew they weren't crying. If you couldn't get a little pleasure out of writing poetry, why go on?

In the meantime he kept staring at *The Bridge* lying unfinished there on the page before him. Blinkless, *The Bridge* stared back. "It's impossible to imagine without undertaking a like problem oneself— what endless problems arise in carrying forward the conception of a theme like *The Bridge*," he lamented to Winters when he could use his eyes again. It took "more than ordinary mental logic . . . to fuse all the multitudinous aspects of such a theme," he explained once more. For six years—*six years*—Crane had "carried the embryonic Idea of the poem about" with him before he'd so much as written a line. If that was true, then the initial inspiration for *The Bridge* had come with his arrival in New York when, at seventeen, he'd beheld the electric force of the city and the sublimity of the bridge rising above the eternal river. Then had come the initial impetus in '23, followed by the work of the previous year—his *annus mirabilis*.

But now he was beginning to think it might take another six years for the rest of the poem to reach "a sufficiently mature organization to be ready for paper." Actually, there was some merit to his thinking in these terms, since, like any poet, he had gleaned his teeming brain down to the stubble and would have to wait for the new sections of the poem to reveal themselves. Structurally, he could see what had to be done to complete the arc of the poem. But "logic or no logic," he could "never do anything . . . worth while without the assent" of his intuitions. And that he would have to wait for. He had a structure in mind, and he could see by that light what had yet to be done. All one could do was to grope forward with a kind of "alert blindness," antennae extended at every moment, waiting for the moment to strike. Aesthetic theory was endlessly fascinating, and he enjoyed talking with anyone willing to engage him in such speculation. But all the theory in the world was useless without that "necessary assimilation of experience." He was even willing to admit to his own biases. That he had, for instance, a "religious attitude toward creation and expression," and responded more to revelation than to learning a style and repeating himself endlessly, no matter how "classic and noble" that style might be.

He thought again of William Carlos Williams, whom Winters admired so much. Except for his most recent stuff—a fragment of something called "Paterson," for instance, which Crane had just read in *The Dial* and found highly disorganized—there was charm in almost everything the man wrote. But in most of Williams's poems he also found repeated the "kind of observations and emotions being 'made'" which he thought were too casually put down. True, even Whitman could be casual at times, though there was also in Whitman "a steady current," a rhythm that constantly bespoke "the ineffable 'word'" at the heart of his utterance. And that was what was important about Whitman: that, despite "all the paradoxes and contradictions" in his work, one always felt the presence of some universal law which could not be expressed by any formula. One either grasped this in a poet or one did not. It was enough simply to quote the opening paragraph of "Out of the Cradle Endlessly Rocking" to sense what Whitman was about. Or just isolated lines, like these:

> *This is the far-off depth and height reflecting my own face;*
> *This is the thoughtful merge of myself, and the outlet again.*

Reading such lines, Crane believed, one knew one was in the presence of a poetry written for the ages. Williams, on the other hand, wrote poems not to the terrible Sublime but merely to the household gods. Crane summed him up as someone "bent on appreciating the best that is given to him" and "dramatizing trifles in the classic manner of the old Chinese poets, and occasionally giving a metaphysical twist to his experience," a trick Crane found "truly marvelous." And besides, the man already had a dozen superb lyrics to his name.

For his part, Winters thought Crane preferred the abstract to the image. But again Crane demurred. A poem, like a painting, needed both design *and* image, he insisted. But an image had to transcend the merely photographic if it was to focus and accentuate the reality of its subject and at the same time flood the consciousness of the reader. Which was where metaphor came in. The trouble with Williams was that he often played with his images, pandering to the fancy rather than the imagination, as he had with some of his more experimental and self-conscious poems in *Spring and All.* Now take Cummings. There was a poet—one far better than Williams, and with a sensibility equal to Donne's. If he could just learn to take "a little more pains and organize," Cummings would be superb.[34]

In mid-March, Crane heard from Moore that *The Dial* had decided to take another piece he'd sent them, "The Dance." Four pages. Money he could use to pay the eye doctor and Addie Turner for the back rent he owed her. ("By the way," he wrote his mother, "if you really meant what you suggested about sending Mrs. Turner some old things I hope you won't forget about it. Some old house dress—even underwear—you've no idea how tattered and forlorn she looks." Nothing fancy, though, since, being sallow and "absolutely toothless," such clothes would only make her look the worse.)[35] To his mother's query as to why he didn't try Veronal powders to get a good night's rest, he told her he'd tried those down on the island "during those mad last days" following the hurricane, only to find himself becoming disoriented.[36] He made no allusion to the Veronal he'd taken twelve years before that had nearly killed him.

He sent his father a copy of *The New Republic*, with Frank's laudatory review of *White Buildings* in it, but even that brought no response. "He probably likes to build up the picture that he's creeping around in utter disgrace on account of the public 'disgrace' his son has made of himself," he complained to his mother. She sent him a photograph of the old Kinsman house in Warren where he'd spent his early years. "Every once in awhile," he told her, he still dreamed of the town where he'd grown up, and of the folks he'd known then: Hall Kirkham, Don Clarke, Katherine Miller, Len Bullus, so-and-so "with her great heart-shaped bosom," Mrs. so-and-so "gasping with her goiter." Where were they all now? he wondered.[37]

When the Browns returned to Robber Rocks, he walked over the receding snows to celebrate their arrival with some of the 150 gallons of hard cider—"successful and highly combustible nectar"—friends of his had brewed the previous fall.[38] That evening the conversation centered on the land reforms President Plutarco Calles of Mexico had instituted over the past two years. Among those reforms had been the nationalization of Mexico's oil fields, which he was now enforcing. Only American oil interests had demurred, and Secretary of State Frank Kellogg had just insinuated that Calles's Bolshevist actions might lead to U.S. Marines intervening there as they had in Nicaragua to protect American interests. Crane's sympathies were all with the Mexicans. He'd followed the issue in the pages of *The Nation* and *The New Repub-*

lic, where Frank and Cowley and others were now publishing, and had read with interest the editorials and articles there defending Calles and denouncing U.S. intervention in the region.

Late that night Crane staggered back to his room to type a letter in Spanish to El Presidente Callas saying how much he admired what he was doing. But when his Corona refused time after time to translate his effusions into Spanish, Crane picked the machine up and hurled it out the second-story window, where it smashed against the frozen ground. Hearing Crane staggering about his room, Addie Turner walked in to find him emptying the room's contents out the window to keep the insolent typewriter company. When she tried to stop him from wrecking any more of her furniture, he swept her to the floor, tripping over her in the process so that they both lay there for a long time afterwards while he "howled imprecations against Coolidge."[39] The next day Brown came over, retrieved the damaged typewriter from the ground where it still lay, and took it into Pawling for repairs. Crane himself remembered none of this afterwards, as he confessed to Winters, though he was relieved to find that the episode had helped him get back to work on *The Bridge.* Comic as the scene was from one angle, the incident marked a new stage of instability in Crane that would become increasingly familiar in the months and years to come.

Two days later the countryside was back in the grip of winter. "Every kind of bird was in full choir around the valley last week," he wrote Underwood on the first day of spring. "Now there is no sound but the cold wind full of icicles." He'd already planted lettuce in some cold-frames as a way of hastening the season, and Addie Turner had promised to go looking for cowslips to make the first salad of the year. "I never ate any," Crane hastened to explain, "but they sound to me always as good as some Shakespearian lyric."[40] As a way of moving forward on *The Bridge,* he was now considering writing a biography of Washington Roebling, the creator of the bridge, with which his own Bridge was so intimately connected. He wrote Tate in New York, asking him to send him the name of an editor he might write at Macauley's about the feasibility of such a book, and then asked him to check, the next time he was at the 42nd Street Library, if such a study had already been done. After all, Roebling was one of his true Spenglerian heroes. Within days, however, he'd moved on to other things and the project was forgotten.

Then the first issue of *transition*, edited by Eugène Jolas from Paris—a magazine Winters had alerted him to—arrived. There were some weak spots in it, Crane wrote Winters, but there was strong work there too by Joyce, Stein, Williams, Laura Riding, MacLeish, Valéry Larbaud, André Gide, Philippe Soupault, and Winters himself. Actually, the magazine was "far better constructed—physically and 'spiritually'"—than he'd had any right to expect and might even last a full year—a "superhuman" span of time in terms of such projects.[41] Soon Crane was sending Jolas his own poems, regardless of Jolas's ability to pay. In fact, of the nearly twenty poems Crane published in 1927, eight appeared in *transition*. After all, Crane could publish a poem there and publish it again in England and yet again in the States, and the magazine supplied him with a much-needed French connection. Then, to his amusement and disbelief, Marianne Moore took another new poem— "Powhatan's Daughter"—and Harriet Monroe took "Cutty Sark," and for a moment his rage against women editors subsided. Next, "O Carib Isle!" was accepted by three magazines in three countries: *Poetry, The Calendar* (England), and *transition* (France). "Hurricanes seem to take with editors," he remarked to Winters. If only there were more "Anglicized countries in the world that poems might pay" his way around it.[42]

By April, reviews of *White Buildings* began appearing in the little magazines. Crane had a hint of what lay ahead when he read an unsigned short review, of which Moore sent a copy along with proofs for "The Dance." Acknowledging that Crane had ability, could write excellent blank verse, and occasionally a good phrase, the anonymous reviewer for *The Dial* also judged the poet guilty of an extremely self-conscious manner and a disingenuous preciosity, and ended by calling him a "high-class intellectual fake." Tate thought Conrad Aiken the author of that review, and Crane concurred. Yet, even if he was, Crane added, what could he do? Aiken had every right to call him whatever he wanted.

There were others. Genevieve Taggard, reviewing the book for the *New York Herald Tribune*, merely aped Aiken, accusing Crane of a "mannered obscurity" and a "slightly faked sonority." The reviewer for the *Saturday Review of Literature* went further. He could hardly understand Tate's "Introduction," let alone Crane's poems. Mark Van Doren, writing for *The Nation*, was more evenhanded. He recognized real distinction and power in the poems, though he too found it difficult often to grasp what they were about. One surprise was a favorable notice in *The*

Times (London) that Underwood sent on. It was, Crane felt, the most satisfying newspaper mention he'd received.

Eight months earlier, he'd written Underwood to thank him for sending him old issues of *The Times*, which he found "a relief after our local stuff." The truth was that the English reviews were far superior to the *New York Times* Sunday literary supplement, which, in spite of dismissing it as a "dirty sheet," Crane still subscribed to. He hated their "behind-the-scenes . . . atrocious snobbism and lickspittle attitude toward writers and factions of writers," and so expected nothing "but shit from them" when *White Buildings* was published.[43] Yet, when at the end of March the *New York Times* did notice his book—in an omnibus review that included books by John Crowe Ransom, Langston Hughes, Richard Aldington, and Ford Madox Ford—Crane was surprised to find the review actually fair.

Surprisingly, Tate's introduction received almost as much attention as Crane's poems, and Crane was generous in seeing the good reviews as a victory for both of them. "Altogether," he wrote Tate, "I think this is the last time in our lives to be badly discouraged. The ice is breaking—for both of us, as near as I can see—in several different quarters—and I'm beginning to detect many salutary signals. Apparently our ideas and idiom evoke some response—however slow."[44] At least now they'd gained a toehold for their sort of poetry. Masters, Bodenheim, Lindsay: each had had their moment and passed into obscurity. Now it was his turn, and he and Tate were sure to gain adherents in the years to come. What, he wondered, would the next five years bring?

Writing in the April issue of *Poetry*, Winters came through as handsomely as he'd promised. Like Frank and Tate, he too saw Crane as one of the country's greatest living poets, and—more—one of the few important American poets of all time, worthy to be judged in the company of Marlowe, Rimbaud, Whitman, and Melville. "Your review has just reached me," Crane wrote Winters on April 2nd. "You and Tate have more courage than any ten other men I could pick. What laurels!" As a token of his appreciation, Crane had put together a collage and sent it on to his friend. He called it "a little two-dimensional toy," an "idol mechanique," and titled it "Musician Apostolic." It was the figure of a man descending a mountain "with a halo and guitar or fiddle." From the time he was five, Crane told Winters, he'd been "drawing and puppet-ing" and had never quite got over it. Throw it away if he wanted, Crane added.[45] Winters responded in kind by sending Crane several small Southwest Native American paintings, which Crane hung next to his African wall hangings. Long after the two men had fought, long after Crane was dead, and until his own death in 1968, Winters would keep Crane's collage in his study as a reminder of their old friendship.

To Crane's immense relief, spring arrived a month earlier than the previous year, and once more his thoughts turned to travel. Spain, he told his mother, then Paris, and—when things had "cooled down" a bit, and they weren't shooting people any more—Mexico.[46] In his imagination he was already traveling down the flooded Mississippi, writing and revising "The River" section of *The Bridge*. But the only place he actually traveled to that spring was out to Cleveland to be with his eighty-year-old grandmother and help his mother through her second divorce. He arrived in Cleveland on April 4th, and endured "a mad harrowing two weeks" filled with "divorces, illness, nervous breakdowns, litigation," before returning to Patterson, exhausted by the effort and relieved to get away again.[47]

Stopping in New York on April 19th, en route to Patterson, he managed to see his father, who was staying at the Roosevelt Hotel on business. "Am leaving for home on the 6:30 and so ends the N.Y. trip," a depressed C.A. wrote his son the following day.[48] He was still mourning the loss of his dear Frances, and now yet another business trip had ended in stalemate. It seemed the rule rather than the exception the way things went these days, for his heart was no longer in buying and selling any more. Still, seeing his boy had done both men some good. In fact, Crane wrote his father afterwards that it had been "the most satisfactory visit we have ever had together," in spite of his father's being "far from gleeful much of the time." If he'd been able "to alleviate, even for only a short period," some of C.A.'s depression, Crane was satisfied, for it was "a good thing to be of some use to one's father," especially when that father had been as good to his son as C.A. had been.[49] "The skies are again blue today," he wrote his mother afterwards, happy to be in his father's good graces and back in Patterson now that spring was here. "After several gloomy days of unbelievable cold and rain," how good to see the woods "full of shad-blows and the loveliest cowslips," and Mrs. Turner cooking him up "bushels of fresh dandelion greens."[50]

On April 29th he sent Winters revised copies of the last two sections of *The Bridge*, though he was still fretting over how he was going to open the hell section he called "The Tunnel." How raw should he leave this New York material? he wondered. The theme demanded "a certain sort of sensitizing introduction"—some hint of Eliotic "wistfulness," but just how much? Two hells: Prufrock's "muttering retreats/Of restless nights in one-night cheap hotels," and "And I have known the eyes already, known them all." Both of these Crane had echoed in his own lines, "Mysterious kitchens . . . You shall search them all." And again, Prufrock's "Let us go then, you and I," chiming with his own, "Then let you reach your hat/and go." On the other hand, he hoped he'd left Eliot's familiar tone of despair behind by the time he reached Poe's hell at Chambers Street. For there he meant to turn the Columbus theme upside down to reveal some poor "Wop washerwoman" riding home on the late night subway to her family in Brooklyn after another night cleaning the empty corridors of those "sky-barracks" sullenly winking in the night sky over Manhattan.

And the place names—Times Square, Columbus Circle, Floral Park, Flatbush, Gravesend, Chambers—all real stops on the New York subway system, which fact he viewed as "something of a miracle." He'd "never been to Floral Park nor Gravesend Manor, but you do actually take the 7th Avenue Interborough to get there," he explained to Winters on the other end of the continent, "and you change for same at Chambers Street. A boozy truckdriver I used to talk with a good deal in a lowdown dive lived out there, used to talk about the girls 'shaping up,' and finally died at Floral Park, Flatbush." He'd added "some new timbres and tonalities" to this nearly impossible poem, which had maddened him for the past three years, until he'd finally "got a few of the acid tremors down on paper." A miracle too that the subway stations should fall into the same symbolic function as the names of his clippers: *Cutty Sark, Thermopylae, Black Prince, Flying Cloud, Rainbow, Nimbus, Taeping, Ariel.*

"Atlantis," he explained, had been written "in a kind of three-days fit," a prolonged ecstasy, the memory alone of which was enough to justify the entire vision of *The Bridge* for him. Looking back, Crane had been astonished to see how that poem contained so much, including "a metaphysical synthesis of . . . aeronautics, telegraphy, psychoanalysis, atomic theory, relativity, and what not!" Perhaps, he had to admit, the poem aspired a little too much "to the famous Pater-ian 'frozen music,'" relying as it did on knowing "the unique architecture of Brooklyn Bridge," for him "the most superb and original example of an American architecture yet hinted at, albeit accidentally." How many times had he walked that bridge hand-in-hand with Emil, gazing up at the stars through the bridge's bound cables, or below into the moon-sequined river, or heard the wind blowing through those wires, or watched the gulls circling overhead or below in ever-widening arcs? All his readers should walk that bridge, Crane felt, just as he had, to get "the marvelous feeling the webbed cables give (as one advances) of a simultaneous forward and upward motion."[51] Even in memory . . .

At the end of April, the Patterson crowd held its first big goodbye-to-winter bash when the New York contingent gathered to celebrate spring's arrival. Daffodils and tulips in the fields, maples shimmering with their translucent youthful leaves, brooks roaring with the spring freshets. Then a telegram and a letter from his mother to say the divorce and alimony had been settled (to her immediate advantage) and that she'd already left for Chicago to visit old friends and start another new life. It was followed by a letter from his father, saying he'd just opened a sort of middlebrow retreat called Canary Cottage in Chagrin Falls, a well-to-do Cleveland suburb, and wondered if Harold would be interested in running it. Crane wrote his father a delicately worded letter, explaining that his hay fever would preclude his ever accepting such an offer. The hills and woods of Patterson, thank God, seemed to protect him from that "nightmare affliction."[52] But the real reason was that he needed to get *The Bridge* finished and off. Boni & Liveright were expecting it for their spring '28 list. Still, he hoped his father would not forget the allowance he'd promised him, money he needed just now for food and heating oil.

Actually, he needed the money for a little vacation in New York. By early May, Crane was back on the scene, staying at the Hotel Albert, using that address from which to make his forays out to the Brooklyn Navy Yard. This time he struck gold almost immediately, within hours picking up a sailor in the quartermasters' division aboard the USS

Shawmut. Together, the two men walked about the ship, enjoying shots of "marvelous old Johnny Walker and Bacardi," thanks to the hospitality of the ship's officers. A good-looking fellow, this sailor—well built, handsome, intelligent—whom he dubbed "Adonis" and "Phoebus Apollo," the god himself "sojourning in Gob blue" (though "that aloof rather chilly deity would hardly have qualified so well").[53] So enthralled was Crane by his Adonis that he was back in New York the following weekend to see him again. "If you are in the city I should like very much to see you," Adonis had written him in Patterson. "I cannot come to you; for the last silver dollar is squandered and gone. Yet *omnia vincit amor.* It is a little life and tomorrow—we may die. *Dum vivimus, vivamus.* May I see you? *A morte.*"[54] That did it for Crane. His correspondence fell off. *The Bridge* lay down again and slept. "I am disabled from everything but the alphabet," he apologized to Winters on May 21st.[55] Love had struck once again, robbing him of all thought of working on his *Bridge.*

That same week a young man two years Crane's junior lumbered down a makeshift runway in Long Island in an airmail plane refurbished with extra gasoline containers and christened *Spirit of St. Louis* for the first nonstop flight across the Atlantic. But for all Crane's keen admiration for modern aviation and the conquest of space, he was so preoccupied with his Adonis that all he could manage was a little hoeing out in Addie Turner's garden. Then, on the 23rd, it began to rain. Four days of it, without stop, until the garden he'd put in so laboriously had to be replanted from scratch. For some days, whenever he looked out the window, all he could see were "several brooks and lakes floating around over the bean and corn rows."[56]

Then a letter from Winters, saying he'd just read Edmund Wilson's essay in *The New Republic* on the current state of American poetry, which was now suffering, Wilson insisted (mentioning Crane's name among others), because American poets were not sufficiently engaged in social issues. This dissociation of poetry and politics had not always been the case, Wilson pointed out, naming three men who had engaged in politics in the long history of English letters: Edmund Waller, Matthew Prior, and Milton. It was dangerous for the poet to give up everything for the Muse and "seclude himself in the country, to live from hand to mouth in Greenwich Village or to escape to the Riviera."[57] That sounded a little too much like Crane. And now Winters, agreeing with the enemy and overstepping his bounds by adding new charges of his own about Crane's manner of living. The poet had to strive to be a "complete man," Winters firmly reminded Crane, and work earnestly to develop an ethical and social conscience.

"You need a good drubbing for all your recent easy talk about 'the complete man,'" Crane warned him. "Wilson's article was just half-baked enough to make one warm around the collar." How easy for someone like that, "born into easy means, [and] graduated from a fashionable university into a critical chair overlooking Washington Square . . . to sit tight and hatch little squibs of advice to poets not to be so 'professional.'" The problem was—as it always was with these easy ideologues—that Wilson had no idea what most writers were actually up against, forced as many of them were "to grub at any kind of work they could manage by hook or crook and the fear of hell to secure!" Crane knew from hard experience what he was talking about. "Yes, why not step into the State Dept. and join the diplomatic corps for a change," he mocked. Of course there were better careers to follow than poetry. "But the circumstances of one's birth, the conduct of one's parents, the current economic structure of society and a thousand other local factors" had more to do with how one made one's living than merely deciding to do a diplomatic stint in Paris, Mexico City, or Washington.

On the other hand, he had to agree that the idea of "the complete man" was a good antidote for modernity's "horrid hysteria for specialization." He also agreed that poets, like anyone else, needed ethical standards. But who wanted to follow the example of a Munson or a Toomer, both "stricken with the same urge" to rush after Gurdjieff and put themselves through all sorts of "Hindu antics, songs, dances, incantations, psychic sessions" until the left lobes of their brains worked in sync with their right lobes? He'd talked himself blue in the face explaining to both men why their platform left him cold, but all to no avail, since both had told him he would never understand their position until he'd allowed himself to undertake the same discipline as themselves. When he'd refused their invitation, he'd been dismissed and "left to roll in the gutter" of his own "ancient predispositions." And yet, look at what had happened to both men, two writers who had shown such early promise. In three years' time, both men had virtually ceased writing altogether.

And besides, Crane did have a code of ethics by which he lived. Admittedly, it was nothing he could reduce to an easy formula, though it seemed obvious to him that "a certain decent carriage and action" was necessary "in any poet, deacon or carpenter." Nor did he have any regrets for his own actions. Then, without telling Winters of his own sexual proclivities, Crane turned to the question of homosexuality. He was unworthy to be linked with poets of the caliber of Christopher Marlowe and Paul Valéry (both homosexuals), "except in some degree . . . 'by kind.'" Nor did one "have to turn to homosexuals to find instances of missing sensibilities." In any event, he was tired "of all this talk about balls and cunts in criticism," though he understood as well as anyone why one needed balls.

The complete man—what the hell was this myth of "the complete man" anyway? And the complete man in whose estimation, since each generation modified its image? Consider Fielding's Tom Jones, a character for whom he had "the utmost affection" and who could certainly stand as representative man for eighteenth-century England; in fact, someone who was still—at least for an Anglo-Saxon—a pretty good model, if one forgot about "calculus, the Darwinian theory, and a few other mental additions." Certainly Tom Jones was more balanced than Hardy's male characters. For good as Hardy was—and Crane thought him "the greatest technician in English verse since Shakespeare"—his heroes hardly filled the bill of the complete man, since not one of them was allowed "to express a single joyous passion without a footnote of Hardian doom entering the immediate description."

To ask Crane to become a more "complete man" was to ask too much. If anybody knew his own limitations, Crane retorted, he certainly knew his. Hadn't he already—under the immense difficulties of trying to finish a major poem—"partially furled" his own flag? The structural weaknesses, for instance, which Winters found in his work, he was willing to admit were real weaknesses. But what the hell. He was only twenty-seven, and in time he might not only write better verse but even extend his "scope and viewpoint." Besides, there was no discipline anyone could offer him—not even Winters's plan for the complete ethical man—that could really help him get on with his writing. The truth was that there were no "shortcuts across the circle." One did what one had to to get the work done. Certainly, *he* was not going to forego any experience he found important. If Winters thought him "aimless and irresponsible" for saying so, so be it. Nature—whatever *that* was—certainly did not seem to hold the answer.

Another thing. Though he'd been labeled a modern Metaphysical,

Crane knew he was no metaphysician, never having read Kant or Descartes. But because the first poem he'd ever written had been too dense to be understood, he'd been tagged a Metaphysical and told that everything he'd written since had been equally dense and futile. The real reason he wrote so little was because he was primarily interested "in recording certain sensations, very rigidly chosen"—sensations he found intense enough for poetry. Prose was different, for there he had the necessary space to give a fuller sense of who he was as a man. Anyone who read only his poems would have a very limited sense of who he was, for you did not get a full sense of someone only from the self that one's poems presented. Still, if he could at last render certain "moments of 'illumination'" in his poems, he would have done what he had set out to do.[58]

And now even letters ceased as work on "The River" finally, mercifully, resumed. "I'm in a 'state' of writing again," Crane told Winters briefly in mid-June, "and am deferring other matters for the time being."[59] That, and gardening, and guests and weekend parties. But by the end of the month his hay fever had become so pronounced that he'd become "a driveling gale of sneezing profanity," unable to work on anything, even "The River." When at last he could see through his puffed eyes, he read Doughty's massive tome, *Travels in Arabia Deserta*, "a very great book," despite the fact that praising it had become as much a fad as playing Mah-Jongg.[60] Finally, on July 1st, he sent Winters a draft of the new poem, with its "long struggle . . . to tell the pioneer experience backward."[61]

To move backwards in time, from the present on back into one's boyhood, like Rip ripped from his twenty-year dream, walking down New York's Avenue A, the Italian organ grinder's hurdy-gurdy recalling an earlier world, when he'd walked to school in rural Warren, Ohio. And flowers along the avenue, behind glass, suddenly recalling the homemade whip fashioned from a lilac branch his father had beat him with. Or the "Sabbatical, unconscious smile" his mother had nearly brought him once as she came back from church. The smile gone like that, even before he could greet her at the door (unlike his aunt Sally Simpson's smile, reminding him of the home he never had).[62]

Hence the hurdy-gurdy overture of "Van Winkle," to be followed by the grand symphony of "The River" itself. Modern time, city time, where time was money. Making time, making money, advertising time and space at so much per, as he himself too well knew:

> Stick your patent name on a signboard
> brother—all over—going west—young man
> Tintex—Japalac—Certain-teed Overalls ads
> and land sakes! under the new playbill ripped
> in the guaranteed corner . . .

Then lines capturing the twentieth century roaring by, where everything was shouted to catch one's attention, even the Good News pounded out daily now by radio evangelists like Aimee McPherson:

> SCIENCE—COMMERCE AND THE HOLYGHOST
> RADIO ROARS IN EVERY HOME WE HAVE THE NORTHPOLE
> WALLSTREET AND VIRGINBIRTH WITHOUT STONES . . .

until it was all too much, and the poet found himself jumping track to let the Limited race on without him, while he and two companions—hoboes—looked for a quieter time, a time closer to the rhythms of a pastoral America, the world of pioneers and early settlers, a time closer to the pulse of the Indian, where names like Ohio and Indiana, Cheyenne and Kalamazoo, might still recall that lost first world.

And other names evoking other lost worlds: Louisiana, Booneville, "a last burr" (Burr) picked from a vest. Hobo-trekkers, children as he once was, "Holding to childhood" for as long as possible, riding the rails, "Blind fists of nothing, humpty-dumpty clods," "old reprobates/With racetrack jargon," in whom the landscape in the shape of a young Indian girl—Pocahontas—was still very much alive. And gods dwindled to the shape of eyeless fishes in sunken pools, living now on the odd kernel of corn dropped by querulous crows passing over, the forests of those ancient gods ravaged to make way for railroad tracks erected in the name of Progress. And the Pullman breakfasters racing down along the Ohio and Mississippi Rivers, through Cairo and on to Memphis: train time running alongside steamboat river time.

And then the river itself, into which all the "grimed tributaries" flowed. The Mississippi: river of ageless time, which carried within itself all authorities and frontiers, the body of the dead DeSoto, sunk in its depths, as well as the bodies of "floating niggers" who for centuries had been made to disappear in its depths. All that weight of history, heavier than those billions of tons of alluvial silt, as the river pushed past New Orleans, that "City storied of three thrones"—Spain, France, the United States, empires vying for the river—and on past the swamped shells of Confederate and Union ironclads. This river, tortured with its own history, crucified by time, merging at last with the salt-stinging, all-embracing, all-obliterating Gulf, which ate all time, and would finally eat even Crane's own troubled century.[63]

And an even older time: glacial, aeonic, the time of the first peoples in America. It was this that Crane was after in "The Dance," its Adirondack landscape recalled in the heat of an island summer. He had written much of the poem quickly in August of '26, seeing it as a reversal, really, of the way he had handled time in "The River," moving here from chthonic time—a time in which valleys were scooped—to a time when the European first traversed the land, shadowed by the Indian. And now the poet travels back across lakes and rivers into the American past, climbing the falls, feet nuzzling "wat'ry webs of upper flows" into an Appalachian Spring, coming at last upon "Grey tepees tufting . . . blue knolls," to find what? To find the Indian medicine man and priest Maquokeeta dancing with abandon, as Crane had seen Isadora Duncan dance with abandon on a stage in Cleveland. Primal energy, an energy linked with the ball-bearing energy of America's turbines and electrical generating plants:

> *A cyclone threshes in the turbine crest,*
> *Swooping in eagle feathers down your back . . .*

It was this music, this early covenant between nature and humanity, the padded foot moving to the ancient rhythm of "black drums thrusting on"—as they would move him again in the last months of his life—which so awed Crane. And now it is himself he sees crucified, tied to the stake as he watches with agony the demise and transformation of the Indian's world into something other. And yet, though we move to other calendars and timetables, he sees, we have *become* the Indian, our deepest dream also being to possess the living landscape that is Powhatan's lovely daughter. For it is she who calls to us in our deepest reveries as she has called to those who came before—Columbus, DeSoto, Whitman, Crane:

> *West, west and south! winds over Cumberland*
> *And winds across the llano grass resume*
> *Her hair's warm sibilance. Her breasts are fanned*
> *O stream by slope and vineyard—into bloom!*

But it is with Maquokeeta that this poet would dance, moving beyond the farms of later interlopers, making his vows with his Indian counterparts—these high priests and sachems of the phallic imagination—all time and space for once washed under as now

> *the strong prayer [is] folded in thine arms,*
> *The serpent with the eagle in the boughs.*[64]

At the end of June he had another letter from Jack Fitzin, back from destroyer duty off the Mediterranean coast. As soon as he could, Crane went back down to New York to meet Jack's ship. First Jack showed him around the destroyer, then it was dinner, then a movie "on hunting in a jungle, full of marvelous tiger close-ups and elephant stampedes." The Fourth, on the other hand, Crane celebrated quietly. Neither he nor the Browns had money for firecrackers or firewater, though he found some of both over at Eleanor Fitzgerald's place in Sherman at a party she threw for some friends. "Sunshine and a certain amount of heat seem to stimulate me to writing," he wrote Aunt Sally that day. "That is, judging by the intensive work I did on the Island with you last summer, and by the returned activity I've been having lately."

He enclosed a copy of "The River," his attempt "to chart the pioneer experience of our forefathers—and to tell the story backwards ... on the 'backs' of hoboes": "psychological ponies" to carry the reader across the country and back to the Mississippi, that great River of Time. It had been "a very complicated thing to do," and he'd worked harder and longer on it than on any other section of *The Bridge*. "You'll find your name in it," he told her, wanting it enshrined there because she'd become for him the very "salt of all pioneers." It was "too damned bad the hurricane came," he sighed, for he'd loved his "little study room there so much, with the mango tree to look at through the back window."[65]

What poetry he'd written there—what glorious poetry! When he sent "The River" on to Winters the following day, Crane was more technical in his explanation, focusing instead on time and timing, "every word and beat . . . measured and weighed," modulating the underlying regularity of the rhythm until it closed in "the hieratic largo of the River" itself, the whole poem flowing "more evenly than any piece of equal length" he'd yet done. He hoped it had the "racial tang of the Great Valley without lapsing into Sandburgian sentimentalities," he added, for he was anxious to make a sharp contrast with "the rapid foot-beat" of "The Dance," which followed it.[66]

When, in mid-July, *The Bridge* stalled again, Crane turned his attention to the group of poems he called "The Hurricane"—lyrics recalling the Isle of Pines disaster of the previous fall. On the 18th, three days before his twenty-eighth birthday, and suffering from a brain-wrenching hangover brought on by too much local hard cider, he sent Winters copies of "The Air Plant," "O Carib Isle!," "The Quarry," "Royal Palm," "The Idiot," and "Eternity." Winters was not impressed. "You are quite right about the relative worth of the recent pieces I've been doing," Crane apologized in early August. After all, these were anthology pieces, written for money. In the past few days, he himself had gotten enough distance on them to see their stature "considerably clipped," so that now he was "in a kind of blue-funk," as much due to a week of hard rain and the coming end of summer as to the failure of the poems themselves. Better to get away from his desk for a while, and begin to think of poetry as some sort of avocation rather than a calling. In fact, if he hadn't been "honor-bound to plug away" at *The Bridge* until it was finished, he had to admit, he would have given the damn thing up months ago.[67]

"Life goes on here pretty evenly and monotonously," he reported to his father on August 12th. Work on *The Bridge* was impossible now, with so many other worries. His mother's "present pathetic circumstances"—living on $150 a month from her alimony settlement, and that for a period of only the next two years—was one worry; the question of where he himself would be come fall another.[68] He needed a job, and needed one badly. In early September, he spent two days in New York looking for work on one of the American shipping lines, again without success. Then, on September 12th, back in Patterson, he wrote Otto Kahn with a progress report on *The Bridge*. He owed him that; but—all else having failed—he hoped to hit Kahn up again for more money.

The Bridge had "reached a stage where its general outline" was evident, he explained. The "Proem" to Brooklyn Bridge and "Ave Maria" Kahn had already seen, both in typescript and in print. Then came "Powhatan's Daughter," representing the symbolic "body of the continent," with its five subsections exploring how the body of America had first been possessed by the Indian, and how that original possession had impacted on all subsequent contact with the continent. He was not approaching his material from a chronological perspective—the sort of thing that might begin with *The Mayflower* and continue on through the Revolution and the conquest of the West. Any history primer could do that. What he was after was to show how the past lived on in the present.

And so a leap from Columbus's dream monologue as he returned to Spain, across four centuries into the dreamlike fogged-in harbor of the East River. Then backwards "through the pioneer period, always in terms of the present—finally to the very core of the nature-world of the Indian." He was handling nothing less than the Myth of America, with himself the pioneer now, sifting through, sorting out, interweaving thousands of strands to build his Bridge. The major difficulty had been to learn to wait until what he'd assembled could assume its proper order, at which point Crane the "sky-gack" could begin welding the pieces into their intrinsic, natural form. The mixed metaphor was his, and by it he signaled that the poem was both a flower, opening with an inner life of its own, and a machine, each section having its "own unique problem of form" (like the precision parts on a Ford assembly line, perhaps, though he did not say this). Each form had to be appropriate to that part of the poem, so that all together they formed a symphony or grand design. As with the ceiling of the Sistine Chapel, he suggested, where each painting stood alone, yet none yielded "its entire significance . . . seen apart from the others."

He offered still other clues—musical clues—to what he was after. The "sea-swell crescendo" and epiphanic moment of Columbus in the "Ave Maria," the legato and blurred images of the waking consciousness of "Harbor Dawn," the "love-motif (in italics)," with its symbols "of the life and ages of man (here the sowing of the seed)," to be picked up and carried forth again in the sections of "Powhatan's Daughter" that followed: Childhood, Youth, Manhood, Age. A man walking, a man getting on the subway, a man landing on the railroad tracks somewhere in the Midwest "in the company of several tramps in the twilight." Crane's jazz "burlesque on the cultural confusion of the present—a great conglomeration of noises analogous to the strident impression of a fast express rushing by." Then the poem slowing again, as the hoboes carried the reader "into interior after interior" to arrive at the great River, and thence to the mythic and smoky world of the Indian in "The Dance."

As for "The Dance" itself, he'd been at pains there to highlight the clash between European and Indian, in which the European would become identified with "the Indian and his world before it is over." It was, after all, the only way "of ever really possessing the Indian and his world." He'd tried in this poem to get "under the skin of this glorious and dying animal" with symbols the Indian himself would comprehend. America—the female, Pocahontas, the land itself: these images Crane saw as the common basis for the European and Indian (male principle) meeting and surviving "the extinction of the Indian, who finally, after being assumed into the elements of nature," would persist "only as a kind of 'eye' in the sky," a star hanging in a twilight suspended between two worlds.

Then "Indiana"—the monologue of an Indiana farmer in the decade following the gold rush and just before the cataclysm of the war that had sundered the nation. This section, which would close "Powhatan's Daughter," he envisioned as a father's farewell to his Prodigal Son, off to return to the sea. Late in the poem's development he would transform the farewell into one between a widowed mother returning empty-handed from the gold rush, and saying good-bye to her grown son, off now to make his fortune as a sailor. On that return trip eastward, she would cross the path of a "half-breed" Indian woman, her child slung on her back, smiling at the widowed mother. Another smile, like Aunt Sally's, not to be forgotten. And so one great cycle in *The Bridge*, beginning with Columbus and ending with the sailor returning once more to the sea, the same sea which Columbus, half a millennium before, had crossed in search of his own brave New World.

Then the poem doubling back on itself, opening once more in a darker vein with "Cutty Sark"—a "phantasy on the period of the whalers and clipper ships." Like "Powhatan's Daughter," it too began in the present and worked backwards into Melville's world and Crane's. He had followed Cummings here, wanting the poem's jazzlike rhythms to suggest "the hallucinations incident to rum-drinking in a South Street dive, as well as the lurch of a boat in heavy seas." A fugue, Time and Eternity, a rambling rum-soaked sailor muttering on like the Ancient Mariner with a nickel-slot Pianola playing in the background, evoking a bastardized version of the myth of Atlantis. A chance meeting with an old derelict (were the young man who'd set out from Indiana sixty years before and this derelict then the same?). Then the old man disappearing in the predawn bustle of crowds already at work along the docks of the Fulton Fish Market. Then the poet himself stumbling in a drunken fog back across the Brooklyn Bridge, astonished to see phantom clipper ships sailing beneath him as he made his way back to Brooklyn.

Next, "Cape Hatteras," Crane's ode to Whitman, still unfinished, though he was confident that soon *The Bridge* would find "its final articulation" in "a continuous and eloquent span" when this poem was at last set in place. The final sections—"The Tunnel" and "Atlantis"— Kahn had also seen. Twelve of *The Bridge's* fifteen sections had now been published or accepted for publication, and these in some of the most prestigious magazines in three countries: *Poetry, The Dial, The American Caravan,* the *Virginia Quarterly, transition, The Calendar,* even Eliot's *Criterion.* Only "Indiana," "Cape Hatteras," and the elegiac "Quaker Hill" had yet to be completed.

There it was, his good-conduct report. But to finish, he would need help. He'd tried—really tried this time—he said, to find work in New York, without success. Part of the trouble was that the only references he could offer for the past two years were his typewriter and a collection of poems. He'd hoped to find work as a writer aboard some liner, but nowadays one needed a degree from Annapolis or an inside line for even the simplest job. He was ready to do whatever it took to find work, as long as it was work he stood a decent chance of doing well in. And since he could still write perfectly good advertising copy, he wondered if Kahn—one of the Metropolitan Opera Company's staunchest patrons—might recommend him to their publicity department. Because he could still count on his grandfather's bequest coming to him some day, he wondered if Kahn might advance him $800 or $1,000 at 6 percent, his inheritance to stand as surety.

"A great poem," Crane ended, might "well be worth at least the expenditure necessary for merely the scenery and costumes of many a flashy and ephemeral play, or for a motor car." The *Aeneid* had certainly not been written overnight, and he felt justified "in comparing the historic and cultural scope" of his own poem to that epic. After all, what he was writing was "at least a symphony with an epic theme, and a work of considerable profundity and inspiration." He'd achieved a great deal in the time he'd been on the Isle of Pines. If he could just find the money to get to Mexico or to Majorca, there was no telling what he might do.[69]

Four weeks later, Crane had his interview with Kahn, still impressed by the poet's work on *The Bridge*. He was eager to see Crane keep on with the poem and finish it, and—learning that Crane's father was willing to give the young man a monthly allowance of fifty dollars—Kahn himself came up with an additional three hundred. That, Crane told his father on October 11th, was enough to get him to Martinique for the winter months, where he would be more comfortable than in a ruined house on the Isle of Pines. There he would be able to pick up some French *and* Spanish, and with those languages under his belt, make his way as a translator when he returned to the States in the spring. He planned on sailing in a week's time.

Within days, however, Crane had changed his plans, settling in again at 110 Columbia Heights and finding part-time work in Sam Loveman's bookstore in midtown Manhattan. A wretched job, really, but at least it was something. Then, through the help of his friend, Fitzi—Eleanor Fitzgerald—he was introduced to Herbert Wise, a neurotic, gay investment broker who had made millions on Wall Street, and who was now interviewing for a combination secretary and traveling companion. Wise, who had recently suffered a nervous breakdown, had been advised by his doctors to take a six-month break from work to travel, and to that end he'd rented a mansion in Altadena, California. Given a copy of *White Buildings*, Wise read it with admiration. Fitzi had also spoken well of Crane, as had Kahn. Wise's secretary set up a series of luncheons and dinners so the two men could get to know one another, and then Crane was invited to take several short trips with Wise, to allow Wise to reach a decision. These tests Crane apparently passed, for in early November, after a final interview, he was picked to serve as Wise's platonic companion. It would be Crane's job, he was informed, to keep his employer abreast of such topics as Eliot, Spengler, and the current state of metaphysics. His duties would not be onerous, Wise's doctors explained, but they would include keeping Mr. Wise as calm as possible. On November 17th Crane would accompany Wise on his trip to California.

There were other incentives. Grace and her mother had relocated to Hollywood, and he would be able to see them both again. He still felt responsible for them—the one unstable, the other closing in on death. In this way he would also please his father, who still hoped Harold would look after them. Another incentive—perhaps the greater one—was that Wise was a globetrotter, and if things worked out, travel to Europe, all expenses paid, was a distinct possibility for the spring of '28. If, on the other hand, things did not work out, either Crane or Wise was free to conclude the arrangement. From time to time Crane would be provided with spending money.

When he actually saw photographs of the Altadena estate, Crane could hardly believe his eyes. Wise had rented the winter home of the president of American Express: a huge California-style red-tiled bungalow with patio, each room replete with private bath and its own heating system. Even the trip cross-country would prove to be an elaborate affair. Wise's limousine and a generous selection of vintage wines from Wise's cellars would be on the same train, along with Wise's chauffeur and valet. Before leaving, Crane was to order as many books to amuse himself and Wise as he wished. Once in California, Crane would be able to play tennis to his heart's content. There were responsibilities, of course, some of them still undefined. But, really, he told the Browns, in the meantime, what fun lay in store for him.

Ain't we got fun? On too many afternoons and evenings over the past twelve months, Crane had taken solace in the isolation of Patterson by imbibing whatever liquor he could lay his hands on, notably hard cider distilled from the local apple orchards. He had long since become a regular at the barn stills and cool stone cellars among the surrounding farms, sometimes drinking himself into near oblivion. Often he joked with the local farmers, sometimes overstepping bounds by telling off-color jokes in the presence of some farmer's wife, which sometimes nearly led to blows. At least once, his beloved typewriter had taken the brunt of his anger; and once, Mrs. Turner. The drinking had continued in New York all that fall, with jugs of hard cider brought down from Patterson, or visits to local speakeasies.

And now he was on his way to California as a kept man, his one job to amuse with hilarious accounts of his own escapades a neurotic millionaire with a flair for the decadent. Over the past twelve months, he'd completed one new section of *The Bridge*, written a few unnotable poems for his "Key West" sheaf, and carried on a literary correspondence with one of the few literary personages left he could still call his friend. He was hardly on speaking terms with either Munson or Tate, and he rarely wrote his parents any more. Even letters to Frank had all but ceased. At twenty-eight, his face already had the swollen, blotched appearance of the alcoholic, and his prematurely gray hair was beginning to turn white. In truth, Crane was no longer in control of his own life, though he would have bristled at anyone telling him so. Several times, in the days before he prepared to leave for California, he mislaid his train ticket. Life, he sighed, had become too goddamn hectic.

On November 8th, nine days before his departure, he spent the evening in a friendly drinking competition with E. E. Cummings and his wife, Anne, in the Village. He was sure, he insisted afterwards—though he could not remember—that he'd managed to outdrink Cummings that night. Returning home by subway at three in the morning, he climbed up out of the Clark Street station in Brooklyn, a ten-minute (sober) walk to his apartment. Somehow, inexplicably, he found himself playing with an Airedale. Then suddenly a cop was standing over him, asking him what he was doing, and Crane was shouting at him, demanding to know why in hell what he was doing was the cop's business anyway. Then he was being thrown into the backseat of a taxi and taken to the police station, "slyly," he told the Browns, "en route tossing all evidence such as billet doux, dangerous addresses, etc., out the window." Then a door slamming and a locked cell.

"I imitated Chaliapin fairly well until dawn leaked in," he joked meekly, "or rather such limited evidences of same as six o'clock whistles and the postulated press of dirty feet to early coffee stands." He was "good and mad," he would tell the Browns on the eve of his departure. "Made an impassioned speech to a crowded court room and was released at 10 o'clock sharp without even a fine." Then it was back to the Village to drink with Cummings again, while Cummings did a round of hilarious takeoffs on Crane's antics of the night before: Crane and the Airedale; Crane and the cop. Crane too found this uproarious, or so he'd been told afterwards, for he could remember none of it now. Never had he had "so much fun jounced into 24 hours before," and—if he could have had his way—he would take both Cummings and his wife along for the ride when he died and went to heaven. It was the first time he'd ever spent a night in jail. It would not be the last.[70]

11 / PINKPOODLE
PARADISE

TWO DAYS AT WISE'S VILLA in Altadena, and Crane was wishing he'd jumped track in the desert outside Albuquerque. He almost had. "Ye Gods!" he wrote Winters on November 23rd, "what a pink vacuum this place . . . is!" It was a bizarre, hybrid world he found himself in, confidant to "a millionaire neurotic (nice as he is) with valet, chauffeur, gardener, and all the rest." The villa itself had been constructed in a neo-gauche California Mediterranean style: a large U replete with working fountain and a central patio onto which each room opened. It was "all bathrooms and bad furniture," he lamented, something sprawling all over a hillside, flanked by hybrid roses, camellias, oleanders, acacias. In two days he'd "limousined around enough to wince at the 'sculptural' advertising" Winters had warned him of. If only the stuccoed bull he'd glimpsed outside some beefeaters' establishment had been "a bit more gilded, not to say gelded," he quipped, it might have served to symbolize the world in which he now found himself a virtual prisoner.

At Winter's suggestion, he paid a brief call on the forty-one-year-old poet and novelist Elizabeth Madox Roberts. It proved an awkward gesture, in spite of Roberts's attempts to be cordial. "A sibyl writhing on a tripod," was how Crane would remember her. Still, they'd managed to speak of Winters, of California, of *The Time of Man,* which Crane had hurriedly paged through the night before. A major achievement, he summed up, a novel with a relentless sense of form right up to the "dying fall" of the close, but no *Ulysses.* No, no *Ulysses.*[1] His first weeks in California he managed to look up "a couple of minor constellations"[2] he'd known in school back in Cleveland, and even ran into someone who'd known Tate at Vanderbilt. He practiced his tennis, a game much in need, he knew, of improvement. Otherwise, his time was taken up visiting movie studios in Hollywood as companion to Wise, who did not seem to be able to get enough glitz. Wise was a perfect host, Crane had to admit, always "agreeable and entertaining," but one of those people who never for one moment allowed you to forget who was paying the bills.[3]

Crane did manage to get some interesting reading in. It was one of the few aspects of his job that had actually been spelled out for him: reading the best that was available and then reporting back to Wise, who read many of the same books and articles, after which they would discuss what each had found. In this fashion Crane perused I. A. Richards's *Principles of Literary Criticism* ("damned good," he thought), and—because Eliot had sent him to it via *The Waste Land*—Jessie Weston's *From Ritual to Romance.* That book had shown him just how many "time-honored symbols" he'd already employed in building *The Bridge.*[4] He even began a correspondence with a Spanish critic, Antonio Marichalar, who wrote the Madrid letter for Eliot's *Criterion* and who had the year before published a favorable review of *White Buildings.* Each night there was Viennese food served with caviar and port, a diet rich enough, Crane groaned, that it was playing hell with his waistline. He slept long and late, waking to a cheery sun already high on the skyline and a glass of Scotch or gin placed in his shaking hand by the butler to help him begin the day in the land of the Lotus Eaters. In the weeks since meeting Wise, he'd written exactly nothing.

Something had to give in such an "egg-stepping"[5] bower of bliss. So it should have come as no surprise to him that, by the end of a month in California, Crane found himself at odds with the boss's weekend guests. These were a ragtag assortment of men and women who made their living in any way they could on the fringes of Hollywood: would-

Hart Crane in white pajamas on the Isle of Pines, summer 1926.

Janet Lewis and Yvor Winters
with their dog, summer 1927,
Altadena, shortly before
meeting Hart Crane.

Harry and Caresse Crosby,
Villefranche, winter 1929.

Sue Jenkins and William Slater
Brown, Patterson ca. March 1927.

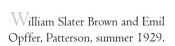

William Slater Brown and Emil
Opffer, Patterson, summer 1929.

Hart Crane smoking a cigar, Villefranche, summer 1929.

Hart Crane on the roof of 110 Columbia Heights with the Brooklyn Bridge as background, as he finished work on *The Bridge,* fall 1929.

Hart Crane. Photo by Walker Evans, late 1929. Sent to Charlotte and Richard Rychtarik, and signed "the 'Heart.'"

Hart Crane with cigar. Photo by Walker Evans, 1930.

Hart Crane (right) with C.A.; C.A.'s third wife, Bess Crane; and C.A.'s employee, Dorothy Smith, at Canary Cottage, Chagrin Falls, outside Cleveland, December 1930.

Hart Crane in animated conversation with Katherine Anne Porter, Mixcoac, late April 1931. Photo probably taken by Gene Pressley, Porter's boyfriend and later husband.

Portrait of Hart Crane executed by David Siqueiros, October 1931. Siqueiros found Crane's gaze so intense that it unnerved him and he asked Crane to lower his eyes. "Astounding," Crane called the huge painting, and done by "the greatest of contemporary Mexican painters." Somehow, he was sure, Siqueiros had managed to spread the very "soil of Mexico . . . on his canvasses." Two weeks before he killed himself, Crane, in a fit of despair, would take a razor to this same canvas and slice it to ribbons, beginning with the eyes.

Hart Crane in the bell tower of St. Prisca in late January 1932, as he worked on his final poem, "The Broken Tower." Behind him is the mestizo sexton who had permitted him to ring the church bells. It is Peggy Cowley's shadow that falls across Crane as she snaps the picture. "The Belles of Taxco —me and the sexton—way up in the air!" Crane wrote on the back of the snapshot before he sent it off to Peggy Robson at the end of January 1932. Despite the jocularity of the sentiment, Crane's downward prayer-like profile is the same as that in the Siqueiros portrait.

Hart Crane decked out with his pre-Conquest silver bells, early 1932.

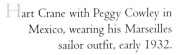

Hart Crane with Peggy Cowley in Mexico, wearing his Marseilles sailor outfit, early 1932.

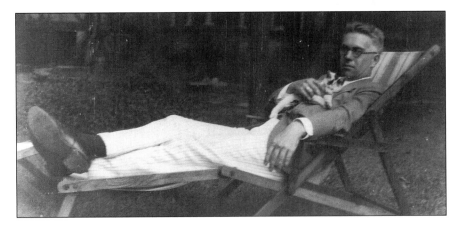

Crane with his house cat at his home in Mixcoac, winter 1932. "Of the 'Epic,'" he confessed to Caresse Crosby three weeks before he ended his life, "I haven't yet written a line. Only a few lyrics. But then, what did I actually write while in Europe—an environment not half so strange and distractingly new-old curious as this?" Here he was, living in an "oldfashioned Mexican residence of 8 rooms, 3 servants, a luxurious garden—with a goat, fighting cock, cat, Spitz dog [Palomo] and an occasional scorpion—all for $50 a month." Speaking of Peggy Cowley, who probably snapped this picture, he added that he'd recently "stretched the dominions of Eros a little with the wife of someone we all know who's here on a mission of divorce."

be actors, starlets, society pimps, figures, some of them, Crane must have thought, straight out of the pages of Petronius' *Satyricon*. Eight days before Christmas, at the start of another weekend orgy, Wise, seeing how Crane was around his guests, told him it was time he took a little vacation and slipped him some cash. Within hours, Crane was in the heart of downtown Los Angeles, crashing a party at the Biltmore ballroom with an aviator he'd already picked up—a Kentuckian living in Riverside—and the two of them were out on the dance floor swinging with "the fair ladies of the haute mondaine." In short order Crane and the aviator managed to get their waiter drunk, at which point they were ejected from the party. Out on Main Street, the two continued their dancing, Crane doing the gotzotzsky, the Kentuckian matching him step for step with a whirling dervish imitation of the Highland Fling.

The following day Crane found himself at the Breakers Club in Santa Monica, overlooking the Pacific, the waves spraying and crashing against the cliffs seven stories below. Most of the day he walked the beaches, staring out at the Pacific and wondering how the hell he'd ever wound up here. "Wall Street seems to carry a slight oppression and madness with it wherever it 'extends,'" he complained to Slater Brown two days later, so that it had been a blessing actually to find this solitude and "hear the gulls cry overhead and watch the solemn pelicans eye you a while and then haul up their legs and sprawl into the air." How he hated this whole phony world with its inane chatter and decadence. "After a good deal of fair 'sailing' since arriving here," he mimicked, "I am now convinced that 'flying' is even better. Right now, however—and until next weekend—I am 'all fives' on the ground and life can run as high as it wants to over in our villa without my batting an eye." It was Beardsley, it was whoops, dearie, all over again. He hated the effeminacy of Wise's guests, the female-mimicking voices bantering back and forth, "Oh you bitch, take that." He had never been able to "stand much falsetto."

What a bizarre assortment of people one met out here, he sighed. There was Tate's friend, the "snappy collegiate," he'd met "hanging around the movie studios." And just that day on the beach up at Venice, he'd run into someone who could discuss "literature, Spengler, Kant, Descartes and Aquinas—to say nothing of [Charles] Maurras and [Henri] Massis." The fellow was a "Bostonian of French descent who knew the editor of *The Dial*" and who turned out to be a terrific scholar, "a great reactionary," and a classicist of the sort Eliot and Wyndham

Lewis were fostering in England at the moment. Hell, Crane had had him "spotted as a Romanist [Catholic] in less than five minutes." Still, he'd enjoyed talking with him even more than all the booze he'd consumed that weekend, for he was starving for good talk to nourish the life of the mind. How boring to have servants picking up after you, continuously serving you food and drinks with "so much tiptoeing and ceremony." The ritual and decorum of weekdays at the villa, and reading, and the occasional talk with Wise: that was the upside of it. The downside: having the house suddenly fill with Hollywood nonentities reveling and stealing anything that wasn't tied down; in short, turning everything upside down while the boss looked on and applauded.

"Whoops! And whoops again, dearie," he mocked, doing his take-off on the female impersonator, Bert Savoy. "And then more warbling, more whiskey and broken crockery and maybe broken necks, for all I know, when I get back and view the ruins!" Wise's present (aging) female "star" out at the villa had played both Peter Pan and Ariel decades before. Silly Peter Pan, with her irritating habit of declaiming "we this" and "we that" when she had something to say. Peter Pan, drunker than Crane himself, mincing how terribly wounded she'd been to find a poem dedicated to that upstart Charlie Chaplin in a copy of *White Buildings* and insisting that Hart dear make immediate amends for neglecting her by writing a sonnet to *her* beauty. It had been Crane's refusal to comply with the dear lady's wishes, in fact, that had exiled him to the Breakers—"mightily pleased," Crane added—where he meant to stay until the storm at Wise's villa had subsided.[6]

A few weeks later, in fact, in mid-January 1928—as could only happen in Hollywood—Crane ran into the mythic Chaplin himself, dining at the star's favorite restaurant. Crane was there with a friend, but he stopped by Chaplin's table to say hello, mentioning Frank's name to help Chaplin recall their New York meeting four years earlier. The following day, the 20th, Crane sent him a copy of *White Buildings*. "To Charles Chaplin," he inscribed the flyleaf, "in memory of *The Kid* from Hart Crane." But the outcome, like so much else about Hollywood, led only to a perfunctory acknowledgment from Chaplin's secretary that the book had been received. When Wise heard about the meeting, he insisted on having Chaplin out to the villa. Crane did what he could, but Chaplin—as usual—demurred. All the stars, in fact, Crane was learning, had built "walls of mystery about themselves as impregnable as Carcassonne."[7]

At Christmas, Winters and his wife, Janet Lewis, drove down from Stanford to visit Winters's parents in nearby Flintridge, overlooking Pasadena, and it was there that Crane finally met the man he'd been corresponding with for the past year. For his part, Winters—scholarly, bespectacled, slight in build—was shocked to find a young man with the red blush of the alcoholic and the ears and knuckles of a pugilist. In truth, though the meeting was quiet and decorous, with Crane on his best behavior, Winters was intimidated by this extraordinary poet who looked like (and could be) a street brawler. Janet Lewis, still recovering from tuberculosis, had to remain in bed each day until four, so that the three of them had tea in her room that first afternoon. The conversation revolved around life in California and, of course, poetry.

After dinner Winters's father drove them down Pasadena's famous Christmas Tree Street. Under the peaceful cedars trimmed with Christmas lights and decorations, sitting now in the backseat with Winters and remembering the fury of the hurricane that had wrecked everything the year before, Crane began declaiming one of his Carib Island poems:

Lo, Lord, Thou ridest!
Lord, Lord, Thy swifting heart

Naught stayeth, naught now bideth
that's smithereened apart! . . . .

Whip sea-kelp screaming on blond
Sky-seethe, high heaven dashing—

Thou ridest to the door, Lord!
Thou bidest wall nor floor, Lord![8]

Over the next week the two men met three more times—each time at the villa—and always the topic came back to poetry. Friendly meetings, serious and comic both, each listening carefully to what the other had to say. Blake was on both their minds, but the real discovery for Crane was a poet completely new to him: Gerard Manley Hopkins, a Victorian Jesuit who had died in almost total obscurity in Dublin forty years before, and whose poems Winters read him from the first (and only) edition, assembled by Hopkins's friend, and England's poet laureate, Robert Bridges, ten years before.[9]

Perhaps it was the similarity in diction and power between Crane's "The Hurricane" and Hopkins's "The Wreck of the *Deutschland*," but in the Jesuit he discovered new thresholds, new anatomies for the poem. Until now, he told Winters, he'd not realized "that words could come so near a transfiguration into pure musical notation—at the same [time] retaining every minute literal signification! What a man—and what daring!"[10] He could hardly "wean" his eyes from one poem to go on to the next. So taken was Crane by what he heard in these poems that he insisted on getting his own copy; meanwhile, Winters lent him his. But when Crane could not locate the book in California, he wrote Sam Loveman back in New York, asking him to help him find a copy. He was willing to pay as much as ten bucks for it, which came to a month's rent at Addie Turner's. If he did not find the book, he added, he would type out the whole volume himself. Never had he felt this enthusiastic about any modern poet before. In fact, it would take two and a half years before Crane finally procured his own copy, and then through an Englishman, Geoffrey Phibbs, a friend of Laura Riding and Robert Graves, who sent the book on to a dumbfounded but delighted Crane.

But Winters himself had a great deal to teach Crane about poetry, especially the French poets, and Crane was hungry to learn. Afternoons, Winters read passages from Baudelaire, Rimbaud, and Valéry in impeccable French and with a sure sense of the poetic line. Then he would translate for Crane, who could read French only with the aid of a dictionary. Crane was amazed at what he found in the French writers, as a whole new world opened to him. Winters also confessed that his own poetry was undergoing a profound change. Earlier he had been sending Crane free verse poems. Now he presented him with a sheaf of sonnets. Sonnets? "Metrically good," Crane wrote him ten days into the new year. "But too skeletal—i.e., like a chemical formula rather than its concrete demonstration," as perhaps his own "Atlantis" had turned out, he was willing now to admit.[11] Years later, Winters would make the offhand comment that he'd only written the sonnets to annoy Crane; in truth, his whole poetic was changing toward a more formalist and conservative bent, leaving behind both Williams (whose free verse experiments he had so ardently championed only a few months before) and—soon—Crane himself.

Then, in the January issue of *transition*, there was a damning attack of *White Buildings* by an American expatriate, Kay Boyle. Winters, who read it, weighed in and went after Boyle in a letter which *transition* also published. What bellowing and ranting, what snottiness on that woman's part, Crane fumed. He was particularly upset that Boyle had attacked not only his grandmother's love letters but his elderly grandmother as well. Was there no pride or integrity in this woman, he wondered, that she should stoop so low? On the other hand, there had been a decent review of the book by his old friend, Laura Riding, who seemed to like his work, though he'd had a devil of a time trying to figure out what she'd actually said in the review. What was she up to? Trying "to evolve a critical style from Gertrude Stein?" If this was what the smart little magazines were allowing to pass for criticism these days, he was going back to the *Saturday Review of Literature* and the popular press.

Phelps Putnam's *Trine*, and Archibald MacLeish's *Streets in the Moon*, and Ramon Fernandez's *Messages* (the last an enormous chore that eventually defeated him): all these he read at Winters's suggestion. Also *Wuthering Heights*, whose Heathcliff now joined Ahab in Crane's "gallery of demon-heroes." And other books: Glenway Wescott's *The Grandmothers*; Gide's *The Counterfeiters*; Proust's *Sodom and Gomorrah*; and Hemingway's "The Killers," a story so good, he had to admit, it made one "doff one's hat."[12] But his own work remained stalled. He could feel the "Cape Hatteras" section trying to be born, but nothing happened. The trouble was that he did not have the uninterrupted leisure he needed, for his time, despite promises to the contrary, was not really his own.

No sooner would he sit down to write than he would be summoned by his boss, or interrupted by a servant asking him if he desired another cocktail, until "the fit" of writing had passed him by, leaving him with "only an irritating collection of notes and phrases defying any semblance of synthesis." Frustrated, he swore to himself that he was going to "take up copywriting, plastering or plumbing," anything so that he would have blocks of time he could call his own.[13] There were simply too many distractions, he told the Cowleys, after ten weeks of it: "the purling of fountains, the drawling of mockingbirds, the roaring of surf, the blazing of movie stars, the barking of dogs, the midnight shakings of geraniums, and, yes, the cruising of warships," arriving weekly now at the naval base in San Pedro.

His philosophic moments were few enough, but to make things worse there was the damned radio to contend with, in particular "the

rasping persuasions of Aimee McPherson, eternally ranting and evan-
gelizing to packed houses at the great palm-flanked arena of Angelus
Temple." Beautiful strawberry-tressed Aimee McPherson, broadcasting
over the airwaves how her followers had to be "carried out in pieces,
arms broken, heads smashed in the stampede for salvation which she
almost nightly stages, thereby emphasizing the need of arriving early (so
as to save one's body as well) and thereupon lifts her voice into a perfectly convulsing chant, coaxing and cuddlingly coy about 'Come, all ye
. . . ,' the chorus of which would make a deacon's bishopric leap crim-
son and triumphant from the grave."

In the short time he'd been in Los Angeles, his brilliant eye had
caught it all: the mix of fantasy, hope, madness, and decadence that
made up the American Dream and the contemporary version of the
gold rush gone awry. "The peculiar mixtures of piety and utter abandon
in this welter of cults, ages, occupations, etc. out here make it a good
deal like Bedlam," he told the Cowleys, anticipating Nathanael West's
Day of the Locust by a decade: "Retired schoolmarms from Iowa, Ohio,
Kansas and all the corn-and-wheat belt along with millions of hobbling
Methuselahs, alfalfa-fringed and querulous, side by side with crowds
of ambitious but none-too-successful strumpets of moviedom, quite
good to look at, and then hordes of rather nondescript people who
seem just bound from nowhere into nothing." How did such people
live, he wondered, and what were they really hoping to find out here?
Midwesterners, New Yorkers, southerners; these Crane could usually
spot. But out here everything was in such flux that people seemed
almost unreal, rather like the labyrinth of villas all about him: "some
pseudo-Spanish, some à la Maya (the colour of stale mayonnaise), others Egyptian with a simply irresistible amphora perched on the terrace,"
and a few gussied up to resemble something vaguely Chinese.[14]

His mother and grandmother he managed to see once or twice a
week, though it took him nearly two hours by bus to reach them at
their small cottage at 1803 North Highland in Hollywood, and that
meant a simple visit ate up the better part of a day. His grandmother
was doing better in the California climate, better than at any time in the
past three years, but the woman Grace had brought out with them to
help with the chores had proved a problem, fretting and sulking most of
the time. By February, it looked as if Wise was finally going to invite
Crane to accompany him to Europe in two months' time, yet now
Crane wondered if he would really be able to leave his mother and

grandmother when the time came. In spite of setbacks, he loved walking the beaches and playing tennis; most of all, he loved the wealth of books and the music with which Wise surrounded himself. Beethoven and Brahms, and hundreds of other albums—symphonies, quintets, concertos: these he listened to for hours.

But his wings were held fast in the honey of sweet degeneration, for Wise's Altadena truly was the fabled Land of the Lotus Eaters. In late February, imbibing his ninth snifter of Scotch, Crane wrote the Browns to congratulate them on the birth of their son. Blessings, he offered, "from the fairy God Mother in her native clime, here where the evenings are made lustful and odorous with the scent of lemon flowers and acacias on the sea-salt air!" He even managed to embed a little poem in the prose of his letter:

> A paean from Venusberg!
> Oy-oy-oy!
> I have just had my ninth snifter of Scotch.
> O shades of Bert Savoy!

"They say he had a glass eye," Crane joked, "as the result of some midnight with a mariner," though he himself had encountered no such dire results as yet with the sailors he'd bedded. He reminded Slater of the thousands of good-looking gobs they'd seen in New York the previous May, then told him to multiply that figure to realize the blessed windfall he'd waded into here in California. "Such a throng of pulchritude and friendliness," he sighed, "as would make your 'hair' stand on end." This had been the way of all flesh with him for the past several months. Wine, sailors, and song. On top of which he'd now met the most bewitching male Circe of them all: a movie actor who had sailors "dancing naked, twenty at a time, around the banquet table." O André Gide and his Counterfeiters, he exclaimed, "No Paris ever yielded such as this." And if you wanted something out of uniform, all you had to do was walk down Hollywood Boulevard, to find "little fairies who can quote Rimbaud before they are 18," or women "who must have the tiniest fay to tickle them in the one and only way!" And then there was the actress, Betty Compson, shaking her boobs and crying, "Apples for a bite!"

Yes, he was reading. Just now it was Wyndham Lewis's *Time and Western Man*. But he still preferred—after a night of wine—waking at dawn to dip once more into *The Tempest*, "that crown of all the Western World,"[15] with its clarities and sonorities, reminding him sadly of a better, simpler time:

> —*The charm dissolves apace*
> *And as the morning steals upon the night,*
> *Melting the darkness, so their rising senses*
> *Begin to chase the ignorant fumes that mantle*
> *Their clearer reason* . . . .

"I have at present a little Spanish port in my noddle," he wrote Winters in late February. "And who knows (*quien sabe*), perhaps the wine is to blame for my conceit of writing you. But enough of bows and furbelows!" He was getting ready to hurl Ramon Fernandez with his epistemology and indirections into the fire, advice his boss (long since fed up with the book) had taken himself. The truth was that writers like Fernandez with their explanations of the twentieth century had actually stopped him from getting on with *The Bridge,* which was why "Cape Hatteras" was still just "a bundle of smoldering notes."[16] Really, this "unmitigated concern with the Future," he told another correspondent, "is one of the most discouraging symptoms of the chaos of our age." It was as if the imagination "had ceased all attempts at any creative activity and had become simply a great bulging eye ogling the foetus of the next century."[17]

The truth was that Crane was now ready to leave Wise and his menagerie as soon as possible. He was becoming irritable and depressed at the honeyed hell he found himself enmeshed in. Again all letters ceased, though he did signal Winters in early March that he was in an "unpleasant state of mind . . . these days," which made him poor company.[18] Then, abruptly, the Altadena experiment was over. On Tuesday, March 20th, after four months of it, Crane packed his things, shook hands with Wise and said good-bye, then left for his mother's cottage across town. It was just as well, he figured, since things had long since soured between himself and his boss. Had he had some real job to perform, he reasoned, he might have been able to keep at least some shred of self-respect. But the constant "tip-toeing, solicitous, willy-nilly uncertainty of everything," besides Wise's "interminable psychoanalysis of every book, person, sausage and blossom" he came across, had finally given him "the heebie-jeebies." Strange as his relationship with Wise had been, it had not included—Crane was quick to point out—calls between the sheets. So, when Wise finally did secure "a quite cultured little piece of Pear's Soap"—"He won't be happy till he gets it"—someone who could "console" him in all ways, Crane knew his own presence had become superfluous.[19]

"Invalid Wall St. brokers have a way of disrupting one's customary mental habits," he wrote Underwood afterwards. Looking back, he could see that he'd been hired on as a sort of "safe and interesting" person to have around. He'd hoped to get some real writing done, but the place had proved "too neurotic to encourage a single strophe." Hollywood—symbol of 1920s glitzy America—had shown itself to be the all-devouring spiritual vacuum it was, "all grease-paint, pretense, expensive motors and chewing gum." Even the "stereotyped sunlight," shining on cue day after day, and which everyone had told him would be so inspiring, had become for him both monotonous and depressing. America, he sighed, America, the land of Babbitts and Polyannas.

Only the fleet had made California bearable. Gobs were "always amusing," he told Underwood, who would understand, and the choice in California had been "positively bewildering in beauty" and friendliness.[20] One of his "duties" each weekend, in fact, had been to come back from San Pedro to regale the crowd at the villa with his misadventures, which had proven plentiful enough. What the hell, half the movie stars were drug addicts, and L.A.'s Pershing Square was a livelier place for meeting a quick lay than Washington's Lafayette Square had ever been, which was saying something. But it was the beaches with their miles of solitude he loved most. He would, he added, be content to live forever by the ocean.

On March 24th, the Saturday after his departure from the Wise menagerie, he hooked up with Emil Opffer, who had just docked in San Pedro for a twenty-four-hour layover. Dear old trusting Emil had taken a job as waiter aboard the SS *California* for the express purpose of making his way out to the West Coast to see Crane. Unfortunately, there had been a mix-up, for Emil had gone up to Altadena looking for Crane while Crane waited at the gangway for Emil to show up. It took Emil eight hours to find his way back to San Pedro, by which time Crane had polished off a bottle of whiskey while Emil had managed a sizable dent in his own bottle of Bacardi.

Reunited at last, they found a booth in a speakeasy, where they continued their drinking. Amidst "many bottles of dubious gin and whiskey" and much "skoling" and laughing back and forth, Emil kept flashing a fat payroll, buying drinks for an assortment of what Crane called those "dubious 'merry andrews.'" At midnight, when the speakeasy closed, Crane and Emil found themselves walking down a dark street with five other men, who insisted Emil spring for a hotel room where they could go on drinking.

By then Crane knew that something was terribly wrong. He sobered up enough to tell the men the night was over, but it was too late. Emil was already being led down an alley by three of them while the other two boxed Crane into a corner. Finally, he managed to break through them and catch up with Emil, only to have all five begin swinging and kicking at him. He put up a fight, but he was too drunk to be effective, and soon he and Emil were both down and their pockets emptied. He had been beaten pretty badly, but Emil had been knocked almost senseless. What stopped them from being killed was a car turning the corner and scaring the muggers off.

At one o'clock in the morning Crane found himself in a police station, trying to remember the details of what had happened. Afterwards, with the help of several sailors, he managed to get Emil back to his ship before it sailed at dawn. Then Crane collapsed in a Salvation Army hotel room. It was five that evening before he could scrape together enough cash for the fare back to his mother's. "I don't mind my losses," he wrote the Browns on the 27th, "but I feel terribly about Emil's luck. He always seems to get the hardest end of things."

For the time being he would stay with his mother and grandmother and help them in any ineffectual way he could. To do that he would need to find a job, preferably in Hollywood, writing. Scenarios, eventually, but to start with he would take anything: "title-writing, gag-writing, 'continuity' writing." Otto Kahn—he had taken to calling him "Papa"—happened to be in Hollywood on vacation for a few weeks, and that same morning Crane had gone to see him at the Ambassador Hotel. Kahn promised to do what he could about finding something suitable, including talking with the movie mogul, Jesse Lasky, at Paramount. As for starring in the movies, it happened that while Kahn and Crane were talking out on the hotel patio, Pathé News Reel had been filming them. How glorious, he thought, if he could only have his profile—decked out in horn-rimmed glasses—thrown up on the silver screen "all the way from Danbury to Hong-Kong and Mozambique!"[21]

But a new theme began entering his letters now, one he'd picked up from his reading of Spengler and Wyndham Lewis and Ramon Fernandez: the general dissolution of the times, the eerie quiet before the coming apocalypse that would tear America to pieces. This mood of desolation, this dark night of the soul, had effectively paralyzed his ability to write anything he could believe in because he no longer knew what he believed in, if anything. Certainly he no longer believed in himself or the poem. Crane mentioned this malaise in letters to Frank, Winters, Munson.

"The spiritual disintegration of our period becomes more painful to me every day," he told Munson a month after leaving Wise. "So much so that I now find myself balked by doubt at the validity of practically every metaphor I coin." Everywhere he looked, including gloom-and-doom Eliot, he saw "a thousand issues . . . raised" for every one settled. And where the odd philosopher offered more hope than despair—as among the neo-Thomists—he saw only "an arbitrary dogmatism," which was too artificial and too European in its premises and values to shape America's future in any positive way. He realized too that he and every pundit and philosopher in the country was spending too much time analyzing what was wrong with America, which was, in its own way, symptomatic of what was wrong with things in general.

Crane turned now to look back again at the program Munson had proposed in *Destinations,* ideas which he himself had long ago pooh-poohed. But what if Munson was right? What if Munson's call for order and a clearer direction in one's life was the only way finally to make sense of things? Placebos! After all, Munson's ideas were "too vaguely articulated to offer any definite system in contrast to the distraction, indifference to major issues, mere intuitiveness," which Munson had complained of in writers whose work he otherwise admired. He was, of course, speaking about himself, and of what was happening to him.

Still, if ever a person distrusted ideologies and platforms, that person was Crane. What he did trust was intuition, and Blake's and Dickinson's insights now seemed "more incontrovertible than ever since

Relativity and a host of other ideologies" had come into being. As for Crane, he knew himself "too well to disagree on as many points" as he had when he'd first read Munson's essay. He was grateful, he told Munson now, for his interest in his work, "especially on the technical side," where Munson had defined his platform with such gusto that Crane had gone back to his poem to find that, yes, here and there he really had caught something in the massive "scrap heap" of *The Bridge*.[22]

This line of troubled introspection continued in a letter Crane wrote Slater Brown at the end of April. "Since the Fleet with its twenty-five thousand gobs has left for Hawaii," he wrote, "I have had a chance to face and recognize the full inconsequence of this Pollyanna greasepaint pinkpoodle paradise with its everlasting stereotyped sunlight and its millions of mechanical accessories and sylphlike robots of the age of celluloid." He was still trying to find "a foothold in this sandstorm," some sort of job, but without success. Worse, his mother was now driving him crazy with her insistence on his becoming a Hollywood film actor. If he could just hold on for a few more weeks he'd been promised an interview at Paramount, and perhaps he might then be able to "creep into some modest dustpan" in Paramount's reading department. Though his hopes weren't high, he'd known some back east who'd made as much as $750 a week writing ads for the movies.

Until then he'd managed to stifle his homesickness for Patterson. But with spring and the Browns back up there once more, he hungered to get back. "Things like that croquet game in the rain, the afternoon at the cider mill, the skeleton surrey ride and the tumble down the hill!" he sighed. He hated having to take buses to get anywhere. He hated the bad liquor, the "rigor mortis of the local hooch," the Wall Street decadence, even the rough and tumble of the San Pedro waterfront. He was by now so starved for decent conversation—locked into the diminished world of a mother reduced in circumstances and grown more garrulous than ever, herself tied to a mother confined to a sickbed—that he sought out whatever pleasures he could find, no matter how marginal and exotic.

In late April it was Alice Barney, "world-famous grande dame and mother of Nathalie Clifford Barney,"[23] a lesbian associate of Gertrude Stein in Paris and friend of Paul Valéry and Wilbur Underwood. By mentioning Underwood's name over the telephone, Crane managed an invitation to one of Barney's soirées on Ogden Drive and Hollywood Boulevard, and prayed for a mildly Proustian evening. He did his best to fit in, but again he was out of his element, listening to one grande dame read Shakespeare while he was kept busy reloading the plate and cup of another. Worse, Barney herself seemed too preoccupied with her other guests to toss him more than a word or two, and those mostly about her dear dear Wilbur. He did not return for more.

Trapped, he would say later. Trapped like a rat. No use trying to hide who he was any more. So, within a few weeks of moving in with his mother, he finally shared with her the fact that he was gay. If Crane thought he could share this secret with her because he suspected that she already knew, or that it would be better for both of them if he no longer had to live a lie, he was wrong. Worse, when arguments arose between them now, in part over his inability to find work in Hollywood, she took the occasion to remind him of what he had become: a drunk and a homosexual. At first she'd even asked him to leave the house and go find a room somewhere else. He tried to see it from her side, but the rejection hurt. She began wondering out loud what his father would think if he learned what had become of Harold.

What happened exactly between Crane and his mother remains misted, because neither of them ever spoke about what precisely had led to the final break between them. "My mother made life so miserable for me with incessant hysterical fits and interminable nagging that I had to steal off east again, like a thief in the night, in order to save my sanity or health from a complete breakdown," he would tell the Rychtariks ten months later.[24] Certainly he felt betrayed, so that by early May he'd made up his mind to leave his mother for good. Quietly, surreptitiously, so as not to arouse her suspicions, he prepared for his departure on the 15th, saying nothing even to most of his friends.

"I carried it through," he would write his aunt Zell once he was back in New York City, "packing by infinitesimal degrees and labyrinthine subterfuges (it sounds like a comedy, but I was ill and nearly dead for sleep) until on the appointed hour the taxi drove up with darkened lights—and I was on my way—'home'—the only one I ever hope to have—this supposedly cruel city, but certainly better for me than either of my parents."[25] With a loan from Frank, he'd arranged to take the train back along the southern route as far as New Orleans—his surrogate mother's home, Aunt Sally's—and from there he boarded a ship for New York. The morning after he left, Grace awoke to find his bed empty and a brief note on the kitchen counter that read, "Gone

East." If it had been her intention to hold him ransom in Hollywood by withholding the $5,000 legacy he was to receive on the death of her mother, the plan failed. After he stole out of the house that night, Grace never again saw her son.

"Friendship agony!" he would write, recalling the new dawn rising as his train approached New Orleans:

> *words came to me*
> *at last shyly. My only final friends—*
> *the wren and thrush, made solid print for me*
> *across dawn's broken arc. No; yes . . . or were they*
> *the audible ransom, ensign of my faith*
> *towards something far, now farther than ever away?*
>
> *Remember the lavender lilies of that dawn,*
> *their ribbon miles, beside the railroad ties*
> *as one nears New Orleans, sweet trenches by the train*
> *after the western desert, and the later cattle country;*
> *and other gratuities, like porters, jokes, roses. . . .*

Aunt Sally and the Isle of Pines: the one mother figure who had accepted him for who he was, and where his gift had flowered in an outpouring so intense he'd managed three years' work in three months' time. Well, the old covenant with Grace was broken now, broken at both ends, as far as he could see, and the one with his surrogate—an old, broken, destitute woman—in the noon of his life recalled and reaffirmed:

> *Dawn's broken arc! and noon's more furbished room!*
> *Yet seldom was there faith in the heart's right kindness.*
> *There were tickets and alarm clocks. There were counters and schedules;*
> *and a paralytic woman on an island of the Indies,*
> *Antillean fingers counting my pulse, my love forever.*[26]

Crane spent twenty-four hours in New Orleans with some friends he'd met there, reporters for the *Times Picayune* who knew his poetry and admired it. Together, they passed the time talking, drinking absinthe, enjoying the French cuisine, and walking about the streets of theVieux Carré. "A beautiful old town," he wrote his father, "full of history and with the kind of mellowness which I prefer to all the boomed-up modernity of Los Angeles and environs."[27] One day in New Orleans had made of him a true believer, he would tell Winters a month later. Never before had he "felt so in the presence of the 'old' America—not baldly 'confronted' with it, as at places like Salem, Mass.—but surrounded and rather permeated by it." Pewter, he supposed, was what most Americans thought of when they thought of colonial America. But then "the old tarnished gold of Orleans" belonged rather "to the traditions of Martinique than to the spirit of the Minute Men."[28] Someday he meant to spend a whole winter in New Orleans.

The boat trip from there to New York took five days, most of it out of sight of land. First there had been the heart-throbbing seven-hour ride down the delta, he told Underwood, with "the great, flat yellow, masculine" Mississippi sprawled out there before him,[29] the same river he'd so often pictured in his imagination and of which he'd written in "The River." There was "something tragically beautiful about the scene," he wrote his father, something tragic indeed about the river approaching the end of its journey, about watching the "great, magnificent Father of Waters pouring itself at last into the oblivion of the Gulf!"[30]

On the other hand, he knew New York too well to shout hosannas when—on the morning of May 23rd—he descended the gangplank with two bucks in his pockets and melted back into the welcome anonymity of the city. After California, the bustle of the harbor looked damned good to him as he watched the tugs ease his ship into place among the gray piers. "Despite all the slogans and catchwords to the contrary," Crane found New Yorkers actually friendlier and more caring than the touted Californians.[31] Nor did it take long to talk his friends into lending him enough to make his way back up to Patterson. With gratitude he found his room ready for him, and meals prepared again by dear old Addie, and all for only six dollars a week. How good to be back "in the old house with the old woman and her cats," he wrote Winters a month after he'd returned, sneezing as strenuously as ever at the roses. How "damned good . . . to rejoin a few human associates who live around here."[32] How good to smell the rank scent of horseshit once again.

"Maybe it's my room," he wrote his father once he'd settled in. Or perhaps it was having "old friends nearby—or the more stimulating mental atmosphere." Whatever it was, he did not miss one bit "the parade of movie actors nor a lot of other artificialities of Hollywood," though for a while he too had been "amused by such matters." He was anxious to have his father understand why he'd left the West Coast so precipitously, especially if Grace was preparing to reveal Harold's secret life. He had wanted to stay out there and help his mother in any way he could, he explained, but he had neither job nor prospect, and so it had seemed best "to go while the going was good."[33] He'd spent everything he had left getting back to Patterson. The trouble was that he did not believe he would be able to find work until after the elections in November, and so was hoping to live here in the country on a shoestring. In the meantime, he wondered if his father might advance him a few dollars.

"I had always imagined that California, with its limpid climate, moving picture stars and shady nooks, was an ideal stamping ground for a vagabond," C.A. joked with his son, twisting the knife a little. How could Harold ever have thought of leaving the land of the lemon trees for "the wild country around New York?" Then he remembered that as a young man he had spent a month at Grandfather Hart's place on the Isle of Pines, and that alone had cured him of ever wanting to live in the tropics again. Boring sunshine day in and day out, he recalled, "the same bird perched on the same spot every morning, singing the same song," until he'd grown "weary of such a methodical climate." On the other hand, hadn't he bought Canary Cottage to get away "from the methodical humdrum life" of business that had been his lot for so long, even as that business was sliding slowly into irrevocable decline?[34] Every week now he found himself getting to the office a little later and not minding it a bit. Only fifty-three, Crane thought, and how tired his father already seemed, how defeated.

The Browns, the Cowleys, the Josephsons, and now the Nathan Asches were all living around Patterson that summer, and soon Crane was enjoying the local applejack (the best liquor he'd tasted north of Cuba, he told one friend), a concoction some cashiered army officer turned bootlegger over on Birch Hill was all too willing to provide.

Once again there were the usual croquet tournaments up at the Browns' place. Williams was going to be staying with the Asches in another month, and Crane was hoping to get to know the good doctor better. Even the fiction writer, Morley Callaghan, was supposed to be coming down from Canada for a visit. Crane was not writing poetry yet, could not, for the electricity was just not there. But he could read, and now, following Winters's promptings, he dove into the Metaphysical poets: Traherne, Vaughan, Herbert. He followed a new magazine called *Outlook*, which featured poets on poets: Cowley on Poe; Tate on Dickinson; Burke on Emerson. And since Tate had "become too pontifical for any discussions whatever," he especially liked talking poetry with Cowley, enjoying that "slow, laborious mind" that refused to "turn out a shoddy sentence."[35]

How he loved this place. Had loved it from the first moment he'd settled here. And now that he'd severed all relations with his mother, now that his childhood home was gone forever, he desperately needed a place he could call his own. At the end of June he wrote his father, asking for a loan against the $5,000 he would receive when his grandmother was finally gone, as he expected to happen at any moment. He wanted the loan, he explained, to buy a house that had come up for sale in the area. But this time C.A. declined. Since 1922, he replied, his failing candy business had eaten up half of what he'd once been worth. The business had flourished during the war, but then taxes, loss of income, and—he admitted—misjudgment on his part had caused it to tumble into a slow but steady decline. He had all he could do now simply to meet expenses. Even the Cottage was not yet making money. Besides, C.A. reminded Harold, he himself had never owned a house until he'd bought the Cottage just two years before.

In any event, the house issue soon became a moot point, for toward the end of July, shortly after Crane's twenty-ninth birthday, after one more wild party in which he began breaking up her furniture again, Addie Turner—realizing she could not handle his outbursts any longer—told him to leave. It was Eleanor Fitzgerald—Fitzi—who came to his rescue by allowing him to stay on at her place just across the state line in Gaylordsville, Connecticut, until he could find something for himself. But Crane was desolate. There was his boss, Herb Wise, off in the Swiss Alps, where he too might have been had things worked out differently, and here he was, without a place to lay his head. True, Fitzi had made him feel "perfectly welcome," but where, he asked his father,

was he going to turn for help next?[36] Mrs. Turner had told him, he
lied, that she couldn't give him any more credit, even though he'd paid
her with the fifty dollars C.A. had sent him a few weeks earlier. He
did not mention the broken furniture or the violence he was more
and more prone to when he got drunk, and he was drunk a good deal
of the time now. All he could do was try to get a job working on the
county roads, earn enough to buy carfare back down to New York,
and see what he could find in the way of work there.

C.A. wrote by return, puzzled at what was happening to his son.
"Of course you don't know where to turn," he explained. "You don't
seem to have enough of the earnest side of life in your make-up." C.A.
knew all too well how he'd made a mess of things in his own life
because he'd been too ambitious for the wrong things, unlike his son,
paying "too much attention to hard work and not enough to play."
But if he was ever going to get through to his son, now was the time.
His own father had scrimped and worked, C.A. reminded Harold, and
he in turn had done the same. It was the American way, and Harold had
shrugged it off as worse than a bad dream. Well, now Harold was learning the hard way what too much playing led to. "Get it out of your
head that you can live in this world and be a good citizen without
paying your way," his father warned him. "People may laugh at your
jokes; they may regard you as a prodigy; they may occasionally buy a
book," but, as old Elbert Hubbard in his wisdom had put it, "Sooner
or later your affections are expressed in beef steaks."[37]

He'd tried breaking Harold into the family business, but it hadn't
taken long to see that his son did not want to work as he had worked.
Yes, Harold could write and write well, but what good was that if it
didn't feed you and put a roof over your head? If Harold could not
make a living by his writing, he would just have to find something
else to do. He could not tell him what to do, and he knew by hard
experience that his advice on that topic had been wrong anyway. He
could hardly give himself advice any more, much less someone else. *His*
father had made money selling maple syrup and he'd made his by selling chocolate. It was all he knew how to do, and now he would just
have to go on doing it until he died. He just hoped Harold found his
own way before it was too late. He enclosed another check for fifty dollars and wished his son well.

At the beginning of August, Crane made his way over to Cro-
ton-on-Hudson north of New York City to stay with his old friends,

the Habichts, who were living now in the barns and stables of the old Horace Greeley estate, recently refurbished into a U-shaped villa, complete with court and patio garden. It was from there, enjoying the best food he'd had since Altadena, that he sent his father a progress report. He was going to New York in a day or so without so much as the prospect of a job, and—since his funds were once again gone—he was going "to take anything on land or sea" he could grab.

He had no idea where he would sleep, so if his father cared to get in touch with him (or rescue him), he would have to write in care of Mrs. Turner, who would at least forward his mail. He thanked his father for all he'd done, adding that he still hoped someday to have a little place of his own, "away from all the contention and fret" that had so beset him these past three years. When he did find that place, he would hang his few pictures, lay down his rug, set his books on a shelf, and get back to work on *The Bridge.* How tired he was of having to leave his few possessions "scattered in all corners of the western hemisphere."[38] Worst was knowing his father thought of him as both lazy and inconsequential. *Someday* he would make him proud. *Someday* he would show him he'd done something of value.

Two days and one wild party later—a party at which Crane once again got so drunk he threatened to kill anyone (including his hosts) if they dared touch the phonograph, even after the needle began wearing a groove in the record—he found himself back in New York. Malcolm Cowley had come through at the last minute, offering him the use of his apartment at 501 East 55th, near the East River. Crane borrowed what money he could from friends in the city and then began pounding the sidewalks in the enervating August heat searching for work. He still hoped to find something with an advertising agency, the one line of work he felt he could do and do well, but no one seemed interested. He looked awful: his hair wild, the gray streaked with white, his cheeks and nose blotched and red. Try as he might, the man who had always been so meticulous about his personal appearance walked about now in rumpled clothes, without even a flatiron to press his shirt and pants. His shoes were dog-eared and his soles flapped. He who a few months earlier had dined nightly on caviar and Viennese food and drunk only vintage wines was now reduced to cooking the simplest of meals to stay alive. "I'm in the big, simmering gluepot Metropolis hunting work," he told Winters. "Not much to say in any direction and slightly dizzy."[39]

Yes, he admitted, when he wrote his father after two weeks of it, it was time to learn "some regular trade like typesetting [or] linotyping."[40] But without money, how was he to pay for the necessary training and eat at the same time? Perhaps he could find work as a plumber's or mechanic's helper. Heavy work, but what could he do about that? Right now, he would be happy to get anything. Heartsick at his son's plight, C.A. sent him a telegram by return. It read, simply: AM SENDING YOU THE MONEY TO COME HOME AT ONCE/FATHER.[41] But, just as suddenly, Crane found a job working for Griffin, Johnson & Mann, a bookstore off Fifth Avenue and 48th. Instead of using his father's check to return home, he cashed it and bought food and a haircut. But he was careful to wire C.A. as soon as he learned he had the job, then followed up the wire with a letter. The job wasn't much, but at least it would do until something better came along. An old friend from Cleveland—Sam Loveman—had offered him the work; and since his friend would be away much of the time buying up collections and rare editions, he'd been hired on to take care of customers as well as write copy for ad catalogues.

He began work on August 20th, in the meantime looking for a place over on Columbia Heights, hoping "the patron saint of rooming houses (St. Anne, I believe!)"[42] felt commodious enough toward him to find him a room with a view. The saint must have been listening, for Crane found a place two weeks later at 77 Willow Street, one block east of his old haunts. The apartment was in a nineteenth-century, five-story, narrow brownstone/brick edifice where Willow intersected with Pineapple Street, and from the window there he could once again view his beloved harbor and his bridge.

But the pressure of writing copy in the sweltering heat of New York had nearly felled him. He was doing ads for all sorts of products: CALOROIL HEATERS, Fos-FoR-Us MINERAL MIXTURE ("for hogs, cattle, poultry"), FLOWER OF LOVE WEDDING RINGS. "The high tension rush of an agency office," he complained to Winters, "is only to be compared with a newspaper office. Inserts, folders, circulars, posters, full pages and half pages, a two-column twentyliner here, there this there that!"[43] Still, he was happy to have a job at all. Happy too to think that someone like Winters was willing to take him seriously enough to make him believe he might still be a poet when everyone else seemed to have given up on him and he had all but given up on himself.

Then he learned from his mother that on September 6th his

grandmother had finally passed away. Grace, prostrate, urged her son to come back out to Hollywood as soon as possible to help her settle her mother's affairs. But this time, though he sent flowers and condolences, Crane refused to return. He felt sorry for his mother, he wrote Aunt Zell, knowing how "miserably unhappy" she would be. But commiserating with her, he knew from long experience, only made her more helpless. He knew she was deeply attached to him, and even loved him in her own strange way, but there were elements in the attachment that were good for neither of them. Psychoanalysis might eventually reveal "many things that it would be well" for his mother to learn, but would she be ready to listen? Alarmed as he was by her condition, he was more alarmed at what she could still do to him.

For twenty years now his family with their incessant problems had robbed him of his vitality, "unmanning" him time and again and threatening to turn him into "one of those emotional derelicts who are nothing but tremulous jellyfish might-have-beens." Perhaps his parents, and especially his mother, had already robbed him of the one thing necessary—his poetry—though he knew he'd done "too much solid writing to believe that to be true." Still, if he kept feeding off "this insatiable demon of morbidity," this preoccupation with the past, he was going to wind up killing himself. He had to learn once more how to believe in himself. He had to become strong enough so that his mother would never again be able to swallow him up. In any event, he did not have the strength just now to trust either her or himself, and he would have to stay away from her until he could. "I won't be dragged into hell—and live there forever for anybody's joke—not even my mother's," he insisted to Aunt Zell. Unless, of course, the hold was already too strong on his "unconscious emotional nature, for hope of escape," and that only time would show. Taking to her bed and pleading helplessness was only going to drive him further away. If his mother kept coming after him, he swore, he was going to disappear. Really disappear.[44]

"Unmanned." The word was Crane's. From the time he returned to New York in August, right through the fall, he made a point of spending more time with one or another woman until, as had happened with Laura Riding earlier, he and that woman had become an item. Lorna Dietz, a friend of Emil Opffer's, the Cowleys, the Browns, and the Provincetown crowd, married to an ad writer but separated now, like Crane a midwesterner from the same sort of ambitious middle-class background, at least made sure Crane got some decent food when he'd arrived down on his luck in New York. Like Crane, Dietz loved a good time, and seemed able to keep up with him drink for drink. Both single, they became the odd couple, seeking out each other's company, though Dietz understood that Crane's first love was still Emil. Crane's and Dietz's was not a sexual relationship, though Crane was attracted to her (she reminded him, ironically enough, of his own mother, "on good days," he added), and she spent a number of evenings with him in Manhattan and Brooklyn.

Often it was at one or other of the local speakeasies, where he liked to play the piano, pounding away time and time again at some tune, especially a miserable but robust rendition of "Too Much Mustard." At the same time, he still had his sailors wherever and whenever he could find them, whether in Hoboken or along the Brooklyn piers, and he had one rouser of a night with a "bluejacket from the *Arkansas*—raving like-a mad," as the two swung together in the "passionate pulchritude of the usual . . . maritime houreths."[45] And then, as dawn flooded the harbor and revealed once more the cyclopean towers across the river, sad-eyed Ulysses stirred himself and prepared to descend into the chasm of the subway, to arise half an hour afterwards into the chill sunlight of Manhattan.

In September, he had heard from the Rychtariks, wondering when he meant to repay the money they'd lent him to buy his hilltop acres. "It has hurt me to think that you thought me indifferent about returning the remainder of the money that you so kindly loaned me," he wrote them in mid-September. True, he might have done so earlier, but certainly at no time since they'd asked for it. But now, tasting the $5,000 bequest his grandfather had left him and about which he'd dreamed for so many years, he assured them they would soon be getting their money. It was probably too late to save their friendship, he added, but he needed them to know he'd always meant to repay his debt, no matter what they thought of him. "As long as I believe in myself," he explained, "I shall insist on my good intentions and with the ultimate faith of putting them into practice."[46] It was the booze talking. Perhaps they would do him the kindness of writing to tell him where he could send them their check.

That same evening he sent Williams a friendly note, wondering why in paradise they didn't get together, especially since he knew Williams got over to New York so often. There were so many things to talk about, especially with a man like Williams. Williams shot back a friendly note, without committing himself. He too had heard a great deal about Crane and was not anxious to go one on one with him. "I promised Hart Crane two months ago to let him know when I should be free to see him," he wrote that other Brooklyn poet, Louis Zukofsky, in early December. What was all "this blather" about getting together anyway?[47] It would be another year before Williams finally took Crane up on his invitation. The reasons for his coolness were complex. Partly it was that, like Winters and others, he felt uncomfortable with Crane's roaring boy, predatory reputation. But what complicated matters even more were his anxieties about Crane as a poetic contender.

"They say Hart Crane is—this or that—a crude homo," Williams had put it bluntly in a letter to Pound in mid-July, about the same time that Addie Turner was throwing Crane out of her house. Williams knew that Marianne Moore detested Crane's work, going so far as to call it "fake-knowledge" (actually, it had been Conrad Aiken who had judged it so, Moore merely providing space for that judgment to be disseminated in the pages of The Dial). "Others think [Crane] is God Almighty," Williams confessed, "which naturally offends anyone, like myself, who pretends to the same distinction. Best poet in U.S. say the Kenneth Burkes, Gorham Munsons, etc. I dunno. Ivor [sic] Winters is plum gaga over him."[48] Stop worrying, Pound wrote back from Italy. What the hell, the whole New York gang—"the Cranes, Ivors, Munsons, Gorhams, Burkes"— had a "peculiar sterility" about them anyway, as the American number the group had put together for Jolas's Paris transition had amply demonstrated.[49] Place their work next to the French avant-garde writers, and you saw at once how lightweight they really were.

And Williams, in mid-August, even as Crane was slogging the streets of New York looking for work: "As to the Hart Crane, Josephson group—to hell with them all," he wrote Pound. Perhaps there was something of value there, but nothing he could see himself using. "As it stands," he added, "Crane is supposed to be the man that puts me on the shelf." But, really, the man was "just as thickheaded" as himself and "quite as helplessly verbose at times." Moreover, Crane came up "into clarity far less often" than he himself did. The truth was that if what Crane put down on the page was "related to design, or thought, or emotion—or anything but disguised sentimentality and sloppy feeling," then his own brand of poetry was "licked and no one more happy to acknowledge it" than himself.

Still, Williams went on, he did not "feel so violently about the group" as Pound seemed to. Let them go on doing what they were doing, for there was nothing there he expected "to be caught copying for the next twenty years." Better after all to give Pound a half million "to do literature with," and let the "Josephsons and Burkes and Cranes" dwindle into obscurity with their old-fashioned rhetoric and ideas. Perhaps Crane's kind of sexual excess was necessary for the artist, which might explain why the Crane school of poetry was "made up of cock suckers." Well, he was a cocksman of sorts himself, he crowed, with more women "willing to throw their cloaks in the mud at my feet" than he knew what to do with.[50] But if Crane was unsure of himself and of his place in the world, Williams—beneath his false bravado—was equally unsure. Wary as the two poets were of each other, each was still very much on the other's mind.

By early October, Crane had once more tired of the New York scene. He'd written nothing of consequence in over a year and his subject—the vital spirit of the American Dream—seemed now completely and "comfortably dead." One saw this death-in-life "in millions of faces," he reported back to Underwood, this sense that there was "nothing left to struggle for except 'respectability.'"[51] Every now and then he still found some sailor who gave him a jolt, but even sex had lost much of its old savor. He felt old, old; and the only thing that kept him going seemed to be his grandfather's legacy of five grand. When he got hold of that, he promised himself, he was going to go off to see Europe.

By the middle of the month he had managed to finagle his way back into his old room at 110 Columbia Heights, where once again he had an unrestricted view of the white buildings of New York and his beloved river. "Rooming houses depress me terribly," he wrote Winters on October 23rd, though this one might get him to "reading and writing a little" as it had in the past. The real problem was time, for with the rush of copywriting at the store, all he could manage to read these days was an occasional review "on the can or in the subway." One of those reviews was Winters's piece on Tate for *The New Republic*, a piece which compared Crane favorably to Tate, and which had struck Crane by its nobility of tone. Still, he felt uncomfortable being compared with

Tate or anyone else "in a kind of All American Lyric Sprint," especially since his own poetry had stalled. Besides, the very idea of a competition between poets seemed foreign to his conception of what poetry was.

Crane knew that Tate possessed "a very complex mind and possibly a wider grasp of ideas" than even he himself did. Still, had the man really come any closer to solving the problems confronting the world than to "simply state the dilemma in a highly inferential manner," something which all poets—himself included—had to do if they were to be worthy of their calling? In fact, Tate's greatest rage against him personally, Crane believed, had been his refusal to succumb to Eliot's despair, to opt instead for a more "positive synthesis" than *The Waste Land* or "The Hollow Men" had offered.[52] Hell, he knew as well as Tate and Eliot that life was ultimately tragic, but he was not going to simply sit back and passively endure life as Eliot seemed willing to do.

A month after writing the Rychtariks, Crane finally received a letter from them telling him not to worry about the loan until he was back on his feet. "I really need to see you, talk with you to explain what a hell the last two years have been," he wrote Charlotte in reply. Then she might see why he'd been unable to write almost anyone for so long now. Who wanted to be bombarded always with troubles? Take his job at the bookstore, which would end in another week, and which would mean tramping the city for some other job. "Moving around, grabbing onto this and that, stupid landladies—never enough sense of security to relax and have a fresh thought—that's about all the years bring besides new and worse manifestations of family hysteria." There were just "too many buttons to button and unbutton" any more.[53] He was tired. He was very tired.

One night, after dining out with Sam Loveman in lower Manhattan, he hailed a taxi for the ride back across the Brooklyn Bridge. Two bucks, he told the cabbie, two bucks was all he was going to pay for the trip. He seemed in high spirits, though he was upset when the cabbie took the Williamsburg Bridge across the river by mistake. On the bridge Crane ordered the cabbie to stop. Then he got out, staggered to one of the bridge supports, and urinated on it, either by way of mock baptism or to mark his displeasure, Loveman wasn't sure. When they got to Columbia Heights, Crane discovered, once again, that he had no money, so Loveman was left to settle the bill. By then Loveman noticed that his friend's mood had shifted into a kind of depression. Screw it, Crane shouted. He was finished, all used up. There was nothing left to do but jump. He took off at a run toward his apartment, the older Loveman in panting pursuit. Crane made it to 110, then began taking the steps by twos—the first floor, the second, the third, then up the ladder and onto the flat tar roof. He headed straight for the roof's edge and was almost over when Loveman managed to reach out and grab his leg. Loveman was shaking with fury. *Don't you ever pull that on me again*, he shouted at Crane. *You sonofabitch, don't ever do something like that to me again.* Finally, when they were off the roof and he had settled down, Crane blurted out the reason for his insane action. What the hell, he said, all he was capable of writing any more was rhetoric. Why live?

When, at the end of October, he lost his job at the bookstore, it was Walker Evans, then a twenty-five-year-old photographer living a few doors down from Crane on Columbia Heights, who helped him find work at the Henry L. Doherty Company's brokerage firm on Wall Street in the same filing department where Evans worked. Crane was glad for the money, but the job turned out to be just another stop-gap measure. It meant the same crowded subway ride under the bridge from Columbia Heights into downtown New York each fall morning, followed by a quick stop at an automat for a cup of coffee to brace himself, and then a lurching rise in a crowded elevator to be deposited on the twentieth floor of some tower where he would spend the next nine hours "sorting securities of cancelled legions ten years back."[54] A booming market with returns of 30 percent a year, and here he was so broke his lunch consisted of a stick of chewing gum. The job lasted only a few weeks until he couldn't take any more. Then, one morning, having made a round of the bars the night before, he marched into the office, unshaven and wearing the same clothes he'd worn the day before, headed straight for the window, opened it, and began shouting the name on the billboard blinking from the roof opposite. Over and over he shouted it, while an astonished cadre of clerks and secretaries stared on. Then he turned, cursing his bosses, capitalism, the whole goddamned age of whoring advertising, and stormed out, scattering piles of securities in his wake. He did not ask for letters of recommendation.

What he really wanted was the blessèd break his grandfather's inheritance would give him. So when, in early December, he learned that his mother had refused to sign the necessary papers releasing the money until he visited her (she was too sick, she'd told the lawyers, to sign on the dotted line), he went into a blind, helpless rage. Immediately he telephoned the Guardian Trust in Cleveland, demanding a five hundred-dollar advance on his inheritance that same day and the balance within a week. The bank replied that there was nothing they could do until Mrs. Crane signed the papers releasing the money. Then he shot a telegram off to Grace demanding she sign immediately or face a lawsuit. Indignant that her own son was threatening her, Grace replied that she'd already signed the papers, at the same time warning him that she was prepared to tell his father what she knew about his way of life. She also promised to urge the bank not to turn over an inheritance to someone as unfit as he had turned out to be. "Grace will probably never hear from me again," he wrote his aunt Zell afterwards. "Nervous strain or simple hysterics could never explain the underhanded and insatiable vanity that has inspired her to crush her nearest of kin. And all for a bucketful of cash! I think I can say that my part in this long melodrama is almost over."[55]

His mother had actually gotten people—lawyers—"who were practically strangers to write me threatening and scolding letters," Crane told the Rychtariks afterwards, "so that I never came home from work without wonder—and trembling about what next I should find awaiting me."[56] She'd already destroyed all the affection he'd ever had for her. But now she'd managed to make him loathe her. He quickly sold the Connecticut property he'd bought three years before back to its original owner—for the same price he'd bought it—and then prepared to do his disappearing act by removing himself as far from his mother as he could, leaving no forwarding address. For weeks, he wrote Winters in late November, he'd been "encircled . . . by the whirlwind hysterics of . . . Fate (if one may allude to one's family in that way)." But now he was sailing for Europe on the *Tuscania* (Cunard Line) on December 8th. If he could work it out, he meant to stay abroad for the next two years, settling in "some quiet and secluded" spot on Majorca.[57]

In the meantime, to thank Cowley for all he'd done for him, Crane spent two days reworking Cowley's manuscript of poems, *Blue Juniata*. His enthusiasm for the lyrics, he wrote Cowley on December 1st, had been heightened rather than diminished by working so closely with them. He took in Jerome Kern's *Show Boat* at the new Ziegfeld Theater with his old boss, Herb Wise, now back in New York, and the two of them enjoyed the "settings, songs, costumes and glistening lithe girlies!" The show had gone by like greased lightning, so mechanically perfect had it all been done.

A few nights later Crane and Lorna Dietz went on "the best bat ever," with two cops joining them at the bar at three in the morning. Drunk, he proposed that he and Dietz get married at once and that she come to Majorca with him. She might just do that, she told him, but first he'd have to wait for her divorce "from the Danish gaucho now on the pampas."[58] Crane was running on nervous energy—partying like mad, joking, waiting desperately for the money from his grandfather's estate. It arrived, finally, or enough of it did, with only hours to spare before his ship sailed. He threw one last party, a big gin blast on the eve of his sailing for England. To it he invited Walker Evans, Sam Loveman, Loveman's business partner (who ran the bookstore) Solomon (Mony) Grunberg, Lorna Dietz, Charmion Habicht, and his other New York friends so they might all join together to give their manic, desperate friend a proper send-off.

12 / LAST STRANDS

To ENGLAND and FRANCE and BACK
DECEMBER 1928–DECEMBER 1929

B
Y THE TIME THE RMS *TUSCANIA* cleared Sandy Hook on
the morning of 8 December 1928, a freezing rain had begun falling,
and for the next two days the seas became an endless series of gargantuan troughs and crests, the ship rearing and bucking, as Crane noted,
like some high-strung bronco. Nothing, however, could dampen his
spirits. He wolfed down each meal as it was served, afterwards strolling
about the quarterdeck, "enjoying the rhythmical lift and plunge of it"
all. "Ahoy Sam!" he wrote Loveman as the *Tuscania* neared Newfound-
land, "O it's great! The bad gin pains are leaving my head and—taking
only the bad memories with them—not the pleasant thoughts of you
and Mony and others." He loved this boat, filled with Englishmen,
Canadians, and Aussies, and fitted out with a British crew who had
proved both efficient and pleasant. He was also delighted that he of all
people should have "the one nearly handsome English waiter in the
salon." The food, as usual on English ships, proved awful. But the
whiskey had turned out to be the very "balm of Gilead—or whatever
Poe said."[1] He passed the time listening to the rhythms of Melville on
the page alternate with the glissando of waves off the ship's sleek sides.

After Halifax, the weather flowered. Sunshine, placid seas (in
December!) and—by the time they reached the Irish coast on the
12th—temperatures "as balmy as May." In spite of heavy drinking, the

ocean voyage, he told himself, had the effect of restoring him. The only American on board, he was delighted to be taken for a Cambridge man by one old Britisher. And what a pleasure it was to find oneself among gentlemen, who knew how to drink. He loved the strong scent of British ale, reminding him of clover meadows, though his own drink of choice this time round was Jamaican rum, which he downed with abandon everywhere he went, even in the foc'sle. At a bal masqué one night he donned a scarlet sergeant major's coat, sailor's hat, and shark swagger stick, and whirled about dervishlike doing the gotzotzsky. Somehow he managed not to offend anyone, and silently prayed that Old King George wouldn't "kick off until after Christmas," for his friends on board had promised him a "Merrie England verily."[2]

Off the coast of Cornwall he watched huge flocks of seagulls following in the wake of the ship, or soaring high overhead in the golden light of dusk in a way that reminded him of his beloved Isle of Pines. Then Le Havre, Plymouth, and—on the 14th—London. By the time he disembarked, Crane was fighting off the flu, quaffing large amounts of rum and quinine to steady himself. London he found sober and impressive, "full of courtesy and deep character," but expensive.[3] After settling into his room at the Royal Hotel on Woburn Place, he went out to Hammersmith in search of Laura Riding, whom he'd not seen since she'd left America three years before. The year before he'd written Cummings from California, telling him he had to get hold of *A Survey of Modernist Poetry* which Riding and her co-author and lover, Robert Graves, had just brought out. There was "more gunpowder" in that book, Crane had told Cummings, "than any other book of contemporary criticism" he'd ever read, and as Cummings and Shakespeare were the book's heroes, he thought Cummings should take the cotton out of his ears and read it.[4] Now he was anxious to see Riding, as she was to see him; and when she realized he was coming down with the flu, insisted he stay at her flat. He spent Christmas with her and Graves and his family on Graves's houseboat moored in the Thames, enjoying a holiday plum pudding with them.

But before long, Crane was itching to be off on his own. Riding, he thought, had become more high-strung and hysterical than ever. So for two weeks he tramped about London on his own, eyes open for any opportunity of finding companionship and enjoying whoever he chanced upon. He drank with charwomen in Bedford Street, with veterans who'd served on the Somme and at Verdun and who regaled him with stories of what the war had really been like. He called on Edgell Rickword, editor of *The Calendar,* who'd been publishing his poems in England. Earlier that fall he had gone with his old patron, Herbert Wise, to see Paul Robeson perform on Broadway in *Show Boat.* Now he went to see Robeson again in another performance of the same show, this time in the West End. Several times he strolled through the National Gallery, coming back again and again to El Greco's *Agony in the Garden.* It was a painting he'd loved at a distance for years, and with its dramatic setting and distinctive planes of light it had served as the model, as he'd once told Frank, for the opening of *The Bridge.* Sometimes he just wandered, admiring the black and white rain-streaked stone and marble facades of the neoclassical buildings. Riding had dismissed London's architecture as mere negative space, but negative space and stolidity were just what Crane needed to clear his head.

If he found Riding hysterical, she found him unstable, one minute telling her that she was the only person who had ever understood him, the next treating her as if she'd somehow betrayed him. Flush with cash, he treated his friends extravagantly, afterwards accusing them of sticking to him just for his money. On the evening of 6 January 1929, Twelfth Night, he attended the theater with Riding and several of her friends. Soon, however, she noticed he was fidgeting, quietly fuming over something until, halfway through the first act, he got up and stomped out to the box office, screaming at the cashier that he'd been shortchanged merely because he was a Yank. Only when the matter was settled to his satisfaction did he quiet down and return to his seat. Then, a few minutes later, he was fidgeting again. This time it was two American sailors enjoying the show. For a few minutes he managed to restrain himself. Finally, turning to Riding, he asked her to lend him a few pounds, got up, and left the theater to do something more to his liking.

He tried duplicating in London what he did nights in New York. He prowled the Limehouse and Whitechapel districts—London's equivalent of Hoboken, Sands Street, South Street, and the Bowery wrapped in one—looking for companionship. In the local pubs he played darts and acted the American thug, partly to protect himself, partly for the sheer hell of it. "Most of the young toughs drank only lemonade," he joked afterwards, "and after I had had several swigs of Scotch they all seemed to be afraid of me!" A knife in the ribs, or in the eye, as the original Kit Marlowe had caught it, might have changed his opinion of his drinking companions, but again fate smiled on him. It was the "damp, raw cold" which set in after the New Year that was the real "knife in [his] throat."[5] And now this awful scene at the theater. It was enough to persuade him to abandon London and take the Dover-Calais boat across the Channel the following morning.

Paris: in 1929 a city still brimming with American expatriates, all searching for something. The real artists and the fringe elements. Surrealism and its manifestos. Notre Dame and the interior of La Sainte Chapelle, so unearthly in its lightness and beauty as to seem unreal.[6] "The greatest work of art here, I think," he told Underwood after he'd observed its traceries and stained glass. "Dinners, soirées, poets, erratic millionaires," Crane reported back to Loveman two weeks into his stay. "Painters, translations, lobsters, absinthe, music, promenades, oysters, sherry, aspirin, pictures, Sapphic heiresses, editors, books, sailors. And How!"[7] Three days later, he sent a similar catalogue crammed onto the back of a postcard to Lorna Dietz, adding the French burlesque dancer, "Kiki," limousines, red pompons, invitations, gendarmes, cathedrals, and fog. By then "sailors" had also been transformed into the more familiar *matelots,* Crane punning on French sailors and a tasty French fish stew laced with wine.[8] For if he was still reeling from the effects of the flu, he was reeling too with the crush of people, including French sailors he undressed nightly up in Montmartre.

Soon after his arrival he'd linked up with Eugène Jolas, who'd published his poems in *transition,* including parts of *The Bridge.* Now Jolas introduced him to Harry Crosby, an expatriate American millionaire approaching forty, and his wife, Caresse, three years younger, who ran the Black Sun Press from the rue Cardinale. It was a small letterhead affair that published avant-garde writers like D. H. Lawrence, E. E. Cummings, and Kay Boyle. The Crosbys in fact were those same "erratic millionaires" Crane had mentioned in his card to Loveman, who by the time he wrote Dietz had become, simply, "mad millionaires." Such bounty, such largesse! By the time Crane met them, they'd already read *The Bridge* in manuscript and offered to publish it just as it stood in a limited de luxe edition, two hundred copies, no expenses spared. Crane was beside himself with delight, for that offer alone had made the entire European jaunt worthwhile. True, the poem still lacked the three sections it had been missing for the past two years, but, yes, he assured them, yes, he could certainly get those done in the next few months.

To allow him the space he needed to finish his poem, the Crosbys set him up with a study and all the amenities—food, service, quiet, booze—at a sixteenth-century stone mill on the estate of the duc de la Rochefoucauld at Ermononville, outside Paris. At the beginning of February, in snow, Crane retired to the estate for a long weekend of work. With a contract for his book, he sent off a letter to the American artist, Joseph Stella, including several requests. Five months earlier, he explained, he'd seen a copy of Stella's *New York*, containing the painter's essay on the Brooklyn Bridge together with his paintings of New York. Would Stella, Crane asked now, be willing to let him use his painting of the Brooklyn Bridge as the frontispiece for the Black Sun edition of *The Bridge*?[9]

That letter had been managed by the proper, businesslike Crane. But there was the other Crane, hell-bent on shocking a city not easily shocked. "As lions come these days, I'm known already, I fear, as the best 'roarer' in Paris," he boasted to Cowley. He'd just returned from Ermononville, where he'd drunk and dined with an amazing crowd. Crosby, "heir to all the Morgan Harjes millions," as he told one friend, had "inherited the famous Walter Berry (London) library." It would take a book to describe people like the Crosbys, but just knowing that such people existed had already inspired him "to new atrocities," like getting drunk and then "making violent love to the Comte de la Rochefoucauld."[10] What made it all the more wicked, he boasted, was that the count was about to be married. Even his old enemy Kay Boyle and her dissolute friend, Lawrence Vail, had been impressed by his sexual prowess. One month into his stay and already he'd given up all thought of Majorca and the Spanish language. He would visit the South of France instead—Villefranche, Toulouse, Marseilles—and learn enough French to seduce as many French gobs as he could.

But in his more sober moments he knew the city was killing his soul. As wild as he was, he was still the midwestern American boy at heart: naive, romantic, idealistic. The world-weary sophistication and decadence that he came up against in Paris and that eventually tempted one to put a gun to one's head he found himself no match for, except to try to outdo the others with the wild antics of some drunken fraternity kid on a lark. "This City, as you know, is the most interesting madhouse in the world," he confessed to Frank, begging him to send along a copy of his *The Re-discovery of America* as soon as possible as an antidote to "the seductions of Europe." The truth was that Crane was afraid he really was being "seduced by the astonishing ease of life" he found all about him.[11]

Hollywood and Pasadena had been one sort of trial—starlets out to erase their Kansas City and Fargo origins, young men from Des Moines and Terre Haute on the move, neurotic Wall Street million-aires anxious to touch the hems of movie stars. But this was different. This was a thousand-year-old culture, where the estates were centuries older than Plymouth or Jamestown or even the California missions. These were men and women who moved easily among three or four languages: brilliant, witty speakers who could suddenly turn on one with a shrug of the shoulder or an aristocratic turn of the head, a ges-ture that had taken a thousand years to perfect. "All sorts of amusing people," he noted. "Scandalous scenes, café encounters . . . writers, painters, heiresses, counts and countesses, Hispano-Suizas, exhibitions, concerts, fights."[12]

But Paris was not, after all, New York. Paris was "a test for an American," Crane confessed, and he was not sure he was "equal to it." Each day he awoke to the reality that he'd written nothing of substance for over a year, torturing himself with the thought that his gift was lost forever, even as some were touting him as the best American poet of his generation. He had loved staying at Ermononville, with its don-keys and bikes to get around on and a whole tower to himself, "and all the service that millionaires are used to having."[13] It was a place where he could be left alone all week to write, with an old peasant couple to prepare his meals and keep the fireplace blazing, and then—when Fri-day came—stroll down to the château for a long weekend party, over which the Crosbys resided with a zany largess. Caresse he came quick-ly to love, though Harry he could not quite figure out. The man seemed to run hot and cold, making extravagant promises one day, forgetting them the next.

Waldo Frank had supplied Crane with letters of introduction to several Paris luminaries: André Gide, Valéry Larbaud, Philippe Soupault, Louis Aragon, Gertrude Stein. But Gide had already left for Africa by the time Crane had arrived in Paris, and Crane simply put off seeing Larbaud, who'd been so important a contact for Williams five years ear-lier.[14] It was Jolas who had taken Crane to meet Soupault and his wife, and Crane had met the elegant Aragon, though neither had had much to say to the other. Although he did not much care for Gertrude Stein's work, he made—using Laura Riding as his contact—the dutiful visit to Stein's apartment at 27 rue de Fleurus. "One is supposed to inevitably change one's mind about her work after meeting her," he told Frank afterwards, but he had not, though he had found Stein herself "beautiful." And then, of course, there were those walls of Picassos to gaze on.[15]

He met others as well: Ford Madox Ford, Glenway Wescott, Richard Aldington, Walter Lowenfels, Emma Goldman, Klaus Mann, Eugene MacCown, Edgar Varèse, René Crevel. Even Allen Tate and Caroline Gordon were in Paris at the moment, Tate on a Guggenheim and staying in Ford's apartment while Ford was away. The Tates loved Paris, they told Crane, and would be happy to stay there forever. Not so Crane, who by then had had enough of the city, with its constant bitching, backbiting, and chatter. He needed to get into himself again, and into his work. The year just past, he believed, had been the most decisive of his life. He'd separated himself from his mother, and he had come up hard against the dark realities of Hollywood and now Paris. He was beginning to fall apart and knew he would need all the strength he could muster.

After all, the reason he had come to Europe was to write; but after ten weeks of Paris, all he'd managed were several drunken and debauched weekends at Ermononville. "Polo with golf sticks on donkeys!" he mused. "Old stagecoaches! Skating on the beautiful grounds of the chateau!" More than once he'd got hung over on absinthe and had even tried opium, though he hadn't much cared for it. Crosby was keeping him supplied with fifths of Cutty Sark. Outside his window he stared at the snow-covered evergreens, like some stage setting, he quipped, for a production of *Pelléas et Mélisande*. And waiting for him at the end of all this: a de luxe edition of *The Bridge* on "sheets as large as a piano score," so that none of his long lines would have to be compromised. And yet for all this, nothing got written.

Wherever he went, it was only himself he found waiting there. It was absolutely imperative, Crane warned his friends, that his mother not find out where he was. Otherwise, he feared he really would never write another word. In particular he wrote the Rychtariks, begging them to say nothing of his whereabouts, not even to mention what continent he was on. "Since my mother has made it impossible for me to live in my own country," he told them, he felt justified by his own indifference toward her. And though he had no particular quarrel with his father, he had no plans to get in touch with him until after *The Bridge* was finished to avoid severe psychological stress. More than anything, he was afraid his mother had already made good on her threat to tell his father about his homosexuality, and he did not want to think about that while he was trying to finish up his long poem. "Twenty-five years of . . . exhausting quibbling" with the two of them had been long enough, and he deserved this one long vacation away from it all. Besides, neither parent really cared "a rap" about him anyway.[16] One night, drunk, he sent a postcard to his mother, saying he was now residing in the Far East. On the card he sketched a pentagram—the devil's mark—and signed the card "Atlantis." Even to himself he seemed a lost city.[17]

"Mob for luncheon," Harry Crosby noted in his diary for one of the Ermononville weekends. "Poets and painters and pederasts and lesbians and Christ knows who and there was a great signing of names on the wall at the foot of the stairs and a firing off of the cannon and bottle after bottle of red wine." Kay Boyle, making fun of Crane as she had in her review of *White Buildings* three years before, and Crane (who'd once told Winters that Boyle's stuff read like a "diluted solution of some kind") picking up a copy of *The American Caravan* and hurling it into the fireplace because it contained a story of hers, for the moment forgetting that it also contained one of his own poems. And loud drinking and "polo harra burra . . . and confusion," so that even Crosby—bemused—found it impossible to get any work done on the Bible he was editing for his press.[18] Or Crane tattooing his face, this time with India ink, and dancing the gotzotzsky. Or declaiming long passages from Marlowe's *Tamburlaine* like some provincial nineteenth-century actor. Or disappearing into the Paris night, a predatory shark's-tooth talisman on a chain about his neck (a gift from Harry), only to reappear at dawn from a night in Montmartre, the stars and anchors of some French sailor pinned to his sweater like shining trophies. This ape, this dancing bear, this wild American boy, goaded on by the jaded applause of the Paris crowd.

Finally, in mid-April, Crane left Paris and hopped the train south to Provence. He spent three weeks in Collioure near the border with Spain, with the eastern Pyrenees as backdrop. The Isle of Pines all over again, he thought, except that here French, Spanish, and Catalan were spoken in the streets and shops. "Nightingales all night and the sound of surf all day," he wrote Loveman on April 23rd.[19] And to Slater Brown two days later: "Here I am, sitting by the shore of the most shockingly beautiful fishing village—with towers, baronial, on the peaks of the Pyrenees all about, wishing more than anything else that you were on the other side of the table. . . . If I could talk Catalan it would be better."[20] And: "Too much wind to notice odors"—this to Gertrude Stein, who had warned him about the town's open sewers—"Feel quite indigenous since spending last night out on a sardine schooner. The dialect isn't so easily assimilated."[21] But beautiful as it was here, overlooking the Mediterranean, in a town with "ancient citadels and fortifications crowning the heights of a lovely white-walled village," his every third thought went back to his room in Patterson.[22] He stayed at the town's one and only boardinghouse—the Hôtel Bougnol-Quintana—along with an international set of painters. But their obsession in continually searching out the picturesque gave him the creeps and he left.

And still nothing kept happening with *The Bridge*. "I'll try to add a few more paragraphs to the flying machine," he had signaled Harry from his room at the Hôtel Jacob in Paris at the beginning of March. By "the flying machine," he'd meant the "Cape Hatteras" section, which still remained a smoldering heap.[23] But six weeks later—in Collioure—all he could do was signal weakly again. "I'm beginning to feel my feet a little nearer the ground already," he wrote Harry on April 25th. "Hot suns and rural surroundings and the sea can almost be counted on to relieve that suspended feeling that cities generally induce. . . . So maybe I can get some work done, after all."[24] By May he was ready to throw in the towel and let the Crosbys publish *The Bridge* as it stood. "If it eventuates that I have the wit or inspiration to add to it later," he wrote Isidor Schneider, an editor at Boni & Liveright, in near despair, "such additions can be incorporated in some later edition." He'd lived with the manuscript for so long he'd grown indifferent to its progress, yet embarrassed by its unfinished state. After all, the poems as arranged did have "a certain progression,"[25] and the gaps were no doubt more evident to him than to anyone else. Why struggle with it anymore? Hadn't it taken three and a half years for *White Buildings* to sell out a mere five hundred copies? Was there anyone out there reading him, anyway?

After Collioure he spent six weeks in Marseilles, with a two-week interlude in nearby Martigues, visiting with the South African poet,

Roy Campbell, and his family. "A sort of Venice and Gloucester combined," was how Crane described Martigues, "being built on three
islands made by canals joining the Etang de Berre with the sea."[26] And
Marseilles: Cannebière, Vieux-Port, drinking steadily, sleeping with
whatever sailors he could find, squandering his inheritance as quickly as
he knew how. Bottles of Cutty Sark—gifts of Harry Crosby—and all
the Pernod he could drink. "Marseilles's a delightful place—to *me*," he
wrote Crosby on May 16th. But Marseilles wasn't a tourist city, and
there was nothing "to gape at—museums or otherwise," the buildings
themselves being so ugly no one seemed to look at them twice. The
denizens he liked better, for they'd turned out to be the least French
of the French he'd so far encountered.

The truth was that Marseilles was a lot more like New York than
Paris had been, for it was an international seaport city, "dirty, vulgar,
noisy, dusty," and—as far as Crane was concerned—"wholesome." He'd
taken to wearing the local sailor suit: striped shirt (white and red) and
tight white pants flared at the bottoms. He went and came as he
pleased, spending one whole Saturday night visiting whorehouses with
an English sailor, "whose great expression of assent and agreement was
'heave Ho!'" Later that evening he'd had a row with a bewhiskered
and besotted elderly Scots officer who kept repeating that he would
"give the 16 . . . remaining years of his life to see America 'humbled in
the dust.'" Crane meanwhile kept his eye on the goodies from a Danish cruiser.[27] The only writing he did manage was confined to his
rhymed gloss running along the left margin of "Powhatan's Daughter,"
an idea he'd borrowed from Coleridge's *Rime of the Ancient Mariner*.

On June 11th—a month into his stay in Marseilles—he wrote
Tate, thanking him for some money he'd lent him until he could free
up some of his grandfather's money from the bank in New York. He
loved Provence, "the wonderful Cézannesque light (you see him everywhere here) and the latinity of the people. Arabs, Negroes, Greeks, with
Italian and Spanish mixtures."[28] The American painter, Marsden Hartley, then in Marseilles, spent an afternoon explaining the intricacies of
the southern coast and the Rhône Valley to Crane, including its allure-
ments and enticements. But Hartley, twenty-two years Crane's senior,
a man reticent, painfully shy, and—like Crane—gay, realized he would
have to steer clear of Crane if he was to survive. A "nice boy," he wrote
one friend. They'd had a good talk about *The Bridge*, but Crane was
just too "flagrant" in the way he stalked his prey, too unpredictable in

his behavior. And though Crane took an instant liking to the tall, deep-browed, blue-eyed, homely, aquiline-beaked artist, Hartley was having none of it. They did manage a water carnival put on in the harbor at Marseilles, but more and more Hartley learned to avoid Crane, whose antics and willingness to brawl frankly terrified him.[29]

Finally, in late June, Crane extricated himself from the black hole Marseilles had become for him and staggered back to Paris and Ermononville. That was where Crosby found him, "back from Marseilles where he had slept with his thirty sailors and he began again to drink Cutty Sark (the last bottle in the house)."[30] "A thick fog still envelops my 'memory' of the latter hours at your side last Saturday," an abject Crane wrote Harry the following Monday, July 1st. "I think Cutty Sark won that bout without the slightest doubt!"[31] He had called at their hotel Sunday morning, only to find Harry and Caresse both gone. He was lonely and he was apologetic, and worse, though he still had a couple of thousand in the bank back in New York, he couldn't touch it and he was now absolutely broke. If he could just get his hands on some money, he pleaded, he was ready to devote the rest of his time in Paris to getting *The Bridge* into final shape.

But if he could not get forward with his own work, he could still reach out to others. "Really, Malcolm," he wrote Cowley shortly afterwards, "if you will excuse me for the egoism—I'm just a little proud at the outcome of my agitations last summer." *Blue Juniata*, he was sure, would "have a considerable sale for a long period to come," for there was a classical quality about the book.[32] He hoped to be out of Paris and back in New York in two months' time. But the next time he sailed to France, he was going to bypass Paris altogether and head right for Marseilles.

But the end of his European odyssey was a lot closer than that. A few nights after he wrote Cowley, Crane was drinking with some friends at Closerie des Lilas, when once again he decided to go off by himself. He wandered down the Boulevard Raspail and stopped at the Café Sélect, where he sat down at a table and began drinking. Hours later, when it came time to pay his bill, he found he had only a few centimes in his pockets. The waiter informed the owner, Madame Sélect, a no-nonsense tower of a woman who disliked Americans intensely. Monsieur had better pay up, she told Crane, if he did not want her to call the police. Other Americans in the café, realizing he was in trouble, offered to pay his bill, but she refused to accept their offer. She seemed intent on humiliating Crane. Furious that he had been cornered, he began shouting at her. When one of the waiters grabbed him to throw him out, Crane hit him hard and sent him sprawling.

That was all it took. Other waiters moved in to hold Crane down, and were also sent sprawling. The blue blur of a gendarme appeared, and Crane hit him as well. There was a whistle for backup and then more police were circling Crane. For a moment he managed to keep them at bay until a club smashed against his head, crumpling him. Dazed, he was dragged out onto the street feet-first, his head bumping and scraping against the curb, and tossed into a paddy wagon. At La Santé—the notorious French prison—he was worked over with a rubber hose for having struck a police officer, and then thrown into a rat-infested cell (he swore afterwards that he'd been bitten several times) and held there incommunicado.

It was three days before someone working at the *Herald Tribune* offices heard via the French press that an American, name unknown, was being held at La Santé. Whit Burnett, the short story anthologist, then a reporter for the *Tribune*, surmised at once who it was and called Crosby, who with several others went to Crane's aid. The American Embassy was notified, lawyers hired, judges spoken to, the sacred name of poetry invoked to explain to the authorities that Crane was—believe it or not—a distinguished American poet who'd unfortunately had too much to drink and had not of course meant to strike a policeman. The embassy promised to take full responsibility for Crane if the courts would free him so he could quietly exit the country.

But a policeman had been assaulted, perhaps several policemen, and a trial would have to take place before Crane could be released. At last one was scheduled, although not until Crane had languished in jail for a week. Crosby, in court for the spectacle, remarked drolly how magnificent Crane had been. "When the Judge announced that it had taken ten gendarmes to hold him . . . all the court burst into laughter. After ten minutes of questioning he was fined 800 francs and 8 days in prison should he ever be arrested again. A letter from the *Nouvelle Revue Française* had a good deal to do with his liberation." Then he was taken back to La Santé. There Crosby and Burnett waited all afternoon and into the evening before the prisoners were released, meanwhile drinking beer, playing checkers, and joking with the gendarmes. Shortly before 9:00 P.M., Crosby noted, "the prisoners began to come out, Hart the last one, unshaved hungry wild. So we stood and drank in the Bar de la Bonne Santé right opposite the prison gate and then drove to the *Herald* office where Burnett got out to write up the story for the newspaper, Hart and I going on to Chicago Inn for cornbread and poached eggs on toast. . . . Hart said that the dirty skunks in the Santé wouldn't give him any paper to write poems on. The bastards."[33]

It was time for Crane to return to the States. Crosby bought him a ticket, and two days later he boarded the USS *Homeric*, bound for New York. The morning of his departure Crane introduced Harry to Peter Christiansen, a gigolo Crane had picked up in Paris. Peter was a "nice Danish boy," he explained to Crosby, temporarily out of work and hungry. He described him as "an expert trainer and keeper of horses (Danish Royal Artillery)," whose English was passable. Could Harry find work for an "honest, industrious" fellow willing to do "anything . . . honorable"?[34]

As he left, Crane gave Harry a small necklace for Caresse as a token of his appreciation for all she'd done for him. Crosby in turn gave him one final bottle of Cutty Sark, which, by careful rationing, Crane was able to make last almost three days. When he left, he promised to have the finished poem in Crosby's hands in ten weeks' time. Somewhere on the high seas, in the company of three college kids returning from a summer abroad, his whiskey gone and drinking bourbon and sodas now (his old Isle of Pines pick-me-up, "palm trees on the horizon" and all that), Crane celebrated his thirtieth birthday by being "politely" thrown out of the first-class bar.[35]

After landing in New York on July 25th in the middle of another New York heat wave, he went back up to Addie Turner's, his drunken behavior of the year before for the time being overlooked. Peter Blume, a twenty-three-year-old painter, had taken over the four rooms (two up and two down) which the Tates had rented three years before, and soon Blume and Crane became friends. When the two men dined at the Cowleys' place in Sherman a few days later, Crane was still fuming about the treatment he'd received at the hands of the Paris police and the needle teeth of the Paris rats. As the evening wore on and Crane became drunker and drunker on the Cowleys' hard cider, he began lashing out once more at Caroline Gordon—"that serpent"—although Tate, he insisted, had redeemed himself by writing that introduction for *White Buildings*. He did not easily forget slights or favors, nor did he tolerate anyone opposing him once he got into his cups.[36]

In early August, Crane went back down to New York to look for an apartment. Because he still had half his $5,000 inheritance in his savings account there, he was still free to work on his poem without having to look for some miserable job in an ad office in the sweltering summer heat. But New York looked very different to him now. The story of his arrest for brawling had made the front page of the *New York Herald Tribune* and Crane was not anxious just now to run into any of the old crowd. How would he ever explain to Cowley, Burke, Cummings, Slater, or the Habitches his seven lost months in France? He avoided his old haunts as much as possible, spending his time at the public beaches (packed, as he noted, "with pulchritude"),[37] until one day, by accident, he ran into Slater down in the Village, who seemed genuinely glad to see him again. Crane was profoundly relieved.

Finally, work on *The Bridge* began inching mercifully forward. On August 8th he sent Caresse the corrected gloss notes for the first two sections of the poem, which were already being set up in print. He promised a corrected typescript in ten days' time, and still hoped to get over to see someone at the Brooklyn Museum about photographing the Stella painting of the Brooklyn Bridge. He begged her not to rush the book into print, and assured her that all 250 copies the Black Sun was printing would go soon enough. On the 20th, he found rooms at 130 Columbia Heights, two buildings down from his old haunts and—better—close to the Brooklyn Navy Yard. "Great housewarmings," he wrote the Crosbys. And the place had a janitor who could actually supply him with all the corn whiskey he wanted at six bucks a gallon. Once more, as he began putting the finishing touches to his poem, he could look out over his beloved harbor and up at his bridge. The only problem was that too much time had been taken up with moving to get away from "two or three rooming houses with farty old spinsters ordering me around."[38] At last, he told Underwood, he was settled in "a very comfortable furnished apartment for very little more than any of the damned rooms cost," and best of all, no landladies keeping their ears to the walls. Which was a blessing, since his first week there his apartment had been "thoroughly 'warmed'" by sailors from the *Cincinnati, Milwaukee,* and *Wyoming* he'd run into down at the Yard.[39]

García Lorca was in New York that fall, taking in American movies, Chinatown, and the Harlem jazz clubs. Like Crane, he was interested in the city, its rivers, its people, and—like Crane—writing his own ode to the brotherhood inspired by Whitman. "Nueva York de cieno," he would write,

> *Nueva York de alambres y de muerte.*
> *¿Qué angel lievas oculto en la mejilla?*
> *¿Qué voz perfecta dirá las verdadas del trigo?*
> *¿Quién el sueño terrible de tus anémonas manchadas?*
>
> *Ni un solo momento, viejo hermoso Walt Whitman,*
> *he dejado de ver tu barba llena de mariposas,*
> *ni tus hombros de pana gastados por la luna,*
> *ni tus muslos de Apolo virginal,*
> *ni tu voz como una columna de ceniza . . .*
>
> *New York, city of filth,*
> *City of wires and death.*
> *What angel do you hide there in your cheek?*
> *Who will utter the truth in an ear of wheat?*
> *Who tell the terrible dream of your blasted anemones?*
>
> *Not for an instant, Walt Whitman, beautiful old man,*
> *have I failed to see your beard full of butterflies,*
> *nor your corduroy shoulders worn out by the moon,*
> *nor your thighs like those of chaste Apollo,*
> *nor your voice like a column of dust . . .*[40]

It was Angel Flores, fluent in Spanish and English and editor of the magazine *Alhambra*, who took Lorca over to Brooklyn one evening to meet Crane. They found him at a local bar holding forth, a party in full swing, Crane already drunk, surrounded by sailors, having a high time. Two of the century's finest poets, two sons of Whitman, sharing between them two of the great languages of America, in the same room together. But as much as Crane loved all things Spanish, he had no more mastery of the language than Lorca had of English, so that it was left to Flores to translate back and forth between them before both poets switched to a pidgin French. For a few moments the conversation continued until all the international courtesies had been extended, at which point Crane turned to talk with one group of sailors, Lorca to another.[41]

Of the three parts of *The Bridge* still left to write, Crane had been trying since before his arrival in Paris to put "Cape Hatteras" into some sort of working order. It was to be his paean to Whitman and the bridging of space, and it had been on his mind in some inchoate form or another for the past three years. Now it was all "being worked out rapidly," he promised the Crosbys, "and the aeronautical sections which you so much admired . . . improved and augmented considerably." The problem was that he was using a more epic sweep to his line, a line longer than any he'd used so far, and that would entail using a larger page if the lines were to be printed unbroken in the Black Sun edition. There was other good news as well. Liveright had finally decided to bring out a second edition of *White Buildings*; the popular *Vanity Fair* was about to bestow laurels on him in their upcoming issue; and both Eliot at *The Criterion* and "Old Mamby Canby," his old bête noire at the *Saturday Review*, had written asking for new work.[42]

On September 6th Crane finally got hold of first proofs for *The Bridge*, delayed because they'd been sent to Patterson where Addie Turner had failed to send them on. Now, having checked them over, he wrote Caresse to set up the poem in the larger of the typefaces that had been sent, at the same time asking her to add a few more lines of verse to each page for balance. He was working like mad on the finale of "Cape Hatteras," with its address to Whitman. He enclosed a draft to show her what he was up to and promised the finished poem in the next few days. Then he would turn his attention to "Quaker Hill," and finally the "Indiana." When he was in one of these fevers of work, he told her, he knew what he was capable of producing. He begged her to be patient. She would have everything by mid-October.

"Cape Hatteras"—three years in the making, and by far the longest poem in *The Bridge*, in fact, the longest single poem Crane ever wrote. It is both palinode and antidote, really, to his "Faustus and Helen," a poem of transformations and metamorphoses, revising the paradigm of the Faustian overreacher in favor of Whitman's more democratic brotherhood of man. In his reading of Spengler and of Western literature and Western history, as in studying his own parents, Crane had come to see both the strengths and weaknesses of the ego-centered drive of Western man to conquer and pacify. The conquest of time, the conquest of space, the conquest of the wilderness, manifest destiny, the age of progress, the race to link East and West. But once "The seas all crossed,/weathered the capes, the voyage done," what then? An age of armaments, the war to end all wars, one empire dying, another striving to be born. Hollywood manifesting once again the gold rush fever. Europe an exhausted whore.

But what of the long view? The gradual replacement of one age with another, the late Jurassic transformed into coal and gas and oil-fields, to be devoured by the late Cambrian in its Western industrial phase. The "dorsal change of energy": frogs' eyes transformed into the giggling whine of greased ball bearings. Explorations, strange languages, the surf of radio static, the "combustion at the astral core." Matter transformed into energy: wind over waters bringing Columbus to the New World. And now what new worlds disclosed with the whirr of engines and the wind playing over canvas wings?

Cutty Sark transformed to Kitty Hawk. Horizontal conquest giving way now to sheer verticality. He was finishing "Cape Hatteras" two years after Lindbergh had made his transatlantic solo flight, reversing Columbus's voyages and covering the same distance backward in a fraction of the time. "The nasal whine of power whips a new universe," Crane wrote, like Williams and other American poets aware of the sheer power of the new electrical stations being built to supply power to entire cities, the stars' energy harnessed by coal and oil, the strop of belts on assembly lines, the boom of spools, the roar of industry with its deafening power. Energy as erotic dynamo.

But consider too the underbelly of this Faustian energy: the urge to conquer space and time implying the urge to conquer other humans as well. The Wright brothers, "windwrestlers" veering like Columbus "Capeward," and the soul, "by naphtha fledged into new reaches," already that much closer to exploring the rocky surface of Mars. Not the space age only, implied in the lifting of that gooneybird over Kill Devil Hills in 1903, but military conquest following inevitably in its wake as well. The most advanced airplane of 1929, not that far removed from its World War I counterpart: biplanes leaving their silver hangars like so many larvae—new Iliads glimmering "through eyes raised in pride." The dogfight, enemy circling enemy in "war's fiery kennel," machine-gun bullets—those "theorems sharp as hail"—grenades exploding, their razor petals carving face and body.

Or the vision of dirigibles like huge whales aboard which planes might land:

> Regard the moving turrets! From grey decks
> See scouting griffons rise through gaseous crepe
> Hung low . . . until a conch of thunder answers
> Cloud belfries, hanging, while searchlights, like fencers,
> Slit the sky's pancreas of foaming anthracite
> Toward thee, O Corsair of the typhoon . . .

A pseudo-epic language here, alas, as out-of-date, really, as da Vinci's drawings of an early helicopter, a Miltonic rhetoric employed to treat the facts of modern air combat. Planes lifting from aircraft carriers circa 1929, swarming through overcast skies, then the sound of anti-aircraft shells and sirens and searchlights zigzagging, swording the skies, trying to pinpoint the enemy, flown by Faustian overreachers, hot-dogs. But the picture in its outlines true for all that, no more far-fetched, really, than the idea of permanent space stations from which manned spacecraft or missiles might be launched. And all this in an elevated Virgilian/Elizabethan language Crane thought of as resonating with the most sublime undertakings of humankind, man drunk on power in the "alcohol of space."

America, Crane rightly understood, had within it the power "to conjugate infinity's dim marge—anew." But first it would have to overcome its bloodlust, its dependency always on force—its destruction of the Indian, slavery, the murder of brother by brother in the epic Civil War which Whitman had witnessed firsthand. "Thou, pallid there as chalk," Crane wrote now, addressing his guide, none other than this same Walt Whitman, "Hast kept of wounds, O Mourner, all that sum/That then from Appomattox stretched to Somme!" All those deaths at Antietam, Fredericksburg, Gettysburg, Chancellorsville, Cold Harbor, the trenches south of Petersburg and Richmond, as well as at the Little Big Horn and San Juan Hill and the even more terrible losses at the Somme, Verdun, Château-Thierry. There had to be another way out of the nightmare of history. If it was death one wanted, then, yes, receive the "benediction of the shell's deep, sure reprieve," the "Sky-gak pilot" hit with a fusillade of machine-gun bullets, as the soaring plane—perforated—suddenly reversed its ascent, spiraling down and down until man and plane hit the Cape again, a heap of "high bravery," yes, but a heap of "mashed and shapeless debris" as well.

Another way was needed, then, another way to ascend those imagined heights and "conjugate infinity's dim marge—anew." That sense of discovery, such as Crane felt, he tells us here, when—like Keats opening Chapman's Homer—he first read Whitman in the spring of 1916 with the Somme offensive about to be unleashed, and fifty thousand men were lost in those first hours alone. Whitman's lines of power and beauty, surging and receding, lines of poetry—"thunder's eloquence" felt in the landscape itself—"as rife as the loam/Of prairies, yet like breakers cliffward leaping," a power Crane was trying to replicate in *The Bridge* with his own thundering lines.

Not division, then, but communion. Not bare-knuckled hands, but a hand extended in friendship. Wasn't that what Whitman, having seen what bullets could do to his brother and to every mother's son, had offered in their stead? *Panis Angelicus!* The new communion of friendship, the radiant host of brotherhood, glimpsed in those "Eyes tranquil with the blaze" not of bullets but "Of love's own diametric gaze, of love's amaze." A gaze steady, democratic, accepting the other not as inferior or superior but as equal, as brother. Walt, seen in the bearded faces of hoboes and beggars behind his father's cannery, or on the tracks, or (closer) the streets of New York. A look both familiar and evasive, the sustaining myth of brotherhood, extended to all, in the all-conquering language of love that just might transcend death itself, a vision bequeathed by Whitman in those marvelous leaves of grass of his:

> *And as to you Death, and you bitter hug of mortality, it is idle*
> *   to try to alarm me . . .*

> *The past and present wilt—I have fill'd them, emptied them,*
> *And proceed to fill my next fold of the future . . .*

> *I bequeath myself to the dirt to grow from the grass I love,*
> *If you want me again look for me under your bootsoles.*

> *You will hardly know who I am or what I mean,*
> *But I shall be good health to you nevertheless,*
> *And filter and fiber your blood.*

> *Failing to fetch me at first keep encouraged,*
> *Missing me one place search another,*
> *I stop somewhere waiting for you.* [43]

Whitman's vision of the Open Road, then—open to all, to be shared by all, the rainbow's arch as promise, a bridge of love connecting past and present. St. Francis Whitman, the "joyous seer" providing a vision of brotherhood, and Crane accepting the open hand extended toward him in friendship across the chasm of time and suffering. For now Crane's hand, but, after him, another's and another's—each reading the Bible of Whitman "by the aureole 'round thy head/Of pasture-shine, *Panis Angelicus!*"[44]

At last the revisions came, sent one after another off to Paris. A final version of "Cape Hatteras," registered. Then the *final* final version with its "necessary improvements." Crane vowed not to trouble Caresse with "further emendations—excepting perhaps a comma or so on the proofs," and patted himself on the back, "highly pleased" with how he'd marshaled "the notes and agonies of the last two years' effort into a rather arresting synthesis."[45] He daydreamed of bottles of Cutty Sark to soothe his excited nerves. By September 10th he was back in Patterson, trying to escape the worst effects of a late summer heat wave.

The countryside as always he found beautiful, though dryer than he'd ever remembered it. The apple crop had already been lost, first to an early frost, then to prolonged drought, and that meant a scarcity of applejack come fall and winter. "I could hear everything through those thin walls which separated us," Peter Blume would recall half a century afterwards, the sounds going on and on far into the night, especially the records, played over and over again. There were the blues, one in particular—"You're the Kind of Man Needs a Kind of Woman Like Me"—and then the classical pieces, especially Ravel's *Boléro*. Over and over Crane played them, for inspiration and comfort, until they became indistinguishable from the hypnotic surge of sea crashing against the shore, as he pounded away at the keys of his typewriter, the tiny bell punctuating the end of each line. *Clickityclack clikkityclack ring.*[46]

At the end of September, Crane returned to 130 Columbia Heights, working "desperately hard"[47] on "Quaker Hill" and "Indiana," and drinking for inspiration. He began calling friends at all hours of the night, denouncing them for their betrayals, at the same time pleading with them not to abandon him when he was so close to completing his long trial. He declaimed passages of "Cape Hatteras" and

"Quaker Hill" into the receiver, then called with his latest revisions and read the poem again. Waking sober and guilty the following morning, he would call yet again, asking for understanding and forgiveness.

For two days he partied with a friend of the Crosbys who was enjoying New York: one Lord Lymington, Gerard Vernon Wallop, ninth earl of Portsmouth, poetaster and good-time fellow. At five in the afternoon on September 25th Crane staggered up to the entrance to Otto Kahn's Fifth Avenue residence with his newfound friend, only to be intercepted by Kahn's servant. It was clear that in his present condition he was not going to see Kahn if Kahn's servant had anything to say about it. Miffed, Crane scribbled a note and handed it to the man. "Lord Lymington and I were sorry to miss you," it read. "It was *not* a business call." He hoped to deliver the first copy of the Black Sun edition of *The Bridge* to Kahn as soon as it arrived, since the edition had been dedicated to Kahn (the poem itself, of course, being dedicated to the Brooklyn Bridge). When he did deliver it, he added, he hoped Kahn's lackeys did not prove "quite so imposing and insulting" as this fellow had.[48]

One morning shortly thereafter, Slater Brown answered his phone, only to hear Crane's voice, weak and flagging, on the other end. Could Brown please come out to see him while there was still time, he pleaded, for he was sure he was dying. When Brown arrived, he found Crane curled up in bed, drunker than usual but certainly not dying . . . yet. Then Crane suffered a case of *delirium tremens* that left him helpless and his apartment in shambles. This time it was Lorna Dietz— his "Twidget"—who stayed with him, straightening up the place and nursing him back to some semblance of health. If anyone dared to tell him to straighten out his life and stop drinking so much, he turned on them in a rage. Only those who took him as he was were allowed near him now. Advice and mirrors he avoided.

On Saturday afternoon, October 19th, he decided on the spur of the moment to return to Patterson, to "weltschmerz"—as he put it— with himself for a few days, and enjoy the fall foliage. Never had he seen "such color as this year's autumnal shades," he wrote Dietz four days into his stay, though the downpour that had begun that morning would no doubt strip the leaves bare of their fall beauty. The *delirium tremens* episode had shaken him badly, he admitted, and he'd come up to the country to try to recover, knowing he needed to practice a little "reserve" after the way he'd been acting in New York for the past few weeks.[49] The deadline for finishing *The Bridge* had come and gone, and still there remained "Quaker Hill"—in fragments—and the elusive "Indiana" to be written.

Then he heard through friends that his mother had found out where he was and was coming east to see him. Had she told his father about his homosexuality? Or would she continue to hold that over his head? One night, he shared a gallon of rhubarb wine he'd bought from the local bootlegger with Peter Blume. As the night wore on, Crane invited Blume into his room to show him a drawerful of photos of his mother. Here she was, he told him, as he held up a photo, here she was, sweet and loving. An angel. And here she was again, a bit older, and a bitch and a blackmailer. Couldn't he see the changes time had wrought in her? On and on he went, drinking steadily, until Blume excused himself and went to bed.

Toward midnight, Crane telephoned Chagrin Falls. It had been more than a year since he and his father had spoken, but—to his relief—his father was eager to talk with him. He was getting married again, C.A. told his son, this time to one Bessie Meachem, a thirty-five-year-old hostess who for the past several years had overseen things at Canary Cottage, and he wanted his boy out there for the wedding. After Crane hung up, he took a lighted kerosene lamp and staggered down to Blume's bedroom. "I've just spoken to my father on the telephone," he mumbled. "Do you know what it means to speak to one's father?" He was almost in tears, so happy was he to be back in C.A.'s good graces again.[50]

In late October, Crane returned to New York, pale and shaken. "Haven't been well lately," he wrote the Crosbys just before Halloween, "but hope to improve as soon as I can get the 5-year load of *The Bridge* off my shoulders." The poem was dragging on his neck like some bloated albatross. No, he could not publish it without the "Indiana" section, for that represented the "metamorphosis of Pocahontas (the Indian) into the pioneer woman, and hence her absorption into our contemporary veins." Moreover, the poem would "round out the cycle, at least historically and psychologically," the pure space of the ocean in "Harbor Dawn" coming full circle as the son turned back to the sea again, the continent crossed once more.[51] The only problem was that he couldn't seem to get the thing written. DEFER PUBLICATION, he telegrammed the Crosbys the following day in a state of paralysis. It would mean a three-month delay for the book.

On the very day that Crane wrote the Crosbys about the precar-

ious state of his health, Wall Street crashed. Serious trouble had begun
five days earlier, when the bull market had begun tumbling precipitously from the opening bell. Within an hour, nearly every stock had
dropped from ten to thirty points, and only a consortium of stock-
holders buying up huge amounts of stock had kept the losses at a reasonable level. But by the close of trading that day, nearly 13 million
shares had been traded, which meant the tickers were still rolling at
seven that night. Friday and the half-day Saturday remained relatively
calm, but on Monday, October 28th, another 10 million shares traded
hands for an additional $14 billion loss, and this at a time when the
entire federal budget was $3 billion. Then, on the 29th, another $15 bil-
lion evaporated like that. In five short days nearly 40 percent of the
value of all Wall Street stocks was gone. The Great Depression had
begun, and soon it would send shock waves heard round the world.
What this would mean for Crane as for millions of other Americans
would become clearer only with each passing day.

For the present, Crane was more concerned about getting out to
Cleveland for his father's wedding. It turned out to be a wonderful time
for him, for he was made to feel special by his father and particularly
by his new stepmother. Canary Cottage, with its superb second-floor
room reserved for him, was all he could have hoped for. Finally, he
sighed, he had a place to come home to. "Six great fireplaces burning," he wrote Sam Loveman on November 11th, "And dad's cigars!"[52]
If his own preferences were for African masks and Oriental rugs and
modernist paintings, he could still appreciate his father's "early American clocks, desks, chairs, tables, beds and highboys."[53] He ate well—
superbly prepared chicken and duck—and took to imitating his father's
sartorial style: the same overcoat, the same sort of cane, the same gray
fedora worn at the same rakish tilt.

He had nearly two weeks of it, and was prepared to go on living
like this for as long as possible. But it all ended when he heard from
his Warren relatives that his mother was on her way east to meet him.
With that, Hart was gone, taking the first train back to New York. When
Grace heard that her son had fled, she cut short her own trip and
returned to Chicago. That her Hart could do this to her stunned her
beyond words. But the sudden departure had taken its toll on Crane as
well. "My melodramatic departure and the attending circumstances sent
me to bed with a backache for three weeks after I got home," he would
tell the Rychtariks later.[54]

He spent a bizarre Thanksgiving in his apartment, alone, afraid to answer the telephone. His father wrote to assure him that he too would have nothing to do with Grace, but he did wonder aloud if perhaps Harold should have her committed. Between Thanksgiving and December 10th, as he traveled back and forth between New York and Patterson, Crane somehow managed to complete drafts of "Indiana" and "Quaker Hill," both shortened from his original intentions. A friend of the Cowleys, Margaret (Peggy) Robson, convinced that, for all Crane's drunken behavior, he'd written a work of genius, saw to it that the manuscript was prepared for the press by typing and retyping the new sections of the poem as he wrote and rewrote them.

If he had one place he could call home now—and even that was questionable by the fall of '29—it was the two rooms he'd furnished and was paying rent on in Addie Turner's farmhouse in Patterson. "Quaker Hill" enacts and holds the complex of emotions he felt toward this pastoral world, which even now was slipping away from him. For this domestic space he evoked the presence of two American women, both of them artists, both of them heroic in his eyes: Isadora Duncan, whom he'd seen dance like Ariel before an unbelieving and startled crowd in Cleveland seven years before; and the reclusive poet, Emily Dickinson. "I see only the ideal," he quoted the first. "But no ideals have ever been fully successful on this earth." His own sentiments exactly. He'd lived long enough to question the very vision that had stirred him to begin *The Bridge* seven years before. And then Dickinson, watching a world of fall blaze into oblivion, the tragic artist signaling the inevitable end: "The gentian weaves her fringes,/The maple's loom is red."

"Cape Hatteras" was all surmise and rhetoric, what the American bard, Crane supposed, might be expected to proclaim. The trouble was that little of it resonated with his own experience: he had never seen military action, never seen Cape Hatteras, never seen a dogfight, never even flown. But "Quaker Hill" was different. He knew Quaker Hill and Patterson intimately; it had been the closest thing to home he had ever experienced, and he knew he was about to lose that, too. Quaker Hill, overlooking the surrounding hills and valleys that make up Patterson, in 1929 was dominated by an empty and decaying Victorian hotel, once bustling, but waiting now to be demolished, as soon it would be.

The very name recalled Patterson's colonial settlers: peaceloving people, visionaries, who had erected on the hill's summit a simple white clapboard gathering place which in time would give way to a hotel for visitors from New York, arriving by carriage from the train station in Pawling. A hotel haunted by memories, atop which rested a widow's walk looking out over the hills, recalling Crane's own lost tower and home in Cleveland. Old Mizzentop, as the grand old hotel came to be known, linking it with Melville and the sea, its long tiers of loose-paned windows staring out toward the west and sunset. How many times had he stalked through the decayed grandeur of those empty rooms and the ghostly ballroom, as Sue Brown would recall forty years later, remembering him leaning out "through a broken window to take in the magnificent view over the Harlem Valley below, where the white church spires of the small town of Pawling showed through the old elms," as he evoked for her "the slow approach of the surreys and 'rigs.'"[55]

And other ghosts as well. Those "Dead rangers [who] bled their comfort on the snow": Washington's soldiers shot up in a skirmish with British regulars and brought to a nearby house to die in the winter of 1779. And those other "resigned factions of the dead" haunting his beloved Patterson: slain Iroquois, scalped Yankees, rangers, in addition to the feminine presences of Emily and Isadora. And all this suffering for what purpose? For the dream of some promised land, where Wall Street czars boarded trains and got off three hours later here in this land of golf courses, laughing their way across manicured lawns "by twos and threes in plaid plusfours/Alight with sticks abristle and cigars"? Twenties America: the Promised Land become so only for "the persuasive suburban land agent," living in "bootleg roadhouses where the gin fizz/Bubbles in time to Hollywood's new love-nest pageant": small-time agents turning a profit on land and illegal booze as they transformed the old farms into building lots.

Everything seemed to be appreciated only in terms of its price tag these days—land in Florida, in California, and now here in Patterson. There was even a price tag, wasn't there? on one's heritage and birthright. And that included a price for which he had been willing to sell himself, or why else the trip to Hollywood to pimp for some neurotic Wall Street millionaire? Adams's auction: one of the old names, the original settlers here, the first man, selling his birthright for the right price ("Tell you what I'm gonna do. Going once, going twice," that "ancient deal/Table" for "only nine-/Ty five" bucks). Or his heavyset, good-natured neighbor, Mrs. Porwitzki, mother of sixteen children—all delivered without benefit of a doctor—of old Burch stock herself, for which Birch Hill Road, off which Crane lived, had been named. Hadn't he waited each day for Andy the postman to deliver his letters, among them the dreaded one from his mother, saying she'd finally written his father about his drinking, his lifestyle, his wastrel ways? "Birthright by blackmail," he called it in the poem, that "arrant page" that would unfold for him "a new destiny to fill." By which he meant what—his own death?

What, after all, was there left to say? The vision of a new world order, the city of Atlantis finally mapped, about which he'd been so sure just seven years before, gone now on the winds of change. What would it mean, after all, to say he was bringing news of his vision back to his readers, like some "guest who knows himself too late,/His news already told?" The bell in the tower tolling, one last orphic angelus announced, the heart wrung, the Hart wrung, the heart rung, the vision extolled turning to dust before him, like some bogus communion offered without God behind it to give it weight.

And now night falling, and leaves falling, "Leaf after autumnal leaf," the "dim elm-chancels" round about hung with autumn dew, the only sound breaking the silence the "triple-noted clause of moonlight" that defined the whippoorwill's song. A song like Crane's: elegiac, breaking the heart, yet—if the truth be told—unhusking it too, "to yield/That patience" (the thought and phrasing Hopkins's, entering at last into a poem of Crane's, as Crane had hoped the good man would). Patience, hard thing, "that is armour and that shields/Love from despair." And love at last defeated, forced to witness to its own demise.[56]

As with Harry and Caresse Crosby, in New York for the two weeks following Thanksgiving. On December 7th Crane held a farewell party for them at 130 Columbia Heights, six days before they were scheduled to return to Europe. He invited all those who'd helped him in any way with *The Bridge*: the Crosbys; Harry Marks, the American distributor for the Black Sun Press; Malcolm and Peggy Cowley; Peggy Robson, who had typed large swatches of the poem; Walker Evans, who'd provided the extraordinary photographs of Brooklyn Bridge and the East River in place of the Stella painting;[57] E. E. and Anne Cummings;

and William Carlos Williams and his wife, Flossie. He also invited at least one sailor. All through the night the party continued, breaking up only toward dawn. Near midnight, Harry had accompanied Peggy Robson over to Pineapple Street to see a bootlegger about refurbishing Crane's dwindling gin supply. She would remember Crosby expatiating eloquently and drunkenly on love and death, of how love could only be fully realized with one's own death. Only afterwards would she understand what he had been trying to tell her.

The following night there was another party, this one given by Harry Marks, which Crane also attended, and on the 10th, dinner followed by a theater party, this affair hosted by the Crosbys. That evening Crane escorted Peggy Robson to join the Crosbys at the Caviar Restaurant in midtown Manhattan, where they were to meet Caresse and Harry's mother. Harry would be along later, they were sure. But when Harry failed to show, the others went ahead and dined before catching Leslie Howard at the Lyceum in a light comedy called *Berkeley Square*. Harry Mortimer, a friend of the Crosbys, thinking Harry might still be at his studio at the Hotel des Artistes on West 67th Street, volunteered to go up there and see what was keeping him. At the box office Crane left his seat number for the phone call from Mortimer.

In the darkened theater a short time later, an usher with a flashlight signaled to Crane that there was a call for him at the front desk. It was Mortimer. He'd gone to the studio and, finding the door locked, had called the superintendent, who then forced the door open. Inside, they'd found Crosby and a young woman, Josephine Rotch, in his arms, lying in bed. Both were fully clothed and a blanket had been drawn up to their shoulders. Each had been shot through the temple with a .25 Belgian automatic, which was still in Crosby's hand. Crane went back to his seat, told Caresse and Harry's mother to come out with him, and then they all went uptown by taxi to the hotel. There they found a crowd, police cars, flashbulbs, pandemonium, and the shock of seeing the street roped off.

The deaths were ruled a double suicide. At the open window of their twenty-seventh-floor apartment at the Savoy Plaza earlier that day, Caresse would remember, Harry had looked at her. "Give me your hand, Caresse," he'd said. "Let's meet the sun death together." Now Harry had flown directly into the black sun . . . with another woman.

On December 13th, after a hasty funeral, Caresse and Harry's mother sailed for Paris as they'd originally planned. Crane sent a bouquet of flowers to the ship, but was too shaken to see them off. "DEAR CARESSE," he had telegrammed her on the eve of her departure, trying to give whatever support he could, "YOU KNOW I WISH TO BE OF HELP CARESSE YOU ARE CARESSE YOU ARE MY FAVORITE FRIEND POLLY CARESSE I SAY CARESSE YOU ARE NOT ONLY ALL BUT YOU UNDERSTAND ALL."[58]

"I've been all broken up about Harry," he wrote Tate the next day. Tate was still in Paris, and Crane took him up now on his offer to proofread the galleys of *The Bridge* to help Caresse. The book was going ahead as scheduled, Crane explained, for Caresse would need to keep busy and would also need all the support she could get. "I had just had a party or so for them—and all our friends immediately fell in love with them both. I was with Caresse and Harry's mother the evening of [the] so-called suicide, and had to break the news to them. I haven't been worth much since."[59]

When he could, he worked on "Quaker Hill" and "Indiana" because he had to, polishing draft after draft in the days leading up to Christmas. The holiday itself he spent with Bob Stewart, a young, tow-haired Alabama boy serving on the USS *Milwaukee*. The day after Christmas, he sent Caresse the final versions of the two poems. He had at long last finished *The Bridge*. "I've been slow, Heaven knows," he told her, "but I know that you will forgive me." He explained that he had not added as much to the "Indiana" section as he'd thought he would, but in any event he preferred the shorter version. It was, after all, only an "accent mark" in the overall scheme of the poem. And besides, he was psychically exhausted and in no mood to think of the promise of America. Harry's death had proven a final, ironic comment on all of that, anyway. "I think of you a great deal," he ended. How brave she'd been, how stalwart and brave.[60] Still, he must have thought to himself, Harry had done it. Flown wide-eyed like some Faustian ace straight into the cauldron of the sun.

PART IV

13 / DOWN AND OUT IN NEW YORK

IN EARLY JANUARY 1930, Crane moved half a block south to a tiny basement apartment at 190 Columbia Heights. Next to his bed, for company, he kept a gallon of bootleg whiskey. He wrote almost no one any more. Defeated by philosophy, he no longer read it. He did read reviews, read Eliot (on Dante), scanned the newspapers. But he no longer carried on long, brilliant exchanges on metrics, theory, or ethical issues. Such things, he told Winters, no longer interested him. He did care about his poem, about the edition Black Sun was bringing out, with its three wonderful photos by Walker Evans, but little more. In mid-January, he wrote "To the Cloud Juggler," ten couplets in memory of Harry Crosby, addressing the sun into which Crosby had disappeared, obliterating himself and his mistress in the process. "Do not claim a friend like him again," he wrote, "Whose arrow must have pierced you beyond pain."[1] He sent the lines on to Caresse, saying they were the best he could find it in himself to write just now. At the end of the month, speaking of Harry's poems to Winters, he admitted that there was "only a little pure ore here and there."[2] Nothing more. Still, he really had been shaken by Harry's death. By then he'd come to accept the death as a suicide, Harry's final insane experiment. But his deepest sympathies went out to the brave wife Harry had so carelessly left behind.

Once again Crane was penniless, his grandfather's inheritance scattered to the winds, his modest advance for *The Bridge* along with it. "I don't want to write anything more for ages," he told Caresse in late January.[3] Three weeks later, he told Charlotte Rychtarik the same thing. "Right here in Babylon"—his new name for New York—"hunting jobs," he wrote her. Not only were his "days of romance thoroughly dead and passed," but he really did not want to write any more just now. Still, it depressed him to think that for the first time in years he didn't have "some ambitious project on hand to take the place of *The Bridge.*"[4]

The only upbeat thing happening on the New York scene was art: the modern French painters at the Museum of Modern Art; gallery shows by Georgia O'Keeffe, John Marin, and his new friend Peter Blume. Otherwise, it was all breadlines, suicides, beggars in alleys, beggars on stoops, including grim mothers with equally grim-looking children, all hoping for handouts. Spring made its mild return, and still he could find no work. "I've really never known so discouraging a time job-hunting," he wrote to Frank. "Insomnia has got me on the rack—and I . . . can't envisage just what is in store." Really, he thought, the disintegrating forces he saw every day around New York struck him as they struck anyone with eyes to see "as pretty severe." Maybe there would be work for him when the reviews of *The Bridge* came out. Surely with his friends reviewing it he could expect some rave notices, and that might give him new confidence in himself and help him "make a better impression in 'the business world.'"[5]

By the end of January, copies of the Black Sun edition (200 copies on Holland Van Gelder at $10, with another 50 on vellum—autographed—at $25, available from Harry F. Marks, bookseller, 31 West 47th) had been sent out to the reviewers. In April, Liveright's trade edition became available for the modest price of $2.50 a copy. Tate would review it for *Hound & Horn*, Cowley for *The New Republic*, Isidor Schneider for the *Chicago Evening Post*. Crane wrote Winters, wondering if he might review it either for *Poetry* or *The Nation*. There weren't really "too many openings for any of us," he added,[6] and reviews had been held up by the press until the trade edition was out. Because of what the book had cost her emotionally in seeing it through the press in the wake of her husband's death, Caresse was naturally upset by the prospect that the limited edition would be overlooked. Crane had to remind her that he had no control over what the press decided in its wisdom to do.

In late April, the reviews began coming in. "You have my sincerest gratitude for your enthusiastic review of *The Bridge*," he wrote Herbert Weinstock on the 22nd from Patterson. He hoped he really was deserving of Weinstock's praise (which had appeared in the *Milwaukee Journal* on the 12th) and could almost believe the book was as densely and symbolically structured as Weinstock had said. Perhaps, as this critic had pointed out, there really was an "essential religious motive" running throughout all Crane's work, though he'd "never consciously approached any subject in a religious mood." And it was only after completing *The Bridge* that he'd noted the book's prevalent piety, though he shuddered at the thought of being pegged as having some "Messianic predisposition."

But Crane was eager to educate his critics, if he could, and told Weinstock, for instance, that with time and familiarity he hoped Weinstock might see the poem "with a clearer and more integrated unity and development" than any first reading could provide. It had, after all, taken him five years to find the essential unity in Eliot's *Waste Land*, and *The Bridge* was "at least as complicated in its structure and inferences" as Eliot's poem had been, and probably more so.[7] To Eda Lou Walton, who'd told him she was including *The Bridge* in a course on Modern Poetry she was giving at NYU, he enclosed an extract from his old letter to Kahn which explained what he was doing in the poem. He tried expanding the letter into an essay for *The New American Caravan*, but like so much he attempted now, the project was soon abandoned.

By early May, he was back at 190 Columbia Heights and cruising the Sands Street dives for sailors. He wrote Caresse about a wild evening he'd recently spent with a sailor named Bob Thompson—"Tommy"—who'd gotten "tired of office work" and expected to "hit the deck again for awhile."[8] In his memoir written half a century after the events, Lincoln Kirstein revealed that Bob Thompson was actually a sailor named Carl Carlsen,[9] and Kirstein provides us with a good sense of the interactions among the maritime homosexual community Crane was drawn to. "Another one of Crane's characters," Walker Evans once summed Carlsen up. "A sphinx without a secret." Evans, himself gay, was to meet Carlsen through Emil Opffer, and it was Evans who suggested that Carlsen send some of his sea stories to Kirstein, then a twenty-one-year-old contributing editor of the Harvard-based *Hound & Horn*. Carlsen lived somewhere between West 16th and 20th, Kirstein would remember half a century later, in a two-storied, unheated, unpainted cold-water flat dating back to the 1840s, a clapboard structure set in from the street, with an outhouse out back and a hand pump for water.

Carlsen was Crane's age, stocky, clean-shaven, leathery, tough. "He had coarse, untrimmed bushy eyebrows fairer than his blonde close-cropped hair," Kirstein would remember, and he wore "well-worn, crisply-laundered old regulation U.S. Navy bell-bottoms, with a drop fly and thirteen buttons, in honor of the thirteen original colonies." By 1934—two years after Crane's death—Carlsen was living with "a stolid, self-contained woman," a piano teacher ten years older than himself. On the fireplace mantel Kirstein remembered a portrait of Crane that Evans had taken in 1930, and beside it a green bottle with a full-rigged sailing ship inside. It was a model of the *Cutty Sark*.

And what kind of a man was Crane attracted to? Someone dependable and close-mouthed about his affairs. More than likely, none of the letters Crane wrote to his sailor lovers still exist. Long ago they were tossed into ashcans or scattered over the sides of ships. It is our loss, for we might have learned much about Crane's most intimate side from them. But there was a quiet dignity about Carlsen, Kirstein noted. He was a man who never drew attention to himself. Nor was he particularly handsome. Like most of Crane's lovers, Carlsen was what he appeared to be, uncomplicated, with no designs on anyone. There was no question of Carlsen's competing intellectually with Crane, who—Carlsen would have been the first to admit—spoke and wrote like an angel. Kirstein, young, callow, self-centered, was attracted to Carlsen and Carlsen's uncomplicated way of life—"slumming," one might call it—though Kirstein feared Crane and what Crane was, even after Crane was dead.

Only once, after he and Kirstein had finally spent a night together, did Carlsen ever ask Kirstein why he didn't like Crane. Hell, he'd hardly known Crane, Kirstein admitted, except to reject his work for *Hound & Horn*. And, besides, Crane frightened him as he'd frightened Winters. The truth was—though it would take him forty years finally to admit it—that he really wasn't up to the energies unleashed by this modern Catullus. "Funny," Carlsen shrugged. "You didn't like him, but you like me." And Kirstein: "Why the hell do you always have to bring Crane into it?" And Carlsen, looking hard at him, giving it to him straight: "Why, you silly son of a bitch. If it wasn't for Hart Crane I wouldn't have given you the sweat off my ass."[10]

But it was Bob Stewart, the twenty-one-year-old sailor from the USS *Milwaukee*, then on maneuvers off Cuba, upon whom Crane doted with a complex affection made up of lust, a lyrical *tristesse*, and perhaps even something like fatherly feeling. That spring, walking the streets, or drinking in his room (because it was cheaper), or staring out at the restless waters of the East River, it was the young Bob Stewart he waited for to come back to him in Brooklyn. And Stewart responded in kind by saying he was saving up all his shore leave so he could be back with Crane as soon as possible. It was a declaration of devotion Crane in his illness and listlessness found "really too good to be true!"[11] But it was true, and the two men spent several days together in Brooklyn toward the end of May. And then, as so often with the men he cared for, his blond-haired boy was off to sea again.

The betrayals came in June. First it was Winters's long-awaited review of *The Bridge* in *Poetry*, in which Winters completely reversed himself, damning Crane and his poetry, adding that Crane would have to change his life if he was ever really going to write anything of lasting value. Poring over *The Bridge*, Winters had written, he could find only one poem that tried "to treat clearly of an individual human relationship," and that was "Indiana," a "mawkish and helpless" piece that had failed miserably. "The fact is unimportant," Winters added, "except that it strengthens one's suspicion that Mr. Crane is temperamentally unable to understand a very wide range of experience."[12] In other words, being homosexual, how could Crane be expected to write about the full range of human experience?

"Dear Winters," Crane wrote from Patterson on June 4th, angry, hurt, and deeply disappointed in his old friend. "Your disparagement of *The Bridge* and friendly counsel . . . surprised me considerably; not so much on account of the wide discrepancies between your public and private opinions . . . as to see to what astonishing lengths of misrepresentations your prejudices toward a biological (or is it autobiographical?) approach to poetry can carry you." Of course Winters had every right to revise his estimate of Crane and his poetry. But to blur the work with the man he'd met in California in 1927, to have appropriated his "ethical and privately expressed aesthetic convictions" and then to have applied these convictions to his reading of the poems: *that* was what rankled. "You had a case to make out," Crane shot back, "and exaggeration, misappropriation—or just confusion, all helped to make it more convincing."

Besides, they'd been through their philosophical differences too many times in too many letters for Winters not to know that what Crane wanted from poetry and what Winters wanted were two very different things. Given that, he'd not been surprised that Winters would "pronounce the performance botched" and end up "with a prognosis . . . more pretentious and weightier" than anything Crane had ever intended. But how could Winters count him out when he'd never even been in the ring Winters had described? Not that others, impressed with Winters's pseudo-arguments, wouldn't follow suit and damn *The Bridge* for a failure. For a failed epic was what Winters had called the poem, something lacking the narrative framework necessary for any epic. But he'd never intended writing an epic, Crane reminded him, and in fact had already told Winters that America wasn't ready for its own epic. Was he out to publicly humiliate Crane by stripping him of pretensions he did not pretend to? Besides, the fact that the poem had failed as an epic did *not* mean that *The Bridge* had failed as "a long lyric poem, with interrelated sections."

Crane was puzzled too that Winters could praise to the "heavens" parts of *The Bridge*, such as "The River," in letters to him, only to have these same passages attacked now as "turgid," "confused," "unmastered," and too much under the insidious influence of Whitman. As for a passage from "The Dance" that Winters had quoted out of context, did he really believe that Crane had "set out to offer some law of the Medes or Persians, or some immutable precept of Nirvana in every other line, mounting gradually to some unapproachable zenith presided over by some Krishna of moral infallibility"? All he'd really attempted in "The Dance" was to imagine himself as one "with the Indian savage while he is in process of absorption into the elements of the pure nature-world about him." But he was tired now, and he'd already been through all this years before with that other true believer, Gorham Munson.

Winters's vision, he could see, had narrowed and congealed since that Christmas week eighteen months before that they'd spent talking poetry. The source of all evil, an emotionally frightened Winters had insisted, lay in the emotions. Therefore, keeping the emotions to a minimum was "the only way to a controlled and harmonious life." Faith itself came down not to a faith in the possibilities of the human race, as *The Bridge* seemed to imply, but rather to faith in existence itself. Period. The ideal point of view, therefore, was—as the Stoics had long ago taught—that of the disinterested observer. The problem with poets like Crane and Jeffers, Eliot and Williams, Whitman and Hopkins, and in fact all Romantics, was that they gave themselves over to "an orgy of emotionalism . . . at the expense of intellect." In every case, Winters would increasingly insist, the poetry had thereby suffered.

Such a return to Calvinism might work for Winters, but it would never work for Crane. As Winters's vision developed, narrowed, or focused—let Winters choose whichever term flattered him the most—Crane wondered if—as had already happened with Munson—that vision wasn't in danger of transcending poetry altogether "in favor of a pseudophilosophical or behavioristic field of speculation." First Munson and now Winters had proclaimed to the world that he—Crane—was capable only of some momentary "inspirational limp." But, goddamn it, couldn't Winters see that it had taken "five years of sustained something-or-other to compose *The Bridge*—with more actual and painful 'differentiation of experience' into the bargain" than Winters would ever willingly take upon himself? Yes, he too would have liked better results; what poet would not wish his poem to be better? But even the "wreckage" that remained had more significance than some mere behavioristic gesture, galvanic tweak, or the "cog-walk gestures of a beetle in a sand pit." Couldn't the man see that he'd managed against the odds to do what every poet yearned to do: make of his art something that transcended his miserable human limitations to build a bridge, perhaps even a bridge of fire? It was the last letter Crane would write Winters.[13]

Four days later, he wrote Isidor Schneider to thank him for his glowing review of *The Bridge*. Then—still smarting—he turned back to Winters's attack. Only their long correspondence had prompted him to write Winters at all, he told Schneider, for how could he allow Winters to believe he would accept such "willful distortions of meaning, misappropriations of opinion, pedantry and pretentious classification—

besides illogic"? Why couldn't he write about subways if he wanted to? And did he really have to "defer alluding to the sea" until Winters had got an invitation for a cruise?[14] The truth was that he felt more like a caged animal than a poet with a major vision, this last Romantic. And here he was, in the summer of 1930, with seven years of his life's spirit wedged between the covers of a book, still forced to live from hand to mouth on a small allowance from his father. It was a pittance that trapped more than freed him, while he waited daily for the economy to turn around so he could find a decent job again.

The worst of it of course was that he still could not write, and now believed he might never write again. There was bootleg gin and cider to occupy his empty days and nights in Patterson, but as depression and alcohol took an ever greater hold on him, there was the inevitable hell which Addie Turner's furnishings had to bear the brunt of. Finally, in early July, after celebrating three Fourth of July parties in Patterson—including one at Peter Blume's place (an abandoned chapel near Eleanor Fitzgerald's house), and another at Slater Brown's (singular, he and Sue having for the time separated), Crane came home late one night and began staggering through the house with a smoking kerosene lamp. This time Addie Turner threw him out for good. She was going to sell the old farmhouse, she told him, and so it was as good a time as any for him to grab his things and clear out. Immediately, he stormed out of the house and walked the mile and a half in the dark to Fitzi's house, returning the next day with a neighbor's wagon and some friends to move his things. "Occasionally I am appalled at my apparently chronic inability to relinquish some hold or connection that has long since ceased to yield me anything but annoyance, until some violence of fates forces my release. That's one of many ways I seem to keep of wasting time."[15] That was how he rationalized his final separation from the woman who had cared for him like a mother for the past five years.

Again it was Fitzi, generous old anarchist that she was, who gave him a room. It was from there on July 13th that Crane finally got around to forcing a grin and thanking Tate for his letter and "admirable review" of The Bridge in the pages of Hound & Horn. He'd read it, he said, in Brentano's bookstore because he hadn't the money to buy the magazine. The essay had been anything but admirable, really, but he did not want to go through what he'd already gone through with Winters. Furling his flag, head bowed, he responded. If Tate placed The

Bridge at the exhausted end of a tradition of Romanticism, so be it, though he was not so sure Romanticism was ready to roll over and die yet. But even if it were, he countered, he would be happy if his poem really did stand as a bridge to whatever new literary movement was in the offing. For if the work contained even the little authentic poetry Winters was willing to grant it, *The Bridge* could still serve to link aspects of the past with aspects of the future. At the very least the mistakes he'd made in attempting a synthesis of the American experience might stand as a warning to other Americans inclined to try to write a long poem.

But the real trouble with the likes of Winters and Munson was that they weren't looking for poetry any more. What they wanted from poets was some sort of cure-all that would right society's wrongs. After all, who really cared any more for poetry? "Away with Kubla Khan, out with Marlowe, and to hell with Keats," he mocked. And yet, "so many true things" had a way "of coming out all the better without the strain to sum up the universe in one impressive little pellet." True, his own poetry was too personal to serve as a clarion for society, and if he ever did write verse again, it would probably be "as personal as the idiom of *White Buildings*," whether or not anyone cared to read it. So be it. And as for Tate's taking him to task for his "sentimental" praise of Whitman, while it was true that his "rhapsodic address" to the father of modern poetry in "Cape Hatteras" might exceed "any exact evaluation of the man," it was also true that Tate himself was too much the hard classicist to assess adequately Whitman's achievement. For Whitman was no more the "hysterical spokesman" for American capitalism than Crane was, and even a cursory reading of *Democratic Vistas* should have put Tate straight on that score at least. He himself still stood by "the positive and universal tendencies" Whitman represented. "You've heard me roar at too many of his lines to doubt that I can spot his worst," he closed. But he did not like being set up as a kind of straw man who was supposed to hold positions he did not hold.[16]

Crane took Lorna Deitz with him when he went to spend a weekend in mid-July with the Cummingses at their summer place in New Hampshire, and it was there that he celebrated his thirty-first birthday. But when he returned to Fitzi's place in Gaylordsville, his right arm was swollen with boils that had made their first appearance under his armpit and spread from there. "The loyal and royal succession of the Plantagenets," Cummings had dubbed them.[17] The upshot was that for the following month, Crane could barely type or lift a pen. A letter arrived from Aunt Sally Simpson, breaking the news to him that the plantation was now being occupied by squatters, who had stripped the place, stealing everything that could be moved. All that was left of any value was the land itself, and his mother would be lucky to get twenty-five dollars an acre for that. He heard from his mother, working as a receptionist at the Carleton Hotel (a modest affair) in Oak Park, Illinois. She wished Hart a happy birthday and enclosed a small photograph of herself. Someday, perhaps, she added plaintively, he might find it in himself to forgive her. It tore him to pieces, this reminder of her, and soon he was on another bender, taking her photo out of his wallet from time to time to trace for his friends the moral degeneration he found there.

In mid-August he sent an inscribed copy of *The Bridge* to John Augustus Roebling, the grandson of the man who had overseen the construction of the very bridge in whose shadow Crane, so many worlds away now, had conceived his poem. "My devotion to the Brooklyn Bridge as the matchless symbol of America and its destiny prompted this dedication," he wrote, at the end of the labor, "as I dare say the particular view of the bridge's span from my window on Columbia Heights . . . inspired the general conception and form of the entire poem." Only now, with the poem already completed, had he learned that he'd actually shared the same address with Washington Roebling, the creator of the bridge. He hoped that the grandson would find something to admire in the poem, which, Crane added modestly, was in its own way "as ambitious and complicated as was the original engineering project."[18] Tate wrote, inviting him down to his place at Benfolly in Tennessee to spend some time. But Crane begged off. "I've got to get located in some office as soon now as possible," he wrote back in early September, "or at least be on the scene of interrogation, prison, palace, and supplication."[19] He was never going to be under the same roof with Caroline Gordon again if he could help it.

Except for the time spent studying Dante, the summer had flown by with nothing to show for it, and already he could taste fall in the air again. It had been T. S. Eliot's essay that had led him to Dante. In fact, he'd followed Eliot's lead and read the Temple Classics prose translation.

Having himself spent five years "with a poem of large proportions and intricate framework,"[20] he'd been particularly curious to see how the medieval Italian had gone about writing his own epic. If this was playing catch-up, or paying homage to the great Western tradition, he did not say so. It was, after all, Eliot (and Poe, and Melville) who had served as his Virgil, as Pocahontas and his mother had served as his spectral, unmanning Beatrice.

In late August he applied for a Guggenheim Fellowship, explaining that if he were awarded one, he would use it to study in Europe. "I am interested in characteristics of European culture, classical and romantic," he wrote the committee, hat in hand, at a loss really as to where he was headed, and using the standard fellowshipese. He was especially interested in "contrasting elements implicit in the emergent features of a distinctive American poetic consciousness." Certainly his one previous visit to Europe had "proved creatively stimulating," he grimaced, as the fruit of that visit—*The Bridge*—would no doubt suggest.[21] He would study modern and medieval French literature and philosophy, this hopeless monoglot told the committee, turning himself (presto!) into another Yvor Winters. He sent the letter off on August 29th, knowing it would be six months before he learned whether his application had been successful.

By mid-September, Crane was back in New York, looking for work. He rented a cheap room at the Hotel St. George, a few blocks from Columbia Heights. This he did because, in a moment of drunken enthusiasm earlier that summer, he'd brought some sailors back to his basement apartment at 190 Columbia Heights and one of them had lifted his black address book with its incriminating names and addresses of sailors and pickups, interlaced with those of relatives and friends. Better just now, prudence reminded him, to leave no forwarding address, and hope the trail of any potential blackmailer would quickly grow cold. But finding work in the fall of 1930 in New York was like "looking for . . . needles in haystacks." All the jobs seemed to hang in some Tantalean midair, always just out of reach. By then the entire first run (one thousand copies) of the trade edition of *The Bridge* had sold out, and a second thousand were being printed. After all the grandiose talk he'd indulged in during the poem's oft-interrupted progress, he wrote Mony Grunberg, no wonder his friends were "appalled at its ultimate shortcomings." Still, to have sold a thousand copies of a poem in a time of severe economic depression! And—he consoled himself—if the spring hadn't "ushered in such a calamitous slump in all books," he knew he could have sold a great many more.[22] In spite of Winters's and Tate's betrayals, in fact, most of the reviews had been positive.

In mid-November, Wilbur Underwood came up to New York. Crane found an evening to spend with his old mentor and friend, his own Brunetto Latini, but he was too preoccupied in trying to write an essay for *Fortune* magazine to do more than bow in his old friend's direction. It was Archibald MacLeish, then on the staff of the powerful magazine, who'd come up with the idea of commissioning Crane to do a feature on the massive construction of the George Washington Bridge, then underway. The singer of the old Brooklyn Bridge would sing now the super new span, one that bridged an even vaster body of water. When MacLeish saw Cummings at a party, he mentioned Crane's difficulties in finishing the piece. Crane? Cummings said, laughing. Why, Crane was incapable now of finishing anything.

Cummings was right. In spite of Crane's going out to the construction site on the Upper West Side and across to the Palisades on the Jersey side, in spite of walking on the bridge platforms in the autumn rain and wind, in spite of his enthusiasm for the din of the building, the crane operators, the massive twisting of the cables, the rising towers, the queue of cement trucks daily pouring concrete, in spite of the interviews with gang bosses, crew foremen, workers, water carriers, and engineers, he could not get forward with the writing. The jazzed-up, popular twenties style that was *Fortune's* signature continued to elude him, frustrating and ultimately silencing him. Not only had his own poetry turned to empty rhetoric, but—called upon to produce it—he could not even write an acceptable popular prose. In spite of his earlier successes at ad writing, the magazine's modern, ironic, streamlined, upbeat style evaded him. The essay remained unwritten.

"All my hectic efforts at concentration . . . have brought me nothing better than a cool turning down from the editor of *Fortune*," Crane wrote Underwood at Thanksgiving. "Perhaps I should call it 'Misfortune.'" So busy had he been, in fact, that he'd seen Bob Stewart, back in port again, only once. He'd interviewed "the oil king," J. Walter Teagle, president of Standard Oil of New Jersey, for a second *Fortune* essay, and thought the interview had gone well. But when it came time to write up the article, he'd frozen once again. He worried constantly about money so much now, in fact, that he was paralyzed, able to write "neither poetry nor the most obvious hack work." Failed deadlines robbed him even of the little sleep he could garner. Surely "a steady job, though a bore," might change all this, he sighed. He ended his letter by hitting up Underwood for a loan of twenty-five or fifty dollars, whatever Underwood could spare.[23]

The depths of the depression had finally hit him. "New York is full of the unemployed, more every day," he wrote Bill Wright, "and the tension evident in thousands of faces isn't cheerful to contemplate." How strange to see New York "so 'grim about the mouth,' as Melville might say." He'd written nothing—not a line—since the elegy for Harry Crosby back in January. Would it be insensitive, he asked Wright, to query the possibility of "a temporary loan" to carry him over until a check from *Fortune* showed up? Twenty-five or fifty would do, if Wright had no scruples about lending a friend in need some money.[24]

Wright sent Crane not one but two checks, one to use immediately, the other in case the check from *Fortune* was held up for any reason. Then he added how much he admired Crane for his willingness to live on the edge for the sake of his art. How many artists would dare to do that? But Crane was too honest to buy into that myth. "By ascribing my almost chronic indigence to so Nietzschean a program as the attitude of 'living life dangerously' infers," he wrote back at the end of November, "you make me blink a little." The truth was that his "exposures to rawness and to risk" had been "far too inadvertent" to serve as a plan for living.[25] Because he was now virtually indistinguishable from the bums he'd portrayed in "The River," he smiled to think his friend would choose to speak of him in such glowing and romantic terms. By then he was not only broke; worse, he'd borrowed from everyone he could think of: Otto Kahn, Caresse Crosby, friends in Cleveland, friends in New York. He had nowhere to turn except to his father. It was time for the Prodigal Son to return home.

When he arrived in Chagrin Falls on December 12th, his father immediately put him to work in the Euclid Avenue store, where he spent the rest of the month wrapping Christmas gift boxes from one end of the day to the other. He had no time for letters and no reason to write any. Finally, four days after Christmas, he wrote Sam Loveman back in New York. The return home had actually done him good, he confessed. He was in high spirits, sleeping soundly at night and staying on the wagon. He pointed to the Canary Cottage stationery he was using, emblazoned with the logo, "The place to bring your guest," and quipped that he would have changed the "bring" to another word likewise beginning with "b," with a lot more action, or he was "no befriender of monks and monkery." Things were quiet around the Cottage just now, without "absinthe, gobs, applevendors [and] breadlines" to throw into the mix. And what had all his enforced virtue produced but "a maidenly complexion and a bulging waist line." Vanished now that "glittering eye of Sands St. midnights," when he'd gone searching for sailors, "erstwhile so compelling" a pastime. Here he was, the Ancient Mariner himself, "facing the new year with all the approved trepidations of the middle west business man, approved panic model of 1931."[26]

When his son returned to Cleveland this time, having failed to find work in the face of staggering unemployment in New York, C.A. was convinced that Harold was finally home to stay. After all, he had a job, a roof over his head—and a terrific one at that—good food and warm clothes, and a stepmother and father who genuinely enjoyed his company. For three months, Crane somehow managed to stay off booze. "My father, of course, expects me to remain in this locality permanently," he wrote Mony Grunberg in New York. "I of course keep all contrary plans very much to myself, including the secret of a bank balance sufficient at least to my carfare east again, whenever my return seems advisable."

He passed his free time in the city's libraries, reading every chance he got: a novel called *Through Traffic* about business and love by Russell Davenport, a friend of his at *Fortune*; John Dos Passos's *42nd Parallel*; and as many of the weeklies and quarterlies as he could lay his hands on, anxious to see what was happening in the world of poetry. For the first time in years, he was reading philosophy again. Just now it was Spinoza ("Einstein's grandpop," he dubbed him),[27] a figure who was keeping him on his toes. Only the Muse refused herself. He could not fool himself there. The few poems he did send out and which appeared from time to time were old things, dating back to his trip to the Isle of Pines four years before.

In mid-January 1931, C.A. and Bess took a winter vacation down to Havana, their pockets stuffed with suggestions from Harold about which wines to order and what places to see. It was the first vacation his father had taken in years and Crane was happy to think of them enjoying themselves. In the meantime, he enjoyed dining and music with the Rychtariks. But except for them and a few family members, he saw no one in Cleveland. Bill Sommer, who had gotten wind of rumors about Crane's wild life back in New York, refused to meet him. "Too bad he isn't a little more stalwart," Crane wrote Loveman in mid-February, "considering the boozing he once indulged in himself." One old friend that Crane had looked up at Christmas had looked "haggard . . . complexion splotched, and thoroughly miserable," in spite of making every effort to look "as suave as possible." When Crane hinted at his friend's sorry appearance, no explanation had been forthcoming, and he'd had to let the matter drop. In his thumbnail sketch of his friend, he seemed to be staring into a mirror.

He looked for permanent work in Cleveland, but was no luckier there than he had been in New York, so that his days were spent puttering about the Cottage doing odd jobs—"hammering, waxing, rubbing, painting and repairing." Still, pleasant as the Cottage could be, there were limitations.[28] "Poetry or anything like that is an offense to mention here," he confessed to Lorna Dietz in mid-February, "something belonging in the category with 'youthful errors,' 'wild oats,' et cetera." Sunday mornings he listened to Roxy's Sunday Concerts on the radio. In fact, his mind was now devolving more and more into a "pleasantly vegetable state . . . that can read Coolidge's daily advice without a tremor of protest." His father, on the other hand, seemed to thrive on the depression. For, though C.A. had lost heavily—like so many others—in the crash, Crane thought his father would "actually be disappointed" if things got better before 1936.[29] In fact, C.A. seemed to relish his new role as doomsayer. The crash, he liked to point out, had been the result of everyone spending too much damned money too quickly, though not, as Crane noted, on his father's chocolates.

And that was how they spent their evenings now, C.A. holding forth on the state of the economy and Harold sitting across from him, nodding his head in agreement, yes, yes, that was so, yes, night after night after night. The enviable news he heard from friends in New York, on the other hand, was that—despite unemployment and hunger—the partying among his old pals went on unabated, along with the flow of booze. The only difference was that every cocktail conversation seemed to revolve around communism as the economic answer to everything. On the other hand, it had not escaped him that *no one* was writing anything of note at the moment. Though he may not yet have realized it, the High Modernism that had shaped his generation was already passing, while the new social realism was still struggling to be born.

No wonder he was confused. These were bewildering times for

everyone, as he wrote Waldo Frank. He couldn't even find anything of substance to say these days, and—what was worse—he no longer much cared. When they got it all decided one way or the other—capitalism or communism—then he would "resume a few intensities." All of life seemed withered and dry. The old battles for a poetic ideal—the struggle for instance to counter Eliot's vision. How far away all that seemed now. "Maybe I'm only a disappointed romantic, after all," he confessed to the one man he could still write to who had shared his vision of America's glorious possibilities.

Had he, he wondered, made "too many affable compromises" with himself and with his vision to speak for America? He hoped to God he found out what was sapping him of his vitality before it was too late. One thing was sure: America in 1931 seemed a hell of a far cry from the destiny Crane had fancied for it when he'd begun writing *The Bridge* eight years before. Perhaps Spengler was right after all about the inevitable decline of the West. Besides, he was thirsty again and tired of his own enforced abstemiousness. "If abstinence is clarifying to the vision," he closed, "then give me back the blindness of my will. It needs a fresh baptism."[30]

Crane was about to get his wish. In mid-March, he was notified by Henry Allen Moe that he'd just been awarded a Guggenheim Fellowship, to take effect as soon as he wished. "As I am at present among the vast horde of the unemployed," he wrote Moe back at once, "and with nothing of consequence to detain me, I should like to situate myself definitely as soon as possible in a favorable environment for constructive work and study."[31] He would sail for France in a month, leaving Depression America as far behind him as he could.

14 / DEATH'S
ADJUSTMENTS

MEXICO CITY/NEW YORK/CHAGRIN FALLS
MARCH–AUGUST 1931

WITHIN DAYS OF ACCEPTING the Guggenheim, Crane had packed his bags, said good-bye to his father and Bess, and returned to New York. But instead of going back to France, where he'd accomplished exactly nothing over a seven-month period, he decided on the spur of the moment to head for Mexico—a more "creative locality"[1]— where he could live cheaply and imbibe the culture and language he'd come to love during his time on the Isle of Pines. Friends who had been to Mexico—among them the Cowleys— had advised him to try it. But the deeper reason for the change, he told Caresse, was that he was after the soul of a people: the mysterious, ineffable Mexican Indian. Lawrence's *The Plumed Serpent* had given him his hint, though even Lawrence had fallen short of what he was looking for. In *The Bridge* Crane had found himself reaching further and further into the Indian consciousness, something he'd tried to evoke in "The Dance," though even there it had been as much miss as hit.

Now he would plunge in even deeper, trying to recover some trace of the authentic Indian world before its contact with the European. And once he had recovered it, he would write a tragedy (in Marlowe's mighty line) which would center on the moment when the two civilizations had collided: Montezuma's Aztecs and Cortés's Spaniards. He had tried to do something similar in *The Bridge*, reaching back into the American experience, bridging time and space to make contact with the spirit of Maquokeeta. But there, in spite of the poem's tragic elements, he'd shaped the strands so that they would lead to a comedic resolution, all resolved in the vision of the bridge. He'd been twenty-three when that vision had come to him and he had seen too much in the intervening years to stay there. This time, the contact between the European and indigenous cultures would take on its proper coloration: the enormous tragedy and waste of it all. To do this he needed Mexico, not France.

He made the change with the Guggenheim Foundation easily enough. As long as he traveled abroad for the tenure of his fellowship, they explained, it didn't much matter which country he sailed for. Crane celebrated his deliverance from Cleveland by going on a bender again. In fact, the entire two weeks he spent in New York before heading for Mexico were one flurry of drunken activity. Lincoln Kirstein would remember seeing him on March 28th, a week into his stay, at a party thrown by the editors of *The New Republic* at a Fifth Avenue penthouse. Edmund Wilson was there, and Paul Rosenfeld, Dwight Macdonald, Walker Evans, and E. E. Cummings. Cummings, aware of Kirstein's dislike of Crane, told Kirstein that, even if Crane's mind were no bigger than a pin, it didn't matter. The man was a born poet and that was that.

For the most part the party was subdued, small groups here and there holding forth in a haze of cigarette smoke and alcohol. Then, suddenly, the hum was broken by an explosion of shouts and fists. Crane, already drunk, had gotten into an argument with someone bigger than himself, and—unwilling to back down—had traded punches with the man, who held him at arm's length and hit him hard, knocking him to the floor. "Chuck the son of a bitch out!" someone shouted, and then Crane was being helped to his feet, rushed out the door and onto an elevator. An hour later, there was a banging at the front door again. It was Crane, followed by a taxi driver demanding that the sonofabitch pay his fare.

Crane had told the driver to take him across the Brooklyn Bridge and over to Sands Street to some sailors' hangout. Only when he got there did he inform the driver that he had no money. It was the perfect opportunity for the taxi driver to show largess, compassion, mercy, love. Instead, he pushed Crane into the gutter. Indignant, Crane told him to drive back to the party, where he was sure his friends would take up a collection to pay for the trip to Sands Street and back and back again to Sands Street. Having returned to the party, he kept apologizing to no one in particular for his earlier behavior. As for the cabby, given a couple of shots, he was soon in a forgiving mood. What a marvelous man this cabby was, Crane was soon proclaiming. Why, he was ready to hire him *and* his taxi to take him to Mexico. And then the two men were out the door again to get Crane back to his sailors.

On Saturday, April 4th, exhausted from drinking and partying, Crane settled his bill at the Hotel Lafayette in the Village and set sail at noon from Pier 4 on the East River aboard the SS *Orizaba*, bound at last for Mexico. It was the same ship that had taken him to Cuba in the spring of 1926. There was "good rum on board," and the captain had turned out to be "very much a Dane," he signaled Slater Brown, though he was not "depending too much on either."[2] New York lay at last behind him, and his sights were set on Mexico and his new project. "Am feeling as at the beginning of *The Bridge*," he wrote Caresse as the ship churned south. "Only fresher and stronger."[3] And to Lorna Dietz: "There are magnificent people and things ahead. How valid it all turns out to be!"[4]

His second day out he met Dr. Hans Zinsser, who held degrees from the University of Heidelberg, the Sorbonne, the Pasteur Institute, "and other places besides American Universities," as Crane reported to Loveman. At present Zinsser was on the faculty at Harvard and probably "the world's greatest bacteriologist," sailing on the *Orizaba* with "letters from the state and war departments and a half dozen rats in the hold loaded with the deadly typhus." Zinsser was on his way to Mexico City to conduct experiments and would return to Harvard in two weeks' time, leaving behind his assistant, Dr. Maximiliano Castaneda, to complete the work which would prove once and for all that rats spread typhoid in human populations, as they had centuries before in Mexico when the conquistadors first came ashore, bringing their rats with them, and the Indian populations had subsequently been decimated.

Soon Crane was referring to Castaneda, a native Mexican, well educated and well connected, as "Max," delighted to know such an eminent physician would be in the Mexican capital should he fall ill. Zinsser especially fascinated him: one of those rare individuals who was not only a recognized expert in his field but who knew literature as well. "What conversations we had," he reported back to Loveman. A man of fifty who looked forty, "bandy legged from riding fast horses," who wrote "damn good poetry," a "thoroughbred," an aristocrat through and through.[5] But it was the rats in Zinsser's cabin, smuggled aboard, that Crane kept coming back to, staring into their steely eyes in the gloom hour after hour.

Late on the afternoon of April 7th the *Orizaba* docked in Havana for six hours to unload freight and pick up supplies, and Crane and his two friends went ashore for dinner at Crane's favorite restaurant, *La Diana*. Over dinner he drank two bottles of Chablis, borrowed some cash from Zinsser for two quarts of Bacardi, and wrote postcards to his friends back in New York. He was no longer merely cutting paper doilies, he wrote Lorna Dietz, by which he meant that he was finally doing something serious again, in just talking with men like Zinsser. By nine-thirty that evening the three were back on ship, and Crane returned to his cabin to enjoy his rum. But when Zinsser and Castaneda returned to Zinsser's cabin, they found two of the rats lying on their sides in their death throes. Nothing for it then but to wrap them in newspaper and toss them overboard as quickly and quietly as possible. The *Orizaba* was still taking on freight, with lighters alongside, and strong lights playing over the water when they threw the rats over the side. To their shock the two men watched as both rats revived and started making for the ropes of the lighters until, to the men's immense relief, the current finally pulled the rats under.

Suddenly, there was Crane, weaving, his eyes riveted on the water below. "The Doctor has thrown rats into the harbor of Havana," he began declaiming. He tried other blank verse variations. "The Doctor has thrown typhus rats into the water./There will be typhus in Havana." Then footsteps, the approach of the first officer, and suddenly the two doctors were hiding in the shadow of a lifeboat while Crane began explaining to the officer that the Doctor had thrown rats into the harbor. Then the arrival of the Cuban port officer, wanting to know what the ruckus was all about, and again Crane, telling him that the Doctor had indeed thrown rats into the typhus harbor. Then Crane being escorted back to his cabin, still ranting on about rats all over the harbor, climbing up ropes into the lighters. In the cold light of morning, when the *Orizaba* was once again on the high seas, Captain Black-adder, informed of the incident with Crane the night before, found him strolling about the deck with a bottle of Mexican beer in his hand. By then the rats had been forgotten and Crane was going on about the excellent service on board. Curious, the captain asked Crane what he did in private life, to which Crane answered proudly, "I am a poet, sir." And the captain, suddenly understanding, shook his head and went back to his post.

The *Orizaba* reached Vera Cruz on the evening of April 12th, and Crane spent the evening on the prowl for sailors, this time without luck. The following morning he proceeded by train into the interior for the five-hour trip up to Mexico City. It was all so marvelous, he thought: the scenery, the people "along the way who swarmed around the train selling fruits, cakes, tortillas, serapes, canes, flowers, pulque, beer and what have you." Higher and higher the coal locomotives strained, hugging narrow ledges that looked down over tropical valleys and waterfalls. At the town of Orizaba, there was a leveling off. The great plateau had finally been reached. "Very austere," he wrote Loveman, with mountains rising on both sides in the distance, crumbling feudal walls, and "burros and brown natives jogging along dry roads."[6] And the faces of the Indians—beautiful faces, kindly, generous, filled with res-ignation and suffering.

His initial reaction to Mexico City was one of delight and awe. His first night there, Crane settled into a room at the Hotel Panuco and enjoyed a good Mexican dinner. But the following morning, when he went to the bank to draw out funds, he learned that all he had left on his first installment was $200, which would have to last him until July. After withdrawing $75 of that (he already owed Zinsser), he fired off a telegram to Moe saying he had to find Eyler Simpson, the Guggenheim representative in Mexico City, at once. Then he settled into his hotel room and proceeded to drink himself into a stupor. It was there that Simpson, alerted by Moe that their new fellow was already in some kind of difficulty, found Crane the following afternoon, still drunk and morose, a helpless monoglot lost in the great city with a baker's dozen words of Español to his name. Simpson greeted Crane as best he could, told him he would notify the papers that a poet was now in their midst, and left. It was Crane's official welcome to Mexico.

The following day—Wednesday, April 15th—having been invited by the forty-one-year-old novelist Katherine Anne Porter—another Guggenheim fellow—to stay with her and her friends, Crane packed up and moved into her villa in Mixcoac, on the outskirts of the city. Porter, who had met Crane in New York a few weeks earlier, had no idea what she was letting herself in for. Mornings Crane could be charming and funny, chatting in the sunny patio or helping with the gardening. But once he began drinking, he turned on Porter's other guests. He especially disliked Gene Pressly, Porter's companion and the man she would later marry, finding him a sourpuss who seemed to distrust everyone.

Later, Porter would remember Crane (sober) telling her that he knew he was killing the poet within him with his drinking, but that he was helpless to stop himself. He knew the life he led was blunting his sensibilities, so that it took greater and greater shocks to himself to feel anything at all any more, and even then he wondered if he really felt anything. He spoke daily of suicide, praising those who had taken that noble step. Harry Crosby's death in particular had been the act of a real poet. "He talked about Baudelaire and Marlowe, and Whitman and Melville and Blake—all the consoling examples he could call to mind of artists who had lived excessively in one way or another." Drunk, he "would weep and shout, shaking his fist. 'I am Baudelaire, I am Whitman, I am Christopher Marlowe, I am Christ.' But never once did I hear him say he was Hart Crane."[7]

On the evening of the 24th, once again drunk, Crane rushed out of his room and up onto the roof of the villa, shouting into the moonlight that he was going to end it all by throwing himself down. Alarmed and annoyed, Porter called out to him that the house, which was after all only a single story, wasn't high enough for him to do the deed and that he would only end up hurting himself. Yes, Crane nodded. Yes, he could see that, and with that he began to laugh, then climbed down from a tree whose branches overhung the roof. Afterwards he talked with her for a while, then went in and began playing the old out-of-tune piano loudly and miserably. Then he took a taxi into the city, roaming from bar to bar until his money ran out and he could pay neither bar bill nor taxi fare and so wound up at La Demarcácion, the local police station, until he could sober up. In the morning he called the vice consul at the U.S. Embassy to explain that he was an American citizen jailed by the Mexican government. Since he had no money with which to pay his fine, he wondered if the consul might locate

Eyler Simpson and have him pay the fine. The fine came to twelve pesos, duly paid by Simpson, after which Crane was released.

Afterwards, Crane went to the Hotel Mancera in downtown Mexico City, where his own credit was still good, and fortified himself with more rum. Then he went out to locate a house for himself. After finding an unfurnished villa around the corner from Porter's, at Number 15 Michoacán, he withdrew another $75 for the lease and other expenses, and returned to Porter's to stay until he could move into his own place at the beginning of May. As if he didn't have enough problems already, he began to break out with another skin eruption that drove him crazy with itching when he tried to sleep. Nothing he tried brought him any relief, so that finally—overhearing Porter saying she wondered what sexually transmitted disease Hart had picked up this time—he stormed out of her house and took a room at the Mancera, where he drank himself into a stupor for the next two days.

DEAR KATHERINE ANNE & GENE—
HAVE GONE TO THE MANCERA UNTIL THE FIRST. EXCUSE MY WAKEFULNESS PLEASE.
    HART
P.S. NO. HAVEN'T BEEN BUSY WITH 'LOVERS.' JUST YEOWLS AND FLEAS. LYSOL ISN'T NECESSARY IN THE BATHTUB. HAVEN'T GOT 'ANYTHING' YET. IF YOU KNEW ANYTHING WHATEVER ABOUT IT, YOU'D KNOW THAT AT LEAST (AND THE LAST THING SYPHILLUS [SIC] DOES) IT DOESN'T ITCH. OTHER MATTERS DO, SOMETIMES.

He sent that off on the evening of April 28th.[8] Thirty-six hours later, when he at last surfaced from his drunken stupor, he followed up with an abject apology. "This is as near as I dare come to you today," he wrote her. "Shame and chagrin overwhelm me. I hope you can sometime forgive."[9] Then he received a note from Simpson asking him to stop by his office for a talk. Crane knew what *that* meant. He was going to have to clean up his act if he was to stay on in Mexico. He had managed to become *persona non grata* in just two short weeks.

The day after Crane withdrew his second $75, he withdrew his last $50 as well. Then he wired his father for help. C.A. responded by sending a wire to the Mancera, along with a check to the bank. "My dear boy," he wrote Harold on May 1st, "Sending money by wire is a new experience to me." He'd not quite understood how the fellowship money would be disbursed, but he did hope his son would be "very careful of . . . expenditures so that . . . receipts and debts will sort of meet." Nor did he think it wise that his son had borrowed money from Zinsser. "You know, Harold," he cautioned, "more friendships are lost by the intrusion of financial obligations than anything else."[10] C.A. was also curious about this Miss Porter with whom Harold was now living. A New York friend, he'd been led to believe, and perhaps an author. But Harold was starting out in a new country and he hoped he would not cause any scandal by having his name linked in some unsavory fashion with a woman. In that way, C.A. assured him, his ambitions as a writer might yet someday be reached. So much did C.A. know of Harold's other life.

In the meantime, Crane had made another new friend, Moisés Sáenz, a young, high-spirited government official and a member of the Guggenheim's Mexican office selection committee. Sáenz had taken an instant liking to Crane and offered now to take him down to Taxco for a three-day holiday to see something more of the country. Crane had just moved over to his new house—the rooms in fact were still bare—and it was there that he wrote Simpson, saying he'd see him on his return. Then he managed a second note, this one to his "Darling Katherine Anne," relieved that she was willing to overlook his recent behavior. He was still "too jittery to write a straight sentence," he explained, but he was at last coming out of his "recent messiness with at least as much consistency as total abstinence can offer." He had one "hell of a bill" still to pay at the Mancera, but would take care of that when his father's check arrived. In the meantime, Hazel Cazes—this was the former Hazel Hasham who'd worked in C.A.'s New York office fourteen years before and who was now married and living in Mexico City, working as Eyler Simpson's assistant—had come through with a loan. The "recent cyclone" he'd caused by his drinking was over, he promised Porter. He was going on the wagon, at least for the remainder of his time in Mexico.[11]

Taxco: city of cathedrals and narrow, twisting streets nestled high in the mountains. City of the old silver mines and now a flourishing silver trade. This was more like the real Mexico Crane was hoping for. He stayed as a guest at the villa of the minister of education and participated in a *gran fiesta* that was already in progress when he and Sáenz arrived. "All 10 cathedrals ablaze with candles, songs," he wrote the Rychtariks. "My bed heaped with confetti. Dancing, wine, *Courvoisier!* Heavenly! And the drive through the mountains!"[12] What a friend Sáenz had turned out to be, he would confide to Cowley. "His innate Aztec refinement; his quiet daring; his generosity . . . has made me love him very much." Sáenz had found him "an ancient silver pony bridle (bells and all!) from the period of the Conquest." How he loved the authenticity and spirit of *this* Mexico. Sáenz had also introduced Crane to another American, Bill Spratling, author of the just-published *Little Mexico,* who was working to restore the old silver industry in Taxco and who took Crane through his impressive pre-Columbian silver art collection. In fact, three weeks later, when Spratling returned to New York for a visit, he left his "precious collection of timeless, or rather dateless, idols" with an awed Crane.[13]

Though he'd been supplied with letters of introduction from Frank, Crane's contacts with the Mexican literati and press were about as effective as they'd been when he had "stormed" Paris in the winter of '29. "The great Yankee poet," one article called him, the "humble workman of the new literature in the Empire of the Dollar."[14] When he wrote Frank in mid-June, he half explained, half apologized for the nonevents the introductions had turned out to be. Shortly after arriving, he'd delivered the letters to two Mexican poets: León Felipe Camino and Genaro Estrada. From Camino he'd heard back at once, then—a few days later—from Estrada. Camino he'd seen several times since and had been "introduced to a flock of writers, doctors, etc., one afternoon at the Café Colon," but since then, Camino himself had dropped him. "Latin-Americans, I've been told (and now I know) have a way of inviting you out on some specific day," Crane reminded Frank, "and then 'letting you down' most beautifully—without notice or subsequent apology or explanation."

Estrada, on the other hand, had presented him with two de luxe volumes of his own poetry in return for Crane's having presented him with a signed Paris edition of *The Bridge.* Crane now had two books of Spanish poetry, neither of which he could make heads or tails of. Still, he had more respect for Estrada than for Camino, "who, as soon as he heard I was about to call on Estrada, began to ridicule both the man and his work in high glee." In any case, he could see that neither poet, nor any of the other writers he'd made contact with, gave a damn about the indigenous culture he was after. All these Mexican pretenders to poesy, Crane summed them up, were still aping Valéry and Eliot, "or more intensely, the Parnassians of 35 years ago." As for himself, he still harbored the "illusion" that there was "a soil, a mythology, a people and a spirit here . . . capable of unique and magnificent utterance." Frank had been right. Mexico *was* "a sick country," probably had always been that way, and he already doubted that he would ever really fathom the Indian soul. He knew now that even to try to touch that world was going to prove dangerous. And yet humanity here was still "so unmechanized," so "immediate and really dignified"—he meant "the Indians, peons, country people," not "the average mestizo"—that being here was already giving Crane "an entirely fresh perspective" on things, and something far more profound than Europe had given him.

For his part, León Felipe Camino would remember the meeting with the North American very differently. Once he'd discovered which hotel Crane was staying at, Camino had gone there, only to be told that Señor Crane was drinking and was not to be disturbed. Letters were exchanged, and when Camino later went out to the house at Mixcoac in early May at Crane's invitation, he found him dressed in white sailor pants (Marseilles cut) and a striped shirt, lying in bed in an unfurnished house with empty bottles of *cerveza* littering the floor and a keg of liquor hunkering in the corner. On the Orthophonic, a Marlene Dietrich song blared over and over, so that conversation was impossible. When Crane got up from his bed to embrace his guest, what Camino saw was a lost boy with the face of an angel, fear darting from his eyes. Crane himself thought it was the sailor suit that finally scared his guest off, but if a man couldn't relax in his own home in whatever clothes he liked, if he didn't fit some goddamn *nordamericano* stereotype of the poet in "stiff black round-shouldered elegance," some "veritable Wall Street gear to impress the Mexican hidalgo," some banker like Eliot, then to hell with all these Mexican literati.[15] The visit was not repeated. When Frank learned how Crane was conducting himself, he was furious. Camino had translated two of Frank's books, and Crane, who had promised Frank he would drink nothing stronger than beer for his first month in Mexico, had clearly broken that promise. With that, letters between Frank and Crane ceased.

On his return from Taxco, Crane met with Simpson, who warned him to stay out of jail or risk losing his fellowship. But by that point Crane was ready to settle down for a bit. Rent on the house came to thirty-five dollars a month, with an additional eight dollars for a *mozo* (servant), a young Mexican Indian named Daniel Hernandez, who moved in with his wife (and two small children) to help with the cooking, cleaning, and gardening. "I found, by advice, that single mozos weren't apt to be much good," Crane would tell Cowley. "Pulque sprees three times a day, and the evenings never certain. Besides I needed a woman to cook. Consequently I have a delightful hide and seek com-

bination—of both functions."[16] Since the Hernandezes had no English
and Crane very little Spanish, communication at first was awkward,
though somehow they managed. He had electric lights installed, he
bought things, he managed to stay off drinking for a few weeks. He
even persuaded Eyler Simpson to get Moe to advance him $100 against
his July installment.

And at last he began getting some writing done: thirty lines of a
prose poem called "Havana Rose." "Let us strip the desk for action," the
poem began, "now we have a house in Mexico." The lines recalled his
one night in Vera Cruz, True Cross, when he'd talked with Zinsser, as
the harbor beacon darkened and brightened, darkened and brightened, and the offshore winds blew the shutters and doors open and
closed, and he'd caught a glimpse of a watchman smoking a cheroot, a
pistol in his waistband, checking the rooms. He recalled the crumbled
palace of Cortés in the great square, sign of that first incursion into
Mexico of the Spanish conquistadors. And of course the rats in their
cages, cousins of those typhus carriers brought ashore with the
Spaniards and which had wreaked havoc with the Aztecs. Rose moles
erupting on the bodies of the infected, and the pink mouths and gleaming white incisors and yellow eyes of the rats watching him from their
cages. And Zinsser, over dinner at *La Diana* that night in Havana, telling
him not to "heed the negative" but to find the "pattern's mastery"—
that major form—to which, when Crane at last did find it in Mexico,
he might give himself fully, just as he had given himself to *The Bridge*,
and so "gain that mastery and happiness" that was his by birthright. This
same Zinsser, this idealist, this egoist, smuggling infected rats into Mexico to prove a thesis. Rose mouths, white teeth. Havana Rose.[17]

For the first time in his life, Crane had a house he could treat as his
own. He would decorate it as he wanted, money be damned, buying
rugs and ornaments and knickknacks for the rooms, much as he had
in Patterson half a dozen years before. He loved the garden that ran
along three sides of the house, which was filled with exotics: roses, lilies,
acanthus, and so many, many more. He walked or rode about Mexico
City, exploring the Diego Rivera frescoes in the Presidential Palace, visiting museums, rug factories, the open markets, the outlying villages.
He studied Spanish. Sometimes—in the evenings—he listened to the

radio, picking up American shows coming in from Los Angeles and San Diego. But what he really liked listening to were classical symphonies and the old Mexican dance songs and Saints' Day songs on his portable Orthophonic, playing them late into the night, hoping for inspiration to revive.

In early June his father sent him one of the new airmail letters the United States had recently begun issuing. The letter had taken only two days to reach him, rather than the usual two weeks, and Crane urged C.A. to continue using them in the future. It was another sign of America's ongoing conquest of time and space. On the other hand, there was nothing new about the advice C.A. doled out with his letter. Harold would have to start living more frugally, it said. After all, he was in Mexico to study and write, not entertain. Business had not been good at Canary Cottage, and the news from Wall Street was especially grim. It may be that C.A. was trying to break the news to his son that he'd suffered serious setbacks with the continuing economic slump. But if this was his intention, he was going to have to shout a lot louder for Harold to hear. "I don't see much of American papers here," Crane wrote back on the 5th, "so anything about the stock market would surprise me." He hoped C.A. was still enjoying the adventures of Sherlock Holmes on the radio. He ended by promising to start being frugal right away, at the same time enclosing a photo of himself as "the bard" in his French sailor's outfit with his silver pony bridle draped about his neck.[18]

But a letter to Malcolm Cowley sent at the same time told a different story. "Maybe it's the altitude (which is a tremendous strain at times) maybe my favorite drink, Tequila; maybe my balls and the beautiful people; or maybe just the flowers that I'm growing or fostering in my garden . . . but it's all too good, so far, to be true," he told Cowley. For the past few weeks he'd been too preoccupied with furnishing the house with everything—"every little nail, griddle, bowl and pillow"—to see much more than a few markets and bars. "No chance to stretch pennies," he added. "Just to spend them." He'd found a drinking buddy in an Irish revolutionary named Ernie O'Malley, "red haired friend of Liam O'Flaherty, shot (and not missed) seventeen times in one conflict and another."[19] They would have made a marvelous pair, Crane and O'Malley, but after three years in Mexico, O'Malley was going back to Dublin.

Weeks before, Crane had sent Harriet Monroe at *Poetry* some of his old poems, which she now returned, at the same time inviting him to send other work and turning him over to the care of her assistant, Morton Zabel. Zabel, enthusiastic about working with him, invited Crane to send prose if he couldn't send poems, and suggested two books of poetry for review: Roy Helton's *Lonesome Water* and James Whaler's *Green River*. Crane accepted the invitation. Zabel also asked him if he'd be interested in doing a Mexican Letter for *Poetry*, but Crane wrote back that he was "too attached to the consciousness" of his own country to attempt tourist sketches.[20] He liked Mexico, but he longed to be back in Patterson. Everyone here, he kept noticing, seemed to love to hate Americans.

Crane in exile, then. Like Hopkins in Dublin. Like Dante, exiled from Florence, wandering the back steps of the houses of the rich, hoping to find a meal and a place to rest his head. By June, Mexico had become Crane's Purgatory. Perhaps it was now that he typed up some twenty lines of a fragment he called "Purgatorio," one of the fruits of his having studied Dante. It was not a polished poem, but there were lines of power and plangency scattered throughout. "My country. O my land, my friends," the poem begins,

> And I apart,—here from you in a land
> Where all your gas lights—faces—sputum gleam
> Like something left, forsaken,—here am I. . . .
> I dream the too-keen cider—the too-soft snow,
> Where are the bayonets that the scorpion may not grow? . . .
> I am unraveled, umbilical anew,
> So ring the church bells here in Mexico . . .[21]

Bells in their towers. How powerful they were, summoning the faithful. But when would he ring out, when summon that heavenly music again, as he had summoned it in the summer of '26? The bells. The bells. To have that power once again. Increasingly, this would become Crane's theme and preoccupation throughout his time in Mexico.

In late June, after nearly two months of relative sobriety, he began drinking heavily again. He was reading Blake by the light of a single candle on the patio of his house just after nightfall one evening when Katherine Anne Porter called from the front gate to tell him how much she liked the flowers he'd had planted around his house. He came in out of the shadows to greet her, declaiming Blake in a drunken voice, then declaiming on the hundreds of flower plants he'd bought that morning at market. This house, he told her, was the only house he'd ever been able to call his own. He loved this house.

The following night, late, he appeared before Porter's gate in a taxi, staggering to keep his balance and shouting that he'd been cheated by yet another goddamned taxi driver and for her to come and pay the bill. It was of course his sad way of crying out, hoping someone would care enough to rescue him. He'd been robbed of every cent he had, he shouted, even as he took a handful of silver coins from his pocket, stared at them, then put them back in his pocket.

Porter paid the driver his fare. She knew from experience Crane would be around in the morning to pay her back. But when he insisted on coming inside to talk and have another drink, she told him flatly to go home and get some sleep. "It was then," she remembered, that he broke into "the monotonous obsessed dull obscenity which was the only language he knew after reaching a certain point of drunkenness." He cursed everyone and everything in sight in that stentorian bellow that could make one's hair stand on edge. *Fuck the moon,* a paraphrase might have run: *And fuck its light. / Fuck the heliotrope, the heaventree, / the sweet-by-night. / Fuck too the air we breathe, / the pool, the sedge. / Fuck too the two small ducks / there huddled at its edge.* "But those were not the things he hated," she understood. "He did not even hate us, for we were nothing to him. He hated and feared himself."[22]

Crane's take on what happened that night was different. He'd spent the afternoon preparing a wonderful meal for Porter and her lover, the ever present, sour-faced Pressly, and when they hadn't shown, he'd passed the time nipping at a bottle of tequila and wondering where the hell his company had disappeared to. Toward evening, he went to a tea at the U.S. Embassy, but arrived so drunk that he had to be forcibly removed from the grounds. Then began a round of stops at the local bars, until he hailed a taxi to take him home. At the gate, sensing he was being overcharged, he refused to pay, insisting that the driver take him to the police station where they would settle the matter. It was on their way there that they'd passed Porter's front gate and he'd shouted out to her to help him. Still upset that they'd stood him up, he told Porter that he certainly had his opinion of her, believing it had been Pressly's intention to humiliate him. He was told that he'd "said something particularly outrageous to her."

What it was he could not now remember, but he did write her a letter of apology, which this time she refused to accept. "Dear Katherine Anne," the note read, "my apologies are becoming so mechanical as (through repetition) to savour of the most negligible insincerity." He placed the blame squarely on "the potency and malfeasance of an overdose of tequila." But he'd already spent a night in a police cell, which was enough of a punishment, surely, for shouting at her. The Mexicans were out to get him, he added, for anti-American feeling was especially strong just now, he realized afterwards, due to recent anti-Mexican episodes north of the border. "I don't ask you to forgive," he pleaded; but since Peggy Cowley was due in Mexico City very shortly to obtain a divorce from Malcolm (the two having separated earlier that year), he hoped for Porter's sake as well as his own that Peggy didn't "step into a truly Greenwich Village scene."[23]

This time, though, the break with Porter was irrevocable. She too had lived in Greenwich Village, she retorted, but never had she been "involved in such a meaningless stupid situation as this." Either he grew up or he should "expect to be treated as a fool." His "emotional hysteria" did not impress her, in fact impressed no one, with the possible exception of "those little hangers-on of literature who feel your tantrums are a mark of genius." They were not, and they added nothing whatever to the value of his poetry. But they did take away the "last shadow of a wish" ever to see him again.[24]

Soon, of course, rumors were circulating around New York about what an ass Hart Crane had made of himself. "It's all very sad and disagreeable," he would try explaining to Lorna Dietz six weeks afterwards. Still, he refused to accept the fact that it was his behavior that had resulted in Porter's inability to get any work done in Mexico. "I'm tired of being made into a bogey or ogre rampant in Mexico and tearing the flesh of delicate ladies," he told Dietz. "I'm also tired of a certain rather southern type of female vanity. And that's about all I ever want to say about Katherine Anne again personally."[25]

At the beginning of July, he received two letters. The first was from Henry Allen Moe, who had by then heard about the fight with Porter. It warned Crane in no uncertain terms to "stay sober, keep out of jail, and get to work." There was "no use or sense in getting mad," Moe explained. Protests had already been filed with "several governmental channels" and he could no longer ignore them, even if he had wanted to, and he didn't. "You are making yourself liable to deportation," he closed, "and, if that happens, your support from the foundation must cease."[26] The message was as bell-clear as Moe could make it. In truth, it was only a miracle that Crane hadn't been knifed in some bar or shot in some back alley for acting as outrageously as he had.

The other letter was from his father, and had been written the same day Moe had written his warning. "My dear Harold," it began. "It isn't surprising to me that after a stay of a few months in Mexico . . . you would find that in this world it isn't all 'tit that titters.'" Life, after all, didn't always work out the way one wanted. There had been a terrible storm in Cleveland that had done a million in damage and left C.A. stranded and shaken on a flooded road in his car. He'd also heard that Hazel's husband was about to lose his job, but then thousands were losing their jobs everywhere now. They'd had two hundred and thirty guests at the Cottage recently, but with prices reduced to attract customers, he didn't know if they'd broken even. He'd begun a new sideline: manufacturing and distributing cheap copies of famous paintings. His own father—now eighty-six—had spent a nice day at the Cottage. Finally, C.A. hoped that Harold would come back to Chagrin Falls once his year in Mexico was over, for Canary Cottage was certainly "the best place on earth" and there were "a lot worse men" than his old father.[27]

It was the last letter Crane was ever to receive from his father. Five days later, on July 6th, there were—suddenly, terribly—two telegrams from his stepmother. The first stated that C.A. had suffered a stroke and urged Crane to return to Chagrin Falls as soon as he could. The second arrived a few hours later, this one informing him that his father had died. Crane went at once to see Simpson and explain what had happened. Then he withdrew all $225 from his Guggenheim account (the money having been made available only days before) and flew out of Mexico City as far as the small plane would take him, which turned out to be Albuquerque. It was the first and only time this poet who had celebrated the advent of the airplane as a twentieth-century phenomenon was ever to fly. But there was no plane out of Albuquerque going anywhere near Cleveland.

Crane telegrammed Bess where he was, then boarded the Santa Fe's Grand Canyon Express, arriving in Chagrin Falls late on the 10th. On the train heading east, he dashed off a letter to Moe, outraged that his character had been so misrepresented by his enemies, and adding that he would make a point of seeing Moe in New York on his way back to Mexico. Just now, however, he had a father to bury.[28] On Saturday, July 11th, C.A. was buried in the family plot in Garrettsville, the town where Harold himself had been born thirty-two years before.

Crane's father was only fifty-six when the stroke killed him. "I don't think he had more than a passing flash of recognition of what had occurred," Crane told Slater Brown afterwards. If there had been misunderstandings between them, most of those had been cleared up during his visit to Chagrin Falls the winter before. In fact, the absence of contact for the past three years with his mother had been more than filled by the affection he felt for Bess, and which she had amply returned. It would take months before his father's estate was settled, but in the meantime he had a roof over his head and the company of people he enjoyed. There would be, he was told by the family lawyer, an annuity of $2,000 a year for the next four years. That was like having four more Guggenheims. After that, he would come into half his father's estate.

For six weeks Crane lived at the Cottage, working with Bess to try to understand how his father's businesses operated on a day-by-day basis. But business matters had always made him nervous, and he was relieved to learn that at least that end of things would be left to Bess. Because the Crane Chocolate Company's assets had been decreasing steadily since 1918, it was decided to terminate that part of the business as soon as possible. And though the Cottage had proven successful, his father had had to borrow against it to open his restaurant. Worse was learning that the depression had rendered all his father's stocks nearly worthless. As it turned out, aside from an initial $500, Crane would receive nothing from what he had supposed was a million-dollar estate.

Nevertheless, that summer he acted the entrepreneur and did what little he could to help Bess straighten out his father's affairs. He saw Loveman (back in Cleveland), the Rychtariks, Bill Wright and his wife. He wrote Morton Zabel about his essay-review, and Louis Untermeyer, asking what Wallace Stevens was up to these days, for the man's poems had meant so much to him. Now there was an original, he noted, and yet what critic had done his work justice? Someday he just might write an essay on Stevens himself. Finally, at the end of August, he said good-bye to Bess and Cleveland and left for New York.

Since his drunken antics in Mexico had been reported in New York, and because he'd not yet recovered from his father's death, Crane holed up at the Hotel Albert, his old familiar. He avoided telling the Patterson crowd that he was in New York, avoided the literati, avoided everyone, in fact, except Carl Carlsen, with whom he spent an evening wandering the Hoboken docks, getting himself blind drunk on needle beer. What he could not avoid were "all the derelicts haunting the streets and alleys" and taking up every bench in the city's parks.[29] How strange to see the new Chrysler Building and the even taller Empire State Building—those brilliant new towers, symbols of the brash old American optimism—looming over the city now in the midst of so much poverty.

Once, walking about the Village, he ran into Slater Brown, now living with his wife and baby over on Twelfth Street. Over lunch at the Browns' apartment, he kept asking Slater if he thought that he— Crane—had ever written a poem worth anything. So much had he come to doubt his own gifts. He saw Moe at the Guggenheim offices in New York and explained as best he could what had happened in Mexico, especially since he hoped to return there shortly. He sent $150 to Peter Christiansen, the Danish sailor he'd met in Paris in the summer of '29 and with whom he had been corresponding, hoping Christiansen might meet him in Mexico; but his friend, richer by a hundred and a half, failed to show, explaining that he had met someone new. Mostly, though, Crane hid in his hotel room and drank.

It was Walker Evans who, finding him in such terrible shape, made sure Crane got his ticket and then deposited him in his cabin on time. At last, on August 29th, Crane set sail once again on the *Orizaba*, bound for the second time in five months for Mexico. At least, he figured, Miss Porter would be on her way to Europe by the time he got back to Mexico City. Good riddance. Of the whole New York crowd, that left only Peggy Cowley—who'd been staying with Porter—to contend with, for she would certainly have been regaled with horror stories by Miss Porter. Well, "CAW! CAW! CAW! for THAT!"[30] Screw them all. He was going after the soul of Mexico.

15 / *VIVA MEXICO!*

Mexico
September 1931–January 1932

He arrived in Vera Cruz on 7 September 1931, in a heat that had sapped him of his strength those last two days on board and now in the city itself: humid, thick weather, which presaged the hurricane that would hit the coast three days later. On the morning of the 8th, he took the train back up to Mexico City and then took a taxi out to his house in Mixcoac. For some time he'd debated whether to return to Mexico at all, finally deciding to stay until the Guggenheim ran out. Within days, however, Daniel and his family had made the house so comfortable and welcoming that he was glad to be back. Everything had been preserved beautifully, and he found the garden a miracle of bloom. "Sunflowers 14 feet high," he crowed, "roses, nasturtiums, violets, dahlias, lilies, cosmos, mignonette."

This time round things would be different. He was going to find the authentic Mexico he had come here in the first place for, the old Mexico buried under a crust of misappellations. This time he would avoid the Mexican literati altogether, as he'd just managed to avoid the New York crowd. He promised himself to "get out more into the smaller cities and pueblos" and become "as thoroughly acquainted with the native Indian population as possible." So when, a few days after his return, he met a young Irish American archeologist from Wisconsin by the name of Milton Rourke who was studying at the University of

Mexico, and who seemed convinced there was a buried Aztec pyramid in the neighborhood of Crane's house, Crane was ecstatic. On September 10th he and Rourke grabbed picks and shovels and spent the
day "digging into the side of a small hill, itself on a vast elevation overlooking the entire valley of Anahuac." It was an area that had long
since been abandoned by the Indians and given over to grazing.

The dig itself had about it the quality of a dream, he told Loveman
afterwards: the marvelous stillness, the sweet scent of grass, and—in
the distance—the two great volcanoes rising, with Lake Texcoco melting into the horizon. And there below: the great city of Mexico. For his
pains, he now had "chips and pieces of the true Aztec pottery picked up
here and there on the surface" and from the dig itself. There was something wonderful and melancholy about finding these shards. It was
like making contact with the past, a sensation no museum could ever
replicate. At one point, he and Rourke had found a fragment of obsidian, "part of a knife blade used either to carve stone and other materials or human flesh." For once, then, something: a taste of the old
Mexico he hungered for.[1]

But the best still lay ahead. On the 12th, he and Rourke packed
up for a five-day visit to Tepotzlán, sixty miles south of Mexico City, a
four-hour trip by train. Crane had read the two books available on the
ancient town: Stuart Chase's *Mexico* and Carleton Beals's *Mexican Maze*,
and now he was anxious to see the place for himself. It lay ten miles east
of Cuernavaca, an Indian settlement isolated by eight-hundred-foot
cliffs that rose precipitously on either side of the town, and far from any
tourist path. The train took them only as far as Porque, after which they
went on by foot, through "tropical verdure forming hanging gardens"
that looked out onto "the beautiful Valley of Morelos," then past the
fortresslike walls "rising in great and irregular ledges covered with tropical foliage . . . flowers, ferns, orchids and waterfalls." The two men
trekked along the mule track in their shabby clothes, each with a bag of
blankets hung over his shoulder, looking for all the world like bums.
Crane was in heaven.

It took three hours by foot—most of it a steep descent—to reach
the town. But it was well worth it, for what they found there was a
Shangri-La of sorts: ancient stone-foundationed houses topped with
brick, tiled roofs and clay-dirt floors. Crane was delighted both by
the laughter of the children and by the open welcome of the Indians.
He and Rourke had been prepared to sleep on the floor of the

monastery, but the local baker invited them to stay with him. And so they slept on a bamboo-slatted bed while the baker, his wife, and two children slept in the only other bed at the other end of the room. Beans and tortillas, long walks in the surrounding fields, evenings at a coffee bar where the young men of the town gathered with guitars after the day's work to sing. And the music of the place, "the strange melancholy tonality" of the Indian men, singing to "the plangent accompaniment of their instruments," dark eyes smiling from beneath great white hats.

They'd arrived, it turned out, on the eve of the Feast of Tepoztecatl, the ancient Aztec god of *pulque*, corn liquor. Crane had noticed the impressive ruins of the god's temple, destroyed centuries earlier by the Spanish, set high on the cliff overlooking one end of the valley. The following day, he and Rourke went out into the cornfields, looking for signs of the older Indian civilization that had flourished here before the coming of the Spanish. Together, they found several fragments of Aztec idols that had been turned over by plows. When they showed these to the elders, they were told some of the legends surrounding Tepoztecatl, even as they were served hot coffee laced with *pulque*. What wonderful people these Indians were, Crane mused, who "still stuck to their ancient rites despite all the oppression of the Spaniards over nearly 400 years." In writing *The Bridge*, except for the New York City cabdriver named Maquokeeta he'd talked with one night, he had had to imagine the Indian through an ersatz American myth and history, and the poem had suffered accordingly. Now he was coming into direct contact with the descendants of the Aztecs. The descent into the essential soil of Mexico had begun in earnest.

That evening, as the sun was setting, Crane and Rourke were drinking tequila at an outdoor coffee bar when they noticed a light on the roof of the cathedral. Suddenly, a drum and flute began playing "the most stirring and haunting kind of savage summons," and they found themselves running toward the cathedral and up the church stairs onto the roof. What they found were several groups of older Indian men—some twenty in all—standing about with lanterns and talking while the drums and flute played on. The musicians, faces turned toward the ruined temple atop its precipice two miles away, played on and on, ceasing only when the sextons rang the great cathedral bells, which called the faithful to prayer at fifteen-minute intervals. When the bells ceased, the drums and flutes resumed. For two hours, this antiphon of response and counterresponse between cathedral gong and tribal flute and drum continued. Then rockets began firing from the parapets of the cathedral, answered by rockets going off from the temple.

"Sitting there," Crane would remember, "on top of that church, with the lightning playing on one horizon, a new moon sinking on the opposite, and with millions of stars overhead and between and with that strange old music beating in one's blood—it was like being in the land of Oz." Two musics, two worlds, each at odds with the other, become now a single reality. "There really did not seem to be a real conflict that amazing night," Crane would tell Bill Wright afterwards, for he'd seen these same Indian elders at mass as well. To witness, as he'd been privileged to witness, such contradictory forces reconciled in the enactments of music! Finally, when the music ended at nine, Crane invited the elders to the bar for a glass of tequila before retiring. In turn they invited the two Americans to join them at 3:00 A.M., when the bells would once again begin ringing in the tower and the drums and flute would play in antiphonal response until sunrise.

It was the music that woke Crane, but not until 5:00 A.M., when he poked Rourke and they ran back to the cathedral for more hot coffee and *pulque* and to "see the sun rise over that marvelous valley to such ringing of bells and wild music as I never expect to hear again." Crane was struck by the presence of an ancient Aztec drum, "a large wooden cylinder, exquisitely carved and showing a figure with animal head, upright, and walking through thick woods." A pre-Conquest drum, "guarded year after year from the destruction of the priests and conquerors, that how many hundreds of times had been beaten to propitiate the god." And here it was, the thing itself, lying on its side, on the roof of the cathedral, while an elder, seated with legs folded, struck it with two heavily padded drumsticks. The night before, this same drum had echoed through the valley from its place of honor in the distant ruined temple. Now it had been brought here to greet the rising god.

And then, as the sun began to come up and the excitement mounted to a near-impossible pitch, the man who had been playing the ancient drum suddenly placed two sticks in Crane's hands and nodded. Crane was stunned. Never had he heard of any American being allowed to participate like this in the *pulque* ceremony before. "It seemed too good to be true, really," he would tell Bill Wright, "that I, who had expected to be thrown off the roof when I entered the evening before, should now be invited to actually participate." Somehow, he managed to maintain "the exact rhythm with all due accents" he'd been listening to for the last several hours, even working in his own rift, "based on the lighter tattoo of the more modern drum of the evening before." And though the heavy drumsticks soon tired his forearms, he believed he'd been a hit, and that the old men would have embraced him had decorum allowed. Several, in fact, did put their arms around his shoulders and walked back and forth with him the entire length of the roof as the bells rang and "the whole place seemed to go mad in the refulgence of full day."

Wonderful as it had been to hear those great bells ringing, however, it had been "inestimably better to see the sextons wield the hammers, swinging on them with the full weight of their entire bodies like frantic acrobats," even as rockets burst into that bell-thronged sunrise before they disappeared.[2] There would be other memories of Tepotzlán: bathing with an Indian lad in a mountain pool and meeting the vicar of the cathedral. But these were dying falls compared to what he had experienced atop the cathedral, where he had helped summon God into this old upon old, ever fresh New World.

A week after his return to Mixcoac, Crane went down to visit Bill Spratling in Taxco for a second time. It was there, in late September, that he met the Mexican painter David Siqueiros, just released from prison and out on bail for his alleged part in some Communist plot. Knowing Siqueiros was desperate for funds, Spratling had commissioned a self-portrait, and Crane—in spite of barely having enough left to pay his rent and other necessary expenses—did his part by buying a small watercolor showing the head of an Indian boy and then commissioning a self-portrait of his own. Siqueiros began work on the portrait at once. It was a large painting—four feet by two and a half—and it showed Crane reading, head bowed as if in prayer. So intense was Crane's gaze, however, that Siqueiros painted the eyes shut. It was, prophetically, as if he were painting Crane's death mask. "Astounding," Crane would tell the Rychtariks after the painting was finished. "When photographs are made I'll have to send you one." He had no idea how he was going to get something that big back north, but he now had a painting by "the greatest of contemporary Mexican painters." Somehow the man had managed to spread the very "soil of Mexico . . . on his canvasses."[3]

The soil of Mexico. *That* was what Crane was after. One night, while at a bar in Taxco, he was talking in his cups with Lesley Simpson, an American historian studying Mexican culture, about what he was in Mexico trying to do. He wanted to write a poem, a poetic drama, on the Conquest, to capture the exact moment of contact between the Spanish and the indigenous populations—Cortés and Montezuma. No, he had no idea yet how he was going to do that beyond absorbing as much of the culture as he could. He knew little Spanish and what he knew of Mexico he'd gleaned from reading Prescott. Lesley, also in his cups, began giving Crane a long reading list, explaining that Crane's ideas about the Conquest were too naive. Finally, Crane exploded. Goddamn it, he shouted, you didn't write poetry by reading goddamn books but by living the life. And with that he stormed out of the bar.

But later that night, in the midst of a tropical downpour, he burst into the room Simpson was sharing with his friend, Paul Taylor, and began arguing again about the poetics of history. Taylor took Simpson's side, maintaining that it would take years of serious reading before Crane could ever write convincingly of a matter as complex as the Conquest. Again Crane shot back. The way one wrote about a place and a people was to let the traditions of a country soak into one's blood and then, with time and patience, one wrote out of that spirit. Back and forth the two went at it until two o'clock in the morning, when Simpson intervened and quietly led Crane back to Spratling's house. By then Crane was feeling awful about the nuisance he'd made of himself. Suddenly, he put his arm around Simpson's neck. "Lesley," he said, "I love you!" He'd poured his heart out to these two men, trying to understand for himself what he was up against in attempting to touch the heart of a country he had come to love, but which—except in isolate flecks—still refused a closer embrace.

Ironically, much of what Crane was looking for in Mexico he found right under his nose. "You should see these native Indian people," he wrote Mony Grunberg. Not the people in power—to hell with them—but the people of "mixed Spanish and Indian blood." Sure they were "dumb as hell in a thousand ways," but they were also wiser "than all our mad, rushing crowd up north." The North was too cerebral, always trying to analyze, sort things out. It was not meaning he was after now, but being, "UN-thought," something closer to the soil, the beautiful brown skin and dark eyes, "white pyjama suits, sandals, dirt, indigestion, faith, doubt, elation, resignation." Something basic, the fundamental hue, "a contact with the soil and earth and the blue of the mountains hereabouts." How glad he was that he hadn't returned to

Europe, for Mexico had proved far stranger than anything Europe could offer. It was far, far more beautiful and more dangerous. It was in fact turning out to be "a perfect Calvary in a thousand ways."[4]

At the beginning of November, Crane watched with fascination as the Indians celebrated the Day of the Dead. "The last two days have been important on the native Indian calendar," he wrote the Rychtariks on the 4th. All over Mexico, as here in Mexico City, the cemeteries were "full of darkskinned men and women, whole families in fact, sitting on tombstones day and night holding lighted candles to the spirits of the dead." How merry these Indians were, whole families drinking and eating with their beloved dead; then, in the evening, "setting off firecrackers made in the image of Judas." Toys in the shapes of skeletons, skulls made of paper and clay: all for sale in the markets, as well as "beautiful trays, crockery, serapes, toys, etc., from all the provinces as would drive you wild," and far better than any museum artifact he'd ever seen.[5]

He watched Daniel and his two brothers—two muscled, uniformed local police officers, who in turn watched over his little walled fortress with its iron gates. And soon Daniel's relatives and friends were coming over to the house in the evenings to sing the old songs and dance the old dances and drink tequila and beer. And the flowers—everywhere flowers, so that it was all Crane could do to keep his rooms from looking like mortuary chapels. Stacks of sugar cane and corn stalks, myrtle wreaths hung on the walls, daisies, nasturtiums, roses, Calla lilies, violets, heliotrope, cannas . . . cosmos, sunflowers, phlox, iris, and scores of other tropical flowers whose names he did not know. He was coming to depend more and more on Daniel, and had now given his *mozo* the additional task of accompanying him whenever he went out in order to take care of Crane's money and bargain with those thieving taxi drivers in advance about the price for getting Señor Crane home after a night on the town. But mostly he did his drinking at home—tequila, or Old Nick Jamaican rum—to avoid spending another night in jail and losing everything.

During his first weeks back in Mexico Crane had steered clear of Peggy Cowley, afraid that Katherine Anne Porter's reports of his behavior had poisoned her toward him. Malcolm had written him that spring, asking him to look in on Peggy and help her get adjusted while she waited for their divorce to come through. But then had come the news of his father's death and his sudden return home. Before leaving, he had sent Peggy a note inviting her to use his house while he was away, but she'd opted instead to stay with Porter until she could find a place of her own. Would she even speak to him now? he wondered.

As it turned out, Peggy was delighted to see him, especially as they were each other's closest link with New York and Patterson. And soon they were going everywhere together, taking long walks—often with Lesley Simpson—through the streets of the city and its great parks. When Peggy got sick, it was Crane who brought her food and read to her. When he went shopping in the open markets, he brought his bargains to her for her to admire. He kept Cowley updated about her health. "I'm glad to be of any help I can to Peggy," he wrote him, "love her as always, and enjoy her company . . . immensely." Old friends were always a godsend, and besides, Peggy had turned out to be one terrific sport.[6]

Elfin, fey, diminutive, with unusual dark yellow eyes. Youthful. That was how Sue Brown remembered her, in spite of the fact that Peggy was forty-four that fall of '31. Peggy was also undemanding and dependent, rather "like a well disposed child." And, Sue believed, Peggy looked rather like the younger Grace Crane, at least in the pictures Crane had shown her, only nicer.[7] In fact, it was Peggy's vulnerability and docility, qualities so unlike Grace Crane, which so appealed to Crane and made him feel protective of this woman twelve years his senior. With $2,000 expected from his father's estate, he could afford for the first time in his life to act like a man of substance. He would spend it all, but not more than he had. Here in Mexico he and Peggy would reenact his parents' relationship as it might have been. He had plans, great plans, and Peggy would be part of those plans.

Peggy would remember the two of them walking the streets of the great city while Crane invented lives for the people they passed. This one was a pimp, he assured her, this one a murderer, this woman a clever whore, this one a femme fatale, and this one—like himself—a veritable prince in disguise. A housewife, shopping bag over her arm: buffo! transformed instantly into a mincing tart, swishing her ass, up to no good. They strolled through the markets, buying whatever caught their fancies: statues of saints, blown glass, even flowers, in spite of Crane's house being already laden down with them. Orchids, he explained. These were orchids and tuberoses, two specimens his garden did *not* have.

When he had cash, Crane could be extremely generous. He had a house, he said, that could fit sixty, so why not fill it? He allowed Milton Rourke to come and go as he wished, and Rourke took ample advantage of the situation. A sponger, Simpson called him, "a queer, a fuzzy Marxist, *and* a sponger, all in one."[8] Crane, who didn't give a damn about abstract theories, often grew tired of Rourke's Marxist tirades, but he liked the man, and that was enough. He gave a party for two young Americans touring Mexico in a Lincoln sedan, in the midst of which one of the boys, a quart of tequila under his belt, suddenly clambered up onto Crane's roof, drew the ladder after him, and began ripping tiles off to hurl down onto his neighbor's courtyard. "I nearly had heart failure before we got him down," Crane confessed to the Rychtariks afterwards, "since my neighbor is a crack shot, and the provocations for shooting are much less here in Mexico than anywhere I know."[9]

As the weather grew colder, he came down with the grippe. To keep warm, he began drinking a brandy and port potion until once again he was raving drunk. Having decided in his intoxicated state that he'd not heard from enough of the friends to whom he'd spent precious hours writing, Crane chose to have it out with the local postal authorities. To make an impression on them, he donned the full Indian regalia he had come to admire: white pajamas, sandals, red waist sash, a serape over his shoulders, and a two-foot straw sombrero tilted on the back of his head and tied under his chin with a colorful cord. To top it all off, he draped his prize silver bridle about his neck. He did not seem to understand that his outfit mocked the Indians he loved.

He was still drinking two days later when he showed up in front of Peggy's apartment late on the afternoon of the 12th. Simpson and Peggy were inside when they heard shouting out on the street and saw a crowd assembling. From the balcony they could see Crane down in the courtyard, red-faced, puffing on a cigar, and shouting at a taxi driver. A few minutes later, he staggered up the stairs and into Peggy's room, goddamning the Mexicans for the thieving sonsofbitches they were. He would *not* pay the outrageous cab fare, cop or no cop!

The mention of a police officer prompted Simpson to go down and try to straighten things out. There was the driver; there was Daniel, trying to melt into the background; and there was the crowd, grinning, along with two police officers. For two and a half hours, the driver insisted—with Daniel nodding—that crazy gringo had had him drive around Mexico City. Now he wanted to be paid. So there it was. When Simpson told Crane he'd have to pay up, Crane cursed him as well. Finally, he took nine *tostones* from his pocket and handed them over to the police officer, who in turn handed them over to the taxi driver.

If Simpson hadn't taken care of matters by giving the driver a large tip in addition to the fare, Crane would have been hauled off to jail for making a public nuisance of himself. Even after the cab left and he was back in Peggy's apartment, Crane was still shouting that he'd been cheated, outraged that Simpson and Peggy had taken sides against him. Peggy had had enough. But when she asked Crane to leave, Simpson prevailed on her to let him stay until dusk. That way Simpson had a better chance of getting Crane home without some Indian killing him for wearing such an insulting and stupid outfit.

On the evening of November 15th, David Siqueiros, ill with malaria, arrived from Taxco, along with his wife and doctors, to stay with Crane. So sick was he, in fact, that he had to be carried into the house on a stretcher. Taxco was too provincial to have the kind of doctors Siqueiros needed now, for his fever had been mounting steadily for a week, and he'd had to be rushed to Mexico City. When Siqueiros's wife had telegrammed, asking Crane to let them stay there until the worst was over, Crane had consented. Siqueiros had contacted a disease while traveling through the tropics of Acapulco, Crane had learned to his amazement: a country so isolated the Indians there wore the same dress Cortés had found their ancestors wearing four centuries earlier. What a land this was: vaster than any map could show, and layered with hundreds of "races and cultures scattered in the million gorges and valleys which make the scenery so plastic and superb."[10] Siqueiros would pull through, he believed, though he would probably have to stay with him for several months until he had sufficiently recovered. But within days Siqueiros was well enough to be hotly debating the fine points of Marxism with his friends there in Crane's living room, Rourke translating so that Crane could join in the discussion.

At first, Crane was delighted to have such distinguished company. After all, he had three rooms he never used, and even now the house didn't feel particularly crowded. But as his guests stayed on and the food and liquor bills mounted, and the debates continued into the early morning hours, Crane bolted. He stayed one night at the Mancera to get some rest, and then, on the morning of November 20th, took the train down to Tepotzlán to spend the weekend wandering through the countryside a second time. He bathed in the cold mountain streams, and on the 22nd walked thirty-five miles, most of it lost in the mountains, until—exhausted—he at last came across a railroad spur and followed it to a water station outside Cuernavaca. He was so parched that he gulped water from an engine trough until he could drink no more. That had been enough adventure for one weekend, and he took the first train he could back to Mexico City. By the time he returned, Siqueiros was up and about. Another week, and Crane would have his house to himself again.

By then he'd managed one review for *Poetry* and was stalled on the second. The Muse he'd waited for daily had still not come. "These are dull times for poetry," he confessed to Eda Lou Walton on the 27th. H. L. Mencken had said it, and he was in no position to disagree. The world really was in a state of social chaos, so what satisfaction could there be in spinning out more lyrics dealing with "mere personal moods and attitudes."[11] He'd already done all of those he wanted in *White Buildings* and the "Key West" sheaf. After all, he'd come here after something deeper and more profound. True, nothing had yet been written, but then he'd been warned repeatedly that it would take time before Mexico gave herself to him. So much to see and do, and still the language to master. And yet, how much better to be here than sitting in some office in New York, going over advertising accounts. In any event, the depression had knocked out any possibility of his finding a decent job up there. Maybe, when he got back, he *would* try teaching English literature at some small private college somewhere.

Three days later, writing to Underwood, Crane picked up again on the theme of the Indian. "The nature of the Mexican Indian, as Lawrence said, isn't exactly 'sunny,'" he began, "but he is more stirred by the moon, if you get what I mean, than any type I've ever known." He was speaking expressly of the Indian's sexual nature. And while Beardsleyan decadence—"the fluttering gait and the powder puff"— were unheard of in Mexico, "ambidexterity"—by which he meant bisexuality—was in "the fullest masculine tradition," as Crane knew now from his own "trials and observations." The "pure Indian type," he'd decided, was "the most beautiful animal imaginable, including the Polynesian." He loved the silken, "rich coffee brown" color of these people; he loved the extraordinary musical pitch of their voices. In fact, the very shape of their heads, he'd been amazed to find out, was identical with those "fragments of ancestral idols" he'd picked up in the cornfields of Tepotzlán.[12]

That was the one side of it. The other was the Indians' profound religious fervor. On the evening of December 12th—the four hundredth anniversary of the Feast of Our Lady of Guadalupe, patroness of Mexico—he reported back to Bess what he'd seen that day in Mexico City. He could still smell the sulfurous whiff of exploded gunpowder in the air and see the rockets "whizzing up sporadically for miles around, and the sound of church bells far and near." Preparations had been going on for weeks as some two hundred thousand pilgrims—most of them Indians—from all over the country continued to pour into the city, and they would be there until New Year's. That very day all of them, plus several hundred thousand from Mexico City itself, had walked out to Guadalupe Hidalgo, a suburb of the city, to the great cathedral there, which had been erected near the site where the Virgin had made her first appearance to an Indian convert named Juan Diego on this day in 1532.

Not wanting to miss any of it, Crane had hired a cab, risen at four, and with Daniel in tow had reached the cathedral just as dawn was breaking. He'd tried to elbow his way inside, but the crowds had been so thick he'd finally given up, settling instead to watch the Indian dances in progress everywhere, right up to the front steps of the cathedral itself. "Certain people are picked from each district or tribe for their marked ability," he explained, fascinated by the whole ritual, "and there is quite a rivalry between districts." He watched amazed as groups of twenty-five to fifty people, dressed in skirts, pantaloons, and feathered crests, danced and danced in circles, swaying and turning, their banners waving, to the music of guitars. And weaving in and out everywhere masked figures, among them Death and the Devil.

For three hours he'd watched, caught up by the bells ringing in the high towers, the flutes and the drums, as he pushed and shoved his way among the churning, protean crowds, one more drop in that massive wave of humanity, until by 9:30 A.M. he was ready to call it quits. Tourist that he was, he'd made the mistake of trying to photograph some of the dancers and had nearly caused a riot, from which Daniel had had to extricate him, explaining to the angry crowds that the gringo had meant no harm. This dancing, Crane had learned, was not your "Mardi-Gras mood . . . despite the flamboyant colors of their costumes," but something "serious and very set and formal," very old and very sacred. All night they had danced, and they would go on dancing all that day, and so on for another two weeks. And all this "for the sake of a ritual and not a cent of money."

Crane could only admire their devotion. To see this too was why he had come to Mexico: the Virgin miraculously uniting "the teachings of the early Catholic missionaries with . . . the old Indian myths and pagan cults." How "illogical and baffling" these people were, he sighed, and yet how appealing. Our Lady of Guadalupe: the beautiful "Goddess of the Mexican masses," her image everywhere—inside the hatbands of sombreros, on postcards, stenciled "above the windshield facing half the taxi drivers of Mexico," offering protection and good luck. He too would have to wear her image now, if only to protect himself "against the wiles and extortions" of some of those same taxi drivers.[13]

At the beginning of December, having caught one too many colds, Peggy abandoned the high thin air of Mexico City for Taxco. Bill Spratling had located a house for her there, on a summit, but still several thousand feet closer to sea level than where she'd been living in the capital. Crane helped her pack and promised to visit her at Christmas. But no sooner had she left than he began to miss her. He kept sending her messages and telegrams until finally—three days before Christmas—he took the bus down to Taxco to see her. She was taking a bath when her maid spied him climbing the steep steps to the house. Quickly she dressed and ran down the steps to embrace him, her maid and gardener looking on and smiling. It would have been "a waste of breath to make it clear," she would note afterwards, that "he wasn't 'mine' in their sense of the word."[14] He needed to be there with her, he told her. He would work quietly, he would give her her space; but he needed to be near her.

When Spratling came over that evening to give her a pair of silver earrings, he and Crane insisted she put them on immediately. When she came back down, she was wearing a dress to match. Crane took one look at her, whirled her about, then looked her over carefully. "I'll fall in love with you," he joked. Then added, "Of course I really am already." After Spratling left, the two sat up talking, Peggy mentioning that it didn't seem like Christmas here without the green and red decorations one found back in the States. The following morning, Crane took Peggy's servants into town, returning later with two hundred green and red poinsettias in a four-foot-long arrangement. The festivities had begun.

There had been *posadas*, large public parties, in Taxco going on for the nine nights preceding Christmas, and now Crane joined in, including attending a dance at the mayor's house with copious brandy toasts. He also attended Christmas midnight mass at the cathedral, and though he was drunk, he managed to keep an air of decorum about himself. But when he saw the Indians kneeling all around him, their faith so real as to be almost palpable, he nearly wept. Christmas Day a dozen guests came down from Mexico City to Peggy's, all of whom returned that night, except for Crane. He stayed on, as it turned out, until after the New Year.

"Peggy and I had the pleasantest Christmas and New Years together that I remember for ages," he wrote Malcolm nine days into the New Year. Her "usual mixed crowd" had been there for Christmas, but he had "stayed long enough to enjoy a week alone with her." Crane said nothing of what went on during that week, except that he loved Taxco and its people, though not the large numbers of Yankees who would ultimately seal the town's doom with their money. Among those who had come down to enjoy Peggy's hospitality, he told Cowley, were Witter Bynner, the American poet; Clinton King, and the woman King would soon marry; and Lady Duff Twysden—prototype for Brett in Hemingway's *The Sun Also Rises*. Christmas night they'd all shouted lewd limericks (Cowley's among them) from the rooftops and in general made fools of themselves. It had been a thoroughly mad crowd, he added, though he'd had "enough Duff—preferring, as I do, the nautical variety." It was a veiled sexual pun, which at this juncture was meant to escape Cowley.

Three dogs, belonging to Natalie Scott, the owner of the house, and two aigrettes "making love continuously to the tune of quack-quack-quack"—Gretchen and Charles, Crane named them—"though I could never distinguish one from the other, except at certain critical moments in their dialogue."[15] It too was code for what had happened between Crane and Peggy that Christmas night in Taxco. After he and

Peggy had seen her guests off on the bus back to Mexico City, the two of them had had a quiet drink in the cantina. They would stay off drinking, they promised each other. And they would work. But the cathedral bells, which seemed to drown out everything, suddenly interrupted their quiet talk.

Back up at the house above the church towers, the sound of bells clanged on and on unimpeded. Nothing for it then but to walk back into town and join the fireworks and dancing in the plaza below. Late into the night they danced and drank and danced some more. "It's all a poem and I shall write it," Peggy thought she remembered him telling her, "with us right in the middle of it, darling." That night they made love together in Peggy's bed while the bells tolled solemnly, insistently, connubially on.

In the morning, Peggy's servant brought a tray of coffee and orange juice to the two of them as they lay there in bed. Had what happened really happened? Crane wondered. Had he really made love to a woman? He kept looking at her and laughing, stunned and delighted with himself. Later that day, he swaggered into Doña Berta's bar, announcing to the small gathering of Americans there, that, yes, he had done it. No. Peggy had done it, Peggy had performed the miracle. Back at her house, he began work on a poem that would come to bear the prophetic title "The Broken Tower." For three days he worked at it, the phonograph playing against the clanging of the bells. He seemed frightened and purified by it all, Peggy would insist many years later. Once, he told her, he'd stood on the Brooklyn Bridge as the fleet steamed up the East River. There he was, he'd sighed, with "the entire Navy streaming between my legs!" And now look at him, sleeping with a woman!

For now they would keep the affair a secret, both when they were together in Mexico City and in their letters. But their letters to each other were a different story. When Grace discovered Peggy's letters to her son among his belongings later that year, she was horrified. She could imagine—barely—a woman saying such things to a man in the heat of passion. But to commit them to paper?! Nothing for it then but to destroy every last letter of Miss Cowley's.

Crane's letters fared better in Peggy's keeping. On 5 January 1932, he returned to Mixcoac to find Daniel "drunk as usual," though he did manage to draw Crane a hot bath before falling asleep. When Crane awoke, he was delighted to find "old Mizzentop"—he meant his phallus, named after the old lookout on Quaker Hill he'd evoked in *The Bridge*—"flaunting the colors still in valiant dreams" of Peggy. He dashed a letter off to her, confessing once more his love for her. He'd been in a state of "sheer delirium," he told her, the whole trip up from Taxco. Already he and Mizzentop missed her.[16] "Old Mizzentop doesn't like air pockets," he wrote her the following day. "Nor standing so long without an occasional tumble."[17]

Because Crane had never laid down strict guidelines with Daniel, who had seen his boss drunk so many times, Daniel no longer cared what Señor Crane thought. Crane was beside himself. Things were so out of control that six nights after Crane's return, Daniel rolled in so drunk he could hardly stand. It was a strange reversal of roles for Crane, who—with his new sense of responsibility—was off liquor for the moment. How he wished he could just rent this damned place, clear out, and get back down to Taxco with Peggy. Worse, it was so cold in the city "that Old Mizzentop would surely have all sorts of excuses for . . . meanderings" around Mixcoac, he told her, though he was still being faithful.[18] "Your love is very precious to me," he wrote her a week later. "It gives me an assurance that I thought long buried. You can give me many things besides—if time proves me fit to receive them: the independence of my mind and soul again, and perhaps a real wholeness to my body."[19]

Although the review he'd promised Morton Zabel months before remained stalled, he still tried to keep up with other literary matters: comments on a group of poems Malcolm Cowley had sent him, articles his friends in Mexico had written and which he tried now to place in magazines back in the States. He followed the literary exchange between Cowley in *The New Republic* and Munson in *Contempo*, though he soon grew embarrassed for them both. He read D. H. Lawrence's novel on the death and sexual resurrection of Christ, *The Man Who Died*—a gift from Underwood—and wrote Underwood on January 15th to explain that the novel had had more to tell him in his "present state of mind—than any book in the Bible." He'd also been perusing the pages of a "burlesque-ad magazine" called *Hooey*, edited by one O. Swish, with ads for *B. Hinds Cream* and a product called *More Bananas*. Finally, he turned serious and confessed to Underwood that he'd just "broken ranks" with the brotherhood for the first time in his life. "The ex-wife of an old friend," he added. Would Underwood ever forgive this betrayal?[20]

After two weeks in Mixcoac, Crane went back down to Taxco on the 20th, arriving just in time for a local fiesta in which animals were decked out in gaudy outfits and paraded through the town to be blessed by the local priest. "Whores," Crane spat. These cats and dogs were nothing but whores dressed up for some Easter parade. A week later, on the 27th, plagued by insomnia, he awoke before daybreak and walked down into the village square. There he met the old Indian bell-ringer on his way to the church of St. Prisca, who invited him up into the tower to help ring the bells. As Crane pulled at the rope, swept up once more by the powerful sound of bells summoning the faithful, the sun rose as it had for the past million years over the mountains. Crane was ecstatic. Afterwards, Lesley Simpson would remember, Crane climbed back up the hill to Peggy's house "in a sort of frenzy, refused his breakfast, and paced up and down the porch" until Simpson could accompany him back down to the plaza, where they sat in the shadow of the church, "Hart the while pouring out a magnificent cascade of words."[21]

Simpson had seen Crane now in both his depressed and manic moods, had remembered his saying, when he'd read aloud a passage from *Moby-Dick* the previous fall, that *that* was what poetry was, and that once he too had written words to rival it. *The Bridge*, he'd added, though he doubted he would ever do anything as good again. Later, Crane had read *The Bridge* for Simpson and his wife—the whole magnificent sweep of the poem from beginning to end—tears in his glittering eyes, and afterwards he'd put the book down and said, quietly, reverently, that, yes, the poem really was great. And it was, Simpson agreed. And immense. That evening was "the high point of Hart's year in Mexico," Simpson would say afterwards, and "in that mood he could have written his epic of the Conquest, or anything else."[22]

And now, for the first time since the summer of '26, Crane was on fire again, really on fire. For several days he worked feverishly at "The Broken Tower" in Peggy's house, trying to put into words the new sense of himself he wanted to believe that his purifying love for Peggy had given him. That and of course so many other things: the poet summoning the Word just as the sexton had summoned the dawn in the ringing of those bells. One afternoon, in fact, Peggy went with him up into the tower and snapped a picture of him with the old sexton standing behind him, impassive as the ages. The poem advanced during those three days, but it was still far from finished when Crane at last left his room on the evening of the 29th to go back into town. Later that evening, Peggy would recall, a tiny *mozo* had come up the hill with a note. Señor Crane had gotten himself into some kind of "scrape" with the law and was now in jail.

Although she would insist that she never did learn what Crane had done, Peggy knew that something more than drinking had gotten him locked up, for she refused to see him off when he paid his fine the following day and took the first bus out of town. Anyone who got drunk publicly in Mexico was subject to jail and a fine, Spratling tried to reassure her after Crane had left Taxco. And being a foreigner, Crane had been fined three times what Spratling's houseboy had been fined. Houseboy? In fact, what had happened was that Crane had been caught groping the boy in some alley and subsequently warned by the local magistrate in no uncertain terms to stay the hell out of town after nightfall. Crane would never see Taxco again.

16 / THE BROKEN TOWER

MEXICO
FEBRUARY–APRIL 1932

WHEN HE RETURNED TO MIXCOAC at the end of January 1932, Crane found his house in shambles and—worse—his typewriter damaged. In his absence, Rourke had managed to break it. Crane, who had himself made typewriters fly, could forgive almost anything, but he could not forgive Rourke this. He was in no mood to listen to Marxist arguments about communal property and he invited Rourke to vacate the house at once. When Rourke refused, claiming he was still weak with jaundice and where would he go, Crane picked him up bodily and threw him off his property. "The crisis," Lesley Simpson later reported, "put Hart squarely back into the middle class."[1] In the absence of his typewriter, Crane began telegramming Peggy, begging her to join him in Mexico City, which after some prompting she finally did.

They met at the Broadway restaurant for lunch, Crane in a white linen suit, she in a dress, for which he provided an orchid corsage. After lunch, he took her by cab to see a film starring Charlie Chaplin at a theater in what—to their dismay—turned out to be one of the worst slums of the city. There were piles of garbage everywhere and the theater itself stank of stale urine. The locals, astonished to see two Americans in such finery, poked each other and stared. But Crane was eager to see the man who had stood in for himself for so many years up there on the samite-sheeted silver screen again, going through his collapses and pirouettes, and soon Crane was once more laughing through his tears. So much, so much had happened in the years since he'd written his poem in honor of two comedians as the letter C.

By the time Peggy returned to Taxco in early February, she and Crane had decided to go public with their relationship. "Don't know how long I'm going to remain here," Crane wrote Mony Grunberg on February 8th. "Hate it and love it alternately." At the moment he was drunk "on the first impressive poem" he'd done in two years and could "feel the old confidence" rising in him again. He'd always been a poet for whom love had served as his first Muse—even more than geography—and now, he believed, poetry had returned because he was "in love again as never quite before." The only difference, he added, was that for the first time in his life, he'd "broken ranks" with his "much advertised 'brotherhood,'" bedding a woman he'd "known for years" who had suddenly and astonishingly claimed "her own." Nor was he sorry, for the relationship had given him "new perspectives, and after many tears and groans . . . something of a reason for living."

He enclosed the still-halting opening stanzas of the poem he was working on, drunk with something he saw there, in this, the first real poem the Muses had sent his way in two years. "The bell cord that gathers God at dawn," it began, "Dispatches me." That angelus, that visionary music, that new language which he had served and which had sent him out as its witness, was also killing him, as surely as God's prophets had been killed, or God's son. It was as if he were falling, as he had fallen in "For the Marriage of Faustus and Helen" ten years—a hundred years—before, but this time he was falling

> down the knell
> Of the new day . . . I could wander the cathedral lawn
> Clear to the crucifix, and back again from hell.

Did no one else hear it, nor see even for a moment what he saw and heard: those great shadows in the tower, calling him to God? *The Bridge.* That had been one great myth, one way to articulate a transcendent reality. And surely these great towers—at Taxco, at Tepotzlán, at Vera Cruz, at Our Lady of Guadalupe, even here in Mixcoac—surely they lent another myth to God? Or was it all one great delusion only?

Haven't you seen—or ever heard those stark
Black shadows in the tower, that drive
The clarion turn of God?—to fall and then embark
On echoes of an ancient, universal hive?

The bells, I say, the bells have broken their tower!
And sing, I know not where . . . Their tongues engrave
My terror mid the unharnessed skies they shower;
I am their scattered—and their sexton slave.

And so it was, I entered the broken world—
To hold the visionary company of love, its voice
An instant in a hurricane (I know not whither hurled)
But never—no, to make a final choice! . . .[2]

A week later, he wrote Underwood an even fuller explanation of the reasons for his affair with Peggy. She was, he phrased it bluntly, an extension of his sexual dominions, language he was sure Underwood would understand. How long the affair would last he had no idea, nor had he "engaged in . . . promises of any sort," but he did think, as he'd told Grunberg, that the affair had done him "considerable good." The old male beauty could still make itself felt, and his eye roamed as much as ever, for he doubted he was ever going to "change very fundamentally." In fact, until recently he'd been seeing some "gorgeous Jorge," that is, until Jorge had run off with one of his suits. For the time being he was keeping his options open, making no final choices.[3] In time he also wrote Bess, the Rychtariks, and then Cowley himself about his new relationship with Peggy.

"Up late for the past two nights, writing countless letters," he wrote Peggy on February 10th. He was sipping tequila and "walking back and forth the length of the room," with the Victrola playing some records he'd earlier played for her. He was working on the opening lines of "The Broken Tower," making change after change, while his little white Spitz, Paloma, lay at his feet, keeping time with her tail to the *clack clicketty clack* of the typewriter. "There's nothing quite like the devotion and obedience of a dog," he wrote Bess, and this dog seemed "to get smarter and more accomplished every day."[4] "The only trouble, he sighed, was Daniel, who strutted about as though *he* were master of the house and Crane some unwelcome guest. He would have loved to sack his goddamned *mozo*, except that Daniel knew enough about his private life to see him behind bars for a long time if Crane ever tried anything like that.

On top of which Crane could not help noticing that Daniel had taken to carrying a knife and a gun in his waistband, so that even when he stumbled in blind drunk late at night, Crane was afraid to reprimand him. Lisa, a friend of Siqueiros's who'd stayed on with Crane after Siqueiros had returned to Taxco, had also warned Crane not to try to fire Daniel, who knew "half the police in Mixcoac," and knew too that Crane did not keep a gun about the place.[5] Because of her own leftist politics, she herself had much to fear from Daniel. Still, something had to be done. So, in spite of perceived threats, Crane called on his landlord to explain the situation with Daniel. Within days Daniel was working for the general who lived next door, though Daniel and his family continued living with Crane. Another *mozo* would be found for Crane, it was half-heartedly determined, and Lisa would stay on to cook.

And then there were Peggy's troubles. When she returned to Taxco after visiting Crane, she found scorpions crawling all over the house. Moreover, the owners were eager now to sell the place rather than continue renting. As soon as Crane heard about this, he invited Peggy to come back up to Mixcoac and live with him, at the same time making it clear that, while he missed her "mucho, mucho, mucho," he did not want either of them urging "the other into anything but the most spontaneous and mutually liberal arrangements."[6] They both knew what that meant. The servant problem, he assured her, would soon be solved. Those assurances he had made on the 11th. But he was in no condition to tell anyone what to do, much less his servant.

Four nights later, having screwed up his courage by getting drunk, Crane finally had his heart-to-heart with Daniel, who was also properly drunk. Far into the night he lectured Daniel on the virtues of sobriety, "meanwhile pouring him glass after glass of Tenampa," while Daniel talked affectionately of "our Pegguié." Crane was also well aware that Peggy could match him drink for drink, and he wondered now if she really was staying off the booze down there, especially with "a great little tanker" like her friend, Luz, around. And just how lonely were her nights with Luz around to keep her company? They were the self-reflexive comments of a man in his cups, haunted by loneliness and rejection. As long as Peggy didn't let her right hand know what her left was doing, he joked, he promised to do the same. "Ahoy and ahoy and AHOY," he closed his letter. That should have let Peggy know where his own thoughts were as he headed out the door for the night.[7]

The domestic truce at Mixcoac, tenuous at best, fell apart within days, and soon Crane was raging at Daniel again, this time because Lisa had discovered Crane's watch and fob in Daniel's cabin, and because Daniel—in spite of being lectured to, had come home drunk once more. He was sick and tired of being run by servants, Crane shouted at Daniel. What he really needed around the house was a nice Indian boy from Taxco. But this was as nothing compared to what he was hearing about goings-on back up north. His friends, it had turned out, were all becoming social reformers. Some were writing for *The New Republic*, others for the more radical *New Masses*, and still others were even taking part in political activities that might get them shot. What had happened to the self-exiled artist in his tower? Cowley and Frank, for instance, along with fifty others, Edmund Wilson improbably among them, had driven all the way to Bell County, Kentucky, in three rickety trucks, bringing food and relief supplies to striking coal miners and their families, hoping to draw national attention in that way to the miners' plight. Cowley and Frank and Bunny Wilson—what an unlikely combination! But common suffering just might "weld a friendship there, after all," he surmised.[8]

Besides, this class struggle thing was really an international affair, he'd learned from his Marxist friends in Mexico. Even here, "in this pre-Columbian World," Crane wrote Cowley, he wondered how much longer the Indians (foremost among them, perhaps, his own servant, Daniel) would "resist a wholesale and picturesque slaughter" of gringos like himself. How had Frank fared "since all the trucks broke down and bird-shot was welcomed by all? Or was it buckshot?" After all, what the hell did he know about guns, despite sojourning "in this gun-toting peninsula"?[9] In fact, as Crane would soon learn from Cowley, the whole group had been arrested in Kentucky and forbidden to talk to the miners, though they had been allowed finally to distribute the three truckloads of food they'd brought before being taken under armed escort to the Tennessee line. Worse, once the locals had realized Frank was a Jew, they'd singled him out for a beating.

In late February, Peggy finally moved in with Crane with the understanding that they would be married once her divorce became final. "I'll make you a good husband yet," she would remember his telling her. And for nearly three whole days he was filled with resolve.

He would cut back on his drinking; he would find literary work; and—
to cap it all—in early March he took her to the old city of Puebla for
a honeymoon of sorts. Before leaving, he withdrew the last $150 of
his Guggenheim funds, opened a bank account with $100 of that, and
set out with Peggy with the rest in his pocket. Puebla turned out to
be "one of the most beautiful places" he'd ever seen, he wrote Bess
afterwards. "Wide streets, pink, blue and terra cotta houses with balconies of wrought iron; a main plaza with lofty trees of a dozen native
varieties; the second largest cathedral on this continent, whose interior
blazes with enough gold railings and gold leaf ornament to pay off Germany's reparation debts."

There were three hundred and sixty-five churches in Puebla, one
for every day of the year, of which he and Peggy had visited a total of
two. A good Catholic, on the other hand, he noted, "might easily wear
out not only shoe leather but his eyes also in trying to do justice to
all." The streets he'd found immaculate, far cleaner than any North
American city he'd ever seen. And the food, clothing, rugs, pottery,
toys—the range and plenitude of it all, so that he and Peggy had been
forced to buy this Indian serape and that piece of hand-blown glass, this
clay pot and that leather belt, at last depositing their plunder back in
Mixcoac. And the flowers! His last day in Puebla he'd returned to the
hotel "with an armful of violets, cornflowers, white carnations and
carmine poppies for Peggy, —four bouquets in all," and all for only
fifteen cents. What was money, after all? He knew he could count on
$125 a month from his father's estate, with a lot more in just a few
years' time. But he would need that money on the first of the month,
he reminded Bess. In fact, he was depending on it. At last he was writing again, and was even now in the midst of "one of the strongest pieces
of poetry" he'd ever done. But it was only because of hers and Peggy's
unconditional love and support that any of this seemed possible.[10]

By mid-March the new batch of Guggenheim fellows had begun
arriving, reminding him once again that his year of subsidized living
was fast coming to an end. Still, living with Peggy, he felt expansive,
domestic. He and Peggy gave several teas with compatriots they liked,
both new and old: the Carleton Beals, Anita Brenner, Marsden Hartley, the Lesley Simpsons, Bill Spratling, even the head of General
Motors. He was not happy to get a letter from Carl Carlsen saying that
the photo Crane had sent of him and Peggy made the two of them
look like "'two waifs' sitting on a strange doorstep." The letter, Crane

wrote Peggy afterwards, was "distinctly below" his friend's "usual level."[11] And yet, with Hartley in particular—whom he'd met in Marseilles in '29—he felt he could speak openly. Despite outward appearances, he had to admit, life with a woman was proving more complicated than he'd expected. For his part, Hartley was convinced he was watching a man spinning rapidly out of control.

Within two weeks of setting up house together, in fact, Crane and Peggy were at each other's throats or screaming at the servants. Worse— as Simpson remembered—was Crane drunk and publicly denouncing the arrangement he'd made with that goddamned woman. On the Puebla expedition, Peggy had lent Crane money to buy a serape. Now she wanted it back. Crane flew into a rage. She wanted the money? She wanted the fucking money?! Then he stormed out of the house and across the street to the telegraph office, where he wired Bess to send money at once, at the same time denouncing Peggy. The next day, after he and Peggy had made their peace, he telegrammed Bess again, making light of the whole affair. Too much tequila, he joked. He'd "misunderstood and misinterpreted Peggy's character." His fault. Apologies.

One night—perhaps the night of the fight with Peggy—there was a knock at Simpson's door. When he opened it, he found Crane swaying there, decked out in his Marseilles sailor's suit and three sheets to the wind. He was shipping out to Frisco, he explained, shipping out to Frisco. A great place. When Simpson took him downtown to get a meal into him, Crane regaled him and the restaurant with stories about Peggy. "She thinks she can reform me, does she?" he shouted to no one in particular as he pounded the table. "I'll show her! God damn her, I'd rather sleep with a man any day than with her!"[12] The scenario was to play itself out a dozen times in the two months Crane lived with Peggy. He would leave Peggy, he screamed out, terrified, before he'd ever let her leave him.

I̶t was in this domestic environment that Crane's poem, conceived in Taxco at Christmas, was born on Good Friday. For three months, whenever he could, he'd worked at it, writing and rewriting lines dozens of times. Except for the detailed and vivid letters he'd written since his return to Mexico, many filled with extraordinary descriptions of the

Mexican landscape and its people, "The Broken Tower" would turn out to be the one notable literary achievement of his year in Mexico.

It is a poem about many things; it is even at odds with itself—as Crane was with himself—but it is preeminently a poem about the poet's awe before a mystery that has the power to silence or to lift him. Even as the bell-rope gathers God at dawn, imaged in the rising of the sun, summoning the faithful, it signals the death of the failed Romantic poet. For the bell-rope that seems to give the sexton/poet the power to summon the sun itself is the same rope that has the power to kill him, rendering him some poor pale ghost wandering the cathedral lawn, staring up at his double: the image of the dead Christ, emptied and self-sacrificed.

"Have you not heard," the poet asks,

> *have you not seen that corps*
> *Of shadows in the tower, whose shoulders sway*
> *Antiphonal carillons launched before*
> *The stars are caught and hived in the sun's ray?*

Crane at Tepotzlán, the bells calling out in antiphonal carillons to drum and flute; Crane at Taxco, swinging from the heavy rope as the cathedral bells rang out in the tower above him; Crane at the Feast of Our Lady of Guadelupe, lost in a crowd of four hundred thousand faithful, summoned by something greater than themselves. The bells clamoring out at dawn, as night lost itself in the morning light, honeyed music hived in the sun's rays. So too himself, a broken man, a broken tower only now, inspiration's slave, who had poured himself out in so many of his poems, this sexton slave to a "long-scattered score of broken intervals," until those very poems had destroyed the very tower of himself, this remnant of a man, his music pealing forth, to touch, to touch, he knew not whom. Christianity and paganism, still both viable here in this land, as the bells announced throughout each blessèd day. But what of the bell of his own voice? Who after all was there to listen? Words, words writ on water.

And those shadows spied there in the tower, whose were they? The shades of the visionary company who had come before, pouring their words too before they in their turn had passed into oblivion? Blake, Baudelaire, Rimbaud, Hopkins, Brother Whitman? How often here in Mexico he had seen the mouths of bells—"oval encyclicals"— calling out, as at Tepotzlán, against the steep canyons, "heaping/The

impasse high with choir." Bell voices, grand resounding sounds, spending themselves endlessly, endlessly, one note, one poem after another,
until every last one of them had at last fallen away, like so many
"Banked voices slain." These bells, these blessèd bells that seemed everywhere, summoning the world over: "Pagodas, campaniles with reveilles
outleaping," become "terraced echoes prostrate on the plain!" And yet
they summoned, as they would again tomorrow and tomorrow and
tomorrow.

So too himself, a bell, one more voice pealing in the long line of
visionary poets, entering this broken world

> *to hold each desperate choice.*
> *To trace the visionary company of love, its voice*
> *An instant in the wind (I know not whither hurled)*
> *But not for long . . .*

Words chosen, words scrapped, other words jostling for position
in the bound cable strands of the line, a bridge, a rope, a bell, rising into
impossible song. A poet pouring out his words, as that figure on the
Cross, that Word, had poured himself out. No doubt about it: He had
given his life for poetry, had taken the risks, put himself in the way of
death, to taste it all, all. Ah, but "was it cognate"? Did his words chime
with that Word; did they touch a sympathetic chord in others, as these
bells so clearly did? Could *his* music summon dawn? As even those
old Indians had, playing their ancient music day and night against the
bells that, like the bread and wine, summoned the god each dawn? Was
there counterresponse in his words, too? Were they likewise "scored,"
composed

> *Of that tribunal monarch of the air*
> *Whose thigh embronzes earth, strikes crystal Word*
> *In wounds pledged once to hope,—cleft to despair?*

And had it all been worth it? Had his own mired wounds managed to strike the authentic note, the benzine-rinsed, immaculate crystal Word? Or had they fallen hollow back to hell? Had it all been folly
after all, this lifelong attempt to touch the empyrean?

Or did the answer lie elsewhere, as these Indians seemed to sense,
in the acceptance of one's death, one's "sweet mortality," which meant
accepting life's rhythms and so the latent power he felt stirring within

again—the creative forces of both eros and song? A stirring within, "Old Mizzentop" rising into a lofty tower, the blood's steep encroachments engorging him, stirred not by another man this time but by her. For the antiphonal carillon he'd felt along his pulse that dawn at Tepotzlán he felt reenacted now, lying on this woman's breast, heart against heart, pulse against pulse. If he was confused, he was glad as well, as he counted the strokes in this "angelus of wars" his chest evoked, believing that the vision had once again been found. In holding her, please God, he could feel himself "healed, original now, and pure."

Not the transcendent, the beyond, his vision now, but a gaze inward and down, down into her. Six months earlier he had written Louis Untermeyer, wondering what Stevens was up to now, for there was a man who could write. "The tomb in Palestine/Is not the porch of spirits lingering," Wallace Stevens had concluded in "Sunday Morning," his own meditation on the loss of one's faith. No, not lingering ghosts, but "the grave of Jesus, where he lay." And if that was so, Stevens had concluded, then what? Death, ambiguities, oblivion, the eye staring at last into a blank sky making a few wavelike empty gestures:

> *in the isolation of the sky,*
> *At evening, casual flocks of pigeons make*
> *Ambiguous undulations as they sink,*
> *Downward to darkness, on extended wings.*

In the wake of the loss of one's vision—religious and transcendent—what remained? Crane was left wondering. Coffee and oranges in a sunny chair? The green freedom of a cockatoo/Upon a rug? Serapes and tequila? Peggy Cowley and a white Spitz named Paloma? Well, that was where he had finally wound up, with love once more buying that silence beyond words that was his special gift:

> *. . . visible wings of silence sown*
> *In azure circles, widening as they dip*
> *The matrix of the heart, lift down the eye*
> *That shrines the quiet lake and swells a tower . . .*
> *The commodious, tall decorum of that sky*
> *Unseals her earth, and lifts love in its shower.*

The matrix of the heart—Hart himself—seeing not sky but earth opening in circle after widening circle. Like pebbles (words) striking the water, much as oval encyclicals struck ever-widening waves of sound upon the air. Let the visionary eye turn modestly away from the heavens then and back toward earth. Let it enshrine instead "the quiet lake" of this woman's love. Turn things over, let up be down and down up, let the phallus swell and let the earth prepare once more to receive its rejuvenating shower. It is a paean—perhaps overly willed, overly determined, because the poet needs some assurance—as the older, transcendent vision gives way at last. But it is a paean nonetheless, a song cracking along its seams addressed to the possibilities of creative renewal and resurrection, and it surely echoes the Good Friday/Easter season in which it was completed.[13]

He signed off on his poem on March 25th, Good Friday. On Easter Sunday, he sent copies to Cowley, Loveman, and Zabel at *Poetry*. "Happiness continues," he wrote Loveman, with "all of the gay incidentals of a Mexican Easter—exploding Judases, rockets, flowers, pappas (excuse me, that's the spelling for Mexican potatoes!), mammas, delicious and infinitesimal children wearing masks and firemen's helmets, flowers galore and a sky that carries you ever upward!"[14] Papas, mammas, children. Maybe, just maybe, Crane might have a family of his own some day and do the damn thing right.

On March 31st, the day his Guggenheim officially ended, Crane wrote Caresse Crosby to thank her for the book of poems honoring her dead husband that she'd written and sent to him earlier. The poems, he told her, were nothing less than "an everlasting litany of chivalry and love" to the memory of Harry. In them she'd somehow managed to write of "the great themes of Love and Tragedy" convincingly in a way he felt few women had. He was going to stay on in Mexico indefinitely, he told her, to take in "its volcanoes, endless ranges, countless flowers, dances, villages, lovely brown-skinned Indians with simple courtesies, and constant sunlight." In his year in the country, he'd "rung bells and beaten pre-Conquistadorial drums in firelit circles at ancient ceremonies, while rockets went zooming up into the dawn over Tepotzlán . . . picked up obsidian arrows and terra-cotta idols from the furrows of corn-fields in far valleys; bathed with creatures more beautiful than the inhabitants of Bali in mountain streams and been in the friendliest jails that ever man got thrown in."

True, he'd written not a single line of his epic. But then, what had he actually written during his time in France, "an environment not half so strange and distractingly new-old curious" as Mexico had turned out to be? Only lately had he begun rapping the typewriter again. Besides, with "the world all going to hell," what could he or anyone "gather together with any confidence" anyway? Sure, he might have gone on writing lyrics and producing a mound of trash; but he'd been trying to grow as a poet as well as a man by taking on new responsibilities, including stretching "the dominions of Eros a little," by entering the "Via Venus" with the wife of someone Caresse knew.[15]

Surely living in Mexico now was better than living back in the depression-riddled States. "Most all the letters we get from the north are pretty damned blue and dubious in tone," he told Grunberg in mid-April. Once in a while he thought of returning to the States to wail "around the grave of capitalism, . . . adopting sackcloth and ashes too," and then thought better of it. No wonder Frank and Cowley *had* turned "a violent pink lately." In fact, he'd been all but convinced to join the Communist Party himself. "By all the laws of logic," Crane had been convinced, except that this seeing "nothing but red on the horizon" went against his deepest grain.[16] He was too much the capitalist at heart, really, a man who enjoyed shopping in the markets and buying whatever he damn well pleased whenever he damn well pleased too much ever to go over to the Marxists.

A capitalist at heart, but a capitalist without cash. The Guggenheim money was gone; worse, the money from Bess had failed to arrive at the beginning of April. He kept wiring her, demanding to know what the holdup was. Worried, he began drinking heavily again. One night he even managed to get into a fight at a bar and had his right palm slashed with a razor as a warning. For a week he went around with his hand wrapped in bandages. Another night, drunk, he accused Daniel of stealing one of his serapes (later he would remember that he'd lent it to a friend), and Daniel, his honor besmirched, had come after him with a butcher's knife.

One of Daniel's policeman brothers had defused that incident by taking Crane down to the police station to sleep it off, which then left Crane feeling *his* honor had been besmirched. Soon he was throwing every stick of furniture in his cell out through the bars of his window. With that, the police released the crazy American, who, still fuming, returned home to find a crowd of Daniel's friends milling about, who'd already heard from Daniel the awful things Crane had accused him of. On that occasion, Lesley Simpson had luckily got Crane downtown to the Hotel Mancera to sleep it off, ordering him not to leave until he came for him in the morning. But at breakfast Simpson received a call from Crane. He was back home, sounding as if nothing had happened, and inviting Simpson and his wife out to lunch that very afternoon with him and Peggy.

When he still failed to hear from Bess, Crane began borrowing money from friends again. Then he heard the unexpected news: there'd been a terrible car accident. One of the women who worked at the Cottage had been killed and two others seriously hurt. On top of losing her husband, the new losses had driven Bess to near despair, but— seeing that Hart was in need—she was sending out a check at once. Crane was not impressed. Damn it, he fumed, couldn't she see he *needed* that money? It was *his* money, after all, his father's one legacy to him, and the installments had to be there for him on the first of the month. When the check finally arrived, he repaid his friends and managed to right himself for a few days. "I'm in a dull mood today," he wrote Grunberg on the 12th, "trying to get back into harness after a couple of feverish weeks spent in running thither and yon every day or so to borrow enough money to keep us going." Why was it he could not get "people to understand that any break in schedule regarding remittances in a foreign country like Mexico" could be catastrophic?[17]

By the middle of April he was working feverishly to get a permanent passport through semi-official channels so he could stay on in Mexico for another six months. Yes, he wrote Lorna Dietz in New York, "the wholesale conversion" of his Brooklyn and Manhattan friends over to the left was making him feel guilty. But rather than don sackcloth and ashes, he preferred sitting around cold evenings in the "most comfortable and flamboyant serapes" he could find and listening to records on his portable, as well as the real thing there in his house.[18] The solemn and eloquent strains of *Las Mañanitas*, he wrote Mony Grunberg that same day, the slangy *La Marihuana*, a song about "the native drug of the same name (generally smoked in cigarettes) and its effects," and *Capulin*, "a wild and throbbing native cancion"—all these could certainly set one prancing.

These singers fascinated him with their ability to produce "heart-wringing vibrations" in ways unknown outside the Orient or Arabia. Yes, they could be shrill, but what range they had, far greater than that "old Hawaiian gargling." How he loved having these amateurs—"masons, plumbers or pickslingers during the day"—come over each night to sing. A little tequila, beer, even coffee, and they'd sing ballad after ballad about "poor Pancho Villa, Zapata and other dead revolutionaries." And then, when they'd all had enough to drink, someone would dance the *jarabe*, "all vibrant gristle, emphasis and exhausting grace." This was the life. If only he could stop drinking, he'd be back on his feet in no time. And Peggy, dear Peggy, with enough "sportsmanship, mentality, taste and sensuality" to meet him on every level. He was learning things from that woman he'd never thought he could learn from anyone.[19]

And yet for all his affection for her, the same day that he was protesting his love for Peggy he'd actually jumped to attention, as he confessed to Sam Loveman, "right into a perfect salute . . . when suddenly—over the neighbor's radio—I caught the chorus of that old favorite of mine, 'The Navy Blues.'" He still thought a great deal about Bob Stewart, that "sweet boy," whose letters for two years had been "so consistently affectionate and nostalgic" that they brought tears to his eyes. And now dear Peggy, late with her period. Twins, he wondered? And was it storks who carried Cranes, or Cranes storks?

Then Claire Spencer Smith showed up in Mixcoac. There was a face from past! After their falling out back in the summer of 1917, she'd become an "enemy for awhile," but now, especially now, when he'd lost so many friends, he was delighted to see her.[20] A published writer, with a novel out, she was on her way to Cuernavaca, traveling with another woman, Katie Seabrook—an old friend of Peggy's—but they promised to stop by on their way back so Claire and he could catch up on old times. They left behind a copy of Dos Passos's sequel to *42nd Parallel*, the big, sprawling *1919*. Back in Chagrin Falls the year before, Crane had plowed through the first novel and found it good, though finally unsatisfying because Dos Passos had failed to create a full portrait of anyone. But *1919* he could not put down, even to eat or sleep, so engrossing did he find it. A great book, he told Grunberg, writing Lorna Dietz that same day that it was "certainly the best book" Dos had ever written. The "same technique as the *42nd Parallel*," but this time "developed and perfected finally into an almost perfect instrument."[21] So the guy had done it, broken through into the sun. A great read, but also Crane's last. For suddenly, unexpectedly, everything began unraveling.

The biggest blow was hearing from Bess that the financial situation over C.A.'s estate was in a lot more difficulty than either of them had realized. Several years before, C.A. had guaranteed a loan on a factory in Kansas City, and now the new owners were refusing to pay. That meant C.A.'s estate would be left holding the bag, which in turn meant C.A.'s assets would be frozen for months, even years, to come. Bess would continue sending Harold his $125 a month out of her own salary, as she had been doing all along, but there would be no other money available for him to draw on. Then he had to accept the bitter pill that "The Broken Tower," the poem he'd banked everything on and which was to have stood as a sign of the recovery of his gifts, the poem he'd sent off to *Poetry* with such high hopes, had been greeted with inexplicable silence. Both his inheritance and his poetic legacy had evaporated into thin air.

The void yawned. His moods grew blacker and blacker. Frightened at what she was seeing, Peggy tried to cheer him up. They would have a leisurely Sunday brunch with two women they both liked: Mary Doherty and Louise Howard. But when the women arrived on the morning of April 17th, they found Crane dressed only in pajamas and a serape, already drunk. Peggy took the women into a back room, hoping to avoid a scene, but within minutes Crane came crashing in on them, bearing the Siqueiros portrait. "A magnificent portrait," he'd called it six months earlier, by a painter he regarded as "superior in depth of conception to both Rivera and Orozco."[22] But that was then. Now he was calling it a piece of shit by someone who dared to call himself one of Mexico's greatest painters. Did they really think anyone was going to remember this jackal in twenty or thirty years? Look at it: the paint not a year old and already cracking. And suddenly he was flashing his father's old razor and slashing his image to shreds, beginning with the eyes.

Stunned silence, as the women looked on in horror at what he'd just done. Then he was gone, shouting for them to come out to the front room. They found him sitting at his desk, making out a will. He wanted Mary and Louise to witness that he was leaving everything to Peggy except for a few trinkets for Bess and his aunt Zell. Then he announced in a steady, dull voice that he was going to kill himself. He disappeared, then reappeared with a bottle of iodine. As he tried to swallow the dark red liquid, Peggy pushed his arm away, so that most of it ran down onto his chin and serape instead. A doctor was summoned, who administered a sedative.

Afterwards, Crane sat down quietly and rewrote his will, this time leaving everything to Bob Stewart, his young sailor-lover, back in Alabama now. "Won't be living any more if this ever reaches you," he wrote Stewart. "Hope you are all right." He was very willfully killing himself, he explained, and wanted Bob to know that he loved him. Yes, it was the "only end."[23] He checked the will and letter carefully for spelling errors and typos, as if it were part of some elaborate fiction, then gave the letter and copies of the wills to Mary Doherty, with instructions to mail the letter as soon as she heard he was dead. Afterwards, he went off and drank a bottle of Mercurochrome. Again the doctor was summoned to clean out his system with emetics. But this time the doctor injected him with a huge dose of morphine and left Peggy with a vial of sleeping pills to administer if Crane stirred before morning.

When Crane did awake the following morning, except for a burning sensation in his throat he seemed in much better spirits. Too much pressure, he explained, shrugging off his behavior of the day before. But attempted suicide in Mexico was a serious offense, punishable by imprisonment. If the authorities learned what he had done, he might not have a choice about leaving Mexico. They were going to have to leave the country, Peggy explained, and they were going to have to do it as soon as possible. Crane nodded. He would book passage for the States at once. Then he went back to his room to put things in order, destroying all the wills and a draft of his letter to Bob, forgetting about the copies of both he'd given to Mary Doherty for safekeeping.

Toward noon, he ran into Lesley Simpson and Marsden Hartley in town and regaled them with stories of his suicide attempt. Neither found the stories very funny. If he was going home, they tried to persuade him, better to go by train than by ship. They knew, though they did not say so, that he stood a better chance that way of getting home alive. Afterwards, Crane and Peggy had lunch with Claire Spencer and Katie Seabrook, who both found him charming one moment and ready to go to pieces the next. He wanted them to return to the States with him on the *Orizaba* on the 24th, he insisted. But both women declined. In fact, they had booked passage for that very trip, but seeing his condition, they changed their plans. Later, when Lesley Simpson's wife, Mary, met him, she became so upset by what she saw in Crane's eyes that her husband had to leave the city with her for the next several days. Crane was a loaded gun waiting to go off.

On the 20th, four days before the *Orizaba* was to leave Vera Cruz, and with still no word from Bess, Crane fired off a telegram to his uncle Byron Madden, begging him to wire $200 at once. BESS INCOMPREHENSIBLE, it fairly screamed, HAVE WIRED TWICE FOR FARE.[24] Then he approached Eyler Simpson. Would the Guggenheim people advance him the money if necessary? Anything, Simpson thought, to get this man the hell out of the country. Next, Crane turned to Mony Grunberg. Having just learned that he'd been living off money meant for Bess, he explained, he was returning to Chagrin Falls and his "middle western exile."[25] He would try to help out with the business, even as several branches of that business were moving toward bankruptcy. Could Mony see his way to lending him something and sending it in care of the Hotel Lafayette on University Place and 8th?

Then it was the Rychtariks and Sam Loveman to the same effect, asking if they could help. It had been "an awful time all round lately."[26] Afterwards, Crane sent off two letters dealing with literary matters. One went to *Contempo*. He was delighted, he told them, that they were going to print his old "Bacardi" poem, and wondered if he could do some reviews for them once he was settled in back home, sometime after May 10th. He was particularly anxious to review MacLeish's *Conquistador*, which dealt with a subject close to his own heart just now. Then he wrote Zabel again at *Poetry*, explaining that he'd been called north on business. Had Zabel received a poem he'd sent him weeks before?

Then buffos and other last-minute complications. When the passage money finally arrived from Bess on Thursday morning, the 21st, Crane and Peggy went at once to the telegraph office, where it was handed over in silver *tostones*, some 600 of them packed in canvas sacks (rather like getting paid off in dimes, he complained; in dimes). These he and Peggy lugged off in a taxi, where they proceeded to the shipping office to buy tickets. After paying six small boys to haul the money inside, they were stunned to learn that the office was permitted to exchange only 20 *tostones* a day. Handwringings, gestures. Then the boys were carrying the bags off to another cab for a trip to the central Bank of Mexico, where still other boys hauled the *tostones* inside.

Knowing he was in no condition to handle bureaucratic inepti-
tude on this scale, Peggy suggested he get some lunch, then return to
the house, while she straightened things out. Inside, she watched dis-
believingly as a clerk counted and then slowly recounted each of the
600-odd *tostones*. When she was herself ready to scream, she demanded to see the president of the bank. Another wait, and then she was
being led down a corridor by two armed uniformed soldiers, who
turned her over to two others. Suddenly, she found herself in the inner
sanctum of the bank in the presence of none other than the former
president of Mexico, Plutarco Calles, for whom Crane had once
destroyed a typewriter trying to send him a fan letter in Spanish. Calles
simply handed her a slip of paper that—presto!—brought her the
money she had come for. There was just enough time to book passage
for herself and Crane before the ship's offices closed.

Back in Mixcoac, Crane had begun drinking again. As the afternoon wore on and no Peggy appeared, he became more and more convinced that someone had seen her with the money and kidnapped
her. Finally, he stumbled off to the police station, where he was of
course already well known, and demanded they dispatch the police to
look for her at once. When they seemed to hold back, he became even
more insistent and shrill, until he was told to leave if he did not wish
to spend another night in jail. Rebuffed, Crane trudged off to the U.S.
Embassy, where he ordered an attaché to telegram President Hoover
that an American citizen had been abducted. He insisted that the
Marines be sent down at once. To appease him, the attaché took him
to the Mexican government's radio station, where a description of
Peggy was broadcast. By the time Crane got back home, it was after
midnight. After all his efforts, he was furious to find Peggy home too,
alive and well.

But he was even more furious that Mexico, as he put it, had finally destroyed him, that he was now a joke among his friends, and that the
poem on which he'd banked so much of his literary credit had been
met with silence.

On Friday night—the 22nd—he wrote Bess. He was sorry about
having wired his uncle for money, but things had gone terribly wrong,
and now he was down with fever and dysentery. He was lying, but
then what did anything matter any more? He lied again. Having
learned of her troubles, he told her, he was rushing home to be of
whatever help he could. Besides, the Mexicans had made it impossible

for a foreigner like himself to remain in the country. He'd placed his passport renewal problems in the hands of a lawyer who had turned out to be a crook, and though it had come out all right in the end, the whole episode had cost him no end of trouble. And then there was Daniel, who'd gotten drunk and returned home to find the gates locked. Daniel had shouted threats at him, Crane told Bess, terrorizing both him and Peggy, until he'd had to call on the U.S. Embassy for police protection. Well, let the Mexicans have their Mexico. He was leaving on the 24th. He mentioned neither his drinking, nor his insane behavior, nor the fact that he had just tried to kill himself.

He knew the sacrifices Bess had made to send him the passage money. Well, he would make it up to her, he promised, once he was back home. He asked her to watch out for a box of books he'd sent collect via Wells Fargo to his father's factory. His other belongings he would send on once he reached New York. He would stay in the city for a few days to see old friends, but promised to telephone her the night of his arrival, after the rates went down. He wanted her to see that he was already thinking economy and responsibility. He was a nervous wreck, he confessed, but he would rest up once the *Orizaba* was out to sea.[27]

Saturday morning, he and Peggy left the empty house and said their final good-byes to his servants who had gathered out in front of the house. As he and Peggy settled into the taxi, bound for the train station, Daniel, bursting into tears, tossed a bouquet of flowers in after them. Later, when they'd deposited their baggage at the station, the two returned to the city for a farewell party in their honor at the Broadway Restaurant. Lesley and Mary Simpson were there, Eyler Simpson, the Beals, Mary Doherty, others. At one point Crane stood up to announce that he and Peggy were going to get married. They would return to Mexico, he promised, in two years' time. Afterwards he took Peggy down to the market and bought her a huge corsage.

Then it was off to the Guggenheim office for the sixty-dollar loan he needed to pay for the train down to Vera Cruz. After Crane left the office, Eyler Simpson wrote a letter to Moe explaining the reason for the loan, which had come out of his own pocket. "A week ago," he wrote, "our friend Hart Crane went off the reservation with a bang," getting himself in so much trouble it had taken the combined resources of Mexico City to get him out of the city alive.[28] Now Crane was on his way to Vera Cruz and would sail, God willing, in the morning.

Even so, Crane almost missed his train. Only as it was about to leave the station did he and Peggy show up, along with several porters and a truckload of baggage. Wavings and blowing of kisses to those who had come to the station to say good-bye. Then the train steamed out of the station and disappeared. Once aboard the *Orizaba*, Crane introduced his intended to the ship's officers. Several eyebrows were raised by those who knew Crane, but otherwise the introductions went smoothly. Drinks, plans, Crane staying over in Peggy's room those first nights out. Then, on the morning of the 26th, a stopover in Havana, with six hours' shore leave. Peggy would go shopping, they decided, while Crane visited some old haunts. They would link up at a place he knew—*La Diana?*—where the waiters spoke English. He wired ahead to New York for a room at the Hotel Lafayette, showed her some of the main sights of the city, told her to be careful, and left her to do her shopping. That morning he got off at least two postcards: one to Lesley Simpson, assuring him that he and Peggy were having a pleasant journey; the other to Aunt Sally Simpson on the Isle of Pines. "Off here for a few hours on my way north," he wrote on the back of a picture postcard of the old Morro Castle in Havana, seen as one approached it from the sea. He was on his way back to Cleveland "to help in the business crisis." He would write when he got home.[29]

Peggy spent the morning buying Crane some records (a surprise) and a few souvenirs for herself, then went to meet him at the restaurant. But as the minutes ticked by and Crane failed to show, she became first worried, then angry that she'd been stood up. Finally, realizing that none of the waiters spoke English and that she just might be in the wrong restaurant, she rushed off to get back to the ship on time. Mr. Crane had been back on board for the last hour, she learned from one of the ship's officers; in fact, he'd been combing the ship looking for her. But by then she was furious, convinced he'd forgotten about her. At the ship's bar she learned he'd stopped by looking for her. Yes, he had been drinking.

Then, as she went to light a cigarette, the box of matches she was holding exploded into flame, burning her hand. It was in the doctor's office that Crane finally found her. He too was upset and angry. She'd gone to the wrong restaurant, he kept telling her, worried sick that

something had happened to her. Then, seeing her burns, he became solicitous. She wanted none of it. Couldn't he see she was in pain? Why didn't he just go away and leave her be? This was more than he could take. The more she rejected him, the louder he became, until finally the doctor ordered him to get out. Peggy was given a sedative and told to rest in the office. But an hour later Crane was back. He would carry her back to her cabin, he offered. Again, she told him to leave.

The second rejection apparently did it. Hurt, he stormed out and began drinking to assuage his pain. Still, twice that evening he came to her room, demanding to know which restaurant she really *had* gone to, and why she hadn't come looking for him when she knew he would be searching everywhere for her. Again she asked him to leave. More time passed for Peggy in a twilight of alcohol, sedatives, and pain. Sometime after midnight, the purser knocked on her door. Mr. Crane had been making a nuisance of himself and had had to be locked in his room and the door nailed shut. Good, she thought. They should have done that hours ago.

But no locked door was going to hold Crane. By 1:00 A.M. he had managed to force his way out of his room. From then until 4:00 A.M., when he was forcibly returned to his room by the steward, he prowled the ship, looking for someone to be with. No one seems to know just where he was or what exactly happened during those three hours. One story was that he'd propositioned a cabin boy. Another said it was a sailor, or even several sailors. But shortly before four o'clock he was back on deck, bruised and bloodied, his right eye swollen shut and turning black, his ring and wallet gone. Once on deck, he stumbled about, disoriented, leaning against the railing and staring out into the black waters breathing beneath him. Suddenly, he began climbing over the rail. But the nightwatchman had been observing him and managed to wrestle him to the deck before he went overboard. Within minutes Crane was turned over to the second steward, who marched him back to his cabin and stayed with him until he had undressed and climbed in under the covers. When the steward left, he secured the door once more behind him.

Six hours later, at 10:00 A.M. on the 27th, the steward returned to unlock Crane's cabin. He looked in to see Crane still in his pajamas, already drinking from a bottle of whiskey. An hour later, this time accompanied by the captain, the steward looked in on him again. Crane

was still in his pajamas and still drinking. Peggy, meanwhile, woozy from her morphine-induced sleep, had gone to the doctor to have her burns rebandaged. By the time she got back to her cabin, Crane was waiting for her. He remembered little of what had happened during the night, he told her, except that his wallet and ring had been taken from him. He was frightened and shaken. She followed him back to his cabin to see if they could find his things, but they could not. Finally, he sat down on his bed beside her and took another drink to steady himself. This time, he told her, he'd really disgraced himself. Everything was lost. It was time to go.

Nonsense, she said. What he needed was a good breakfast, which she proceeded to order. While he wolfed down his food, he told her exactly what he'd done in Havana. He'd not had anything to drink, he insisted, until he was back on the ship. And, he insisted, she really *had* gone to the wrong restaurant. She had to understand that. The wrong restaurant. Then Peggy got up and went back to her own cabin to dress. A few minutes before noon, there was a knock at her door. It was Crane, still in pajamas, but wearing a light topcoat over them. She told him to shave and get dressed and join her for lunch. "I'm not going to make it, dear," he told her, his voice already drifting. "I'm utterly disgraced." Nonsense, she told him. How much better he'd feel once he was dressed. "All right, dear," he said. He leaned over, kissed her good-bye, and closed the door behind him. Then he walked along the promenade deck toward the stern of the ship.[30]

Gertrude Vogt, one of the passengers sitting on deck chairs by the stern, was waiting along with others to hear the results of the ship's pool, which would be announced at noon. She looked up to see a man walking toward her. Earlier that day, she would recall forty years later, one of the ship's officers had told her and some of the others that a man "had been in the sailors' quarters the previous night, trying to make one of the men, and had been badly beaten." Now she watched as that man, in coat and pajamas, walked up to the railing, took off his coat, and folded it over the railing. Then he "placed both hands on the railing, raised himself on his toes, and . . . dropped back again. We all fell silent and watched him, wondering what in the world he was up to. Then, suddenly, he vaulted over the railing and jumped into the sea. For what seemed like five minutes, but was more like five seconds, no one was able to move; then cries of 'man overboard' went up. Just once I saw Crane, swimming strongly, but never again."[31]

What happened when he hit the water? Was he swept back into the powerful wake of the ship, then under, and caught in the ship's propeller? Did he struggle to regain the surface, suddenly sobered by what he'd done, the fury of brinewater smarting eyes and mouth? If he was swimming strongly, as Gertrude Vogt says he was, was he swimming toward one of the life preservers or away from it? And why did he suddenly disappear? Did he feel something brush his leg, the file-sharp streaking side of concentrated muscle, before the silver flash and teeth pulled him under?

The official report says the *Orizaba* was 275 miles north of Havana and 10 miles east of the Florida coast when Hart Crane jumped. Eight bells had just sounded—high noon—followed by bells signaling that someone had gone overboard. Lifesavers were sent whirling down and down, the engines were ground into reverse to slow the ship down, then one, two, and finally four lifeboats lowered. Some thought they saw an arm raised, others that a life preserver had been turned over by a hand, though the officer in charge of the bridge insisted it was only a wave. For two hours the ship circled *Pequod*-like while the lifeboats bobbed or rowed in zigzags, the crew—some of whom must have known what had transpired the previous night—talking among themselves or staring down into the impenetrable waters off which the noon sun gleamed. But this time the calyx of death's bounty gave back neither scattered chapter nor livid hieroglyph, gave back nothing anyone could read. At last Captain Blackadder called off the search, ordered the sailors to return to ship, and once more the *Orizaba* churned on, heading north toward the teeming harbor of New York.

CODA

Late on the morning of 28 April 1932, Bess Crane heard through her brother-in-law, Byron Madden, that Hart had been lost at sea. Grace, still working as a hostess at the Carleton Hotel, learned of her son's death in the newspapers. So it was over, and she would have to accept the fact that she would never see her Hart again. For the next fifteen years, until her own death, Grace would work unceasingly to see that neither her boy nor his poetry was ever forgotten. She would collect his correspondence and she would work with those who sought to remember his work: Philip Horton, his first biographer, and Waldo Frank, as they assembled her son's *Collected Poems*. She worked especially hard to reconstruct the blank of her son's last years, hoping to find some clue that he had not forgotten her. If almost his last words were any indication—"I'm utterly disgraced"—at some deep level he had not.

"About three years ago," Grace would write Charlotte Rychtarik a week after Hart's death, "we had a cruel experience which has separated us ever since, altho I have made repeated efforts to get in touch with him by letter & other ways. I had been living in hopes that perhaps this summer something would bring us together when I knew everything would be forgotten instantly. Knowing him as I did, I was certain he was suffering remorse over the affair. But now he is gone—forever—and those past years will be a blank to me, regarding his movements and actions. Would you please write me what you know of his life during that time & if he ever talked of me."[1]

Grace herself went from small job to smaller, from living in Oak Park to Leonia, New Jersey, where she earned fifteen dollars a month working as a common drudge. From there she moved to a one-room apartment on 38th Street on New York's East Side, until she could no longer care for herself and was moved to a Catholic hospital in Tenafly, New Jersey. When Sam Loveman visited her there in the late summer of 1947, he found her comatose and very near death. The mother of a very great poet, he told the nurse in attendance that day, to which Grace, for the moment stirring, shook her head. "Poor Hart. Poor Hart," was all she said. After her death at the age of sixty-seven on 30 August 1947, Loveman, whom she had made her son's literary executor, and who was with her when she died, had her body cremated and—with the help of several women—scattered the ashes from the bridge his old friend had turned to myth. From the curved span he watched Grace's dust fall into the river below. Perhaps, in the ages to come, it might somehow mingle with her son's diced bones.

William Carlos Williams—of all Crane's major contemporaries the one who watched Crane most closely—was in the midst of writing a comment on the state of American poetry for his own magazine, *Contact*, when he learned of Crane's death. Such a death as Crane had suffered, he knew very well, made Crane more of a threat to American poetry now than when he'd been alive. "Certainly Hart Crane bumped himself off with no thought of improving or marring his condition," he understood. The reports had spoken of suicide; but what if it had all been some terrible accident? What if he'd just been drunk and had rolled off the boat? In any event he was dead, and already being transformed into some myth of the last Romantic. Well, if Crane's poetry shaped up after there was time to evaluate it, so much the better. But he had his doubts.[2]

A month later, in the pages of *Contempo*, Williams came at Crane's death a second time. Even someone like himself, intent on making a totally different kind of American poem, even he had to admit there was something to admire in Crane. Those poems in *White Buildings*, for instance, with "the sound of continual surf" running through them, "the alternate peak and back rush of waves in them." Still, even there one felt the sense of someone writing poetry to please the editor of some New York Sunday book supplement. For what, after all, was Crane's vaunted poetic language when all was said and done, but a "direct step backward to the bad poetry of any age but especially to the triumphant regression" of the French Symbolistes who had followed Whitman, a poetry content to imitate Mallarmé and which had come "to a head in T. S. Eliot excellently."

What a poor fool Crane had been, trying to sound more and more cosmic instead of looking at the waste his life had become, especially in his last years. Williams hated Crane's rhapsodies, particularly a poem like "Atlantis," because he so deeply distrusted that sort of orphic music. "I cannot grow rhapsodic with him," he insisted, this "evangel of the post-war, the replier to the romantic apostle of *The Waste Land.*" But the really unforgivable sin Crane had committed was turning his life into the stuff of myth, living the life of the roaring boy, drinking nightly and cruising the Brooklyn and Hoboken docks after sailors, only to end up jumping from a ship at the age of thirty-two. It rankled Williams, who at forty-nine still had almost no following, that he would now have to watch as Crane's life and death—in the best tradition of Villon and Rimbaud—threw "a white glare" over Crane's best work, as had happened with Van Gogh when he'd killed himself.[3]

Fourteen years later, Williams returned to the vexing problem of Crane once again in a piece for the *Kenyon Review*. Crane had "got to the end of his method," he saw now, a poetic method that had never been "more than an excrescence." He'd tried it every way he could: "written it right and left, front and back, up and down and round in a circle both ways, criss cross and at varying speeds," until he'd exhausted himself and all his options. He'd gone to Mexico to recover his vision and found he could not. When he died, "he was returning to create and had finished creating. Peggy said that in the last three hours he beat at her cabin door—after being deceived and thrashed. He didn't know where to turn—that was the end of it. That he had the guts to go over the rail in his pyjamas, unable to sleep or even rest, was, to me (though what do I know—more than another?) a failure to find anywhere *in his 'rime'* an outlet. He had tried in Mexico merely to write—to write anything. He couldn't."

True, "love might have saved him." But at what cost to others, and the bomb a part of everyone's life now, and Williams in the midst of asking himself the same questions in his own belated epic, *Paterson*. Nor was Williams very comfortable with the answers he was coming up with as to what constituted a viable response to Whitman's *Leaves of Grass*. "Anyone who has seen 2,000 infants born as I have and pulled them one way or another into the world must know that man, as such, is doomed to disappear in not too many thousand years. He just can't go on. No woman will stand for it. Why should she?" At least Crane had been smart enough to leave the party early.[4]

Williams's old friend, Marsden Hartley, was also deeply shaken by Crane's death. During his year's sojourn in Mexico as a Guggenheim recipient (1932–33), Hartley watched the country warily, believing it to be primarily responsible for Crane's death. Indeed, in the months following the suicide, he was obsessed by Crane. Besides his letters, Hartley wrote three essays and a lengthy verse elegy to his "brother" Hart; and—in late 1932—he painted a powerful work entitled *Eight Bells' Folly*, eight bells signaling high noon, the hour when Crane had leaped to his death. "He should have respected life," Hartley would write, "and the surging life in himself," not destroyed it.[5] But Mexico had been too vivid, too primitive, too unforgiving. Like the old gods, it demanded everything from you, and finally it killed you. Seventeen years before, Hartley had lost his German lover in the trenches of the Great War and had tried to deal with that loss in several paintings that focused on symbolic numerology. Now, for the last time in his life, he tried to deal with a death by once again incorporating numbers into his painting, a painting that even Hartley thought had a "very mad look" about it.

A sailing ship foundering—*Cutty Sark?*—"a sun, a moon, two triangles, clouds,"[6] and a shark racing up toward the ship and its drowned voyager, its jaws red with human blood. At the lower right, a red bell with the number 8—eight bells—and (above the bell) eight haunted eyes belonging to drowned mariners, all focused on the "new lodger" come to join them. Other numbers: 33 written across the sail of the foundering ship—Christ's age, and Crane's too, nearly. And then an 8 on one of the portal clouds above the sea's horizon, and—where the shark was torpedoing itself upward—the number 9. Three times three, for body, mind, soul. Whatever the numerology, Hartley seemed to say here, there was finally the mouth of voracious death to consider, and that Crane could not escape.

But let Crane's estranged friend Yvor Winters have the final word. In 1947, Professor Winters published an essay entitled "The Significance of *The Bridge* by Hart Crane, or What Are We to Think of Professor X?" It was his final assessment of Crane as a failure, or perhaps—if *he* was Professor X—then himself. Certainly some nagging residuum, some small adamantine substance, of admiration remained. "Professor X says, or since he is a gentleman and a scholar, he implies, that Crane was merely a fool, that he ought to have known better." But Crane was not a fool. Winters had known Crane and, by 1947, as a distinguished presence at Stanford University who'd been in the world of academia long enough to know, he also knew Professor X. Winters—with that acerbic, terrifying irony that could wither all but the strongest opponent—was therefore reasonably certain that Crane was "incomparably the more intelligent" of the two.

As for Crane's ideas, "they were merely those of Professor X, neither better nor worse." Ideas finally, no more, no less. The all-important difference was that Crane—unlike Professor X—had also been capable of writing great poetry. Whatever else, and "in spite of popular and even academic prejudices to the contrary," Winters knew as well as anyone that it took "a very highly developed intelligence to write great poetry, even a little of it." How gladly, he ended—speaking for any number of poets who have come after and who have read Crane with puzzlement, awe, passion, and gratitude—how gladly he would emulate Odysseus, if only he could, "and go down to the shadows for another hour's conversation with Crane on the subject of poetry."[7]

The subsequent lives of Crane's sailor-lovers must remain shadowy and indistinct. Almost none of Crane's letters to them—not even to Emil Opffer—has ever surfaced. It is a pity, for they would surely throw a much-needed light on Crane's most intimate side. Except in the most general way, Opffer never spoke of his love for Crane. In fact, the love Crane felt for Opffer, enfleshed in the "Voyages" sequence, was never returned with anything like the same intensity. That was not the way it was among most of the sailors Crane knew. He liked Crane a great deal, Opffer once told Sue Brown, and he loved to hear him recite his poems. But he had never been "in love" with the man. In 1978, at the age of eighty-two, Opffer returned to his native Denmark to be married. Hart Crane belonged to another chapter in his life, and that chapter had long since closed.

And the others? Relative longevities, mostly. Otto Kahn died two years after Crane, at the age of sixty-seven. Wilbur Underwood retired a civil servant from the Department of State's Division of Communications and Records in 1932 after thirty-two years (he'd begun working there the same year Crane had been born) and died three years later. He was sixty-one. Whether Crane ever learned the story or not, the Baroness predeceased him, killed by a French boyfriend in a Paris tenement in December 1927, who turned the gas on full one morning while she slept, walked out of the apartment, and closed the door behind him. A joke, perhaps, and right in line with the Baroness's brand of Dadaism. Caresse Crosby outlived her husband by forty years and died in 1970, aged seventy-seven. Bess Crane remarried after World War II and lived to the ripe age of eighty-four. After the Browns' divorce in 1932, Sue continued working for various New York publishing houses, and in 1969, in her seventies, published Crane's letters to her and her ex-husband. She died in 1982 at the age of eighty-six. Slater Brown served on the editorial board of *The New Republic* and *New Masses*, stopped drinking (and later smoking), gave up all his old literary friends, turned his life around, and in 1957, age 59, married the grandniece of Henry James, by whom he had a daughter. He outlived everyone, dying at the age of one hundred in his bed in Rockport, Massachusetts. He wrote ten books in his time, including a novel, a biography for children, and a study of parapsychology and the occult. Charmion von Wiegand served as a journalist stationed in Russia, afterwards editing *Art Front* and serving as art critic for *New Masses*. She died in 1985 in her ninetieth year.

The irrepressible Peggy Baird Cowley, married first to the New York poet, Orrick Johns, and then to Malcolm Cowley, married twice more after her divorce from Cowley, and spent her last years at Tivoli, a home for the destitute in upstate New York founded by her long-time friend, the sainted Dorothy Day. She died there in 1970 in her eighty-third year. After a rocky twenty-year marriage, Caroline Gordon and Allen Tate divorced in 1946. They remarried each other later that same year and remained more or less together until 1959, when they divorced for a second and final time. In 1956, Gordon published *The Malefactors*, a novel whose main characters were based on Crane, Tate, and herself. She died in 1981 at eighty-six. Tate continued to publish: poetry, biography, fiction, criticism. He was a master teacher, a formalist, and always a Southern conservative, who taught at Princeton, the University of Minnesota, and the University of the South, and had a great impact on any number of younger poets, including Berryman and Lowell. Cranky until the end, he broke with them as he had with Crane. He died in 1979 in his eighty-first year. Yvor Winters continued to write eloquently, learnedly, and wrong-headedly against the direction modern poetry had taken, taking swipes at every great poetic innovator of the twentieth century. By the time he died in 1968, he had long become a venerable institution at Stanford.

Gorham Munson continued on as a disciple of Gurdjieff and his disciple, A. R. Orage, writing and editing various magazines until his death in 1969. His memoir of the 1920s and of Crane was published sixteen years after Hart Crane's death as *The Awakening Twenties: A Memoir-History of a Literary Period*. Matthew Josephson continued to write leftist-inspired studies of American culture. In 1962, his memoir of the twenties, *Among the Surrealists*, was published. He died in 1978, nearing eighty. Jean Toomer published sporadically but never so well as he had in *Cane*, and died in 1967. Waldo Frank continued to publish his leftist cultural studies: *Dawn in Russia* the year Crane died; followed by *In the American Jungle* in 1937, and *The Prophetic Island: A Portrait of Cuba* in 1961. He was seventy-seven when he died in 1967.

Malcolm Cowley became literary editor of *The New Republic* in 1929, and stayed on until 1944. In 1948, he became the literary adviser to Viking Press, editing their Portable Editions of Hawthorne, Faulkner, and Hemingway. He wrote two well-known memoirs, *Exile's Return: A Literary Odyssey of the 1920s,* published just two years after Crane's death; and *The Dream of the Golden Mountains: Remembering the 1930s,* published forty-six years later. He was ninety-one when he died in 1989. Kenneth Burke (*Permanence and Change; A Grammar of Motives; A Rhetoric of Motives; Language as Symbolic Action*) went on writing and lecturing—intense blue eyes in a swirl of energies—until well into his eighties. He died in 1993 in his ninety-seventh year. Cummings was sixty-eight, Williams seventy-nine, Katherine Anne Porter ninety when each of them passed from the scene.

And what of Crane's Cleveland friends? After Charlotte Rychtarik's death in the 1960s, Richard continued to paint until his own death in 1982. Bill Sommer designed murals for various public buildings in Cleveland and Akron as part of the Federal Arts Project in the thirties and died in 1949 at the age of eighty-two. Sam Loveman, who did so much for Crane's memory, died in 1976, approaching his ninetieth birthday. And Bill Wright worked his way up to become owner of a department store back in Crane's childhood home in Warren, Ohio. In April 1953, he killed himself. He was fifty-two. *Requiescant in pace.*[8]

NOTES

The following abbreviations are used throughout the Notes for works by or about Hart Crane:

Poems   *Complete Poems of Hart Crane*, ed. Marc Simon. New York: Liveright, 1986.

Letters I   *The Letters of Hart Crane 1916–1932*, ed. Brom Weber. Berkeley & Los Angeles: University of California Press, 1952.

Letters II   *Letters of Hart Crane and His Family*, ed. Thomas S. W. Lewis. New York: Columbia University Press, 1974.

Letters III   *O My Land, My Friends: The Selected Letters of Hart Crane*, ed. Langdon Hammer and Brom Weber. New York & London: Four Walls Eight Windows, 1997.

H   Philip Horton, *Hart Crane: The Life of an American Poet*. New York: W. W. Norton, 1937.

RR   Susan Jenkins Brown, *Robber Rocks: Letters and Memories of Hart Crane: 1923–1932*. Middletown, Conn.: Wesleyan University Press, 1969.

U   John Unterecker, *Voyager: A Life of Hart Crane*. New York & London: Liveright, 1987 (first publ. Farrar, Straus & Giroux, 1969).

YW   Thomas Parkinson, *Hart Crane and Yvor Winters: Their Literary Correspondence*. Berkeley: University of California Press, 1978.

S/b   SUNY Buffalo Collection: William Carlos Williams papers, State University of Buffalo Collection.

The following abbreviations are used throughout the Notes for names:

SA	Sherwood Anderson
SJB	Susan Jenkins Brown
WSB	William Slater Brown
GB	George Bryan
MC	Malcolm Cowley
PC	Peggy Cowley
CA	Clarence Arthur Crane
GC	Grace Crane
HC	Hart Crane
LD	Lorna Dietz
WF	Waldo Frank
SG	Solomon Grunberg
EBH	Elizabeth Belden Hart
MJ	Matthew Josephson
OK	Otto Kahn
SL	Sam Loveman
GM	Gorham Munson
KAP	Katherine Anne Porter
CR	Charlotte Rychtarik
RR	Richard Rychtarik
CS	Carl Schmitt
AS	Alfred Stieglitz
TWS	Mrs. T.W. (Aunt Sally) Simpson
AT	Allen Tate
JT	Jean Toomer
WU	Wilbur Underwood
CW	Charmion von Wiegand
WCW	William Carlos Williams
YW	Yvor Winters
WW	William Wright

Prolegomenon

1. HC to WF, 21 April 1924, *Letters III*, p. 187.

2. "To Brooklyn Bridge," *Poems*, p. 43.

3. "Song of Myself," in Richard Ellmann and Robert O'Clair, ed., *The Norton Anthology of Modern Poetry*, Second ed. (New York: W.W. Norton, 1988), p. 27.

4.   "Perpetuum Mobile: The City," in A. Walton Litz and Christopher MacGowan, ed., *The Collected Poems of William Carlos Williams*, Vol. I (1909–1939), (New York: New Directions, 1986), p. 430.

5.   "Body and Soul," *New and Selected Poems* (New York: Knopf, 1995), p. 15.

PART I

Chapter 1:   *Starting Out*

1.   From "The River" section of *The Bridge*, *Poems*, p. 58.

2.   From "Porphyro in Akron," *Poems*, p. 152.

3.   Ibid., p. 55.

4.   CA to HC, 24 January 1915, *Letters II*, pp. 7–8.

5.   "The Moth That God Made Blind," *Poems*, p. 168.

6.   "C 33," ibid., p. 135.

7.   Williams to HC, 16 November 1916, SUNY Buffalo Collection.

8.   HC to CS, late November 1916, quoted in H, p. 36.

9.   HC to CA, 31 December 1916, *Letters II*, p. 17.

10.   HC to CA, 5 January 1917, ibid., pp. 21–22.

11.   HC to GC and EBH, 26 January 1917, ibid., p. 31.

12.   HC to GC and EBH, 26 January 1917, ibid.

13.   CA to HC, 20 January 1917, ibid., pp. 27–30.

14.   CA to HC, 29 January 1917, ibid., pp. 32–33.

15.   "The Hive," *Poems*, p. 137.

16.   GC to HC, 30 January 1917, *Letters II*, p. 34.

17.   GC to HC, 29 March 1917, ibid., pp. 53–56.

18.   CA to HC, 16 April 1917, ibid., p. 57.

19.   CA to HC, 1 August 1917, ibid., p. 65.

20.   HC to CA, 8 August 1917, ibid., p. 66.

21.   HC to CA, 8 August 1917, ibid., pp. 66–67.

22. CA to GC, 21 August 1917, quoted in U, p. 82.

23. HC to CA, 18 September 1917, *Letters II*, p. 68.

24. GC to CA, 23 September 1917, ibid.

25. HC to GC, 28 September 1917, ibid., pp. 69–70.

26. HC to GC, 28 September 1917, ibid., p. 70.

27. WCW to HC, 19 April 1917, SUNY Buffalo Collection.

28. HC to GC, 3 October 1917, *Letters II*, p. 74.

29. HC to CS, October 1917, quoted in U, p. 99.

30. HC to GC, 9 October 1917, *Letters II*, pp. 81–82.

31. HC to CS, late November 1917, quoted in H, p. 55.

32. HC to GC, 26 October 1917, *Letters II*, p. 88.

33. HC to GC, 31 October 1917, ibid., p. 91.

34. Margaret Anderson to HC, undated (about 20 September 1917), quoted in U, p. 89.

35. "In Shadow," *Poems*, p. 13.

36. Quoted in H, pp. 57–58. HC pasted Pound's letter into his own copy of Pound's *Lustra*.

37. HC to CS, March 1918, quoted in H, p. 58.

38. HC to George Bryan, 23 April 1918, *Letters III*, pp. 13–14.

Chapter 2: Shuttlecock

1. HC to WW, 17 July 1918, quoted in U, pp. 113–14.

2. HC, "Joyce and Ethics," *The Little Review* (July 1918), repr. in *Letters III*, pp. 14–15.

3. HC to WW, 12 August 1918, *Letters I*, p. 11.

4. HC to Charles C. Bubb, 13 November 1918, ibid., pp. 11–12.

5. HC to GB, 14 December 1918, quoted in U, p. 118.

6. HC to GB, 4 January 1919, ibid.

7. HC to GB, 21 February 1919, ibid., p. 123.

8. HC to GC, 22 February 1919, *Letters II*, pp. 110–12.

9. HC to GB, 25 February 1919, quoted in U, p. 137.

10. HC to GB, 2 March 1919, *Letters III*, pp. 19–20.

11. HC to GC, 11 March 1919, *Letters II*, pp. 118–19.

12. HC to GB, 17 March 1919, *Letters III*, p. 20.

13. HC to GC, 7 March 1919, *Letters II*, p. 115.

14. HC to GC, 2 April 1919, ibid., p. 125.

15. HC to WW, 2 May 1919, *Letters I*, p. 16.

16. HC to WW, 2 May 1919, ibid., pp. 16–17.

17. "To Portapovich," *Poems*, p. 147.

18. HC to GC, 30 May 1919, Decoration Day, *Letters II*, pp. 135–36.

19. HC to GC, 30 May 1919, ibid., pp. 136.

20. HC to WW, 17 June 1919, *Letters III*, p. 24.

21. HC to WW, 14 May 1919, *Letters I*, p. 17.

22. HC to WW, 17 June 1919, *Letters III*, p. 23.

23. HC to GM, 22 August 1919, *Letters I*, p. 22.

24. *Poems*, p. 148.

25. Ibid., p. 15.

26. HC to CW, 5 November 1919, *Letters I*, p. 22.

Chapter 3: *About My Father's Business*

1. HC to GM, 13 November 1919, *Letters I*, pp. 23–24.

2. *The Pagan* (September 1919), repr. in Brom Weber, ed., *The Complete Poems and Selected Letters and Prose of Hart Crane* (Garden City, N.Y.: Doubleday, 1966), pp. 205–06.

3. SA to HC, 3 December 1919, quoted in U, p. 157.

4. HC to GM, 13 December 1919, *Letters III*, pp. 28–29.

5. HC to GM, 22 November 1919, ibid., p. 26.

6. HC to GM, 28 November 1919, ibid., p. 27.

7. HC to GM, 13 December 1919, ibid., pp. 28–29.

8. HC to WW, 14 December 1919, quoted in U, pp. 154–55.

9. SA to HC, 17 December 1919, ibid., p. 158.

10. HC to GM, 27 December 1919, *Letters III*, pp. 27–29.

11. Quoted in U, p. 156.

12. HC to GM, 13 December 1919, *Letters III*, p. 28.

13. HC to GM, 27 December 1919, ibid., pp. 29–30.

14. HC to GM, 27 December 1919, ibid., p. 30.

15. "Porphyro in Akron," *Poems*, pp. 150–52.

16. HC to GM, 9 January 1920, *Letters III*, p. 32.

17. HC to WW, 24 February 1920, *Letters I*, p. 33.

18. HC to GM, 14 April 1920, *Letters III*, p. 39.

19. HC to GM, mid-February 1920, ibid., pp. 33–34.

20. HC to GM, 28 November 1919, ibid., p. 27.

21. HC to GM, 22 November 1919, ibid., p. 26.

22. *Poems*, p. 6.

23. HC to GM, 28 January 1920, *Letters I*, pp. 31–32.

24. HC to GM, 6 March 1920, ibid., pp. 33–35.

25. HC to GM, 9 January 1920, *Letters III*, p. 31.

26. HC to GM, 14 April 1920, ibid., p. 39.

27. HC to GM, 6 March 1920, ibid., pp. 34–35.

28. HC to GM, 6 March 1920, ibid., p. 35.

29. HC to GM, 6 March 1920, ibid., p. 36.

30. HC to GM, 6 March 1920, ibid.

31. *Poems*, p. 173.

32. HC to GM, 14 April 1920, *Letters III*, pp. 39–40.

33. HC to GM, 18 August 1920, *Letters I*, p. 41.

34. HC to GM, 18 August 1920, ibid.

35. "Porphyro in Akron," *Poems*, p. 152.

36. HC to MJ, 15 March 1920, *Letters III*, p. 38.

37. *Poems*, p. 9.

38. HC to GM, 30 July 1920, *Letters I*, p. 41.

39. HC to GM, 13 September 1920, ibid., p. 42.

40. HC to GM, 24 September 1920, ibid., pp. 42–43.

41. HC to GM, 24 September 1920, *Letters III*, p. 41.

42. HC to GM, 20 October 1920, ibid., p. 43.

43. HC to GM, 20 October 1920, ibid.

44. HC to GM, 20 October 1920, ibid.

45. HC to GM, 20 October 1920, ibid., p. 42.

46. HC to WU, 31 January 1921, ibid., pp. 59–60.

47. HC to GM, 20 October 1920, ibid., p. 44.

48. HC to GM, 9 November 1920, *Letters I*, p. 45.

49. HC to GM, 23 November 1920, ibid., p. 48.

50. HC to WU, 22 December 1920, *Letters III*, p. 56.

51. HC to GM, 5 December 1920, *Letters I*, p. 48.

52. HC to WU, 22 December 1920, *Letters III*, p. 55.

53. HC to GM, 14 January 1921, ibid., pp. 50–51.

54. HC to GM, 14 January 1921, ibid., p. 51.

55. HC to WU, 2 January 1921, ibid., pp. 56–57.

56. HC to MJ, 14 January 1921, ibid., p. 57.

57. HC to MJ, 14 January 1921, ibid., pp. 57–58.

58. HC to GM, 28 January 1920, ibid., p. 58.

59. HC to GM, 21 May 1921, *Letters I*, p. 58.

60. HC to GM, 20 April 1921, *Letters III*, p. 61.

61. "Black Tambourine," *Poems*, p. 4.

62. HC to GM, 20 April 1921, *Letters III*, p. 62.

Chapter 4:   Breakthrough

1. HC to GM, 16 May 1921, *Letters I*, p. 57.

2. HC to WU, 31 January 1921, *Letters III*, p. 61.

3. HC to GM, 12 June 1921, *Letters I*, pp. 58–59.

4. HC to WU, 14 May 1921, *Letters III*, p. 63.

5. HC to GM, 16 May 1921, *Letters I*, p. 56.

6. HC to GM, 21 May 1921, ibid., p. 58.

7. HC to GM, 22 July 1921, ibid., p. 63.

8. HC to GM, 22 July 1921, ibid., p. 62.

9. HC to GM, 22 July 1921, ibid., pp. 62–63.

10. HC to GM, 9 August 1921, ibid., p. 63.

11. HC to GM, 1 October 1921, *Letters III*, p. 65.

12. *Poems*, p. 11.

13. HC to WW, 17 October 1921, *Letters III*, p. 70.

14. *Poems*, p. 11.

15. HC to GM, 6 October 1921, *Letters III*, p. 68.

16. HC to GM, 3 November 1921, *Letters I*, p. 69.

17. HC to GM, 3 November 1921, ibid., p. 70.

18. HC to WW, 17 October 1921, *Letters III*, pp. 69–70.

19. HC to GM, 26 November 1921, ibid., pp. 71–72.

20. HC to GM, 23 January 1922, ibid., p. 81.

21. HC to SA, 10 January 1922, ibid., p. 79.

22. HC to GM, 21 November 1921, *Letters I*, p. 71.

23. HC to GM, 10 December 1921, *Letters III*, pp. 73–74.

24. HC to GM, 2 January 1922, quoted in U, p. 225.

25. HC to GM, 23 January 1922, *Letters III*, p. 80.

26. HC to GM, 23 January 1922, ibid.

27. HC to GM, 2 March 1922, *Letters I*, p. 82.

28. HC to GM, 23 January 1922, *Letters III*, p. 80.

29. HC to WW, 11 February 1922, ibid., p. 82.

30. HC to GM, 25 December 1921, ibid., pp. 76–77.

31. HC to GM, 25 December 1921, ibid., p. 76.

32. HC to WU, 4 July 1922, ibid., pp. 94–95.

33. "Praise for an Urn," *Poems*, p. 8.

34. HC to GM, 12 March 1922, *Letters I*, p. 82 (misdated 2 March 1922).

35. HC to GM, 29 March 1922, ibid., p. 83.

36. HC to GM, 25 February 1922, ibid., p. 80.

37. HC to GM, 19 April 1922, quoted in H, p. 104.

38. HC to CW, 6 May 1922, *Letters I*, pp. 85–86.

39. HC to WU, 15 June 1922, *Letters III*, p. 91.

40. HC to GM, 16 May 1922, ibid., p. 83.

41. *Poems*, p. 154.

42. HC to AT, 16 May 1922, *Letters III*, p. 85.

43. HC to AT, 16 May 1922, ibid., p. 86.

44. HC to GM, 16 May 1922 (2nd letter), ibid., p. 84.

45. HC to GM, 4 June 1922, ibid., p. 88.

46. HC to GM, 18 June 1922, ibid., p. 93.

47. "For the Marriage of Faustus and Helen," Part II, *Poems*, p. 29.

48. HC to WU, 15 June 1922, *Letters III*, p. 91.

49. HC to GM, 18 June 1922, ibid., pp. 91–93.

50. "For the Marriage of Faustus and Helen," Part II, *Poems*, p. 30.

51. HC to GM, 18 June 1922, *Letters III*, pp. 92–93.

52. "Praise for an Urn," *Poems*, p. 8.

53. HC to GM, 18 June 1922, *Letters III*, p. 93.

Chapter 5: *The Higher Consciousness*

1. "For the Marriage of Faustus and Helen," Part II, *Poems*, p. 29.

2. HC to WU, 4 July 1922, *Letters III*, pp. 94–95.

3. "Voyages I," *Poems*, p. 34.

4. HC to GM, "Monday," probably 28 August 1922, *Letters I*, p. 99.

5. HC to AT, 19 July 1922, *Letters III*, p. 96.

6. "For the Marriage of Faustus and Helen," Part I, *Poems*, pp. 26–28.

7. HC to WU, 27 July 1922, *Letters III*, pp. 97–98.

8. HC to GM, 10 December 1921, ibid., p. 73.

9. HC to GM, 7 August 1922, *Letters I*, p. 95.

10. HC to CW, 15 August 1922, ibid., p. 97.

11. HC to GM, 5 January 1923, *Letters III*, p. 117.

12. HC to GM, 7 August 1922, *Letters I*, p. 96.

13. "Sunday Morning Apples," *Poems*, p. 7.

14. HC to GM, Friday night, late August 1922, *Letters III*, p. 98.

15. HC to WU, 2 September 1922, ibid., pp. 102–03.

16. HC to GM, 12 October 1922, *Letters I*, p. 102.

17. HC to WU, 19 September 1922, *Letters III*, p. 105.

18. HC to GM, Tuesday, probably 20 September 1922, *Letters I*, p. 100.

19. HC to GM, 7 November 1922, ibid., p. 103–04.

20. HC to WCW, Wednesday, probably 19 September 1922, *Letters III*, pp. 104–05.

21. HC to GM, 12 October 1922, ibid., p. 102.

22. HC to GM, Thanksgiving Day 1922, ibid., p. 109.

23. HC to GM, 25 October 1922, *Letters I*, p. 103.

24. HC to WU, 10 December 1922, *Letters III*, p. 114.

25. HC to GM, 20 November 1922, ibid., p. 108.

26. HC to GM, Thanksgiving Day 1922, ibid., p. 109.

27. HC to WW, 4 December 1922, ibid., p. 111.

28. HC to WU, 10 December 1922, ibid., pp. 112–13.

29. HC to GM, 5 January 1923, , ibid., pp. 115–16.

30. "America's Plutonic Ecstasies," *Poems*, p. 157.

31. HC to GM, 12 December 1922, *Letters III*, pp. 114–15.

32. HC to GM, 29 September 1922, ibid., p. 106.

33. HC to GM, Friday night, late August 1922, ibid., p. 99.

34. HC to GM, 14 January 1923, ibid., pp. 118–19.

35. HC to GM, 20 November 1922, ibid., p. 108.

36. HC to GM, 5 January 1922, ibid., pp. 117–18.

37. "For the Marriage of Faustus and Helen," Part III, *Poems*, pp. 31–32.

38. HC to GM, 7 December 1922, *Letters I*, p. 107.

39. HC to WU, 10 December 1922, *Letters III*, p. 113.

40. HC to Louis Untermeyer, 19 January 1923, ibid., pp. 119–20.

41. Quoted in U, p. 277.

42. HC quoting AT in letter to GM, 6 February 1923, *Letters III*, p. 123.

43. HC to GM, 24 January 1923, ibid., p. 117.

44. *Poems*, p. 10.

45. HC to GM, 9 February 1923, *Letters III*, p. 127.

46. HC to WU, 20 February 1923, ibid., pp. 133–34.

47. HC to GM, 18 February 1923, ibid., pp. 131–32.

48. HC to GM, 27 February 1923, *Letters I*, p. 128.

49. HC to WF, 27 February 1923, *Letters III*, p. 135.

50. HC to GM, 2 March 1923, ibid., p. 137.

51. "For the Marriage of Faustus and Helen," Part II, *Poems*, p. 30.

52. HC to GM, 2 March 1923, *Letters III*, p. 137.

53. HC to GM, 2 March 1923, ibid., p. 138.

Part II

Chapter 6: *White Buildings*

1. HC to WF, Easter, 1 April 1923, *Letters III*, pp. 147–48.

2. HC to William Sommer, 9 May 1923, ibid., pp. 150–51.

3. *Poems*, p. 207.

4. HC to CR and RR, 4 April 1923, quoted in U, p. 288.

5. HC to CR, 13 April 1923, *Letters I*, p. 131.

6. HC to AS, 15 April 1923, *Letters III*, pp. 148–49.

7. "To Brooklyn Bridge," *Poems*, p. 43.

8. GC to HC, 4 May 1923, *Letters II*, pp. 150–51.

9. HC to William Sommer, 9 May 1923, *Letters III*, pp. 149–50.

10. HC to WU, 9 May 1923, ibid., pp. 151–52.

11. HC to Charles Harris, 11 May 1923, quoted in U, p. 296.

12. *Poems*, p. 208.

13. HC to GC and EBH, 25 May 1923, *Letters III*, pp. 166–67.

14. HC to GC, 1 June 1923, *Letters II*, p. 172.

15. HC quoting WF in letter to GC, 10 June 1923, ibid., p. 175.

16. HC to CR, 21 July 1923, *Letters III*, pp. 157–59.

17. HC to AS, 4 July 1923, ibid., pp. 154–57.

18. HC to Charles Harris, 8 July 1923, quoted in U, p. 304.

19. HC to CR, 21 July 1923, *Letters III*, pp. 157–58.

20. HC to Alfred Stieglitz, 11 August 1923, ibid., pp. 160–61.

21. HC to JT, 19 August 1923, ibid., p. 161.

22. "The Tunnel," *Poems*, pp. 98–99.

23. HC to GC and EBH, 18 August 1923, *Letters II*, pp. 193–94.

24. HC to AS, 25 August 1923, *Letters III*, p. 162.

25. HC to GC and EBH, 8 September 1923, *Letters II*, p. 200.

26. HC to GC and EBH, 8 September 1923, ibid., p. 199.

27. HC to GC, 21 September 1923, ibid., p. 204.

28. HC to CR, 23 September 1923, *Letters I*, p. 148.

29. HC to CW, 6 May 1922, ibid., p. 85.

30. Charlie Chaplin, *My Autobiography* (New York: Simon & Schuster, 1959), pp. 248–50.

31. HC to GC, 5 October 1923, *Letters II*, p. 211.

32. HC to GC and EBH, 12 October 1923, ibid., p. 215.

33. HC to GC, 12 October 1923, ibid., p. 217.

34. HC to GM, 18/19 October 1923, quoted in U, pp. 314, 320.

35. Matthew Josephson to Harold Loeb, quoted in U, p. 315. See also Mal-

colm Cowley, *Exile's Return: A Literary Odyssey of the 1920s* (New York: Viking Press, 1951).

36. HC to GM, 28 October 1923, *Letters I*, pp. 154–55.

37. CA to HC, 27 October 1923, *Letters II*, p. 224. HC's letter is missing and was probably destroyed by an infuriated CA himself.

38. CA to HC, 27 October 1923, ibid., pp. 222–24.

39. HC to GC and EBH, 20 October 1923, ibid., p. 219.

40. HC to GM, 24 October 1923, quoted in U, p. 321.

41. HC to GC and EBH, 1 November 1923, *Letters II*, p. 225.

42. HC to WU, 3 November 1923, *Letters III*, p. 168. "I never even undressed," Crane added, still stunned, "and it will be weeks before I can get the thing out of my mind....The most perfect gifts are shattered before you have seen them whole!"

43. HC to JT, 4 November 1923, ibid., p. 168.

44. HC to JT, 23 November 1923, ibid., p. 169.

45. Cf. *Poems*, p. 192, where the fragment is titled by its first line, "This Way Where November . . ." See also *Letters III*, p. 170, the fragment included in HC's letter to JT of 23 November 1923.

46. "Possessions," *Poems*, p. 18.

47. HC to GM, 31 November 1923, quoted in U, p. 333.

48. "Recitative," *Poems*, p. 25.

49. Quoted in U, p. 334.

50. HC to AT, 1 March 1924, *Letters III*, pp. 182–83.

51. HC to SJB, 13 November 1923, *RR*, pp. 16–17.

52. HC to EBH, 5 December 1923, *Letters II*, pp. 235–36.

53. HC to AS, 5 December 1923, *Letters I*, p. 157.

54. CA to HC, 10 December 1923, *Letters II*, p. 239.

55. HC to GC, 14 December 1923, ibid., p. 240.

56. HC to GM, 20 December 1923, *Letters I*, pp. 162–63.

57. "Emblems of Conduct," *Poems*, p. 5.

58. HC to GM, 9 January 1924, *Letters III*, p. 176.

59. HC to CA, 12 January 1924, *Letters* II, pp. 258–61.

60. HC to GC, 19 January 1924, ibid., p. 266, in reference to CA's letter of 15 January 1924.

61. HC to GC and EBH, 24 January 1924, ibid., pp. 268–69.

62. HC to GC and EBH, 29 January 1924, ibid., pp. 269–71.

63. Malcolm Cowley to Kenneth Burke, 19 February 1924, Paul Jay, ed., *The Selected Correspondence of Kenneth Burke and Malcom Cowley, 1915–1981* (New York: Viking, 1988), p. 159.

Chapter 7:   *In the Shadow of the Bridge*

1. HC to AT, 1 March 1924, *Letters III*, p. 182.

2. HC to CR and RR, 5 March 1924, *Letters I*, p. 176.

3. HC to GC, 23 March 1924, *Letters II*, p. 294.

4. HC to GC, 29 March 1924, ibid., pp. 294–95.

5. HC to GC, 3 April 1924, ibid., p. 295.

6. HC to GC, 3 April 1924, ibid., p. 296.

7. HC to GC, 21 December 1923, ibid., p. 243.

8. "Lachrymae Christi," *Poems*, pp. 19–20.

9. WF to HC, 28 March 1924, repr. in *Letters II*, pp. 300–02.

10. HC to GC and EBH, Easter, 20 April 1924, ibid., pp. 305–06.

11. Cf. *Letters III*, pp. 143–44. Cf. also Sam Loveman's remembrances of what Emil Opffer told him about his first meeting with Crane, recounted in *Hart Crane: A Conversation with Sam Loveman* (New York: Interim Books, 1964), *passim*.

12. HC to WF, 21 April 1924, ibid., pp. 186–87.

13. "Voyages II," *Poems*, p. 35.

14. "Voyages III," ibid., p. 36.

15. HC to GC and EBH, 11 May 1924, *Letters II*, p. 312.

16. HC to JT, 16 June 1924, *Letters III*, pp. 192–93.

17. "Voyages IV," *Poems*, p. 37.

18. HC to JT, 16 June 1924, *Letters III*, pp. 192–93.

19. HC to GC, 19 June 1924, *Letters II*, p. 323.

20. HC to GM, 9 July 1924, *Letters I*, pp. 184–85.

21. HC to GC, 3 February 1924, *Letters II*, p. 275.

22. HC to GM, 9 July 1924, *Letters I*, p. 185.

23. HC to GC and EBH, 12 August 1924, *Letters II*, p. 337.

24. HC to GC, 17 August 1924, ibid., p. 339.

25. HC to GC and EBH, 12 August 1924, ibid., p. 337.

26. "Voyages V," *Poems*, p. 38.

27. "Voyages VI," *Poems*, pp. 39–40.

28. HC to GC and EBH, 14 September 1924, *Letters II*, p. 345.

29. HC to GC, 23 September 1924, ibid., pp. 349–50.

30. HC to GC, 23 September 1924, ibid., p. 348.

31. HC to GC, 14 October 1924, ibid., p. 355.

32. "Paraphrase," *Poems*, p. 17.

33. HC to GC, 23 September 1924, *Letters II*, p. 348.

34. HC to GC and EBH, 21 October 1924, ibid., p. 359.

35. "Legend," *Poems*, p. 3.

36. HC to GC, 14 October 1924, *Letters II*, p. 354.

37. H. P. Lovecraft, journal entry, 29 September 1924, quoted in U, p. 372.

38. H. P. Lovecraft, journal entry, 4/5 November 1924, quoted in ibid.

39. Robert Lowell, *Life Studies* (New York: Farrar, Straus & Cudahy, 1959), p. 55.

40. HC to GC and EBH, 9 November 1924, *Letters II*, p. 367.

41. HC to GC and EBH, 26 November 1924, ibid., pp. 376–77.

42. HC to GC and EBH, 16 November 1924, ibid., p. 372.

43. HC to GC and EBH, 9 November 1924, ibid., p. 367.

44. HC to GC and EBH, 16 November 1924, ibid., p. 372.

45. HC to GC and EBH, 16 November 1924, ibid., pp. 372–73.

46. "The Harbor Dawn," *Poems*, pp. 53–54.

47. GC to HC, 18 November 1924, *Letters II*, p. 374.

48. HC to GC, 20 November 1924, ibid., p. 374.

49. HC to GC and EBH, 26 November 1924, ibid., p. 376.

50. HC to GC, 30 November 1924, ibid., pp. 377–79.

51. HC to GC and EBH, 26 November 1924, ibid., p. 376.

52. HC to GM, 5 December 1924, *Letters III*, p. 201.

53. HC to GM, 9 July 1924, ibid., p. 194.

54. HC to GM, 5 December 1924, ibid., pp. 201–02.

55. HC to GM, 8 December 1924, *Letters II*, p. 202.

56. HC to GC and EBH, 4 January 1925, ibid., p. 381.

57. HC to GC. 10 February 1925, ibid., p. 389.

58. HC to CR and RR, 1 March 1925, *Letters I*, p. 200.

59. HC to CR and RR, 28 February 1925, ibid., p. 199.

60. HC to GC and EBH, 23 February 1925, *Letters II*, p. 391.

61. HC to GC, 10 March 1925, ibid., p. 393.

62. HC to CR and RR, 9 April 1925, *Letters I*, p. 202.

63. HC to GC and EBH, Easter Monday, 13 April 1925, *Letters II*, pp. 309–10.

64. HC to GC and EBH, 2 May 1925, ibid., p. 404.

65. HC to GC and EBH, 21 April 1925, ibid., p. 401.

66. HC to GC, 28 May 1925, ibid., p. 408.

Chapter 8: *The Hawk's Far Stemming View*

1. HC to EBH, 17 June 1925, *Letters II*, pp. 417–18.

2. HC to GC and EBH, 10 July 1925, ibid., p. 424.

3. HC to GC and EBH, 10 July 1925, ibid., pp. 425–26.

4. "Passage," *Poems*, pp. 21–22.

5. HC to WF, Friday, 14 July 1925, *Letters I*, p. 213.

6. Quoted in letter HC sent to WF, 19 August 1925, ibid., p. 215.

7. HC to WF, Friday, 14 July 1925, ibid., p. 213.

8. HC to WF, 19 August 1925, ibid., p. 214.

9. HC to SJB and WSB, *RR*, 3 August 1925, pp. 29–30.

10. HC to SJB and WSB, 3 August 1925, *RR*, p. 29.

11. HC to SJB and WSB, ? 19 August 1925, *RR*, p. 31.

12. HC to WF, 19 August 1925, *Letters I*, p. 214.

13. Quoted in U, p. 404.

14. "The Wine Menagerie," *Poems*, pp. 23–24.

15. HC to CR and RR, Sunday, 4 October 1925, *Letters I*, p. 216.

16. HC to CR and RR, Sunday, 4 October 1925, ibid., p. 217.

17. H. P. Lovecraft's journal, ? 11 October 1925, quoted in U, p. 402.

18. HC to SJB and WSB, 21 October 1925, *RR*, pp. 36–37.

19. Ibid., p. 37.

20. HC to WS, 27 October 1925, *Letters I*, pp. 218–19.

21. "At Melville's Tomb," *Poems*, p. 33.

22. Reprinted in various collections of Crane's prose writings. Cf. *Letters III*, pp. 278–82.

23. "General Aims and Theories," Brom Weber, ed., *The Complete Poems and Selected Letters and Prose of Hart Crane* (Garden City, N.Y.: Doubleday, 1966), pp. 217–23.

24. HC to WF, 18 January 1926, *Letters III*, pp. 226–27. "Symphonic" was the word Crane repeated over and over in describing the condensed music of "Atlantis."

25. "Atlantis," *Poems*, pp. 105–08.

26. HC to CA, 21 November 1925, *Letters II*, p. 442.

27. HC to CA, 3 December 1925, ibid., pp. 445–46.

28. HC to CR and RR, 1 December 1925, *Letters III*, p. 209.

29. HC to YW, 5 October 1926, ibid., pp. 283–84.

30. Marianne Moore, *Writers at Work: The Paris Review Interviews, Second Series* (New York: Viking Press, 1963), p. 80.

31. HC to Otto H. Kahn, 3 December 1925, *Letters III*, pp. 212–14.

32. CA to HC, 16 December 1925, *Letters II*, p. 450.

33. HC to CA, 25 December 1925, ibid., p. 451.

34. HC to WU, 25 December 1925, "Wind-blown Flames: Letters of Hart Crane to Wilbur Underwood," ed. Warren Herendeen and Donald G. Parker, *Southern Review*, vol. 16, no. 2 (1980, cited hereafter as "Wind-blown Flames"), pp. 360–62.

35. HC to CR and RR, 31 December 1925, *Letters III*, pp. 224–25.

36. HC to EBH, 5 January 1926, *Letters II*, p. 458.

37. HC to GC and EBH, 7 January 1926, ibid., p. 459.

38. HC to MC, 3 January 1926, *Letters III*, p. 226.

39. This list was provided by HC in a letter to Yvor Winters, 2 April 1927, *YW*, p. 77.

40. HC to WF, 18 January 1926, *Letters III*, p. 227.

41. HC to GM, 5 March 1926, ibid., pp. 230–31.

42. HC to EBH, 27 January 1926, *Letters II*, p. 471.

43. HC to GC, 26 January 1926, ibid., p. 467.

44. HC to Gaston Lachaise, 10 February 1926, *Letters III*, p. 227.

45. HC to CR and RR, 2 March 1926, ibid., p. 229.

46. HC to GM, 5 March 1926, ibid., pp. 230–31.

47. HC to MC, 28 March 1926, ibid., p. 238.

48. HC to GM, 17 March 1926, ibid., p. 231.

49. HC to MC, 28 March 1926, ibid., p. 238.

50. HC to GM, 17 March 1926, ibid., pp. 232–34.

51. HC to Otto H. Kahn, 18 March 1926, ibid., pp. 235–37.

52. "Ave Maria," *Poems*, pp. 47–50.

53. HC to GC, Sunday, 28 March 1926, *Letters III*, p. 476.

54. HC to GM, 5 April 1926, ibid., pp. 239–40.

55. HC to GC, 18 April 1926, *Letters II*, pp. 478–83.

56. The Tates' letters to Crane and Crane's two letters to the Tates that follow are all reprinted in *Letters III*, pp. 246–49. As one who saw himself as a Southern gentleman, Tate was not averse to throwing down

the gauntlet. He did it in his twenties, and he was still doing it in his sixties with two of his younger protégés and friends, Robert Lowell and John Berryman.

57.   HC to GC, 18 April 1926, *Letters II*, p. 478.

58.   Caroline Blackwood to Sally Wood, 15 May 1926. Sally Wood, ed., *Letters of Caroline Gordon to Sally Wood, 1924–1937* (Baton Rouge: Louisiana State University, 1984), pp. 21–22. "We had material for a Eugene O'Neill play in this house this winter," Gordon added. "Our landlady, a worthy soul of sixty-four, fell violently in love with Hart."

59.   HC to SJB and WSB, 7 May 1926, *RR*, p. 55.

60.   CA to HC, 10 May 1926, *Letters II*, p. 490.

Chapter 9:   Clenched Beaks Coughing for the Surge Again!

1.   HC to GC and Charles Curtis, 3 May 1926, *Letters II*, p. 486.

2.   HC to SJB and WSB, 7 May 1926, *RR*, pp. 53–54.

3.   "Voyages II," *Poems*, p. 35.

4.   HC to SJB and WSB, 7 May 1926, *RR*, p. 54.

5.   HC to CA, 20 May 1926, *Letters II*, p. 493.

6.   HC to SJB and WSB, 7 May 1926, *RR*, p. 54.

7.   HC to SJB, 22 May 1926, ibid., p. 59.

8.   HC to SJB and WSB, 7 May 1926, ibid., pp. 54–55.

9.   HC to GC, 8 May 1926, *Letters II*, p. 488.

10.   HC to SJB and WSB, 7 May 1926, *RR*, p. 55.

11.   HC to GC, 8 May 1926, *Letters II*, p. 490.

12.   HC to CA, 20 May 1926, ibid., p. 494.

13.   HC to GC and EBH, 14 May 1926, ibid., pp. 491–92.

14.   HC to WF, 19 June 1926, *Letters III*, p. 256.

15.   HC to SJB, 22 May 1926, *RR*, p. 59.

16.   HC to WF, 22 May 1926, *Letters III*, p. 253. An "accidental calligramme" is what he called it in his letter to Sue Brown written that same day.

17.   HC to GC, 1 June 1926, *Letters II*, pp. 497–98.

18. HC to WF, 19 June 1926, *Letters III*, p. 255.

19. HC to WF, 20 June 1926, ibid., pp. 258–59.

20. CA to HC, 7 July 1926, *Letters II*, p. 499.

21. "Repose of Rivers," *Poems*, p. 16.

22. HC to WU, ca. 8 July 1926, *Letters III*, pp. 260–61. Hammer's proposed date of 1 July is too early.

23. HC to WW, 16 July 1926, *Letters I*, p. 267. and U, p. 443.

24. HC to EBH, 29 July 1926, *Letters II*, p. 505.

25. HC to WF, 24 July 1926, *Letters III*, p. 263.

26. "To Brooklyn Bridge," *Poems*, pp. 43–44.

27. HC to WF, 26 July 1926, *Letters III*, p. 265.

28. HC to MC and PC, 29 July 1926, ibid., p. 266.

29. HC to WU, "Wind-blown Flames," 3 August 1926, pp. 363–64.

30. "Cutty Sark," *Poems*, p. 71.

31. HC to GC, 30 July 1926, *Letters II*, p. 507.

32. HC to WF, 3 August 1926, *Letters III*, p. 267.

33. HC to WU, "Wind-blown Flames," 3 August 1926, pp. 363–64.

34. HC to WU, ibid., p. 364.

35. HC to WF, 3 August 1926, *Letters III*, p. 267.

36. HC to GC, 30 July 1926, *Letters II*, p. 507.

37. HC to WF, 3 August 1926, *Letters III*, p. 267.

38. HC to GC, 30 July 1926, *Letters II*, p. 507.

39. HC to WF, 12 August 1926, ibid., p. 268.

40. HC to WF, 12 August 1926, ibid., p. 268.

41. HC to CR and RR, 14 August 1926, quoted in U, p. 451.

42. HC to WF, 19 August 1926, *Letters III*, p. 271.

43. HC to WF, 19 August 1926, ibid., p. 270.

44. HC to WF, 23 August 1926, ibid., p. 272.

45. "The Tunnel," *Poems*, pp. 97–101.

46. HC to Isabel and Gaston Lachaise, p.c. early August 1926, *Letters III*, p. 266.

47. "Island Quarry," *Poems*, p. 116.

48. HC to WF, 19 August 1926, *Letters III*, p. 270.

49. "The Idiot," *Poems*, p. 118.

50. HC to GC, 28 August 1926, *Letters II*, p. 509.

51. HC to CA, 2 September 1926, ibid., p. 510.

52. HC to WF, 3 September 1926, *Letters III*, p. 274.

53. HC to WF, 5 September 1926, ibid., p. 275.

54. HC to GC, 6 September 1926, *Letters II*, p. 512.

55. HC to GC, 19 September 1926, *Letters III*, pp. 513–14.

56. HC to YW, 27 January 1927, ibid., pp. 313–14.

57. "O Carib Isle!," *Poems*, pp. 111–12.

58. HC to Otto Kahn, late September 1926, quoted in H, p. 214.

59. HC to YW, 5 October 1926, *Letters III*, pp. 283–84.

60. HC to YW, 9 October 1926, *YW*, p. 14.

61. Quoted in *RR*, pp. 66–67.

62. "Eternity," *Poems*, pp. 186–87.

63. HC to TWS, 5 December 1926, *Letters III*, pp. 292–93.

64. GC to HC, 30 October 1926, *Letters II*, p. 515.

65. HC to CA, 31 October 1926, ibid.

66. CA to HC, 2 November 1926, ibid., p. 517.

67. HC to CR, 1 November 1926, *Letters I*, p. 277.

PART III

Chapter 10: *Aftermath*

1. HC to YW, 12 November 1926, *Letters III*, p. 285.

2. HC to AT, 1 March 1924, ibid., p. 182.

3. HC to YW, 12 November 1926, ibid., p. 286.

4. HC to WF, 21 November 1926, ibid., pp. 289–90.

5. HC to YW, 15 November 1926, ibid., p. 287.

6. "A Name for All," *Poems*, p. 119.

7. HC to WF, 21 November 1926, *Letters III*, p. 289.

8. "To Emily Dickinson," *Poems*, p. 128.

9. HC to TWS, 5 December 1926, *Letters III*, p. 292.

10. HC to TWS, 5 December 1926, ibid.

11. HC to YW, 27 March 1927, *YW*, p. 74.

12. HC to TWS, 5 December 1926, *Letters III*, pp. 292–93.

13. HC to WU, 16 December 1926, ibid., pp. 293–94.

14. HC to GC, 22 December 1926, *Letters II*, pp. 518–19.

15. HC to WU, 3 January 1927, *Letters III*, p. 304.

16. HC to WU, 11 January 1927, ibid., p. 308.

17. HC to GC, 23 January 1927, *Letters II*, p. 520.

18. HC to GC, 19 March 1927, ibid., p. 534.

19. Crane quoted this passage in a letter to his mother, 23 January 1927, ibid., p. 521.

20. Also quoted in Crane's letter to his mother for 23 January 1927, ibid.

21. HC to WF, 28 January 1927, *Letters III*, p. 317.

22. HC to GC, 19 March 1927, *Letters II*, pp. 533–34.

23. HC to SJB and WSB, 16 February 1927, *Letters III*, pp. 317–18.

24. HC to Sam Loveman, no date, but probably mid-February 1927, ibid., p. 317.

25. HC to SJB and WSB, 16 February 1927, ibid., p. 318.

26. HC to Isidor Schneider, 19 February 1927, *Letters I*, pp. 287–88.

27. HC to AT, 24 February 1927, *Letters III*, p. 319.

28. HC to YW, 23 February 1927, *YW*, p. 55.

29. HC to YW, 26 February 1927, *Letters III*, pp. 320–23.

30. HC to WSB, 9 March 1927, *RR*, p. 70.

31. Quoted in, ibid., p. 71.

32. HC to AT, 10 March 1927, *Letters III*, p. 324.

33. HC to AT, 14 March 1927, ibid., p. 325.

34. HC to YW, 19 March 1927, ibid., pp. 326–29.

35. HC to GC and EBH, 28 March 1927, *Letters II*, pp. 540–41.

36. HC to GC, 19 March 1927, ibid., p. 534.

37. HC to GC, 19 March 1927, ibid., p. 535.

38. HC to AT, 21 March 1927, *Letters III*, p. 330.

39. HC to YW, 27 March 1927, *YW*, p. 73.

40. HC to WU, "Wind-blown Flames," 21 March 1927, p. 366.

41. HC to YW, 27 March 1927, *YW*, p. 73.

42. HC to YW, 27 March 1927, ibid., p. 74.

43. HC to WU, "Wind-blown Flames," 3 August 1926, pp. 363–64.

44. HC to AT, 30 March 1927, *Letters III*, p. 332.

45. HC to YW, 2 April 1927, *YW*, p. 76.

46. HC to GC and EBH, 28 March 1927, *Letters II*, p. 540.

47. HC to YW, 18 April 1927, *YW*, pp. 77–78.

48. CA to HC, 20 April 1927, *Letters II*, p. 544.

49. HC to CA, 23 April 1927, ibid., pp. 544–45.

50. HC to GC, 28 April 1927, *Letters III*, p. 550.

51. HC to YW, 29 April 1927, ibid., pp. 333–34.

52. HC to CA, 7 May 1927, *Letters II*, p. 558.

53. HC to WU, 4 May 1927, *Letters III*, pp. 334–35.

54. Quoted in HC's letter to WU, 12 May 1927, ibid., p. 335.

55. HC to YW, 21 May 1927, *YW*, p. 81.

56. HC to GC, 27 May 1927, *Letters II*, p. 572.

57. Edmund Wilson, "The Muses Out of Work," *New Republic*, 11 May 1927.

58. HC to YW, 29 May 1927, *Letters III*, pp. 335–40.

59. HC to YW, 14 June 1927, *YW*, p. 92.

60. HC to YW, 25 June 1927, ibid., pp. 93–94. Crane, suffering from aggravated hay fever, ended this letter by withdrawing from the battle he had engaged in with Winters in his letter of 29 May. Since Winters was in quest of "a convincing ethic for contemporary tragic poetry," he could see that his own remarks now looked "superfluous and trifling." They were neither, but Crane realized he would get nowhere trying to argue with someone with Winters's bulldog tenacity.

61. HC to YW, 1 July 1927, *YW*, p. 94.

62. "Van Winkle," *Poems*, pp. 55–56.

63. "The River," ibid., pp. 57–61.

64. "The Dance," ibid., pp. 62–65.

65. HC to TWS, 4 July 1927, *Letters III*, pp. 341–43.

66. HC to YW, 5 July 1927, *YW*, pp. 95–97.

67. HC to YW, 3 August 1927, ibid., p. 101.

68. HC to CA, 12 August 1927, *Letters II*, p. 604.

69. HC to Otto Kahn, 12 September 1927, *Letters III*, pp. 344–50.

70. HC to SJB and WSB, 16 November 1927, ibid., pp. 351–52.

Chapter 11: Pinkpoodle Paradise

1. HC to YW, 23 November 1927, *Letters III*, pp. 352–53.

2. HC to YW, 8 December 1927, ibid., pp. 353–54.

3. HC to Sam Loveman, 5 February 1928, *Letters I*, p. 316.

4. HC to YW, 8 December 1927, *Letters III*, p. 354.

5. HC to YW, 23 November 1927, ibid., p. 353.

6. HC to WSB, 19 December 1927, ibid., pp. 354–56.

7. HC to WF, 12 June 1928, *Letters I*, p. 328.

8. "The Hurricane," *Poems*, p. 124.

9. Crane was much taken with Hopkins's curtal sonnet, "Pied Beauty," in particular; he carefully copied the poem and sent it to Sam Loveman in New York.

10. HC to YW, 27 January 1928, *Letters III*, p. 359.

11. HC to YW, 10 January 1928, ibid., p. 111.

12. HC to YW, 20 January 1928, ibid., p. 358.

13. HC to YW, 27 January 1928, ibid., pp. 359–60.

14. HC to PC and MC, 31 January 1928, ibid., pp. 360–61.

15. HC to WSB, 22 February 1928, ibid., pp. 362–63.

16. HC to YW, 23 February 1928, ibid., pp. 363–64.

17. HC to Isidor Schneider, 28 March 1928, *Letters I*, p. 322.

18. HC to YW, 7 March 1928, *YW*, p. 117.

19. HC to SJB and WSB, 27 March 1928, *Letters III*, pp. 365–67.

20. HC to WU, 27 April 1928, ibid., pp. 372–73.

21. HC to SJB and WSB, 27 March 1928, ibid., pp. 365–66.

22. HC to GM, 17 April 1928, ibid., pp. 370–72.

23. HC to WSB, 27 April 1928, *Letters I*, pp. 324–25.

24. HC to CR and RR, 26 February 1929, ibid., p. 337.

25. HC to Aunt Zell Deming, n.d., but probably June 1928, quoted in H, p. 244.

26. "A Postscript," *Poems*, p. 196.

27. HC to CA, 14 June 1928, *Letters II*, pp. 619–20.

28. HC to YW, 27 June 1928, *Letters III*, pp. 374–75.

29. HC to WU, "Wind-blown Flames," 5 June 1928, pp. 369–70.

30. HC to CA, 14 June 1928, *Letters II*, p. 620.

31. HC to YW, 27 June 1928, *Letters III*, p. 374.

32. Ibid.

33. HC to CA, 14 June 1928, *Letters II*, p. 619.

34. CA to HC, 18 June 1928, ibid., pp. 621–22.

35. HC to YW, 27 June 1928, *Letters III*, p. 376.

36. HC to CA, 25 July 1928, ibid., p. 626.

37. CA to HC, 27 July 1928, ibid., pp. 627–28.

38. HC to CA, 2 August 1928, *Letters II*, p. 629.

39. HC to YW, 17 August 1928, *YW*, p. 125.

40. HC to CA, 14 August 1928, *Letters III*, p. 630.

41. CA to HC, 16 August 1928, ibid., p. 631.

42. HC to MC, ? 20 August 1928, *RR*, p. 98.

43. HC to YW, 9 September 1928, *Letters III*, p. 377.

44. HC to Aunt Zell Deming, ? early November 1928, quoted in H, pp. 248–49.

45. HC to MC, 20 November 1928, *Letters III*, p. 382.

46. HC to CR and RR, 16 September 1928, ibid., pp. 377–78.

47. WCW to Louis Zukofsky, 2 December 1928. When Crane's first biographer, Philip Horton, asked Williams in the mid-1930s why he didn't see more of Crane, Williams answered testily and defensively that he was "a bit off homos and had heard that [Crane] was fairly assertive on that score. That may have influenced me. After all, I was living too." Quoted in *Letters III*, p. 379.

48. WCW to Ezra Pound, 12 July 1928, quoted in Paul Mariani, *William Carlos Williams: A New World Naked* (New York: W. W. Norton, 1990), p. 278.

49. Ezra Pound to WCW, 27 July 1928, ibid., pp. 278–79.

50. WCW to Ezra Pound, 11 August 1928, ibid., p. 279. See also Hugh Witemeyer, ed., *Pound / Williams: Selected Letters of Ezra Pound and William Carlos Williams* (New York: New Directions, 1996), pp. 88–93.

51. HC to WU, 5 October 1928, *Letters III*, p. 379.

52. HC to YW, 23 October 1928, ibid., p. 380.

53. HC to CR, 23 October 1928, ibid., p. 381.

54. HC to MC, 20 November 1928, ibid., p. 382.

55. HC to Aunt Zell Deming, ? early November 1928, quoted in H, p. 250.

56. HC to CR and RR, 26 February 1929, *Letters III*, pp. 399–400.

57. HC to YW, 29 November 1928, *YW*, p. 129.

58. HC to MC, 1 December 1928, *Letters III*, p. 383.

Chapter 12: Last Strands

1. HC to SL, 9 December 1928, *Letters I*, p. 331.

2. HC to WU, 12 December 1928, "Wind-blown Flames," p. 371.

3. HC to WF, 28 December 1928, *Letters III*, p. 394.

4. HC to E. E. Cummings, 21 December 1927, ibid., p. 357.

5. HC to CR and RR, 26 February 1929, ibid., p. 400.

6. HC to WU, p.c., n.d., February 1929, ibid., p. 398.

7. HC to SL, 23 January 1929, *Letters I*, p. 333.

8. HC to LD, 26 January 1929, *Letters III*, pp. 395–96.

9. HC to Joseph Stella, 24 January 1929, ibid., p. 395.

10. HC to MC, 4 February 1929, ibid., pp. 396–97.

11. HC to WF, 7 February 1929, *Letters I*, p. 335.

12. HC to CR and RR, 26 February 1929, *Letters III*, p. 400.

13. HC to WF, 7 February 1929, *Letters I*, pp. 335–36.

14. Cf. the Père Sebastian Rasles chapter of *In the American Grain* (New York: New Directions, 1956), pp. 105–29. Originally published 1925.

15. HC to WF, 7 February 1929, *Letters I*, p. 336.

16. HC to CR and RR, 26 February 1929, *Letters III*, p. 400.

17. Cf. H, p. 251.

18. Cf. ibid., p. 257.

19. HC to SL, 23 April 1929, *Letters I*, p. 339.

20. HC to WSB, 25 April 1929, ibid.

21. HC to Gertrude Stein, p.c. postmarked 29 April 1929, *Letters III*, p. 404.

22. HC to Isidor Schneider, 1 May 1929, ibid., pp. 405–07.

23. HC to Harry Crosby, Sunday morning, ? 3 March 1929, ibid., p. 402.

24. HC to Harry Crosby, 25 April 1929, ibid., p. 403.

25. HC to Isidor Schneider, 1 May 1929, ibid., pp. 405–07.

26. HC to AT, 11 June 1929, ibid., p. 409.

27. HC to Harry Crosby, 16 May 1929, ibid., pp. 407–08.

28. HC to AT, 11 June 1929, ibid., p. 409.

29. Quoted in Townsend Ludington, *Marsden Hartley: The Biography of an American Artist* (Boston: Little, Brown, 1992), p. 195.

30. Harry Crosby's diary for late June 1929, quoted in H, p. 258.

31. HC to Harry Crosby, 1 July 1929, *Letters III*, p. 410.

32. HC to MC, 3 July 1929, ibid., p. 411.

33. Quoted in H, pp. 258–59.

34. HC to CC, 8 August 1929, *Letters III*, p. 414.

35. HC to Harry Crosby, 23 July 1929, ibid., p. 412.

36. Peter Blume, "A Recollection of Hart Crane," *Yale Review*, vol. 76, no. 2 (Winter 1987), p. 153.

37. HC to CC, 8 August 1929, *Letters III*, p. 414.

38. HC to Harry Crosby and CC, 30 August 1929, ibid., p. 415.

39. HC to WU, 27 August 1929, "Wind-blown Flames," pp. 371–72.

40. From "Ode to Walt Whitman," *Poeta en Nueva York*. Translation by Paul Mariani.

41. Ian Gibson, *Federico García Lorca: A Life* (New York: Pantheon Books, 1989), p. 271.

42. HC to Harry and CC, 30 August 1929, *Letters III*, p. 415.

43. Song of Myself, in Richard Ellman and Robert O'Clair, ed., *The Norton Anthology of Modern Poetry*, Second ed. (New York: W. W. Norton, 1988), pp. 33–35.

44. "Cape Hatteras," *Poems*, pp. 77–84.

45. HC to CC, 17 September 1929, *Letters III*, p. 417.

46. Blume, "A Recollection of Hart Crane," p. 154.

47. HC to WU, 17 October 1929, "Wind-blown Flames," pp. 372–73.

48. HC to OK, 25 September 1929, *Letters III*, p. 417.

49. HC to LD, 25 October 1929, ibid., p. 418.

50. Blume, "A Recollection of Hart Crane," p. 155.

51. HC to Harry and CC, 29 October 1929, *Letters III*, pp. 418–19.

52. HC to SL, 11 November 1929, quoted in U, p. 606.

53. HC to WSB, 11 November 1929, ibid.

54. HC to CR and RR, 11 February 1930, *Letters I*, p. 348.

55. *Robber Rocks*, pp. 69–70.

56. "Quaker Hill," *Poems*, pp. 92–94.

57. "I think that Evans is the most living, vital photographer of any whose work I know," Crane told Caresse Crosby. "More and more I rejoice that we decided on his pictures rather than Stella's." HC to CC, 2 January 1930, *Letters III*, p. 422.

58. HC to CC, 12 December 1929, ibid., pp. 419–20.

59. HC to AT, 14 December 1929, ibid., p. 420.

60. HC to CC, 26 December 1929, ibid., p. 421.

PART IV

Chapter 13: Down and Out in New York

1. "To the Cloud Juggler," *Poems*, p. 114.

2. HC to YW, 27 January 1930, *Letters III*, p. 424.

3. HC to CC, 22 January 1930, quoted in U, p. 614.

4. HC to CR, 11 February 1930, *Letters I*, p. 349.

5. HC to WF, 16 March 1930, ibid., p. 349.

6. HC to YW, 27 January 1930, *Letters III*, p. 424.

7. HC to Herbert Weinstock, 22 April 1930, ibid., pp. 426–27.

8. HC to CC, 13 May 1930, quoted in U, p. 613.

9. Lincoln Kirstein, "Crane and Carlsen: A Memoir, 1926–1934," *Raritan*, vol. 1, no. 3 (Winter 1982), p. 15.

10. Ibid., p. 40.

11. HC to CC, 8 February 1930, quoted in U, p. 613.

12. Yvor Winters, "The Progress of Hart Crane," *Poetry*, 36 (June 1930), pp. 157–58.

13. HC to YW, 4 June 1930, *Letters III*, pp. 427–30.

14. HC to Isidor Schneider, 8 June 1930, ibid., pp. 430–31.

15. HC to AT, 13 July 1930, ibid., p. 433.

16. HC to AT, 13 July 1930, ibid., pp. 431–32.

17. HC to AT, 7 September 1930, ibid., p. 435.

18. HC to John Roebling, 18 August 1930, ibid., p. 434.

19. HC to AT, 7 September 1930, ibid., p. 435.

20. HC to SG, 30 September 1930, *Letters I*, p. 356.

21. HC to the John Simon Guggenheim Foundation, 29 August 1930, *Letters III*, pp. 434–35.

22. HC to SG, 30 September 1930, *Letters I*, p. 356.

23. HC to WU, 20 November 1930, *Letters III*, p. 437.

24. HC to WW, 21 November 1930, ibid., pp. 438–30.

25. HC to WW, 29 November 1930, ibid., p. 440.

26. HC to SL, 29 December 1930, ibid., pp. 440–41.

27. HC to SG, 10 January 1931, , ibid., p. 442.

28. HC to SL, 16 February 1931, *Letters I*, pp. 363–64.

29. HC to LD, 10 February 1931, *Letters III*, pp. 444–45.

30. HC to WF, 19 February 1931, ibid., pp. 446–47.

31. HC to Henry Allen Moe, 16 March 1931, ibid., pp. 447–48.

Chapter 14: Death's Adjustments

1. HC to CR and RR, 30 March 1931, *Letters III*, p. 459.

2. HC to WSB, 6 April 1931, *RR*, pp. 123–24.

3. HC to CC, 5 April 1931, *Letters III*, p. 460.

4. HC to LD, 7 April 1931, quoted in U, p. 652.

5. HC to SL, 12 April 1931, *Letters III*, pp. 461–62.

6. HC to SL, 12 April 1931, ibid.

7. Katherine Anne Porter, quoted in H, pp. 286–87.

8. HC to KAP, Tuesday, 28 April 1931, *Letters III*, p. 464.

9. HC to KAP, Thursday morning, 30 April 1931, ibid.

10. CA to HC, 1 May 1931, *Letters II*, p. 642.

11. HC to KAP, Friday, 1 May 1931, *Letters III*, pp. 464–65.

12. HC to CR and RR, 14 May 1931, quoted in U, p. 662.

13. HC to MC, 2 June 1931, *Letters III*, pp. 465–66.

14. Quoted in U, p. 663.

15. HC to WF, 13 June 1931, *Letters III*, pp. 468–70.

16. HC to MC, 2 June 1931, ibid., pp. 466–67.

17. "Havana Rose," *Poems*, pp. 200–01.

18. HC to CA, 5 June 1931, *Letters II*, pp. 645–46.

19. HC to MC, 2 June 1931, *Letters III*, pp. 465–66.

20. HC to Morton Dauwen Zabel, 20 June 1931, ibid., p. 471.

21. "Purgatorio," *Poems*, p. 202.

22. Quoted in H, pp. 285–86.

23. HC to KAP, 22 June 1931, *Letters III*, pp. 471–72.

24. KAP to HC, quoted in ibid., p. 472.

25. HC to LD, 15 July 1931, ibid., pp. 475–77.

26. Henry Allen Moe to HC, 29 June 1931, ibid., p. 473.

27. CA to HC, 29 June 1931, *Letters II*, pp. 646–47.

28. HC to Henry Allen Moe, 8 July 1931, *Letters III*, p. 474.

29. HC to WU, 30 November 1931, ibid., p. 494.

30. HC to Margaret Robson, 29 July 1931, quoted in U, p. 682.

Chapter 15: Viva Mexico!

1. HC to SL, 11 September 1931, *Letters III*, pp. 478–79.

2. HC to WW, 21 September 1931, ibid., pp. 479–83.

3. HC to CR and RR, 4 November 1931, *Letters I*, pp. 384–85.

4. HC to SG, 20 October 1931, *Letters III*, pp. 485–86.

5. HC to CR and RR, 4 November 1931, *Letters I*, p. 385.

6. HC to MC, 5 October 1931, *Letters III*, p. 484.

7. SJB, *RR*, pp. 140–41.

8. Quoted in U, p. 697.

9. HC to CR and RR, 4 November 1931, *Letters I*, p. 385.

10. HC to SL, 17 November 1931, *Letters III*, p. 491.

11. HC to Eda Lou Walton, 27 November 1931, ibid., p. 493.

12. HC to WU, 30 November 1931, ibid., pp. 493–94.

13. HC to Bess Meachem Crane, 12 December 1931, ibid., pp. 495–96.

14. Cf. Peggy Baird Cowley's memoir, "The Last Days of Hart Crane," reprinted in *RR*, pp. 147–73. Originally published in *Venture*, vol. 4, no. 1 (1961).

15. HC to MC, 9 January 1932, *Letters III*, p. 500.

16. HC to PC, 6 January 1932, ibid., pp. 497–98.

17. HC to PC, 7 January 1932, ibid., pp. 498–99.

18. HC to PC, Tuesday, 12 January 1932, quoted in U, p. 718.

19. HC to PC, Wednesday, ? 20 January 1932, *Letters III*, pp. 502–03.

20. HC to WU, 15 January 1932, ibid., p. 501.

21. Quoted in U, p. 722. Lesley Simpson wrote up his recollections in September 1932, only eight months after the events.

22. Ibid., p. 698.

Chapter 16:   The Broken Tower

1. Quoted in U, p. 724.

2. To SG, 8 February 1932, *Letters III*, pp. 503–04.

3. HC to WU, 14 February 1932, ibid., p. 507.

4. HC to Bess Meachem Crane, 17 February 1932, ibid., p. 509.

5. HC to PC, 10 February 1932, ibid., p. 505.

6. HC to PC, Thursday, 11 February 1932, ibid., pp. 506–07.

7. HC to PC, Tuesday, 16 February 1932, ibid., pp. 507–08.

8. HC to PC, 16 February 1932, ibid., p. 508.

9. HC to MC and Muriel Maurer, 18 February 1932, ibid., p. 512. Letter typed on rose-colored paper with an image of Our Lady of Guadalupe in the center. Crane typed around the image, leaving it intact.

10. HC to Bess Meachem Crane, 8 March 1932, *Letters II*, p. 650.

11. HC to PC, 16 February 1932, *Letters III*, p. 507.

12. Quoted in U, p. 736.

13. "The Broken Tower," *Poems*, pp. 160–61.

14. HC to SL, Easter, 27 March 1932, *Letters III*, p. 517.

15. HC to CC, 31 March 1932, *Letters I*, p. 405.

16. HC to SG, 12 April 1932, *Letters III*, pp. 518–19.

17. HC to SG, 12 April 1932, ibid., p. 517.

18. HC to LD, 12 April 1932, ibid., pp. 520–21.

19. HC to LD, 12 April 1932, ibid., pp. 517–19.

20. HC to SL, 13 April 1932, *Letters I*, p. 409.

21. HC to SG, 12 April 1932, and to LD, 12 April 1932, *Letters III*, pp. 518–20.

22. HC to SG, 20 October 1931, *Letters III*, p. 488.

23. Quoted in U, p. 747.

24. HC to Byron Madden, 20 April 1932, quoted in ibid., p. 748.

25. HC to SG, 20 April 1932, *Letters III*, p. 522.

26. HC to SG, 20 April 1932, ibid.

27. HC to BC, 22 April 1932, ibid., pp. 653–55.

28. Eyler Simpson to Henry Allen Moe, 23 April 1932, quoted in U, p. 753.

29. HC to TWS, p.c. 26 April 1932, *Letters III*, p. 524.

30. "The Last Days of Hart Crane," *RR*, p. 172.

31. Mrs. C. G. Vogt in a letter to Unterecker, 27 September 1969, quoted in U, p. 812.

Coda

1. GC to CR, 3 May 1932, quoted in *Letters II*, p. 656.

2. WCW, "Comment," *Contact*, vol. 1, no. 2 (May 1932), pp. 109–10.

3. WCW, "Hart Crane (1899–1932)," *Contempo*, vol. 1, no. 4 (July 1932), pp. 1, 4.

4. WCW, "Shapiro Is All Right," *Kenyon Review* (1944), reprinted in William Carlos Williams, *Selected Essays* (New York: New Directions, 1954), pp. 261–62.

5. Marsden Hartley, quoted in Ludington, *Marsden Hartley*, p. 216.

6. Marsden Hartley's description of his painting, *Eight Bells' Folly, Memorial for Hart Crane*, 1933. University Gallery, University of Minnesota, Minneapolis.

7. Yvor Winters, *In Defense of Reason* (New York: The Swallow Press and William Morrow, 1947), pp. 589–90.

8. A word of thanks to Langdon Hammer for information contained in the biographical appendix to his *O My Land, My Friends,* some of which is used here in a different configuration.

ACKNOWLEDGMENTS

CRANE *at* 100

ANYONE WRITING A BIOGRAPHY of Hart Crane owes a debt to Philip Horton for his crisp, powerful, fast-moving, focused life first published in 1937, just five years after Crane's death. Horton's biography had the benefits of many living witnesses—including Crane's mother, his relatives (especially his aunt Zell Deming), and his many friends and acquaintances. It also had the disadvantages of having to be published while many of those same people—jealous of their prerogatives, each sure they best understood Hart, and wanting to protect him—were still very much alive. One sometimes feels their presence—especially Grace Crane's—looking over Horton's shoulder, each telling him how to paint Crane's portrait. Luckily for his readers, most of these pitfalls—except for his own deep-wired prejudices—his narrative style managed to overcome.

Even John Unterecker, whose biography came out in 1969 (initially without notes) and who began his interviews and research in the 1950s, could still call on many who knew Crane, though by then the images were becoming distended by myth. Still, Unterecker went after every fact he could, every source, every living witness, insisting on getting it all in there, until Crane's thirty-two years exceeded eight hundred pages. The amount of material he uncovered was staggering—obsessional, one might say—but he didn't (alas) learn the trick of sufficiently focusing and dramatizing what he found, and many have found the book longer even than it is. Still, Unterecker was, and remains, an authority on Crane long after his death.

My task, as I saw it, was different. In the past thirty years, more material on Crane—letters, memoirs, critical commentary—has become available, so that both Horton and Unterecker must be revised and Unterecker streamlined. Both biographers wrote around Crane's homosexuality, Horton seeing it as an aberration and offering Monday morning advice on how Crane should have lived his life; Unterecker at pains to show how "normal" Hart Crane really was. Now, as Crane approaches his hundredth birthday, it seems time to tell his story with something of the grittiness, humor, accuracy, and sublimity one finds in the letters and in his brilliant poems.

Crane has fascinated me since I first became interested in poetry, and writing this biography has been on my mind since I first put down Unterecker's biography back in the summer of '69, both with a mixture of amazement at the prodigious scholarship and disappointment with the life I found portrayed there. My own intentions have been, first, to incorporate the materials that have become available in the past thirty years, including the names of Crane's enemies and lovers and other associates where these were edited or erased. Second, to provide a read-ing of the poems that would elucidate Crane's complex language and music and show why Crane wrote as he did. And third, to provide the reader with a book he or she might enjoy, even if Crane's poetry—or poetry in general—remains a foreign country with land mines to be gingerly traversed. Crane's life reads like a great Greek tragedy, and I have tried to capture something of the meteoric rise and fall of this brilliant and tragic poet.

For many years now, I have talked with other poets and scholars about Hart Crane. There were David Clark and David Porter, older col-leagues at the University of Massachusetts, who taught Crane when I first arrived here thirty years ago. That was when English departments still taught literature. There were talks with Harold Bloom, both real and imagined. One in particular, as we walked about the Yale campus twenty years ago, Bloom waxing eloquently—as usual—about Hart Crane. Did he write poetry himself, I asked ingenuously. No, but if he did, Bloom remarked, furrowing his brow, it would probably sound like bad Crane. From that I have extrapolated that Crane was for him the *sine qua non*, the real touchstone for judging American Romantic poetry.

And other figures, whom I know only by their work: Waldo Frank and Malcolm Cowley; Gorham Munson and Jean Toomer; Yvor Winters and Allen Tate and Waldo Frank and Kenneth Burke. Thomas Parkinson. R. W. Butterfield. Geoffrey Wolff for *Black Sun*, his biography of Harry Crosby. Thomas S. W. Lewis for his important work in making the Crane family letters available. Brom Weber for his pioneering editions of the letters and the poetry. Marc Simon for his edition of Crane's poems. Susan Jenkins Brown, Lincoln Kirstein, Sherman Paul, Warren Herendeen, Donald Parker. Ann Douglas for her study, *Terrible Honesty: Mongrel Manhattan in the 1920s*. And especially Langdon Hammer, both for his *Hart Crane and Allen Tate: Janus-Faced Modernism*, and more recently, his very welcome edition of Crane's selected letters: *O My Land, My Friends,* a text that finally gives us many of the letters as they were written.

There were talks with others: Robert Bagg, Bob Creeley, Kate Daniels, Martín Espada, Allen Ginsberg, Bill Heyen, Ed Hirsch, Mark Jarman, Donald Justice, Philip Levine, Allen Mandelbaum, Bill Matthews, Bob Pack, Agha Shahid Ali, Jim Tate, Dara Weir, John Wideman. Other talks, too, with Barry Moser and Fred Turner. These I remember, but whom have I missed? And my students at U. Mass for the past thirty years—so many. Brilliant, feisty, argumentative, witty, helpful. Others: the indefatigable library staff here at the University of Massachusetts and—since these are the nineties and word processors a fact of life—the young staff at the computer center who have helped me deal with the manuscript many times over. In particular, John Burk, who saved me long hours and probably an ulcer. And university administrators, who make the writing of biographies, with their enormous expenses, at least possible: Provost F. W. Byron, Dean Lee Edwards, and my indefatigable chair, Stephen Clingman. Thanks to all of them.

I also want to thank three friends who went out of their way to read and comment on the first draft of the manuscript. My colleague Vincent DiMarco, who has been through it all with me at U. Mass for thirty years now and carefully read the manuscript, even though he believes that all real literature ended with the death of Chaucer. Ron Hansen, who read the manuscript with the eye of the first-rate novelist he is. And finally and especially Philip Levine, who provided his always astute and brilliant comments, all of which helped shape the form of the book. I am lucky to have such friends. My editor at Norton, Jill Bialosky, has been a support for years now, and read the manuscript with the eye of the poet she is. And her very able assistant, Eve Grubin, and my copy editor, Ann Adelman. And then my three sons. Paul, for probing into the philosophical and ethical conditions of the human animal; John for his crisp insights into the psychological quagmire of the human mind; and Mark for the care and feeding of sentences and paragraphs. And finally my dear wife, Eileen, who has been through all this with me before—with Hopkins and Williams, Berryman and Lowell—and who as usual helped see me through yet another obsession-ridden life: Crane's life, my obsessions.

PHOTOGRAPH CREDITS

Section 2

9. Hart Crane in white pajamas on the Isle of Pines, summer 1926. *Butler Library, Columbia University*

10a. Janet Lewis and Yvor Winters. *Janet Lewis Papers, Special Collections, Stanford University Libraries*

10b. Harry and Caresse Crosby, Villefranche, winter 1929. *Special Collections, Morris Library, Southern Illinois, University at Carbondale*

11a. Sue Jenkins and William Slater Brown, Patterson, ca. March 1927. *Butler Library, Columbia University*

11b. William Slater Brown and Emil Opffer, Patterson, ca. March 1927. *Butler Library, Columbia University*

12a. Hart Crane smoking a cigar, Villefranche, summer 1929. *Butler Library, Columbia University*

12b. Hart Crane on the roof of 110 Columbia Heights, fall 1929. *Butler Library, Columbia University*

13a. Hart Crane. Photo by Walker Evans, late 1929. *Butler Library, Columbia University*

13b. Hart Crane with cigar, sitting in chair. Photo by Walker Evans, 1930. *Butler Library, Columbia University*

14a. Hart Crane (right) with C.A.; C.A.'s third wife, Bess Crane; and C.A.'s employee, Dorothy Smith; at Canary Cottage, Chagrin Falls, outside Cleveland, December 1930. *Butler Library, Columbia University*

14b. Hart Crane in animated conversation with Katherine Anne Porter, Mixcoac, late April 1931. *Katharine Anne Porter Collection, University of Maryland, College Park*

15a. Portrait of Hart Crane by David Siqueiros, October 1931. *Butler Library, Columbia University*

15b. Hart Crane in the bell tower of St. Prisca in late January 1932. *Photo taken by Peggy Cowley*

16a. Hart Crane decked out with his pre-Conquest silver bells, early 1932. *Butler Library, Columbia University*

16b. Hart Crane with Peggy Cowley in Mexico, wearing his Marseilles sailor outfit, early 1932. *Butler Library, Columbia University*

16c. Hart Crane with his house cats at his home in Mixcoac, winter 1932. *Butler Library, Columbia University*

INDEX